Active Directory Administration Cookbook

Actionable, proven solutions to identity management and authentication on servers and in the cloud

Sander Berkouwer

BIRMINGHAM - MUMBAI

Active Directory Administration Cookbook

Commissioning Editor: Pavan Ramchandani
Acquisition Editor: Rohit Rajkumar
Content Development Editor: Aishwarya Moray
Technical Editor: Rutuja Patade
Copy Editor: Safis Editing
Project Coordinator: Jagdish Prabhu
Proofreader: Safis Editing
Indexer: Priyanka Dhadke
Graphics: Tom Scaria
Production Coordinator: Deepika Naik

First published: May 2019

Production reference: 1030519

Published by Packt Publishing Ltd.
Livery Place
35 Livery Street
Birmingham
B3 2PB, UK.

ISBN 978-1-78980-698-4

www.packtpub.com

`mapt.io`

Mapt is an online digital library that gives you full access to over 5,000 books and videos, as well as industry leading tools to help you plan your personal development and advance your career. For more information, please visit our website.

Why subscribe?

- Spend less time learning and more time coding with practical eBooks and Videos from over 4,000 industry professionals

- Improve your learning with Skill Plans built especially for you

- Get a free eBook or video every month

- Mapt is fully searchable

- Copy and paste, print, and bookmark content

Packt.com

Did you know that Packt offers eBook versions of every book published, with PDF and ePub files available? You can upgrade to the eBook version at `www.packt.com` and as a print book customer, you are entitled to a discount on the eBook copy. Get in touch with us at `customercare@packtpub.com` for more details.

At `www.packt.com`, you can also read a collection of free technical articles, sign up for a range of free newsletters, and receive exclusive discounts and offers on Packt books and eBooks.

Contributors

About the author

Sander Berkouwer calls himself an Active Directory aficionado; he's done everything with Active Directory and Azure Active Directory, including decommissioning. He has been MCSA, MCSE, and MCITP-certified for ages, an MCT for the past 5 years and a Microsoft Most Valuable Professional (MVP) on Directory Services and Enterprise Mobility for over a decade. As the CTO at SCCT, Sander leads a team of architects performing many projects, most of them identity-related, throughout Europe.

About the reviewer

Brian Svidergol designs and builds infrastructure, cloud, and hybrid solutions. He holds many industry certifications, including Microsoft Certified Solutions Expert (MCSE) – Cloud Platform and Infrastructure. Brian is the author of several books, covering everything from on-premises infrastructure technologies to hybrid cloud environments. He has extensive real-world experience, from start-up organizations to large Fortune 500 companies on design, implementation, and migration projects.

Packt is searching for authors like you

If you're interested in becoming an author for Packt, please visit authors.packtpub.com and apply today. We have worked with thousands of developers and tech professionals, just like you, to help them share their insight with the global tech community. You can make a general application, apply for a specific hot topic that we are recruiting an author for, or submit your own idea.

Table of Contents

Preface

Active Directory is an administration system for Windows administrators to automate network, security, and access management tasks in Microsoft-oriented networking infrastructures. Bundled with Microsoft's cloud-based Azure Active Directory (AD) service, it offers a comprehensive **Identity and Access Management (IAM)** solution to organizations that want to manage on-premises and cloud-based resources.

Who this book is for

Active Directory can be overwhelming, but the straightforward recipes in this cookbook break it down into easy-to-follow tasks, backed by substantial real-world experience and clear explanations of what's going on under the hood.

This cookbook offers essential recipes for day-to-day Active Directory and Azure AD administration for both novices in managing Active Directory and Azure AD, and seasoned administrators with several Active Directory migrations and consolidations under their belts.

Because today's identity in the world of Microsoft technologies is no longer about just on-premises Active Directory, this book also offers three chapters with recipes for Azure AD, as well as an entire chapter dedicated to **Active Directory Federation Services (ADFS)**.

Whether you just need a hand, want to take out the guesswork, or have a read-up before messing it up, this book helps admins at each stage of their careers to make the right choices, check the right boxes, and automate the repeatable tasks that become tedious after some time.

What this book covers

This book consists of fourteen chapters:

Chapter 1, *Optimizing Forests, Domains, and Trusts*, provides recipes for structuring the logical components of Active Directory, including UPN suffixes, trusts, domains, and forests. Several recipes help lift Active Directory to new heights, where others help expand the functionality of Active Directory in terms of collaboration.

Chapter 2, *Managing Domain Controllers*, shows how to promote, demote, and inventory both domain controllers and read-only domain controllers; these are Active Directory's physical components.

Chapter 3, *Managing Active Directory Roles and Features*, covers **Flexible Single Operations Master (FSOM)** roles and global catalog servers for addressing all your organization's multi-forest and multi-domain needs.

Chapter 4, *Managing Containers and Organizational Units*, provides Active Directory admins who like cleanliness, with the rationale and steps necessary to categorize objects into organizational units and containers. Lazy admins learn how to properly delegate, too.

Chapter 5, *Managing Active Directory Sites and Troubleshooting Replication*, details how to optimize multiple domain controllers in multiple geographic locations using sites, site links, and bridgehead servers, and how to troubleshoot replication.

Chapter 6, *Managing Active Directory Users*, contains recipes to help out colleagues when they start working, leave the organization, and every change in between. The proactive recipe on finding locked-out accounts helps admins to stay ahead of the game.

Chapter 7, *Managing Active Directory Groups*, covers all types of groups in Active Directory, along with how to create, modify, and delete them, no matter how nested these groups are. Getting rid of empty groups is easy with the last recipe in this chapter.

Chapter 8, *Managing Active Directory Computers*, provides ways to keep your organization's devices in check. Of course, it also details how to prevent non-privileged users to join devices to your environment.

Chapter 9, *Getting the Most Out of Group Policy*, enables admins to get the most out of Group Policy! Managing tens or thousands of devices won't be an issue anymore with the recipes in this chapter.

Chapter 10, *Securing Active Directory*, provides ways to improve the security stance of your Active Directory environment. Each recipe in this chapter makes your environment less attractive to attackers.

Chapter 11, *Managing Federation*, covers ADFS. Build the perfect ADFS farm using the recipes, or decommission one.

Chapter 12, *Handling Authentication in a Hybrid World (AD FS, PHS, PTA, and 3SO)*, details hybrid identity between Active Directory and Azure AD in terms of ADFS, **Password Hash Synchronization (PHS)**, **Pass-Through Authentication (PTA)**, and **Seamless Single Sign-on (SSO)**.

Chapter 13, *Handling Synchronization in a Hybrid World (Azure AD Connect)*, covers Azure AD Connect and the key role it plays in synchronizing between Active Directory and Azure AD.

Chapter 14, *Hardening Azure AD*, provides recipes to keep your organization's Azure AD tenant in check. The recipes explore the many possibilities of Azure AD, including conditional access and Azure AD Identity Protection.

To get the most out of this book

To get the most out of the book, it helps to have basic knowledge of Windows Server and Active Directory.

Many recipes are written to lift an aging Active Directory environment to new heights. It helps in these cases to know the old protocols, such as **NT Lan Manager (NTLM)**, but an open mind is a more valuable asset when engaging with the recipes.

Some recipes in this cookbook require significant hardware, so if you're staging changes in development, test, or acceptance environments, make sure you have the computational power and storage to do so.

Download the example code files

You can download the example code files for this book from your account at www.packt.com. If you purchased this book elsewhere, you can visit www.packt.com/support and register to have the files emailed directly to you.

You can download the code files by following these steps:

1. Log in or register at www.packt.com.
2. Select the **SUPPORT** tab.
3. Click on **Code Downloads & Errata**.
4. Enter the name of the book in the **Search** box and follow the onscreen instructions.

Once the file is downloaded, please make sure that you unzip or extract the folder using the latest version of:

- WinRAR/7-Zip for Windows
- Zipeg/iZip/UnRarX for Mac
- 7-Zip/PeaZip for Linux

The code bundle for the book is also hosted on GitHub at `https://github.com/PacktPublishing/Active-Directory-Administration-Cookbook`. In case there's an update to the code, it will be updated on the existing GitHub repository.

We also have other code bundles from our rich catalog of books and videos available at `https://github.com/PacktPublishing/`. Check them out!

Download the color images

We also provide a PDF file that has color images of the screenshots/diagrams used in this book. You can download it here: `http://www.packtpub.com/sites/default/files/downloads/Bookname_ColorImages.pdf`.

Conventions used

There are a number of text conventions used throughout this book.

`CodeInText`: Indicates code words in text, database table names, folder names, filenames, file extensions, pathnames, dummy URLs, user input, and Twitter handles. Here is an example: "To work with `repadmin.exe`, sign into a domain controller."

```
New-AdfsWebTheme -Name custom -SourceName default
```

Bold: Indicates a new term, an important word, or words that you see onscreen. For example, words in menus or dialog boxes appear in the text like this. Here is an example: "The **Multiple Users** window appears:"

Warnings or important notes appear like this.

Tips and tricks appear like this.

Sections

In this book, you will find several headings that appear frequently (*Getting ready*, *How to do it...*, *How it works...*, *There's more...*, and *See also*).

To give clear instructions on how to complete a recipe, use these sections as follows:

Getting ready

This section tells you what to expect in the recipe and describes how to set up any software or any preliminary settings required for the recipe.

How to do it...

This section contains the steps required to follow the recipe.

How it works...

This section usually consists of a detailed explanation of what happened in the previous section.

There's more...

This section consists of additional information about the recipe in order to make you more knowledgeable about the recipe.

See also

This section provides helpful links to other useful information for the recipe.

Get in touch

Feedback from our readers is always welcome.

General feedback: If you have questions about any aspect of this book, mention the book title in the subject of your message and email us at customercare@packtpub.com.

Errata: Although we have taken every care to ensure the accuracy of our content, mistakes do happen. If you have found a mistake in this book, we would be grateful if you would report this to us. Please visit www.packt.com/submit-errata, selecting your book, clicking on the Errata Submission Form link, and entering the details.

Piracy: If you come across any illegal copies of our works in any form on the Internet, we would be grateful if you would provide us with the location address or website name. Please contact us at copyright@packt.com with a link to the material.

If you are interested in becoming an author: If there is a topic that you have expertise in and you are interested in either writing or contributing to a book, please visit authors.packtpub.com.

Reviews

Please leave a review. Once you have read and used this book, why not leave a review on the site that you purchased it from? Potential readers can then see and use your unbiased opinion to make purchase decisions, we at Packt can understand what you think about our products, and our authors can see your feedback on their book. Thank you!

For more information about Packt, please visit packt.com.

1
Optimizing Forests, Domains, and Trusts

Back in the year 2000, when Active Directory was introduced to the larger public, we lived in a different world. The internet was only just starting to deliver value to businesses. That's why, in Windows 2000 Server, Active Directory was largely disconnected from the internet. Windows 2000 Server's default **Domain Name System (DNS)** settings even came with a root domain; so, if you wanted to connect to the internet, you'd need to delete the . DNS zone manually.

Fast forward to today, and the internet and cloud services seem omnipresent. The default . DNS zone has disappeared from Windows Server, but the concepts of trees and forests in Active Directory has persisted, and they still allow for some confusion among Active Directory admins.

To explain domains, trees, and forests in Active Directory, we need to acknowledge Active Directory's past. To create anything in Active Directory, you'll need to create a domain. It starts with the name. For a hypothetical organization, Lucern Publishing, four typical domain names would be as follows:

Type	Domain Name
Public DNS domain name	`lucernpub.com`
Internal part of a public DNS domain name	`ad.lucernpub.com`
Non-public DNS domain name	`lucernpub.local`
Single-label domain name	`lucernpubcom`

The first two options are the preferred options, as they adhere to RFC 822 (`https://www.w3.org/Protocols/rfc822`). The third option is a common option, but doesn't comply with RFC 2606 (`https://tools.ietf.org/html/rfc2606`) and should be avoided. The fourth option is a typical single-label domain. They are usually the result of a common error among Active Directory admins migrating from Windows NT 4 Server's model to Active Directory. Products that once supported Windows NT 4 Server's single-label domains are no longer around, or they no longer support single-label domain names, including Microsoft.

Lucern Publishing may be quite a successful organization, so they might expand their operations from Switzerland to Europe, North America, and Asia. For reasons that we'll discuss later, they might want to separate Active Directory domains for each of their territories, but they want them to keep working together like one organization. This is where a domain tree comes into play. Now, Lucern Publishing might choose to create three subdomains under `lucernpub.com`:

- `eu.lucernpub.com`
- `usa.lucernpub.com`
- `asia.lucernpub.com`

They've created a tree of Active Directory domains, sharing the same DNS namespace. Of course, Lucern Publishing might also choose to create multiple trees, next to the `lucernpub.com` domain or tree, to accommodate an organizational layout with different names for their global expansions, such as Austin Publishing and Wuhan Publishing. In this case, it will make sense to create separate domains such as `austinpub.com` and `wuhanpub.com`. Effectively, Lucern Publishing will create three trees this way, belonging to the same Active Directory forest. Yes, some Active Directory environments are large structures with many large trees, but the default Active Directory forest consists of just one tree, with one Active Directory domain.

In this chapter, we'll discuss the reasoning behind creating domains and forests. We'll also discuss **userPrincipalName (UPN)** suffixes and trusts. The goal of this chapter is to help you make the right choices in terms of your Active Directory structure.

The following recipes will be covered in the chapter:

- Listing the domains in your forest
- Using adprep.exe to prepare for new AD functionality
- Raising the domain functional level to Windows Server 2016
- Raising the forest functional level to Windows Server 2016
- Creating the right trust

- Verifying a trust
- Securing a trust
- Extending the schema
- Enabling the Active Directory Recycle Bin
- Managing UPN suffixes

Before going through these recipes, we will look at a few aspects that you will need to know for this chapter.

Let's begin!

Choosing between a new domain or forest

In organizations, sometimes, an expansion or business change requires changes in Active Directory too. In Active Directory terms, the change might require creating a new Active Directory domain or a new Active Directory forest. In this recipe, we'll look at the reasoning between these two choices, taking the entire life cycle of Active Directory into consideration.

Why would you have a new domain?

A new Active Directory domain—as either a subdomain of an existing domain, or a new domain tree in an existing forest—provides a boundary.

The boundary of domains in Active Directory relates to the following:

- **DNS name**: An additional domain tree offers the possibility to add a DNS domain name to the organization to, for instance, correctly label a new business venture. An alternative might be to add an additional UPN suffix.
- **Domain DNS zones replication**: Throughout an Active Directory forest, all domain controllers replicate to exchange information on objects, schema, and configuration. Between domains, a distinction can be made to limit the replication of information on Active Directory-integrated DNS zones. That way, this information is only replicated within the domain.
- **Password and account lock-out policies**: Fine-grained password and account lock-out policies can only be applied within an Active Directory domain. The information can be viewed by any account in the domain. If you want to shield this information or create completely separate policies, an additional domain is the route to go.

- **Group Policy**: **Group Policy Objects (GPOs)** only replicate within a domain. The only exception is the GPOs that are linked to Active Directory sites; these are copied between domains instead, since Active Directory sites are created at the forest level.

However, the boundary of domains in Active Directory does not include the following:

- An Active Directory schema
- The scope of the enterprise administrators group

Essentially, a new Active Directory domain is an administrative boundary, which you can create for an organization to allow for delegated management.

What are the downsides of a new domain?

Microsoft's advice is to keep Active Directory as simple as possible. When you create additional domains, the organization ends up with the following:

- At least two additional domain controllers
- Active Directory trusts between the current domain(s) and the new domain
- An increase in administrative burden

Why would you create a new forest?

A new Active Directory forest is basically a completely new Active Directory environment. When you create it, it does not have a relationship with an existing Active Directory environment, unless you choose to create Active Directory trusts afterward.

Since the new Active Directory forest is separate, a boundary is created for the following reasons:

- **Schema and configuration partitions**: The schema and configuration partitions hold information on the way that objects can be created, what attributes are required for these objects, what attributes are optional for these objects, and the domains within the forest. Since many applications require Active Directory schema extensions, introducing a legacy or cutting-edge application might result in schema conflicts. In these types of scenarios, creating an additional Active Directory forest is the best way forward. An alternative might be to add an **Active Directory Lightweight Directory Services (AD-LDS)** instance to the environment.

- **Global catalog replication**: Domain controllers with the additional global catalog role hold partial information on the most requested attributes for objects in Active Directory. With multiple global catalogs, the information is replicated throughout the forest. To shield this information, an additional Active Directory forest can be created.
- **Forest DNS zones replication**: To overcome the default boundary for Active Directory-integrated DNS zones, the Forest DNS zone replication scope, an additional Active Directory forest can be created.

When requirements apply in terms of schema or replication, creating an Active Directory forest is the right choice. One thing that might be good here is to state that the forest is a security boundary as well as an administrative boundary.

Additionally, since the forest is a separate environment, by default, it can also be separated afterward. In acquisition and divestiture scenarios that can be overseen for the life cycle of Active Directory, an Active Directory forest is also the right choice.

What are the downsides of a new forest?

A separate Active Directory environment, of course, requires double the administrative effort of Active Directory admins. Additionally, since the environments are separate, creating an address list in Microsoft Exchange Server or sharing common applications, services, and/or systems is hard.

Now we can look at the recipes covered in this chapter.

Listing the domains in your forest

In an Active Directory environment with multiple domains and forests, it can be hard to distinguish the trees from the forest. As authentication is often per forest, an easy way to list the domains per forest will be welcome.

Getting ready

Alas, the only reliable way to list the domains in a forest is to use PowerShell.

For this recipe, we'll need one of the following:

- A domain controller running Windows Server 2012 with Desktop Experience (or a newer version of Windows Server)
- A domain-joined member server running Windows Server 2012 with Desktop Experience (or a newer version of Windows Server) with the Active Directory module for Windows PowerShell installed
- A domain-joined device running Windows 8.1 (or a newer version of Windows) with the Active Directory module for Windows PowerShell installed

On domain controllers running Windows Server 2012 with Desktop Experience (and on newer versions of Windows Server), the Active Directory module for the Windows PowerShell feature is automatically installed, when promoted to domain controller.

On domain controllers running Server Core installations of Windows Server 2012 (and on newer versions of Windows Server), the availability of the Active Directory module for Windows PowerShell depends on the `-IncludeManagementTools` option for the `Install-WindowsFeature` Windows PowerShell cmdlet used to install the Active Directory Domain Services role.

Installing the Active Directory module for Windows PowerShell on Windows Server

To install the Active Directory module for Windows PowerShell on a Windows Server with Desktop Experience, follow these steps:

1. Open **Server Manager** (`servermanager.exe`).
2. In the top gray pane, click **Manage.**
3. Select **Add Roles and Features** from the context menu.
4. In **Add Roles and Features Wizard**, click **Next >** until you reach the **Select Features** screen.
5. On the **Select Features** screen, scroll down in the list of features until you reach **Remote Server Administration Tools.**
6. Expand **Remote Server Administration Tools.**

7. Expand **Role Administration Tools.**
8. Expand **AD DS and AD LDS Tools**.
9. Select the **Active Directory module for Windows PowerShell** feature:

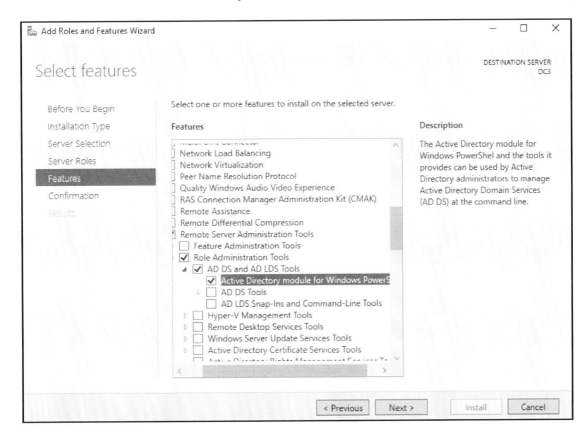

10. Click **Next >** until you reach the **Confirm installation** selections page.
11. Click **Install.**
12. Click **Close.**

To install the Active Directory module for Windows PowerShell on a Server Core installation of Windows Server, run these two commands:

```
PowerShell
Install-WindowsFeature RSAT-AD-PowerShell
```

Installing the Active Directory module for Windows PowerShell on Windows

To install the Active Directory module for Windows PowerShell on a Windows device, download the separately available **Remote Server Administration Tools (RSAT)** package for your version of Windows. After you install the package, all the RSAT will be available, including the Active Directory module for Windows PowerShell.

Required permissions

To list all the domains in a forest, use an account that is a member of the Enterprise Admins group in Active Directory.

How to do it...

On the system, start an elevated Windows PowerShell window or Windows PowerShell ISE window using the domain credentials for any account.

Then, type the following lines of PowerShell:

```
Import-Module ActiveDirectory
Get-ADForest | select domains
```

How it works...

On the first line, we verify that the Active Directory module for Windows PowerShell is installed, correctly configured, and ready.

On the second line, we use the `Get-ADForest` cmdlet from the Active Directory module to get the information for the current Active Directory forest. Then, we pipe the output of that command to select only the domains, since that's what we're after.

You can now make the best choices for implementing new domains and/or forests, and/or decommissioning domains and/or forests.

Using adprep.exe to prepare for new Active Directory functionality

The Active Directory schema defines the way that objects can be created, and what attributes are required or are optional for these objects. With every version of Windows Server, the base schema has been improved and extended.

Many features require certain schema versions for Active Directory. For instance, when you want to deploy a Windows Server 2016-based **Active Directory Federation Services (AD FS)** farm, you'll need the Windows Server 2016 schema.

Since Windows Server 2012, Microsoft updates the Active Directory schema automatically when you promote the first Windows Server 2012-based member server to an Active Directory domain controller.

However, consider what will happen if you want to do any of the following:

- Update the Active Directory schema only, because your organization doesn't want domain controllers running the latest version
- Delegate the promotion of the first domain controller to a lesser-privileged user, instead of an admin that is a member of the Schema Admins group
- Control the proper replication of the schema update to all domain controllers, before promoting the first domain controller
- Avoid the default time-out that the Active Directory Configuration Wizard provides for proper replication
- Perform all Active Directory preparations, including the Group Policy preparation step

In these situations, you'll want to update the Active Directory schema manually, using `adprep.exe` from the Windows Server installation media.

Getting ready

Copy the entire contents of the `\support\adprep` folder from the Windows Server installation media to a temporary folder on your system's hard disk.

Required permissions

The Active Directory preparation process consists of four separate stages. You'll need an account with the following group memberships for each stage:

Stage	Required group memberships
Preparing the forest	Enterprise Admins Schema Admins Domain Admins in the forest root domain
Preparing the forest for **Read-only Domain Controllers (RODCs)**	Domain Admins in the forest root domain
Preparing the domain	Domain Admins
Fixing up Group Policy permissions	Domain Admins

How to do it...

Start Command Prompt in the file explorer window of the folder where you've copied the files to.

On Windows 10 version 1803 and up, you can simply type cmd in the address bar to achieve this.

The Active Directory preparation process consists of four separate stages:

- Preparing the forest
- Preparing the forest for RODCs
- Preparing the domain
- Fixing up Group Policy permissions

After these steps, you'll want to check proper Active Directory replication.

Preparing the forest

Perform these steps to prepare the Active Directory forest:

To prepare the Active Directory forest, run the following command:

```
adprep.exe /forestprep /forest lucernpub.com /user EntAdmin /userdomain
lucernpub.com /password P@ssw0rd
```

Replace the value for the domain and the values for the credentials with values that make sense for your Active Directory environment.

Next, you issue the `c` command type, followed by *Enter*.

The following line at the end of the output indicates the successful preparation of the Active Directory forest:

```
Adprep successfully updated the forest-wide information
```

Preparing the forest for RODCs

The `/rodcprep` switch for `adprep.exe` triggers the preparation of the forest for RODCs. This action only needs to be performed when the intention is to run RODCs in the Active Directory forest:

To prepare the Active Directory forest for RODCs, run the following command:

```
adprep.exe /rodcprep /forest lucernpub.com /user DomAdmin /userdomain
lucernpub.com /password P@ssw0rd
```

Replace the value for the domain and the values for the credentials with values that make sense for your Active Directory environment.

The following line at the end of the output indicates the successful preparation of the Active Directory forest for RODCs:

```
Rodcprep completed without errors. All partitions are updated. See the
ADPrep.log in directory C:\Windows\debug\adprep\logs\ <date> for more
information.
```

Preparing the domain

Perform these steps to prepare the domain:

To prepare the Active Directory domain, run the following command:

```
adprep.exe /domainprep /domain lucernpub.com /user DomAdm /userdomain
lucernpub /password P@ssw0rd
```

Replace the value for the domain and the values for the credentials with values that make sense for your Active Directory environment.

The following line at the end of the output indicates the successful preparation of the Active Directory domain:

```
Adprep successfully updated the domain-wide information
```

Fixing up Group Policy permissions

Group Policy preparation, as part of `adprep.exe`, adds two pieces of functionality to Active Directory:

- Cross-domain planning functionality for Group Policy
- **Resultant Set of Policy (RSoP)** planning mode

GPOs are stored in both the **System Volume (SYSVOL)** and Active Directory. Both locations require an update of the permissions for existing GPOs, in order to take advantage of the preceding functionality.

If the Active Directory domain already contains custom or delegated permissions, Group Policy preparation kicks off the replication of all Group Policy files in the SYSVOL, and may deny the functionality of RSoP to delegated admins until their permissions are recreated.

 Group Policy preparation does not need to be run with every upgrade. Admins need to run Group Policy preparation only once, and they only need to run it if an Active Directory domain has run on Windows 2000 Server-based domain controllers at one point in its existence. If an environment was created with domain controllers running Windows Server 2003, or newer versions of Windows Server, the Group Policy preparation step can be skipped.

To fix up Group Policy permissions, run the following command:

```
adprep.exe /domainprep /gpprep /domain lucernpub.com /user DomAdm
/userdomain lucernpub.com /password P@ssw0rd
```

Replace the value for the domain and the values for the credentials with values that make sense for your Active Directory environment.

The following line at the end of the output indicates the successful preparation of the Active Directory domain:

```
Adprep successfully updated the Group Policy Object (GPO) information.
```

Checking the preparation replication

When done with the preparation steps, the Active Directory schema base version should be upgraded to a higher number, corresponding to the new schema version.

The following table shows the version numbers in accordance to the Active Directory level:

Windows Server version	Schema version
Windows 2000 Server	13
Windows Server 2003	30
Windows Server 2003 R2	31
Windows Server 2008	44
Windows Server 2008 R2	47
Windows Server 2012	56
Windows Server 2012 R2	69
Windows Server 2016	87
Windows Server 2019	88

You can manually check the schema version per domain controller with the following command from any of your domain controllers:

```
repadmin.exe /showattr * "cn=schema,cn=configuration,dc=lucernpub,dc=com"
/atts:objectVersion
```

Replace lucernpub and com with values for your Active Directory environment.

When all domain controllers report the same schema version, the Active Directory preparation has replicated successfully to all domain controllers.

How it works...

In Windows Server 2012 (and later versions), the whole Active Directory preparation process is automated. When you promote a Windows Server 2012-based member server (or any newer version of Windows Server) to an additional domain controller for a domain, or upgrade a domain controller running a previous version to Windows Server 2012 (or any newer version of Windows Server), the Active Directory Domain Services Configuration Wizard determines whether the environment needs to be prepared as part of the promotion process.

Larger organizations often separate the schema or preparation work from the actual domain controller-promotion process work to minimize risk, adhere to small change windows, and more.

However, `adprep.exe` is still available to prepare the Active Directory forest and/or Active Directory domain(s) manually.

There's more...

Unless there is a big reason not to, preparing for the latest available Active Directory schema version is the best way to go. A reason not to do this is when an organization doesn't want to enable the promotion of the latest version(s) of Windows Server to domain controllers in a delegated environment.

Raising the domain functional level to Windows Server 2016

When implementing new Active Directory domain controllers and removing domain controllers running previous versions of Windows Server, many admins forget to raise the Active Directory **domain functional level** (**DFL**) to the earliest Windows Server version still running as domain controllers. After upgrading all domain controllers from Windows Server 2008 R2 to Windows Server 2012 R2, for instance, they would not raise the DFL to Windows Server 2012 R2, but keep it at the Windows Server 2008 R2 level.

 The Windows 2016 domain is the highest available DFL for Active Directory; there is no Windows 2019 domain level.

It's a shame, really, because many new Active Directory features and optional Active Directory features are only available when the functional level is raised. Furthermore, the DFL dictates the lowest version of Windows Server that admins can use to promote new domain controllers. In addition, since Windows Server 2008 R2, the DFL can also be reverted, as long as no new optional features have been enabled and the Active Directory **forest functional level (FFL)** is the same as the DFL that you want to revert to, or lower.

From an Active Directory point of view, the Windows Server 2008 DFL (or any newer version of the DFL), is required when you want to deploy Windows Server 2016-based domain controllers.

Getting ready

Microsoft recommends raising the DFL from the Active Directory domain controller that holds the **Primary Domain Controller emulator (PDCe) Flexible Single Master Operations (FSMO)** role.

To locate this domain controller, run the following command on any domain-joined device, member server, or domain controller:

```
netdom.exe query fsmo
```

Alternatively, use the following lines of PowerShell on a domain-joined system that has the Active Directory module for Windows PowerShell installed:

```
Import-Module ActiveDirectory

Get-ADDomain | Format-List PDCEmulator
```

Required permissions

Use an account that is a member of the Domain Admins group in the Active Directory domain for which you want to raise the DFL.

How to do it...

On domain controllers running Windows Server with the Desktop Experience, follow these steps:

1. Sign in to the domain controller holding the PDC emulator FSMO role.
2. Open **Active Directory Domains and Trusts** (domain.msc).
3. In the left navigation pane, right-click the domain for which you want to raise the functional level, and then click **Raise Domain Functional Level**.
   The **Raise domain functional level** window appears:

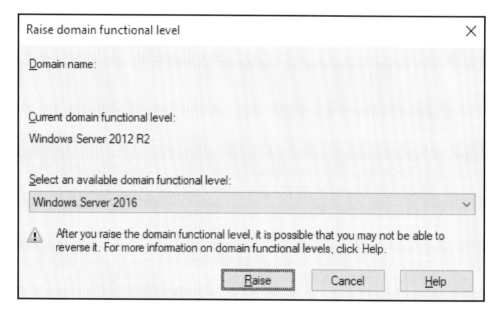

4. From the **Select an available forest functional level** drop-down list, select the desired DFL, and then click **Raise**.

Alternatively, you can use the following two PowerShell commands:

```
Import-Module ActiveDirectory
Set-ADDomainMode lucernpub.com Windows2016Domain
```

Replace lucernpub.com with values for your Active Directory environment.

Even when under time pressure, you'll want to check for the proper replication of changes to Active Directory functional levels before making any other changes in Active Directory that might depend on them. Especially in large environments with elaborate replication technologies, replication might take a while.

To check for the proper replication of changes to Active Directory functional levels, use the following command:

```
repadmin.exe /showattr *.lucernpub.com "dc=lucernpub,dc=com" /atts:msDS-
Behavior-Version
```

Replace `lucernpub.com`, `lucernpub`, and `com` with values for your Active Directory environment.

The command checks the value for the `msDS-Behavior-Version` attribute on each of the domain controllers in the respective Active Directory domain, and return the value.

The following table shows the `msDS-Behavior-Version` attribute value per Active Directory DFL:

DFL	msDS-Behavior-Version
Windows 2000 Server	0
Windows Server 2003 Mixed	1
Windows Server 2003	2
Windows Server 2008	3
Windows Server 2008 R2	4
Windows Server 2012	5
Windows Server 2012 R2	6
Windows Server 2016	7
Windows Server 2019	8

The output shows you the domain controllers that are replicating a change from a lower value to a higher value. When each domain controller returns the same value, the DFL has successfully replicated throughout the Active Directory environment.

How it works...

When a domain controller operates, it references the DFL to know how it can optimally interoperate with other domain controllers in the Active Directory domain. Additionally, when you want to enable optional Active Directory features, the `msDS-Behavior-Version` attribute is referenced to see whether it's a permittable action.

If there is a domain controller running a version of Windows Server that does not meet the requirements of a certain DFL, the level is grayed out in **Active Directory Domains and Trusts** and the level cannot be raised to this level (DFL). When you try to raise the DFL using Windows PowerShell or other programmatic means, it will error out.

Raising the forest functional level to Windows Server 2016

Just like the Active Directory DFL, the FFL also determines the availability of new Active Directory functionality. Where the DFL dictates the minimum version of Windows Server to run as domain controllers, the FFL dictates the minimum version of the DFL in the Active Directory forest.

The new functionality that is unlocked by raising the FFL includes the following:

- **Privileged Access Management (PAM)** that requires the Windows Server 2016 FFL
- Active Directory Recycle Bin that requires the Windows Server 2008 R2 FFL
- Linked-value replication that requires the Windows Server 2003 FFL

Getting ready

Microsoft recommends raising the FFL from the Active Directory domain controller that holds the Domain Naming Master FSMO role.

To locate this domain controller, run the following command on any domain-joined device, member server, or domain controller:

```
netdom.exe query fsmo
```

Alternatively, use the following PowerShell commands on a domain-joined system that has the Active Directory module for Windows PowerShell installed:

```
Import-Module ActiveDirectory

Get-ADForest | Format-List DomainNamingMaster
```

Required permissions

Use an account that is a member of the Enterprise Admins group in the Active Directory forest for which you want to raise the FFL.

How to do it...

On domain controllers running Windows Server with the Desktop Experience, follow these steps:

1. Sign in to the domain controller holding the Domain Naming Master FSMO role.
2. Open **Active Directory Domains and Trusts** (`domain.msc`).
3. In the left navigation pane, right-click **Active Directory Domains and Trusts**, and then click **Raise Forest Functional Level**.
   The **Raise forest functional level** window appears:

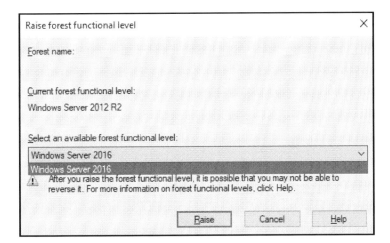

4. From the **Select an available forest functional level** drop-down list, select the desired FFL, and then click **Raise**.

Alternatively, you can use the following two lines of PowerShell:

```
Import-Module ActiveDirectory

Set-ADForestMode lucernpub.com Windows2016Forest
```

Replace `lucernpub.com` with values for your Active Directory environment.

How it works...

When a domain controller operates, it references the FFL to know how it can optimally interoperate with other domain controllers in the Active Directory forest. Additionally, when you want to enable optional Active Directory features, the `msDS-Behavior-Version` attribute is referenced to see whether it's a permittable action.

When a new Active Directory domain is added to an Active Directory forest, the available DFLs for the domain are shown, based on the `msDS-Behavior-Version` attribute for the forest too.

If there is a domain running a DFL that does not meet the requirements of a certain FFL, the level is grayed out in **Active Directory Domains and Trusts** and the level cannot be raised to this level. When you try to raise the FFL using Windows PowerShell or other programmatic means, it will error out.

Creating the right trust

In an Active Directory environment with multiple domains, you're bound to have trusts. Trusts allow people to access resources in a domain or forest other than the domain or forest where their user accounts reside.

When Active Directory domains are added to an existing Active Directory domain, two-way transitive trusts are automatically created. However, in other situations, trusts have to be created manually. With many different types of trusts, two trust directions, and a choice in transitivity, which trust is the right trust for which situation?

Let's take a look at the six types of trusts first:

- **Parent-child trust**: The parent-child trust is a trust type that is automatically created when you add a domain to a tree root. For example, a parent-child trust is automatically created between `adatum.com` and `sub.adatum.com`. You cannot manually create a parent-child trust.

- **Tree-root trust**: The tree-root trust is a trust type that is also automatically created, just like the parent-child trust. However, the tree-root trust is created when you add a new domain tree to an Active Directory forest. For example, when you add the domain to a forest that contains only the `adatum.com` domain. The difference between the tree-root trust and the parent-child trust is that with the former, you break the domain tree, whereas with the latter, you expand on it. You cannot manually create a tree-root trust.

- **Forest trust**: A forest trust is a trust type that you will have to create manually. When accounts in two separate Active Directory forests want to work together on each other's resources, then this is the right trust type to create between the two forest root domains. Creating a forest trust is highly preferable over creating an external trust, because the latter only supports older authentication schemes, whereas a forest trust supports Kerberos authentication.

- **Realm trust**: The realm trust type exists to help you connect with non-Active Directory environments, such as Samba-based environments and Novell eDirectory-based environments. The requirement for the other side of the trust is that it needs to support the Kerberos version.

- **External trust**: An external trust is a trust type that you will have to create manually. This trust type is truly versatile, as you can create a trust with any other environment, including Windows NT 4.0 Server-based environments. The downside is that it leverages NTLM as its authentication protocol; this is considered an outdated and weak protocol.

- **Shortcut trust**: In large Active Directory environments, authentication to access a resource may take a long time. As a user traverses trusts within an Active Directory forest, they have to perform Kerberos authentication up and down trees until they reach the domain with the resource they want to access. The rule of thumb is to create a shortcut trust when users in one domain regularly use resources in another domain (but within the same forest), and they have to traverse five, or more, trusts to get from the domain where their user accounts reside to the domain where the resources reside.

This creates the following flowchart:

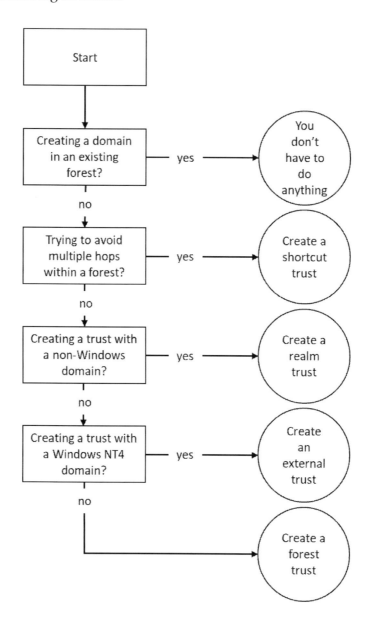

Trust direction

The right direction of a trust can be simply explained with an analogy. Suppose that a friend wants to borrow your car; you share your keys to the car with them and then you give them permission to use the car.

In terms of the Active Directory trust, the friend will map to the *user account*, the car to a *resource*, and you will be the *resource owner*. The trust flows from the resource to the user. The admin of the resource has to create the trust.

Trust transitivity

The same analogy also works for transitivity. Suppose that you want to lend your car to a friend, but they also want to lend the car to their friends. If you trust the friend enough, you will probably allow them to do so. If you don't have this level of trust in your friend, or you know some of their friends and you don't trust them with your car, then it's a bad idea.

In terms of Active Directory trusts, the trust type where you trust all the user accounts in all the domains to access the resource, is a transitive trust; parent-child trusts, tree-root trusts, and forest trusts are transitive, by default.

The trust type where you only trust your friend and not all of their friends to access the resource is a non-transitive trust. Realm trusts and external trusts are non-transitive, by default.

One-way or two-way trust

Essentially, every trust is a one-way trust. All the trusts that you create manually are one-way trusts, by default. However, you can combine two one-way trusts in opposite directions to create a two-way trust. In the scope of a two-way trust, people on both sides of the trust can access resources on both sides of the trust using their user accounts.

Microsoft recommends creating a two-way trust when your goal is to migrate accounts and resources using the **Active Directory Migration Tool** (**ADMT**). After migrating everything over, the two-way trust can be torn down.

Getting ready

To create a trust between two environments, make sure that the two environments know how to find each other. In DNS, create any necessary (conditional) forwarders or stub zones to point domain controllers from one environment to the domain controllers or Kerberos **Key Distribution Centers (KDCs)** of the other environment.

Additionally, take care of proper networking; the domain controller holding the PDCe FSMO role and at least one global catalog for each domain on the route of the trust should be reachable from the device that someone uses to access the resource. The following firewall ports should be opened:

Service	Protocol	Port
Kerberos authentication	TCP and UDP	88
RPC endpoint mapper	TCP	135
NetBIOS name service	TCP and UDP	137
File Replication Service (FRS) between domain controllers	UDP	138
Distributed File System Replication (DFSR), NetBIOS session service	TCP	139
Lightweight Directory Access Protocol (LDAP)	TCP and UDP	389
Server Message Block (SMB)	TCP and UDP	445
Kerberos password change	TCP and UDP	464
Lightweight Directory Access Protocol over SSL (LDAPS)	TCP and UDP	636
LDAP to global catalogs	TCP	3269
LDAPs to global catalogs	TCP	3269

Preferably, you should sign in to the domain controller that is running the Domain Naming Master FSMO role, or connect the **Active Directory Domains and Trusts** console to this specific domain controller.

To find this domain controller, right-click the **Active Directory Domains and Trusts** node and select **Operations Master...** from the menu. Alternatively, run the following command from any domain-joined device, member server, or domain controller:

```
netdom.exe query fsmo
```

Otherwise, you can use the following PowerShell commands on a domain-joined system that has the Active Directory module for Windows PowerShell installed:

```
Import-Module ActiveDirectory

Get-ADForest | Format-List DomainNamingMaster
```

Required permissions

For shortcut trusts, sign in with the credentials of an admin account that is a member of the Domain Admins group. For all other accounts, sign in with the credentials of an admin account that is a member of the Enterprise Admins group.

How to do it...

To create a trust on Windows devices or Windows Servers with the Desktop Experience use the **Active Directory Domains and Trusts** tool for the domain you (as a resource owner) want to give access to:

1. Open **Active Directory Domains and Trusts** (`domain.msc`).
2. In the console tree, right-click the domain that you want to allow access to, and then click **Properties....**
3. Navigate to the **Trusts** tab, as follows:

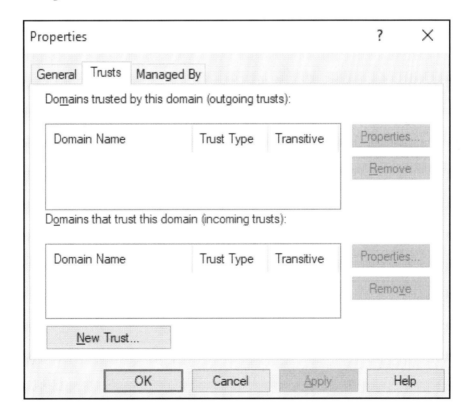

4. Click the **New Trust...** button.
5. Run through the **New Trust Wizard**.
6. In the **Welcome to the New Trust Wizard** screen, click <u>N</u>ext >.
7. In the **Trust Name** screen, type a name for the trust in the **N<u>a</u>me:** field. Then, click <u>N</u>ext > when done.
8. In the **Trust Type** screen, choose between a **Realm trust** or a **Trust with a Windows domain**. For the latter, type the name of the domain, in case it's different to the trust name. Click <u>N</u>ext >.
9. In the **Trust Type** screen, choose between an **External trust** or a **Forest trust**. Click <u>N</u>ext >.
10. In the **Direction of Trust** screen, choose between a **Two-way**, **One-way: incoming**, or **One-way: outgoing** trust. Click <u>N</u>ext >.
11. In the **Sides of Trust** screen, choose between creating the trust for this domain only, or both this domain and the specified domain. Click <u>N</u>ext >.
12. In the **User Name and Password** screen, provide the credentials of an account that has administrative privileges in the Active Directory domain on the other side of the trust. Click <u>N</u>ext >.
13. In the **Outgoing Trust Authentication Level-Local Forest** and/or **Outgoing Trust Authentication Level - Specified Forest** screens, choose between **Forest-wide authentication** and **Selective authentication**. Click <u>N</u>ext >.
14. In the **Trust Selections Complete** screen, review the settings, and click <u>N</u>ext > to create the trust.

15. In the **Trust Creation Complete** screen, click **Next** >:

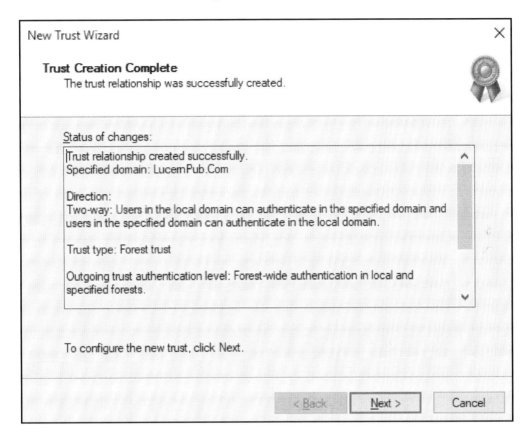

16. In the **Confirm Outgoing Trust** and/or **Confirm Incoming Trust** screens, choose between **No, do not confirm the outgoing trust** and **Yes, confirm the outgoing trust**. Click **Next** >.
17. In the **Completing the New Trust Wizard** screen, click **Finish**.

Alternatively, you can use the following commands:

```
netdom.exe trust TrustingDomain.tld /Domain:TrustedDomain.tld /TwoWay /Add
```

Replace `TrustingDomain.tld` with the DNS domain name of the Active Directory environment that gives access to its resources, and then replace `TrustedDomain.tld` with the DNS domain name of the Active Directory environment that gains access to the resources.

In the preceding example, a two-way trust is created where both Active Directory environments give and gain access to the other Active Directory environment.

It's a recommended practice in Active Directory to remove objects and settings that have no use.

When a trust is no longer needed, it can be deleted. To do so, follow these steps:

1. Open **Active Directory Domains and Trusts**.
2. In the console tree, right-click the domain that you want to allow access to, and then click **Properties**.
3. Navigate to the **Trusts** tab.
4. From the list of **Domains trusts by this domain (outgoing trusts):**, or from the list of **Domains that trust this domain (incoming trusts):** select the trust that you want to remove.
5. Click the **Remove** button next to the corresponding list.

Verifying and resetting a trust

After you create a trust, you might regularly want to check if the trust is working properly. You might be triggered by people who report that they can no longer access resources in other domains or forests, or it might be an activity that you perform on a regular basis.

When a trust is broken, there is a way to reset it. Also, when you want to reset the shared secret on both sides of the trust, a reset of the trust is needed.

Getting ready

It is recommended that you sign in to the domain controller that is running the Domain Naming Master FSMO role, or connect the **Active Directory Domains and Trusts** console to this specific domain controller, by right-clicking in the console on the **Active Directory Domains and Trusts** node and selecting **Change Active Directory Domain Controller...** from the context menu.

To find this domain controller, right-click the **Active Directory Domains and Trusts** node and select the **Operations Master...** from the context menu, or run the following command from any domain-joined device, member server, or domain controller:

```
netdom.exe query fsmo
```

Alternatively, use the following PowerShell commands on a domain-joined system that has the Active Directory module for Windows PowerShell installed:

```
Import-Module ActiveDirectory

Get-ADForest | Format-List DomainNamingMaster
```

Required permissions

For shortcut trusts, sign in with the credentials of an account that is a member of the Domain Admins group.

For all other accounts, sign in with the credentials of an account that is a member of the Enterprise Admins group.

How to do it...

Perform these steps:

1. Open **Active Directory Domains and Trusts**.
2. In the console tree, right-click the domain that you want to allow access to, and then click **Properties**.
3. Navigate to the **Trusts** tab.
4. From the list of **Domains trusts by this domain (outgoing trusts):**, or from the list of **Domains that trust this domain (incoming trusts):**, select the trust you want to verify.

5. Click the **Properties** button next to the corresponding list.
   The **Properties** window appears:

6. Click the **Validate** button.
7. For a two-way trust, choose between **No, do not validate the incoming trust** and **Yes, validate the incoming trust**. For the latter, provide the credentials of an account that has administrative privileges in the Active Directory domain on the other side of the trust. Click **OK**.

8. In the **Active Directory Domain Services** popup window, click **OK** to confirm that the outgoing trust has been validated. It is now in place and active.

9. In the **Active Directory Domain Services** popup window, notifying you of `UserPrincipalName` suffix routing, click **Yes**.

Alternatively, you can use the following command:

```
netdom.exe trust TrustingDomain.tld /Domain:TrustedDomain.tld /TwoWay
/Verify /verbose
```

Replace `TrustingDomain.tld` with the DNS domain name of the Active Directory environment that gives access to its resources, and then replace `TrustedDomain.tld` with the DNS domain name of the Active Directory environment that gains access to the resources.

 In the preceding example, a two-way trust is created where both Active Directory environments give and gain access to the other Active Directory environment.

The option to reset the trust will be presented only if a problem has been identified during the process of verifying the trust relationship.

How it works...

When a trust is verified, the following characteristics of the trust are verified:

- Networking connectivity between both sides of the trust
- Existence of the trust on the far side of the trust
- Synchronization of the shared secret on both sides of the trust

Therefore, verifying a trust is a good point to start troubleshooting, because it might quickly be able to identify changes made by network admins or the Active Directory admin on the other side of the trust.

When a trust relationship cannot be verified, the option to reset it is displayed, as indicated previously.

Securing a trust

Trusts in Active Directory can be misused for purposes not intended by the admin of the trusting domain. There are three ways to secure a trust to make it more secure:

- Enable SID Filtering
- Enable Quarantine
- Enable Selective Authentication

SID Filtering is enabled on all trust relationships, by default. SID Filtering operates on the same surface as trust transitivity. When enabled, SID Filtering filters the user accounts over the trust to user accounts from the domain tree that is explicitly trusted, only. In a way, it allows for more granular transitivity.

Quarantine is enabled on all trust relationships, by default. Quarantine for a trust allows granular access, too. Where SID Filtering allows for limiting access to a trusted domain tree, quarantine limits access to a trusted domain.

Selective authentication is not enabled, by default. Where SID Filtering and Quarantine limit access to user accounts from trusted domains, selective authentication limits access to devices, member servers and domain controllers in trusting domains. This means that in a default trust, all resources in the trusting domain can be accessed.

By default, Active Directory trusts are pretty secure, since the SID Filtering and Quarantine features are automatically enabled. You can heighten this default level of security by enabling and managing selective authentication.

Getting ready

To use the selective authentication feature, both Active Directory forests on either side of the trust need to run the Windows Server 2003 FFL, or a higher forest functional level.

It is recommended that you sign in to the domain controller that is running the Domain Naming Master FSMO role, or connect the **Active Directory Domains and Trusts** console to this specific domain controller, by right-clicking in the console on the **Active Directory Domains and Trusts** node and selecting **Change Active Directory Domain Controller...** from the context menu.

To find this domain controller, right-click the **Active Directory Domains and Trusts** node and select the **Operations Master...** from the context menu. Alternatively, run the following command from any domain-joined device, member server, or domain controller:

```
netdom.exe query fsmo
```

Otherwise, you can use the following PowerShell commands on a domain-joined system that has the Active Directory module for Windows PowerShell installed:

```
Import-Module ActiveDirectory

Get-ADForest | Format-List DomainNamingMaster
```

Required permissions

Sign in with the credentials of an admin account that is a member of the Enterprise Admins group.

How to do it...

SID Filtering and Quarantine on trusts can only be managed using netdom.exe:

1. To enable SID Filtering for a trust, use the following command:

   ```
   netdom.exe trust TrustingDomain.tld /Domain:TrustedDomain.tld
   /EnableSIDHistory:yes
   ```

   Replace TrustingDomain.tld with the DNS domain name of the Active Directory environment that gives access to its resources, and then replace TrustedDomain.tld with the DNS domain name of the Active Directory environment that gains access to the resources.

2. To disable SID Filtering for a trust, use the following command:

   ```
   netdom.exe trust TrustingDomain.tld /Domain:TrustedDomain.tld
   /EnableSIDHistory:no
   ```

   Replace TrustingDomain.tld with the DNS domain name of the Active Directory environment that gives access to its resources, and then replace TrustedDomain.tld with the DNS domain name of the Active Directory environment that gains access to the resources.

3. To enable Quarantine on a trust, use the following command:

```
netdom.exe trust TrustingDomain.tld /Domain:TrustedDomain.tld
/Quarantine:yes
```

Replace `TrustingDomain.tld` with the DNS domain name of the Active Directory environment that gives access to its resources, and then replace `TrustedDomain.tld` with the DNS domain name of the Active Directory environment that gains access to the resources.

4. To disable Quarantine on a trust, use the following command:

```
netdom.exe trust TrustingDomain.tld /Domain:TrustedDomain.tld
/Quarantine:no
```

Replace `TrustingDomain.tld` with the DNS domain name of the Active Directory environment that gives access to its resources, and then replace `TrustedDomain.tld` with the DNS domain name of the Active Directory environment that gains access to the resources.

To manage Selective Authentication, we can use the **graphical user interface (GUI)**. To do so, follow these steps:

1. Open **Active Directory Domains and Trusts.**
2. In the console tree, right-click the domain that you want to configure selective authentication for, and then click **Properties.**
3. Navigate to the **Trusts** tab.
4. From the list of **Domains trusts by this domain (outgoing trusts):** or from the list of **Domains that trust this domain (incoming trusts):**, select the trust that you want to configure selective authentication for.
5. Click the **Properties** button next to the corresponding list.

6. Navigate to the **Authentication** tab as follows:

7. On the **Authentication** tab, select or deselect **Selective Authentication.**
8. Click **OK** to finish.

Of course, selective authentication for trusts is also available on the command line.

To enable selective authentication for a trust, use the following command:

```
netdom.exe trust TrustingDomain.tld /Domain:TrustedDomain.tld
/SelectiveAuth:yes
```

Replace `TrustingDomain.tld` with the DNS domain name of the Active Directory environment that gives access to its resources, and then replace `TrustedDomain.tld` with the DNS domain name of the Active Directory environment that gains access to the resources.

To disable selective authentication for a trust, use the following command:

```
netdom.exe trust TrustingDomain.tld /Domain:TrustedDomain.tld /
SelectiveAuth:no
```

Replace `TrustingDomain.tld` with the DNS domain name of the Active Directory environment that gives access to its resources, and then replace `TrustedDomain.tld` with the DNS domain name of the Active Directory environment that gains access to the resources.

Now, the actual domain-joined resources, which a user from another domain or forest has access to, is governed per object. Follow these steps to manage this setting:

1. Open the **Active Directory Administrative Center**.
2. Search for the domain-joined device, member server, or domain controller that you want to grant access to over the trust. Use the search box in the **Global Search** field on the **Overview** screen of the **Active Directory Administrative Center**, or use the left navigation pane.
3. Right-click the object and select **Properties** from the context menu.
4. In the left navigation pane of the object's properties, click **Extensions**.
5. Click the **Security** tab.

6. Select the user object(s) and/or group(s) that you want to grant access to, wielding the **Add...** and **Remove** buttons underneath the field for **Groups and user names**:

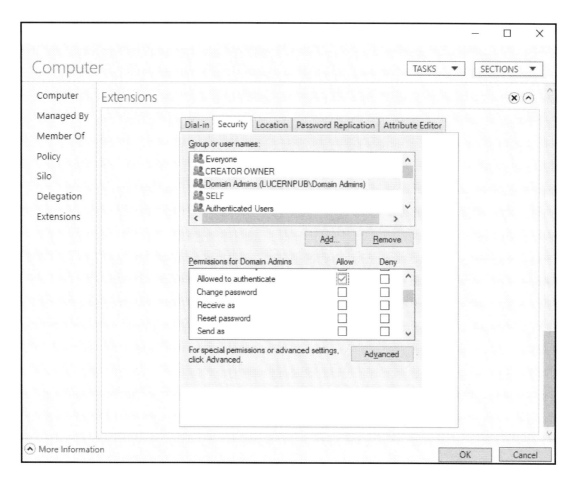

7. Select the **Allow** checkbox that is next to the **Allowed to Authenticate** permission.
8. Click **OK** when you're done.

How it works...

Selective authentication leverages the **Allowed to Authenticate** option to give permission to allow or disallow requests coming from user accounts over the trust, because they are automatically added to the Authenticated Users group. When selective authentication is disabled (the default), every user account on the other side is allowed to authenticate. However, after selective authentication is enabled, only the user accounts with the **Allowed to Authenticate** permission explicitly set can authenticate to it over the trust, because they are not automatically added to the Authenticated Users group.

There's more...

To make managing the Active Directory trust possible for a trust that has selective authentication enabled, make sure that admins on both sides have the **Allowed to Authenticate** permission on each other's domain controllers. You can specify specific domain controllers only by fiddling with the DNS SRV records for domain controllers. However, make sure that you always include the domain controller holding the PDCe FSMO role, and at least one global catalog.

Extending the schema

Some applications require additional object types and/or attributes to store their information in Active Directory. Some good examples of these type of applications are Microsoft Exchange Server and Microsoft's free **Local Administration Password Solution (LAPS)**.

These applications and their schema changes are thoroughly tested, but there's also the option to create your own custom Active Directory schema extension. For instance, you can introduce your own employee or customer ID type attribute to the user object class.

Getting ready

The domain controller holding the Schema Master FSMO role is authoritative for the Active Directory schema throughout an Active Directory forest. Microsoft recommends that you perform the following actions on the domain controller that is holding the Schema Master FSMO role.

To find this domain controller, run the following command on any domain-joined device, member server, or domain controller:

```
netdom.exe  query fsmo
```

Alternatively, use the following PowerShell commands on a domain-joined system that has the Active Directory module for Windows PowerShell installed:

```
Import-Module ActiveDirectory

Get-ADForest | Format-List SchemaMaster
```

To gain access to the Active Directory schema using Microsoft tools, look on the domain controller holding the Schema Master FSMO role, the Schema MMC Snap-in needs to be registered. By default, this MMC Snap-in is hidden from view, due to its sensitive nature.

Run the following command to register the Schema MMC Snap-in:

```
regsvr32.exe C:\windows\system32\schmmgmt.dll
```

Required permissions

To extend the schema, perform the following actions using an account that is a member of the schema admins group.

To request permission to use an **official identifier (OID)** for your schema attribute or object, you will need to create it as part of your organization's OID branch. The following two websites allow you to view whether your organization has an official OID branch: www.iana.org/assignments/enterprise-numbers and www.alvestrand.no/object id/.

If your organization does not have an assigned OID, go to your country's national registry to request one. Make sure that the registration is correct, but also leave room for further expansions, relocations, mergers, acquisitions, and divestitures.

OIDs are hierarchical, so you should create it as part of your organization's branch.

How to do it...

Perform these steps to extend the Active Directory schema with a new attribute:

1. Open a **Microsoft Management Console** window (`mmc.exe`).
2. From the **File** menu, select **Add/Remove Snap-in**.
3. From the left-hand list of **Available snap-ins:**, select the **Active Directory Schema** snap-in. Click the **Add >** button to add it to the right-hand list of **Selected snap-ins**:

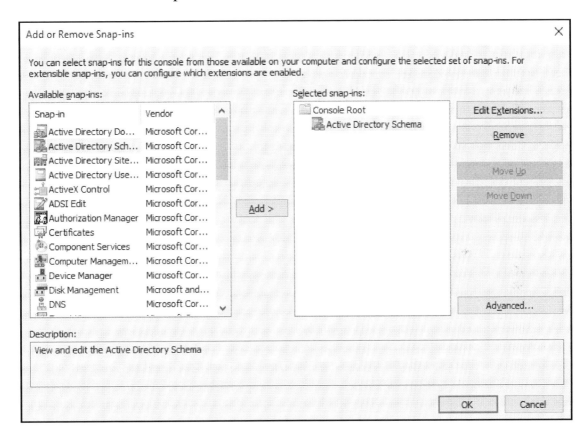

4. Click **OK**.
5. In the left navigation pane, expand **Active Directory Schema**.

6. Right-click the **Attributes** folder and select **Create Attribute** from the context menu:

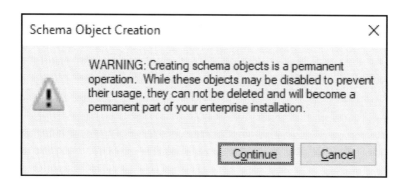

7. Click the **Continue** button to confirm that you want to extend the schema:

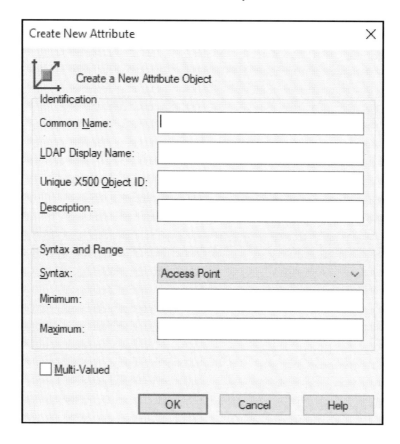

8. Enter the information for the new attribute.
9. Click **OK** when done.

Perform these steps to extend the Active Directory schema with a new object class:

1. Open the **Active Directory Schema** snap-in.
2. In the left navigation pane, expand **Active Directory Schema**.
3. Right-click the **Classes** folder, and select **Create Class** from the context menu.
4. Click the **Continue** button to confirm that you want to extend the schema. The **Create New Schema Class** window appears:

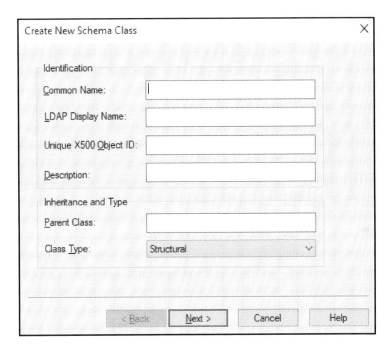

5. Enter the information for the new class.
6. Click **Next>** when done.
7. Enter any mandatory and optional attributes and click **Finish**.

There's more...

Any attributes and classes added to Active Directory cannot be removed. However, they can be defunct when they are no longer needed.

It's a best practice to keep the Schema Administrators group in Active Directory as empty as possible for as long as possible. When you're done, remove any accounts that you may have added to the Schema Administrators group.

If you want your Active Directory schema extension attributes to extend into Azure Active Directory as well, make sure it's a single-valued attribute.

Enabling the Active Directory Recycle Bin

The Active Directory Recycle Bin was introduced as a new Active Directory feature with Windows Server 2008 R2. It enables administrators to restore (accidentally) deleted objects.

There were features available to administrators before the advent of the Active Directory Recycle Bin – such as the **Directory Services Restore Mode (DSRM)** mode and object reanimation. In contrast to booting into the DSRM, the Active Directory Recycle Bin saves admins time. In contrast to reanimating objects, the Active Directory Recycle Bin prevents the typical loss of attributes and group memberships.

There are also numerous third-party solutions that are available to restore objects and their attributes. They typically expand on the functionality that is offered by the Active Directory Recycle Bin, by offering granular attribute restore and group policy versioning. These are two areas where the Active Directory Recycle Bin doesn't offer a solution.

Getting ready

The Active Directory forest needs to run the Windows Server 2008 R2 FFL (or a later version).

Microsoft recommends enabling the Active Directory Recycle Bin on the Active Directory domain controller that holds the Domain Naming Master FSMO role.

To find this domain controller, run the following command on any domain-joined device, member server, or domain controller:

```
netdom.exe query fsmo
```

Alternatively, use the following PowerShell commands on a domain-joined system that has the Active Directory module for Windows PowerShell installed:

```
Import-Module ActiveDirectory

Get-ADForest | Format-List DomainNamingMaster
```

Required permissions

Sign in to the preceding domain controller using an account that is a member of the Enterprise Admins group in Active Directory.

How to do it...

You can enable the Active Directory Recycle Bin from within the Active Directory Administrative Center, when you're signed in with an account that is a member of the Enterprise Admins group on a domain controller that runs Windows Server with Desktop Experience. To do this, perform the following steps:

1. Open the **Active Directory Administrative Center** (dsac.exe).
2. Select the forest name in the left navigation pane.

3. In the action pane on the right, click the **Enable Recycle Bin** link. Alternatively, you can right-click the domain name in the left navigation pane, and select the **Enable Recycle Bin...** option from the context menu. The **Enable Recycle Bin Confirmation** popup appears:

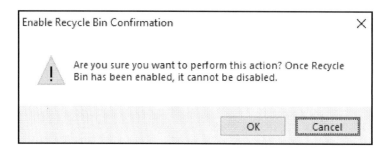

4. In the **Enable Recycle Bin Confirmation** pop up, click **OK**.
5. The popup message labeled **Active Directory Administrative Center** appears:

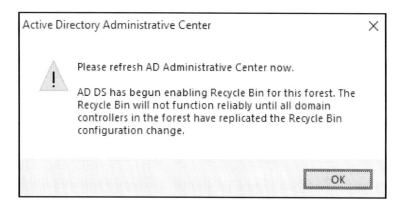

6. Click **OK**:

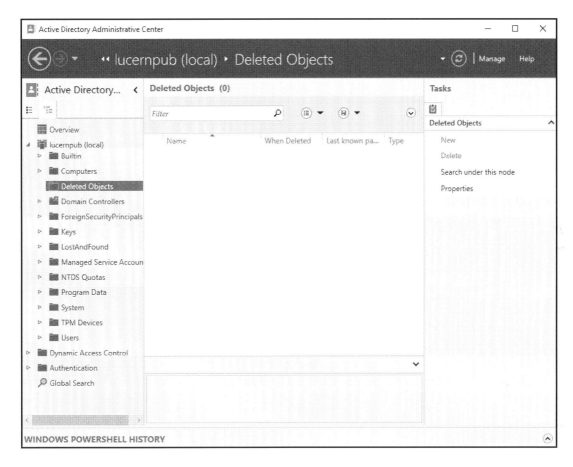

7. After you refresh, a new container underneath the domain root named **Deleted Objects** appears.

On Server Core installations of Windows Server, use the following PowerShell commands:

```
Import-Module ActiveDirectory

Enable-ADOptionalFeature -Identity "CN=Recycle Bin Feature,CN=Optional
Features,CN=Directory Service,CN=Windows
NT,CN=Services,CN=Configuration,DC=lucernpub,DC=com" -Scope
ForestOrConfigurationSet -Target "lucernpub.com"
```

Replace `lucernpub`, `lucernpub`, and `com` with values for your Active Directory environment.

How it works...

Since the inception of Active Directory, when an object such as a computer or a user is deleted, the **isDeleted** attribute is set to `true`. This allows the domain controller to replicate the change for the object. Each domain controller has the time configured as the tombstone lifetime period to replicate this change. Only after the tombstone lifetime period is the object removed from the database by each domain controller.

The Active Directory Recycle Bin introduces a new recycle lifetime and a new attribute: `isRecycled`. With the Active Directory Recycle Bin enabled, when an object is deleted it's `isDeleted` attribute is still set to `true`, but it's `isRecycled` attribute is untouched. This is the period where the object is visible in the deleted objects container, where it can be restored by simply right-clicking on it. After the recycle lifetime has expired, the `isRecycled` attribute is also set to `true`. This is when the tombstone lifetime kicks in. Only after the tombstone lifetime period has expired the object is removed from the database by each domain controller.

Managing UPN suffixes

In Active Directory, users and services can sign in using their pre-Windows 2000 logon name (the value of the **sAMAccountName** attribute) or their Kerberos user principal name (the value of the **userPrincipalName** attribute). As Kerberos relies heavily on DNS, the user principal name features an **userPrincipalName** suffix, in the form of a DNS domain name.

These **userPrincipalName** suffixes can be added to the list of available UPN suffixes for each Active Directory forest.

By default, this list already contains the DNS domain names of the Active Directory domains in the forest.

UPN suffixes in on-premises Active Directory environments do not need to be publicly routable. Only if you intend to use them with the federation and/or hybrid identity then they need to be. In many organizations, a cloud journey begins with changing the UPN suffix on all the user objects that need to be cloud-enabled to a publicly-routable UPN suffix. Some organizations have adopted `.local` as their top-level domain name, and this is the prime example of a non-publicly-routable top-level domain name.

Getting ready

To make the most of UPN suffixes, make sure that you have an overview of the domain names and the publicly registered domain names for the organization.

How to do it...

UPN suffixes can be managed using **Active Directory Domains and Trusts**.

To do so, perform the following steps:

1. Open **Active Directory Domains and Trusts** (`domain.msc`).
2. Right-click **Active Directory Domains and Trusts** in the left navigation pane, and select **Properties** from the context menu:

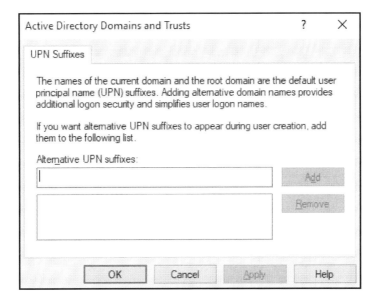

3. Type the new UPN suffix that you would like to add to the Active Directory forest, select the UPN suffix that you would like to remove, or simply glance over the list of UPN suffixes.
4. Click **Add** or **Remove**, and then click **OK.**

How it works...

Both **userPrincipalName** and pre-Windows 2000 logon names can be used to sign in interactively to Windows. Windows' sign-in screen can handle both. However, in cloud scenarios, the **userPrincipalName** suffix is used, by default.

There's more...

An admin cannot assign a non-existing **userPrincipalName** suffix. However, when a UPN suffix is assigned to one or more accounts, there's no alert that mentions this when you remove a UPN suffix.

Managing Domain Controllers

2

Active Directory domain controllers are your network's castles of identity. They offer services, such as LDAP, Kerberos, and NTLM, to people using devices, appliances, and servers. The previous chapter introduced the concepts of forests, trees, and domains. In this chapter, we are going to provide some more tangible things, such as server machines. But please don't take that literally; domain controllers these days are found to be virtual machines, more than physical machines.

I'll walk through creating new domain controllers and show you which type of domain controller to implement. I'll also show you how to create domain controllers quickly, even when there's only a slow connection between the location with existing domain controllers and the location where you want to implement a new domain controller. We'll also look at creating hundreds of domain controllers quickly.

The following recipes will be covered in this chapter:

- Promoting a server to a domain controller
- Promoting a server to a read-only domain controller
- Using Install From Media
- Using domain controller cloning
- Determining whether a virtual domain controller has a VM-GenerationID
- Demoting a domain controller
- Demoting a domain controller forcefully
- Inventory domain controllers
- Decommissioning a compromised read-only domain controller

Preparing a Windows Server to become a domain controller

To make Active Directory a reliable service in any networking environment, the domain controllers need to be available with high integrity. Any changes an administrator needs to make to a deployed domain controller might diminish the availability. Any component or configuration that is misbehaving might diminish the integrity. Therefore, let's look at how to properly prepare a Windows Server installation to become a domain controller, before we actually promote it to becoming a domain controller.

The following steps are my time-tested recommended practices for production domain controllers within enterprises. I highly recommend these steps to create highly reliable domain controllers.

Intending to do the right thing

The first few items on the list of preparations is to have the right ideas for promoting domain controllers throughout their life cycles:

- **Intend to create at least two domain controllers per Active Directory domain**: This way, both servers can be advertised to networking clients as LDAP servers and DNS servers. Then, when you have to reboot one of at least two servers, these clients wouldn't be hindered. Also, restoring a domain controller while another domain controller is still available allows for scenarios such as non-authoritative restores, domain controller cloning, and domain controller re-promotion.
- **Intend to implement role separation**: By all means, do not misuse a domain controller as an Exchange Server or SQL Server, unless it's a Windows Small Business Server. The DNS Server, DHCP Server, and NPS server roles are gray areas here, which should be addressed with common sense: if it means a domain controller will be harder to restore, manage, or decommission, separate the roles.

Dimensioning the servers properly

Now, let's look at how to actually dimension intended domain controllers:

- **Intend to create equal domain controllers in terms of hardware dimensions**: It's tempting to place one big server and one smaller server as domain controllers, but consider the possibility of having to move FSMO roles or other loads from one domain controller to another. Since domain controllers are randomly assigned to networking clients inside an Active Directory site, networking clients accessing the smaller server might not enjoy the same performance.

- **Dimension the intended domain controllers properly in terms of hardware**: Domain controllers offer the best performance, when they can cache the Active Directory database, `ntds.dit`, in RAM. Plan for ample room in RAM to cache up to 4 KB per Active Directory object plus a 10 MB minimum for the main objects and partitions. You should start with the minimum RAM required to install Windows Server then add on the additional memory for AD DS. For physical servers, use RAID and separate spindles for storage of Active Directory related data, when possible. Use hardware that will be covered by the manufacturer's (extended) guarantee, support, and life cycle policies for the period in which you need to rely on the domain controller.

- **Dimension the intended domain controllers properly in terms of software**: Use a version of Windows Server that will be covered by Microsoft's (extended) support and life cycle policies for the period in which you need to rely on the domain controller.

- **Implement the Server Core version of Windows Server, when possible**: Server Core installations of Windows Server offer higher availability and smaller attack surface compared to Windows Server installations with the Desktop Experience feature. However, some agents or other software components in use within the organization might not properly run on Server Core installations. In the latter scenario, Windows Server installations with the Desktop Experience feature (called full installations in previous versions of Windows Server) should be performed, obviously.

- **Install the latest firmware for devices and/or integration components**: On physical boxes you intend to use as a domain controller, install the latest stable firmware for the **Basic Input/Output System (BIOS)**, the storage controller(s), the video card(s) and network interface card(s) (NICs). On virtual machines, implement the latest stable version of the integration components or VMware tools and follow the recommended practices from the vendor of the hypervisor platform.

- **Use a virtualization platform that offers the VM-GenerationID feature**: Place virtual domain controllers on a virtualization platform that offers the VM-GenerationID feature. This will offer the domain controller virtualization safeguards that allows administrators to take snapshots of domain controllers without compromising the integrity of the Active Directory database. Also, domain controller cloning is available on these virtualization platforms.

Preparing the Windows Server installations

Before you install Windows Server on intended domain controllers, perform these actions:

- **Run the memory diagnostics from the Windows Server installation media**: The Windows Server DVD allows administrators to check the RAM of physical and virtual machines to make sure that the memory used by the Windows Server installation is not faulty. Checking beforehand means you don't have to replace faulty memory after going live.
- **Run** `sysprep.exe` **on cloned disks**: When the Windows Server installation is the result of the cloning of a disk with a Windows Server installation on it, make sure the Windows Server installation is Sysprepped. You wouldn't want the SID of the cloned disk to become the SID for the new Active Directory forest or domain you might be creating.

Preconfigure the Windows Servers

After Windows Server is installed, configure these items on the Windows Server, either through the Server Manager on Windows Server installations with the Desktop Experience feature or by using `sconfig.cmd` on Server Core installations:

- Change the hostname for the Windows Server installation. Leverage the server naming convention and/or policy within the organization.
- Check for proper Windows Activation of the Windows Server operating system.
- Update the Windows Server installation with the latest updates.
- Configure the server with at least one static IPv4 address and/or a static IPv6 address. Leverage the networking plan and zone assignment policies within the organization. Avoid multi-homing domain controllers.

When the intended domain controller is to run as a virtual machine within a cloud environment, such as Amazon's AWS or Microsoft's Azure, let the cloud provider assign the IPv4 and/or IPv6 addresses, because manually setting these addresses might break the connectivity of the Windows Server installation. Instead, use IP address reservations to make sure intended domain controllers remain reachable over the same addresses.

- **Check for at least one connected LAN connection**: Without a connected LAN connection, the promotion of a domain controller will fail. This is by design.
- **Configure proper naming resolution**: As DNS plays a vital role in locating Active Directory, make sure DNS is properly configured. Plan for Active Directory-integrated DNS. Don't forget the DNS stub zones and/or conditional forwarders when creating a new Active Directory domain and/or forest. Deploy WINS or GlobalNames zones in legacy environments.
- Configure the pagefile correctly.
- **Implement information security measures**: Deploy agents for anti-malware, uninterruptible power supplies, backup and restore, **Security Incident and Event Management (SIEM)**, **Technology State and Compliance Monitoring (TSCM)**, advanced threat analytics, and other information security measures your organization's policies might require.

Document the passwords

In large organizations, you can't get anything done without the proper changes being filed through change management. Even if your organization doesn't require these steps, it's still a recommended practice to document at least these items:

- **Document the password for the built-in administrator account**: When deploying a new Active Directory forest or domain, deploy using a pre-configured password for the built-in administrator account. After successful promotion, change the password to one that you intend to assign to this account for a longer period of time. Document the latter password in a password vault.

As domain controllers are promoted using scripts, there is a chance the password for the built-in account lingers around unintentionally. Also, the password initially set for this account is stored with a weaker hashing algorithm than changed passwords.

- **Document the Directory Services Restore Mode (DSRM) password**: In dire situations, when the Active Directory-related services are no longer able to start, an administrator can sign in to the server using a fallback account with the DSRM password. Intend to use different DSRM passwords for each domain controller and document these properly in a password vault.

Now we will look at the recipes covered in this chapter.

Promoting a server to a domain controller

There are three ways to promote a Windows Server installation to a domain controller:

- Using Server Manager and the Active Directory Domain Services Configuration Wizard
- Using `dcpromo.exe` with an answer file
- Using the `Install-DDSDomainController`, `Install-ADDSDomain` or `Install-ADDSForest` cmdlets from the Active Directory module for Windows PowerShell

In this recipe, we will cover the steps to promote a server using the preceding three ways.

Getting ready

In some organizations, changes can only be made using scripts and must be accompanied by roll-back scripts. In these cases, the answer file and the PowerShell cmdlets offer the best method. On Server Core installations of Windows Server, only the last two options are available, unless you use Server Manager to remotely manage the server you intend to promote to a domain controller.

The Active Directory Domain Services Configuration Wizard no longer features the option to not reboot the Windows Server installation intended as a domain controller after successful promotion. If you need this option, for instance to harden the domain controller before the first boot with custom scripts, then you can't use the wizard. Use `dcpromo.exe` or the PowerShell cmdlets in these cases.

How to do it...

This recipe details how to promote a server to a domain controller using the wizard, `dcpromo.exe`, and PowerShell.

Promoting a domain controller using the wizard

When you've properly prepared the Windows Server installation you intend to promote to a domain controller, or when you've successfully managed such a Windows Server installation, you can use the graphical user interface of the Server Manager tool, to promote it.

Promoting a domain controller using the GUI consists of two parts:

- Executing the Add Roles and Features Wizard to install the Active Directory Domain Services role
- Executing the Active Directory Domain Services Configuration Wizard to promote the server to a domain controller

Installing the Active Directory Domain Services role

Follow these steps to install the **Active Directory Domain Services** role:

1. Open **Server Manager** (`servermanager.exe`).
2. In the gray top bar of **Server Manager**, click **Manage**.
3. Select **Add Roles and Features** from the menu.

4. The **Before you begin** screen appears, as shown in the following screenshot:

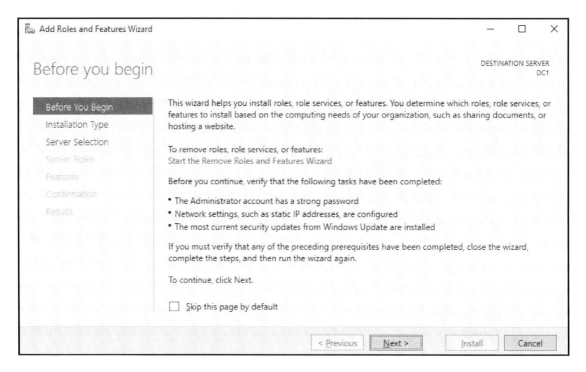

5. On the **Before you begin** screen, click **Next >**.
6. On the **Select installation type** screen, select **Role-based or feature-based installation**.
7. Click **Next >**.
8. On the **Select destination server** screen, select the local Windows Server installation from the server pool list, select the remote Windows Server installation you intend to promote to domain controller from the server pool list, or make a selection of both types of resources.
9. Click **Next >**.
10. On the **Select server roles** screen, select the Active Directory Domain Services role from the list of available roles.

11. The **Add Roles and Features Wizard** popup appears, as shown in the following screenshot:

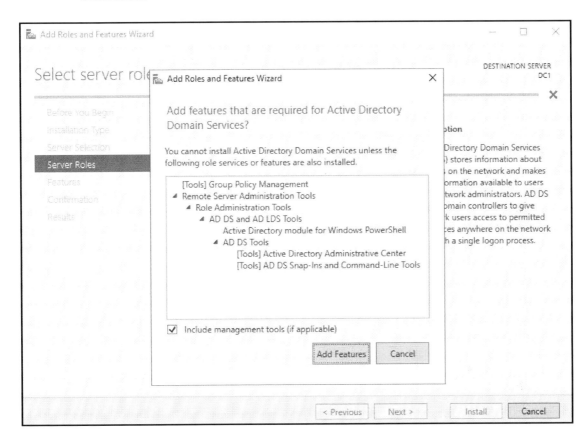

12. In the popup screen, click the **Add features** button to **Add features that are required for Active Directory Domain Services**. These features include the Group Policy Management tool, the **Active Directory module for Windows PowerShell**, the **Active Directory Administrative Center**, and the **AD DS Snap-Ins and Command-Line Tools**.

13. Back on the **Select server roles** screen, click **Next >**.

14. On the **Select server features** screen, click **Next >**.

15. On the **Active Directory Domain Services** screen, providing an overview of Active Directory and Azure AD, click **Next >**.

16. On the Confirm installation selections screen, click **Install**.

17. When configuration of the **Active Directory Domain Services** server role is done, click **Close** to close the **Add Roles and Features Wizard**:

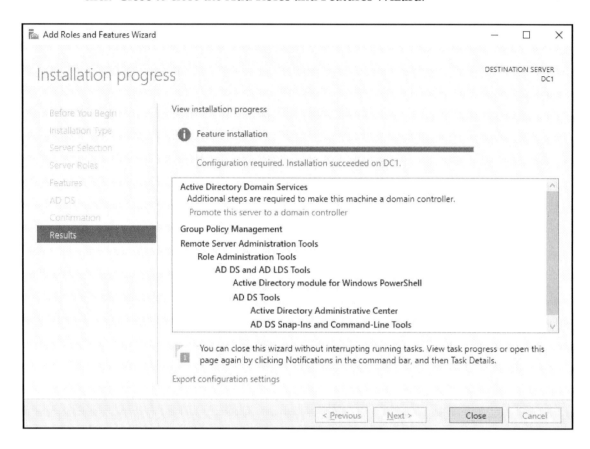

Promoting the server to a domain controller

Follow these steps to promote the server to a domain controller:

1. Open **Server Manager** (`servermanager.exe`) or return to it, when you've accomplished the previous steps.
2. In the left navigation pane, click **AD DS**.
3. Click the **More...** link in the yellow ribbon (as shown in the following screenshot) titled **Configuration required for Active Directory Domain Services at server:**

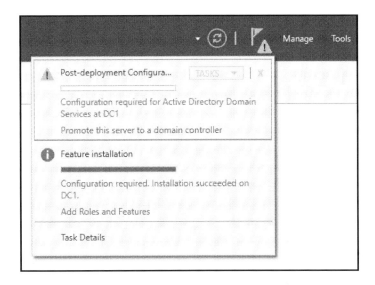

4. In the **All servers Task Details and Notifications** screen, follow the link to **Promote this server to a domain controller**. This starts the **Active Directory Domain Services Configuration Wizard**.

In the top-right corner of every **Active Directory Domain Services Configuration Wizard** screen, it shows you the hostname of the Windows Server installation you're promoting to a domain controller.

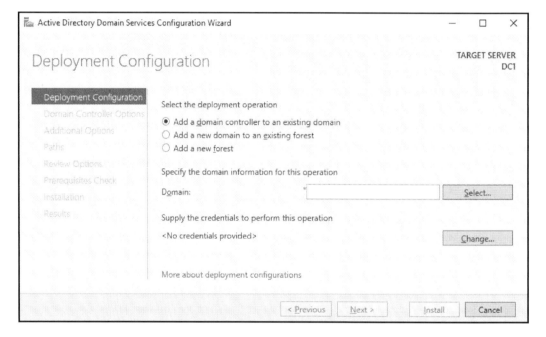

5. On the **Deployment Configuration** screen (as shown in the preceding screenshot), select the type of deployment you intend:

- **Add a domain controller to an existing domain**
- **Add a new domain to an existing domain**
- **Add a new forest**

The option, **Add a domain controller to an existing domain**, is the default one. It will create a replica domain controller in the domain. If this is not your preferred choice, and you are unsure of the choice to make, please refer to the *Choosing between a new domain or forest* recipe from `Chapter 1`, *Optimizing Forests, Domains, and Trusts*. The **More about deployment configurations** link at the bottom of the **Deployment configurations** screen offers a web page from Microsoft with more information, too.

6. Depending on your choices on the **Deployment configuration** screen, supply information for the **Domain** or **Credentials** fields. Click **Next** to proceed to the next screen.

7. In all of the other screens for the **Active Directory Domain Services Configuration Wizard**, make the appropriate choices for the deployment scenario. Click **Next >** every time to proceed to the next screen, until you reach the **Review Options** screen:

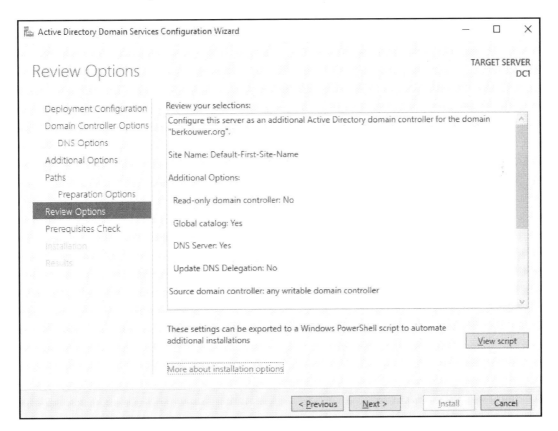

8. On the **Review Options** screen, as shown in the preceding screenshot, review the choices made. Click **Next** to proceed to the **Prerequisites Check** screen.

The **Review options** screen features a button labeled **View script**. This button displays the Windows PowerShell script used to execute the domain controller promotion. Especially when adding several domain controllers to an existing domain, this reusable script may be a real time-saver.

9. After the prerequisites checks have been performed, click **Install** on the **Prerequisites Check** screen to start promotion.

After successful promotion, the Windows Server installation will reboot as a domain controller.

Promoting a domain controller using dcpromo.exe

Despite many news outlets reporting that dcpromo is dead, the popular option to promote a Windows Server installation to a domain controller is alive and well, even in the latest Windows Server versions. One change to the functionality of dcpromo.exe, when compared to previous version of Windows Server, is that you can no longer use dcpromo.exe to launch the Active Directory Domain Services Configuration Wizard. You'll need to use dcpromo.exe with an answer file or with all of the installation arguments specified.

Benefits of using dcpromo.exe include the use of a slew of options that are not available when using the Active Directory Domain Services Configuration Wizard, but also a wide array of sample answer files and scripts, because the type of answer files used when using dcpromo.exe, and the arguments to use on the command line, have been available since the early days of Windows Server. Many people have used them and many people have written them.

Using dcpromo.exe with an answer file consists of running the following Command Prompt line:

```
dcpromo.exe /unattend: C:\install\dcpromo.txt
```

Simply replace the text file location with the file of your choice.

You can also use network paths such as
`\\server\promotiontext$\dcpromo.txt` to supply an answer file
to `dcpromo.txt`. This makes for an ideal scenario where files don't
remain lingering on domain controllers promoted this way.

The `answer` file consists of several arguments. Typical arguments found in the answer file
include the `ReplicaOrNewDomain`, `InstallDNS`, and `ConfirmGC` arguments. A prime
example of an answer file to add an additional domain controller to an existing domain
would look like the following:

```
[DCINSTALL]
ReplicaorNewDomain= replica
ReplicaDomainDNSName= lucernpub.com
UserDomain= LUCERNPUB
UserName= Administrator
SiteName= RemoteLocation
Password= "P@$$w0rd"
InstallDNS= Yes
ConfirmGC= Yes
CreateDNSDelegation= No
DatabasePath= E:\NTDS
LogPath= E:\Logs
SYSVOLPath= E:\SYSVOL
SafeModeAdminPassword= "P@$$w0rd"
RebootOnSuccess= true
```

This will add a domain controller to the `lucernpub.com` Active Directory domain, using
the credentials for the administrator account with the password, `P@$$w0rd`. The domain
controller will be installed with a DNS Server and configured as a global catalog server. All
of the Active Directory-related files are stored in corresponding folders on the `E:\` drive,
and when successful, the Windows Server installation you intend as domain controller will
be rebooted automatically.

Replace the values in the preceding sample file with the values of your choice.

When promotion is successful, the passwords specified as the values for
the `Password` and `SafeModeAdminPassword` arguments are cleared from
the answer file. However, when promotion is unsuccessful, these values
remain and may cause harm when falling into the wrong hands.

The arguments in the answer file can also be specified as command line arguments. The arguments can be reused one-on-one, so the preceding sample `answer` file would correspond to the following command line:

```
dcpromo.exe /unattend /replicaornewdomain:Replica
/replicadomaindnsname:lucernpub.com /userdomain:LUCERNPUB
/username:administrator /password:"P@$$w0rd" /sitename:RemoteLocation
/installdns:yes /confirmgc:yes /databasepath:"E:\NTDS" /logpath:"E:\logs"
/sysvolpath:"E:\sysvol" /safemodeadminpassword:"P@$$w0rd"
```

Promoting a domain controller using Windows PowerShell

For the Active Directory Module for Windows PowerShell, Microsoft has decided to take a slightly different route. Instead of using a single PowerShell cmdlet to promote a domain controller, there are three separate PowerShell cmdlets for each of the three scenarios, as presented as part of the Active Directory Domain Services Configuration Wizard:

Scenario	PowerShell cmdlet
Add a domain controller to an existing domain	Install-ADDSDomainController
Add a new domain to an existing forest	Install-ADDSDomain
Add a new forest	Install-ADDSForest

To add a domain controller to an existing domain, the simplest script would look like that shown in the following example:

```
Install-WindowsFeature AD-Domain-Services -IncludeManagementTools

Import-Module ADDSDeployment

Install-ADDSDomainController -DomainName lucernpub.com
```

However, to add a domain controller to an existing domain, as you would in the previous three examples, the following script would suffice:

```
Install-WindowsFeature AD-Domain-Services -IncludeManagementTools

Import-Module ADDSDeployment

Install-ADDSDomainController -DomainName lucernpub.com -Credential
(Get-Credential) -installDNS:$true -NoGlobalCatalog:$false -DatabasePath
"E:\NTDS" -Logpath "E:\Logs" -SysvolPath "E:\SYSVOL" -Sitename
RemoteLocation
```

This will add a domain controller to the `lucernpub.com` Active Directory domain, using credentials you will be prompted for securely. The domain controller will be installed with a DNS Server and configured as a global catalog server. All the Active Directory-related files are stored in corresponding folders on the `E:\` drive, and when successful, the Windows Server installation you intend as domain controller will be rebooted automatically.

Replace the values in the preceding sample file with the values of your choice.

Checking proper promotion

After promoting a Windows Server installation to domain controller, it's recommended to check for proper promotion. Follow these steps to check:

1. **Check the logs**: The following two files contain all of the actions performed when promoting the Windows Server installation to domain controller. A good way to check against improper promotion is to search for lines containing error and warning:
   - `C:\Windows\Debug\dcpromo.log`
   - `C:\Windows\Debug\dcpromoui.log`

2. **Check the event viewer**: In event viewer (`eventvwr.exe`), new dedicated logs are created for Active Directory. Search these logs for any Active Directory-related errors.

3. **Run Windows Update**: Even though one of the recommended steps is to update the Windows Server installation you intend to promote to a domain controller, it's also a recommended step to install Windows Updates after the Windows Server installation has been promoted, as updates apply to the newly installed server roles and features, too. These role-specific updates are only applied after the role is installed.

See also

For more information refer to the following recipes:

- See *Preparing a Windows Server to become a domain controller* recipe.
- See *Promoting a server to a read-only domain controller* recipe.

Promoting a server to a read-only domain controller

Read-only domain controllers were introduced with Windows Server 2008. They have been hugely popular for providing Active Directory Domain Services to branch offices and small perimeter networks.

Read-only domain controllers are the ideal type of domain controllers for environments with the following:

- Poor physical security
- Relatively few user accounts and/or devices
- Relatively poor bandwidth to central datacenters with domain controllers
- Little local IT knowledge and/or experience

These characteristics are typically true for branch offices. Before read-only domain controllers, administrators had to make the hard choice between doing nothing, placing fully (read-write) domain controllers in these locations, or upgrading the available bandwidth and/or resiliency of the networking connections between the branch offices and the head office or central datacenter(s).

Some organizations have opted to deploy read-only domain controllers in perimeter networks. Microsoft supports only one read-only domain controller per Active Directory site. This way, any perimeter network deployment would not have much Active Directory resiliency. Many organizations have, therefore, opted for a separate Active Directory forest, for these implementation scenarios.

Getting ready

Read-only domain controllers have requirements that we need to adhere to, before we can deploy and use them:

- At least one domain controller running Windows Server 2008 (or a newer version of Windows Server)
- The Windows Server 2003 FFL, or a higher FFL
- The Windows Server 2008 DFL, or a higher DFL, for the Active Directory domain(s) in which you intend to implement read-only domain controllers

- `ADPrep/rodcprep` needs to have run at least once on the domain controller holding the Domain Naming Master FSMO role, but this step may be skipped when the Active Directory environment was never set up or has never run with pre-Windows Server 2008-based domain controllers
- When implementing read-only domain controllers for branch offices, create the corresponding Active Directory sites and site connections first

As read-only domain controllers allow for scoped replication, as a *Getting ready* step, it's a recommended practice to determine the user accounts and computer accounts that are strictly needed in the branch office location. The read-only domain controller will be able to cache the passwords for these accounts to speed up authentication for these accounts in the branch office. The **Allowed RODC Password Replication Group** is the default group to add (groups of) user accounts and computer accounts to for this functionality.

> If you desire strict group memberships for this functionality per read-only domain controller, create the groups you need before you promote the Windows Server installation to a read-only domain controller for which you need the group scope.

Another way to think about security before promoting the first read-only domain controller is to determine the privileged accounts and otherwise sensitive accounts for which you do not want passwords replicated to the read-only domain controller you intend to create. These (groups of) accounts can be specified as the accounts that are denied from replicating passwords to the RODC.

How to do it...

When you've properly prepared the Windows Server installation you intend to promote to a read-only domain controller, or when you've successfully managed such a Windows Server installation, you can use the GUI of the Server Manager tool, to promote it.

Promoting a domain controller using the GUI consists of two parts:

- Executing the Add Roles and Features Wizard to install the Active Directory Domain Services role
- Executing the Active Directory Domain Services Configuration Wizard to promote the server to a read-only domain controller

Installing the Active Directory Domain Services role

Follow these steps to install the Active Directory Domain Services role:

1. Open **Server Manager**, (`servermanager.exe`).

2. In the gray top bar of **Server Manager**, click **Manage**.

3. Select **Add Roles and Features** from the menu. The **Add Roles and Features Wizard** appears.

4. On the **Before you begin** screen, click **Next**.

5. On the **Select installation type** screen, select **Role-based or feature-based installation**. Click **Next** afterward.

6. On the **Select destination server** screen, select the local Windows Server installation from the server pool list, select the remote Windows Server installation you intend to promote to domain controller from the server pool list, or make a selection of both types of resources. Click **Next** when done.

7. On the **Select server roles** screen, select the **Active Directory Domain Services** role from the list of available roles.

8. In the popup screen, click the **Add features** button to **Add features that are required for Active Directory Domain Services**. These features include the **Group Policy Management tool**, the **Active Directory module for Windows PowerShell**, the **Active Directory Administrative Center**, and the **AD DS Snap-Ins and Command-Line Tools**.

9. Back on the **Select server roles screen**, click **Next**.

10. On the **Select server features** screen, click **Next**.

11. On the **Active Directory Domain Services** screen, click **Next**.

12. On the **Confirm installation selections** screen, click **Install**:

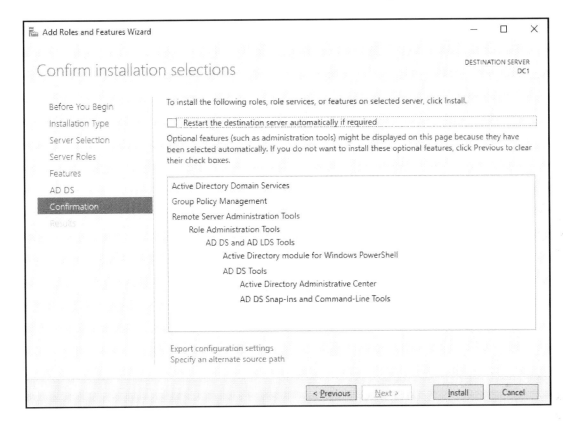

13. When configuration of the **Active Directory Domain Services** server role is done, click **Close** to close the **Add Roles and Features Wizard**.

Promoting the server to a read-only domain controller

Follow these steps to promote the server to a domain controller:

1. Open **Server Manager** or return to it when you've accomplished the previous steps
2. In the left navigation pane, click **AD DS**.
3. Click the **More...** link in the yellow ribbon titled: **Configuration required for Active Directory Domain Services at server**.

4. In the All Servers Task Details and Notifications, follow the link to Promote this server to a domain controller:

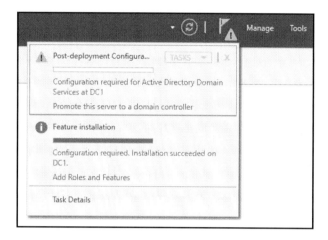

5. This starts the **Active Directory Domain Services Configuration Wizard**.

In the top-right corner of every **Active Directory Domain Services Configuration Wizard** screen, it shows you the hostname of the Windows Server installation you're promoting to a domain controller.

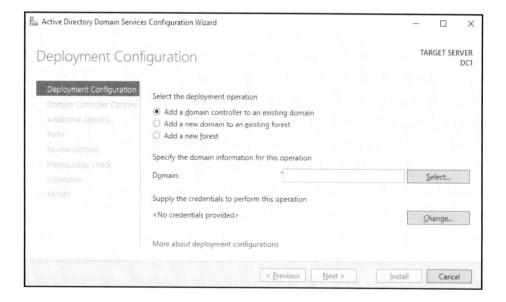

6. On the **Deployment configuration** screen, as seen in the preceding screenshot, select **Add a domain controller to an existing domain**. Then, input the DNS domain name and administrator credentials for the Active Directory domain for which you intend to add a read-only domain controller. Click **Next >** to proceed to the **Domain Controller Options** screen:

7. On the **Domain Controller Options** screen, we're presented with a couple of options:

- Select the option to add a **Read only domain controller (RODC)**: When preferred, select the options to install the **Domain Name System (DNS) Server** and configure the intended read-only domain controller as a global catalog, too.
- Select a site name from the drop-down list of available Active Directory sites.
- Enter the Directory Service Restore Mode password for the intended read-only domain controller

8. Click **Next** > to proceed to the next screen.
9. On the **RODC options** page, perform the following optional actions:
   1. Select a user account for delegation.
   2. Select the **accounts that are allowed to replicate passwords to the RODC**.
   3. Select the **accounts that are denied from replicating passwords to the RODC**.

If a group or an account features on both the accounts that are allowed to replicate passwords to the RODC and accounts that are denied from replicating passwords to the RODC, then the group or account is denied from replicating the password to the RODC.

10. Click **Next** > to proceed to the next screen.
11. On the **Additional Options** screen, select a fully writable domain controller to replicate the Active Directory database and the Active Directory SYSVOL from. Click **Next** > to continue to the **Paths** screen:

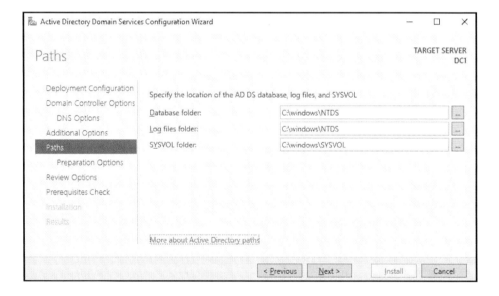

12. On the **Paths** screen, verify the default locations underneath `C:\Windows` or change the values to store Active Directory-related files somewhere else.

13. Click **Next >** to proceed.

14. On the **Review options** screen, review the choices made. Click **Next >** to proceed to the **Prerequisites Checks** screen.

> The **Review options** screen features a button labeled **View script**. This button displays the Windows PowerShell script used to execute the read-only domain controller promotion. This reusable script may be a real time-saver, especially when adding several read-only domain controllers to an existing domain.

15. After the prerequisites checks have been performed, click **Install** on the **Prerequisites checks** screen to start promotion.

After successful promotion, the Windows Server installation will reboot as a read-only domain controller.

Promoting a read-only domain controller using dcpromo.exe

Read-only domain controllers can be promoted using `dcpromo.exe` with an answer file or with all of the installation arguments specified, just like fully-writable domain controllers. An added benefit is that `dcpromo.exe` will install the Active Directory Domain Services server role automatically when it's not yet present.

Using `dcpromo.exe` with an answer file consists of running the following command line:

```
dcpromo.exe /unattend: C:\install\dcpromo.txt
```

A prime example of an answer file to add a read-only domain controller would look like the following:

```
[DCINSTALL]
ReplicaorNewDomain= readonlyreplica
ReplicaDomainDNSName= lucernpub.com
UserDomain= LUCERNPUB
UserName= Administrator
SiteName= "Remote Location"
Password= "P@$$w0rd"
InstallDNS= Yes
ConfirmGC= Yes
CreateDNSDelegation= No
```

```
DatabasePath= E:\NTDS
LogPath= E:\Logs
SYSVOLPath= E:\SYSVOL
SafeModeAdminPassword= "P@$$w0rd"
RebootOnSuccess= true
```

This will add a read-only domain controller to the `lucernpub.com` Active Directory domain, using the credentials for the administrator account with the password, `P@$$w0rd`. The read-only domain controller will be installed with a DNS Server and configured as a global catalog server. All the Active Directory-related files are stored in corresponding folders on the `E:\` drive, and when successful, the Windows Server installation you intend as the read-only domain controller will be rebooted automatically. Replace the values in the preceding sample file with the values of your choice.

The arguments in the answer file can also be specified as command-line arguments. The arguments can be reused one on one, so the preceding sample answer file would correspond to the following command line:

```
dcpromo.exe /unattend /replicaornewdomain:ReadOnlyReplica
/replicadomaindnsname:lucernpub.com /userdomain:LUCERNPUB
/username:administrator /password:"P@$$w0rd" /sitename:RemoteLocation
/installdns:yes /confirmgc:yes /databasepath:"E:\NTDS" /logpath:"E:\logs"
/sysvolpath:"E:\sysvol" /safemodeadminpassword:"P@$$w0rd"
```

Promoting a domain controller using Windows PowerShell

For the Active Directory Module for Windows PowerShell, Microsoft does not offer a dedicated PowerShell cmdlet to add a read-only domain controller. Instead, `Install-ADDSDomainController` is used with the dedicated `-ReadOnlyReplica` parameter. The simplest script would look like the following code:

```
Import-Module ADDSDeployment

Install-WindowsFeature AD-Domain-Services -IncludeManagementTools

Install-ADDSDomainController -DomainName lucernpub.com -Sitename
RemoteLocation -ReadOnlyReplica
```

However, to add a read-only domain controller to an existing domain as you would in the previous examples, the following script would be needed:

```
Import-Module ADDSDeployment

Install-WindowsFeature AD-Domain-Services -IncludeManagementTools

Install-ADDSDomainController -DomainName lucernpub.com -Credential
(Get-Credential) -ReadOnlyReplica -installDNS:$true
-NoGlobalCatalog:$false -DatabasePath "E:\NTDS" -Logpath "E:\Logs" -
SysvolPath "E:\SYSVOL"
-Sitename RemoteLocation
```

This will add a read-only domain controller to the lucernpub.com Active Directory domain using credentials you will be prompted for securely. The domain controller will be installed with a DNS Server and configured as a global catalog server. All of the Active Directory-related files are stored in corresponding folders on the E:\ drive, and, when successful, the Windows Server installation you intend as the domain controller will be rebooted automatically.

Replace the values in the preceding sample file with the values of your choice.

Checking proper promotion

After promoting a Windows Server installation to a read-only domain controller, it's recommended practice to check for proper promotion. Follow these steps to check:

1. **Check the logs**: The following two files contain all of the actions performed when promoting the Windows Server installation to a domain controller. A good way to check against improper promotion is to search for lines containing error and warning, as shown in the following example:
   - C:\Windows\Debug\dcpromo.log
   - C:\Windows\Debug\dcpromoui.log

2. **Check the event viewer**: In the event viewer, eventvwr.exe, new dedicated logs are created for Active Directory Domain Services. Search these logs for any Active Directory-related errors.

3. **Run Windows updates:** Even though one of the recommended steps is to update the Windows Server installation you intend to promote to a read-only domain controller, it's also a recommended step to install Windows updates after the Windows Server installation has been promoted, as updates apply to the newly installed server roles and features, too. These role-specific updates are only applied after the role is installed.

How it works...

Read-only domain controllers are different to normal domain controllers in the following ways:

- They allow read-only access to the Active Directory database and SYSVOL. Read-only domain controllers refer to other domain controllers for write operations such as SYSVOL.
- They allow read-only access to the DNS records. Read-only domain controllers refer to other domain controllers for DNS registration requests.
- They allow for scoped replication, so only the accounts that are needed are synchronized. This way, only privileged accounts and other sensitive accounts remain in the central datacenter.
- They allow for a quick change of passwords for synchronized users, when the read-only domain controller is stolen or otherwise compromised.
- They use their own dedicated account to encrypt their Kerberos tickets. This prevents attackers from decrypting a Kerberos **Ticket Granting Ticket (TGT)**, issued by a read-only domain controller, to obtain the secret of the Kerberos account (`krbtgt`).

Additionally, because no updates are expected from read-only domain controllers, normal domain controllers don't replicate from them.

See also

For more information refer to the following recipes:

- See *Preparing a Windows Server to become a domain controller* recipe.
- See *Promoting a server to a domain controller* recipe.

Using Install From Media

For Active Directory environments with really low bandwidth or networking resiliency between locations with domain controllers, regardless of whether these are read-only domain controllers or fully-writable domain controllers, promoting a Windows Server installation to a domain controller can take a long time or even fail.

In these kinds of scenarios, for adding an additional domain controller or read-only domain controller to an existing domain, Microsoft offers the **Install From Media (IFM)** option.

How to do it...

IFM consists of two steps:

- Creating the IFM package
- Leveraging the IFM package

Creating the IFM package

To create the IFM package, perform the following actions on a domain controller in a well-connected networking location, running the same version of Windows Server on which you intend to use the IFM package to swiftly promote to a domain controller in a low-bandwidth scenario:

> IFM packages to create read-only domain controllers can be created on both read-only domain controllers and on fully-writable domain controllers. IFM packages to create fully-writable domain controllers can only be created on fully-writable domain controllers.

1. Open Command Prompt with administrative privileges.
2. Run the following command to start the NTDS utility in interactive mode:

   ```
   ntdsutil.exe
   ```

3. Type the following command in interactive mode to select the Active Directory database:

   ```
   activate instance ntds
   ```

4. Type the following command in interactive mode to enter the IFM creation context:

   ```
   IFM
   ```

5. Type the following command in interactive mode to create IFM, including the contents of the Active Directory SYSVOL for a read-only domain controller, and place it in the C:\IFM folder:

   ```
   create RODC C:\IFM
   ```

6. Type the following command in interactive mode to exit the IFM context:

   ```
   quit
   ```

7. Type the following command in interactive mode to exit the NTDS utility itself:

```
quit
```

8. Close the Command Prompt window.

Leveraging the IFM package

To leverage the `IFM` package in the remote location, choose one of the following methods:

- Using the Active Directory Domain Services Configuration Wizard after you've installed the **Active Directory Domain Services** role
- Using `dcpromo.exe`
- Using the `Install-ADDSDomainController` PowerShell cmdlet

Using the Active Directory Domain Services Configuration Wizard

Perform these steps to leverage the install using the Active Directory Domain Services Configuration Wizard:

1. Promote the Windows Server installation as you would normally.
2. On the **Additional Options** screen, click the **Install from Media** option:

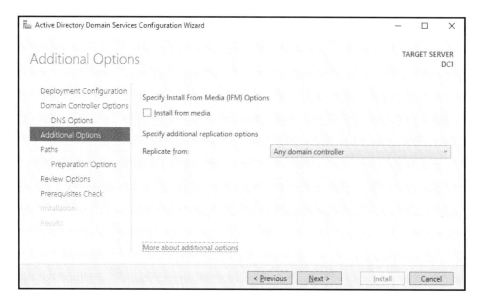

3. On the **Install from Media** screen, specify the location on the drive of the Windows Server installation you intend to promote to a (read-only) domain controller using **Install from Media**.
4. Optionally, specify the fully-writable domain controller you want to **Replicate from:**. Specify a domain controller that is best reachable from the intended domain controller.
5. Click **Next >** to proceed to the next screens as you normally would.

Using dcpromo.exe

Perform the following steps:

1. Promote the Windows Server installation, as you would normally.
2. When using an answer file, add the following line:

```
ReplicationSourcePath= "C:\Install"
```

3. When using unattended mode, add the following argument:

```
/ReplicationSourcePath:"C:\Install"
```

Using the Install-ADDSDomainController PowerShell cmdlet

Just as when using `dcpromo.exe`, the `Install-ADDSDomainController` PowerShell cmdlet only needs an additional parameter to leverage the `IFM` package, as shown in the following code:

```
InstallationMediaPath
```

When combining it with the sample PowerShell command for adding an additional fully-writable domain controller to an existing domain, the following script emerges:

```
Install-WindowsFeature AD-Domain-Services -IncludeManagementTools

Import-Module ADDSDeployment

Install-ADDSDomainController -DomainName lucernpub.com -
InstallationMediaPath "C:\Install"
```

How it works...

As a Windows Server installation becomes a domain controller, it replicates contents of the Active Directory database and the Active Directory SYSVOL to its local hard drive(s). The entire package needed for this replication can also be assembled before promotion. Then, the package can be delivered to the remote location, or even carried by the technician that will promote the (read-only) domain controller.

The amount of network traffic needed when using the **Install from Media** option is heavily reduced, but is certainly not zero. As the IFM package represents a point in time snapshot of the contents of the Active Directory database and the Active Directory SYSVOL, any changes between the time of creation of the IFM package and using it will need to replicate before promotion of the domain controller is successfully completed.

Using domain controller cloning

The IFM feature for promoting domain controllers leverages the fact that the contents of the Active Directory database and the Active Directory SYSVOL are largely identical throughout all domain controllers within the domain. The domain controller cloning feature takes this one step further, and leverages the fact that all domain controllers are largely identical; not just the Active Directory-related files, but all operating system files, most agent installations, information security measures, and most configuration items.

When a domain controller is properly prepared and promoted, it can serve as a template.

Getting ready

The domain controller cloning feature requires the following:

- A hypervisor platform offering the VM-GenerationID functionality
- At least one domain controller running Windows Server 2012 or a newer version of Windows Server, promoted to a domain controller, holding the PDCe FSMO role

The domain controller you intend to clone needs to adhere to the following requirements:

- Running Windows Server 2012 or a newer version of Windows Server
- Running on top of the VM-GenerationID-capable hypervisor platform
- Running the latest stable integration components or VMware tools
- Promoted as a domain controller
- Not holding the PDCe FSMO role
- Not holding the RID FSMO role

How to do it...

There are four steps to cloning a domain controller:

1. Making sure all agents and software packages are cloneable
2. Supplying the information for the new domain controller configuration
3. Adding the domain controller to the Cloneable Domain Controllers group
4. Cloning the domain controller from the hypervisor

Making sure all agents and software packages are cloneable

To successfully clone a domain controller, all agents and software packages that you've installed and configured on the domain controller you intend to clone, need to support it.

When you install the Active Directory Domain Services role on a Windows Server 2012 installation, or on any newer version of Windows Server, there is the `Get-ADDCCloningExcludedApplicationList` PowerShell cmdlet that you can use. When you run this PowerShell cmdlet, it will return the applications and services that Microsoft does not know if you can successfully clone.

All Microsoft services and add-on packages that ship with Windows Server are tested, so these are already part of the `DefaultDCCloneAllowList.xml` file. The contents of the `DefaultDCCloneAllowList.xml` file is shown as follows:

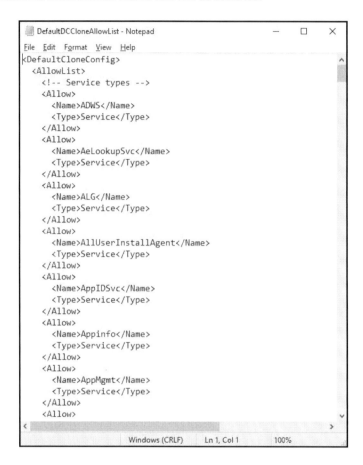

For any other service and/or application, the recommended practice is to ask the vendor if domain controller cloning is supported. When all services and applications check out, you can run the following line of PowerShell to add them to your organization's `CustomDCCloneAllowList.xml` file:

```
Get-ADDCCloningExcludedApplicationList –GenerateXml –Path C:\Windows\NTDS –
Force
```

In the preceding Windows PowerShell example, the default path for the Active Directory database is supplied. Change it accordingly before running the lines of PowerShell.

After cloning, the domain controller you intend to clone will pick up this file when you store it on removable media or in the same path as the Active Directory database.

Supplying the information for the new domain controller configuration

The new domain controller that will be created when an existing domain controller is cloned, will need to be different from the existing one. It will need a different hostname, IPv4 address(es), IPv6 address(es), possible different DNS Server allocations, or a different Active Directory site.

Microsoft provides a way to supply this information through the `DCCloneConfig.xml` file. Again, after cloning, the domain controller you intend to clone will pick up this file when you store it on removable media or in the same path as the Active Directory database.

If no `DCCloneConfig.xml` file is supplied, the new domain controller will boot into Directory Services Restore Mode.

If an empty `DCCloneConfig.xml` file is supplied, the new domain controller will be assigned the following:

- IP addresses through DHCP
- An automatically assigned hostname
- The same Active Directory site as the source domain controller

If a specific hostname, Active Directory site, or IP address is needed, take a look at the parameters you can specify for `New-ADDCCloningConfig`, such as the `-SiteName`, `-CloneComputerName`, and `-Static -IPv4Address` parameters.

A sample PowerShell one-liner to create a new domain controller with the name `DC04` in the Active Directory site named `RemoteLocation` with the correct IPv4 information would look like the following code:

```
New-ADDCCloneConfigFile -CloneComputerName "DC04" -SiteName RemoteLocation
-Static -IPv4Address "10.0.1.3" -IPv4SubnetMask "255.255.255.0" -
IPv4DefaultGateway "10.0.1.1" -IPv4DNSResolver "10.0.0.2"
```

Adding the domain controller to the Cloneable Domain Controllers group

In large organizations, the team responsible for managing Active Directory is usually a different team from the one managing the hypervisor platform. Through the integration components and/or VMware tools, the latter team might configure domain controllers for cloning and clone them, adding to the management burden of the Active Directory management team.

Therefore, the Active Directory team has to explicitly allow a domain controller to be cloned in Active Directory. The mechanism to do so is to add source domain controllers to the **Cloneable Domain Controllers** group.

The following line of PowerShell accomplish this for a source domain controller named DC03 in the `lucernpub.com` Active Directory domain:

```
Add-ADGroupMember "Cloneable Domain Controllers" "CN=DC03,OU=Domain
Controllers,DC=lucernpub,DC=com"
```

Cloning the domain controller from the hypervisor

Now, the hypervisor platform team can clone the source domain controller.

As an Active Directory administrator, shut down the domain controller you intend to clone. After cloning has been successful, remove the source domain controller from the Cloneable Domain Controllers group and start it again as one of the domain controllers for the domain, or leave it off and allow it to be cloned over and over again for a maximum time period of 60 to 180 days, depending on the current tombstone lifetime period settings.

How it works...

Domain controller cloning leverages the VM-GenerationID feature found in most modern hypervisor platforms. Through the specifications that Microsoft wrote for this feature, this ID is stored in every virtual machine's RAM and only changes under certain circumstances. These circumstances are the following:

- When a virtual machine's hard disk is attached to a different virtual machine
- When a previous snapshot for a virtual machine is applied

Active Directory Domain Services is the first server role to take advantage of the VM-GenerationID feature to do the following:

- Increase the integrity of the contents of the Active Directory database and the Active Directory SYSVOL by employing virtualization safeguards
- Clone a perfectly prepared domain controller using domain controller cloning

By storing the 128-bit value for the VM-GenerationID in RAM in the Active Directory database, and the domain controller checking the value stored in the database with the value in RAM before each major action, the domain controller can sense when a snapshot is applied or when the hard disk is reused.

 As the VM-GenerationID feature is a hypervisor platform feature, a domain controller cannot sense a snapshot is applied or that the hard disk is reused when these actions originate from the storage fabric or otherwise outside of the hypervisor platform.

When a hard disk is reused and the domain controller is properly prepared to be cloned, domain controller cloning creates a perfect clone of the source domain controller.

 Domain controller cloning only allows cloning of fully-writable domain controllers. Domain controller cloning does not apply to read-only domain controllers.

See also

Use the information in the *Determining if a virtual domain controller has a VM-GenerationID* recipe to see whether the hypervisor platform supports domain controller cloning. Refer to the *Modify the tombstone lifetime period* recipe from Chapter 14, *Hardening Azure AD,* to find out whether domain controllers can be cloned for 60 or 180 days.

Determining whether a virtual domain controller has a VM-GenerationID

One of the requirements for Active Directory Virtualization Safeguards and domain controller cloning is the ability of the hypervisor platform to provide the VM-GenerationID to the virtual domain controller.

How to do it...

To determine whether a virtual domain controller has the VM-GenerationID, perform these steps:

1. Sign in to the virtual domain controller.
2. Open **Device Manager** (`devmgmt.msc`).
3. In the taskbar of **Device Manager**, open the **View** menu and select **Show hidden devices**.
4. In the main pane of **Device Manager**, expand **System devices**.
5. Search for the **Microsoft Hyper-V Generation Counter** system device. The existence of such a device means the virtual domain controller has a VM-GenerationID.
6. Close **Device Manager**.

How it works...

When the hypervisor platform supports the VM-GenerationID feature, it will create a device to place the value of the VM-GenerationID in the virtual memory of the virtual domain controller.

To determine whether a virtual domain controller has a VM-GenerationID, look for this system device.

Demoting a domain controller

Every domain controller has a life cycle. After a certain period of time, it should make room for newer, better, more agile, or even more cost-efficient, domain controllers or other solutions, such as Azure Active Directory (Domain Services).

Getting ready

Before you can demote a domain controller, you should make sure of the following:

- It no longer hosts any FSMO roles.
- It no longer offers networking services, such as DNS, LDAP, RADIUS, or WINS. These protocols are largely manually configured on networking devices and other servers. Demoting a domain controller that offers these services might negatively impact the networking infrastructure. Reconfigure networking devices and servers to use alternative domain controllers or services, first.
- It is not an Enterprise Root **Certification Authority** (**CA**). When a domain controller is configured as an Enterprise Root CA using **Active Directory Certificate Services** (**AD CS**), it cannot be demoted. First, the CA needs to be migrated.
- There are other global catalog servers available when you remove a domain controller that is also configured to be a global catalog server.

For successful demotions, the domain controller you intend to demote needs to have at least one network interface card attached to the network. Other domain controllers should be reachable.

How to do it...

There are two supported ways to demote a domain controller graciously:

- Using the wizard
- Using the Active Directory Module for Windows PowerShell

Using the wizard

To demote a domain controller graciously using Server Manager, follow these steps:

1. Open **Server Manager**, (`servermanager.exe`).
2. In the gray top bar of **Server Manager**, click **Manage**.
3. Select **Remove Server Roles and Features** from the context menu. The, **Remove Roles and Features Wizard** appears.
4. On the **Before you begin** screen, click **Next**.
5. On the **Select destination server** screen, select the local Windows Server installation from the server pool list, and then click **Next**.

6. On the **Select server roles** screen, deselect the **Active Directory Domain Services** role from the list of installed roles.

7. In the popup screen, click the **Remove features** button to **Remove features that are required for Active Directory Domain Services**:

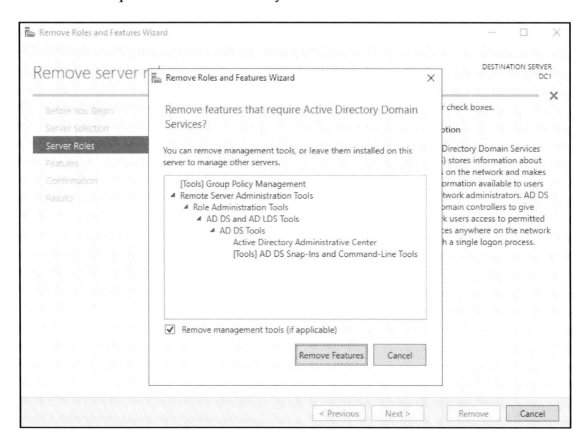

8. On the **Validation Results** screen, follow the **Demote this Domain Controller** link to acknowledge that the domain controller needs to be demoted before the Active Directory Domain Services role can be removed:

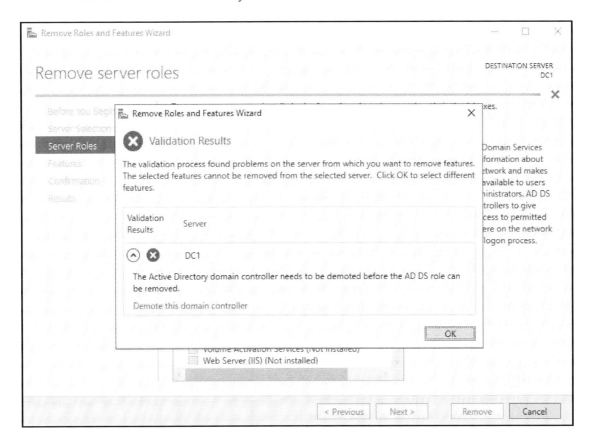

9. The **Active Directory Domain Services Configuration Wizard** appears.

10. On the **Credentials** screen, optionally enter the credentials to perform the demotion, or click **Next >** to perform the operation with the credentials of the account you signed in with:

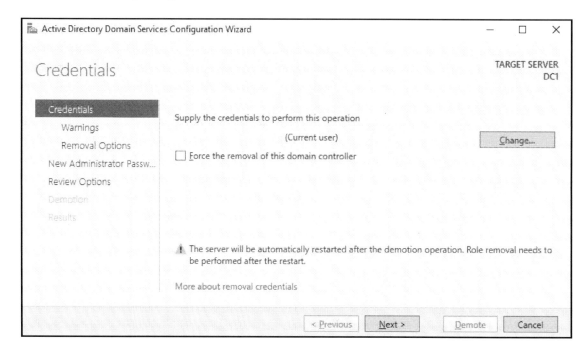

11. On the **Removal options** screen, select the **Proceed with removal** option and click <u>Next</u> >:

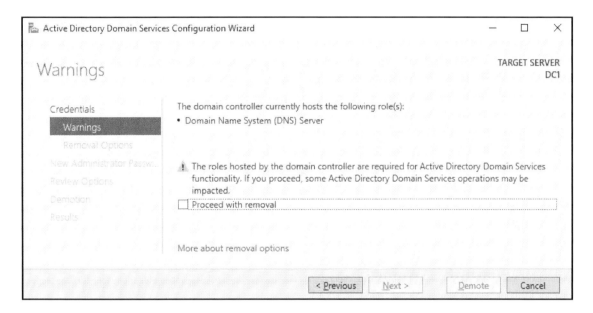

12. On the **New administrator password** screen, enter the new password for the built-in administrator account. Click <u>Next</u> > to proceed to the next screen.
13. On the **Review Options** screen, click **Demote**.
14. When configuration of the **Active Directory Domain Services** server role is done, click **Close** to close the **Remove Roles and Features wizard**.

Using the Active Directory module for Windows PowerShell

To graciously demote a domain controller, you can use the Uninstall-ADDSDomainController PowerShell cmdlet. The simplest script would look like that shown in the following example:

```
Import-Module ADDSDeployment

Uninstall-ADDSDomainController
```

This will remove the domain controller from the Active Directory domain and prompt you for the new password for the built-in administrator account after demotion. Replace the values in the previous sample file with the values of your choice.

To remove the Active Directory Domain Services role, use the following PowerShell line:

```
Uninstall-WindowsFeature AD-Domain-Services -IncludeManagementTools
```

How it works...

Every domain controller has its information stored in numerous places throughout the Active Directory database.

To remove this information and stop other domain controllers replicating to non-existing domain controllers, domain controllers should be demoted.

There's more...

Proper demotion of a domain controller will remove all of the references to the domain controller from Active Directory.

However, it is recommended practice to check the following tools manually after demotion:

- **DNS**: (dnsmgmt.msc)
- **Active Directory Sites and Services**: (dssite.msc)

Demoting a domain controller forcefully

It's also an option to forcefully remove a domain controller from Active Directory. While graciously demoting should be the preferred option, you might have to resort to this option.

The process of demoting a domain controller forcefully, consists of these steps:

1. Performing a metadata cleanup
2. Deleting the domain controller from DNS
3. Deleting the computer object for the domain controller
4. Deleting the SYSVOL replication membership

5. Deleting the domain controller from Active Directory Sites and Services
6. Seizing any FSMO roles that were hosted by the domain controller (you can do this first to ensure no impacts for domain members)
7. Taking care of the existence of global catalog servers

If the domain controller was the last domain controller for a domain in an existing forest, the domain will need to be removed as it is now an orphaned domain.

How to do it...

There are two ways to do it:

- Using the Active Directory Domain Services Configuration Wizard
- Using manual steps

Using the Active Directory Domain Services Configuration Wizard

The Active Directory Domain Services Configuration Wizard can be used to forcefully demote a domain controller when the Windows Server installation is still bootable and you are able to sign into it with administrative credentials.

Follow these steps:

1. Open **Server Manager**, (`servermanager.exe`).
2. In the gray top bar of **Server Manager**, click **Manage**.
3. Select **Remove Server Roles and Features** from the menu.
4. On the **Before you begin** screen, click **Next >**.
5. On the **Select destination server** screen, select the local Windows Server installation from the server pool list.
6. Click **Next >**.
7. On the **Select server roles** screen, deselect the **Active Directory Domain Services** role from the list of installed roles.
8. In the popup screen, click the **Remove features** button to **Remove features that are required for Active Directory Domain Services**.

9. On the **Validation Results** screen, follow the demote this domain controller link to acknowledge that the domain controller needs to be demoted before the Active Directory Domain Services role can be removed.

10. On the **Credentials** screen, elect the option **Force the removal of this domain controller**:

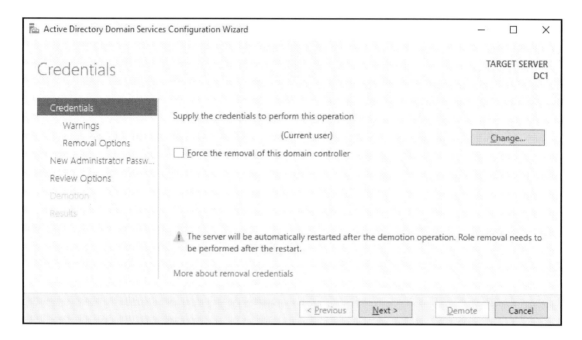

11. Click **Next >**.

12. On the **Removal options** screen, select the **Proceed with removal** option and click **Next >**.

13. On the **New administrator password** screen, enter the new password for the built-in administrator account.

14. Click **Next >** to proceed to the next screen.

15. On the **Review Options** screen, click **Demote**.

16. When configuration of the Active Directory Domain Services server role is done, click **Close** to close the **Remove Roles and Features Wizard**.

Using manual steps

Sometimes, the Active Directory Domain Services Configuration Wizard cannot be used, such as when in the following situations:

- You can no longer sign in interactively or remotely to the domain controller.
- The physical hardware of the domain controller has been damaged beyond repair.
- The domain controller is no longer reachable for other domain controllers.
- The domain controller, for some reason, can no longer be trusted to provide Active Directory Domain Services in a meaningful way.

In these scenarios, the following manual steps can be performed to remove the domain controller from Active Directory.

Performing metadata cleanup

Perform these steps to perform a metadata cleanup:

1. Open **Command Prompt** (cmd.exe) with administrative privileges on a domain controller that is known to be good. The domain controller holding the Domain Naming Master is preferred.
2. Run the following command to start the NTDS utility in interactive mode:

   ```
   ntdsutil.exe
   ```

3. Type the following command in interactive mode to start the metadata cleanup:

   ```
   metadata cleanup
   ```

4. Type the following command to remove the server, DC04.lucernpub.com:

   ```
   remove selected server
   "CN=DC04,CN=Servers,CN=RemoteLocation,CN=Sites,CN=Configuration,DC=lucernpub,DC=com"
   ```

5. Type the following command in interactive mode to exit the metadata cleanup context:

   ```
   quit
   ```

6. Type the following command in interactive mode to exit the NTDS utility itself:

```
quit
```

7. Close the Command Prompt window.

Deleting the domain controller from DNS

After the metadata cleanup, the DNS records for the domain controller may still be present. Use the DNS MMC Snap-in to remove the DNS A, AAAA, PTR and SRV records for the domain controller.

Deleting the computer object for the domain controller

To delete the computer object for the domain controller, use the Active Directory Administrative Center:

1. Open the **Active Directory Administrative Center** (dsac.exe).
2. In the main **Welcome to Active Directory Administrative Center** pane, in the **Global Search** field, enter the search criteria of the desired object and then click the **Search** button:

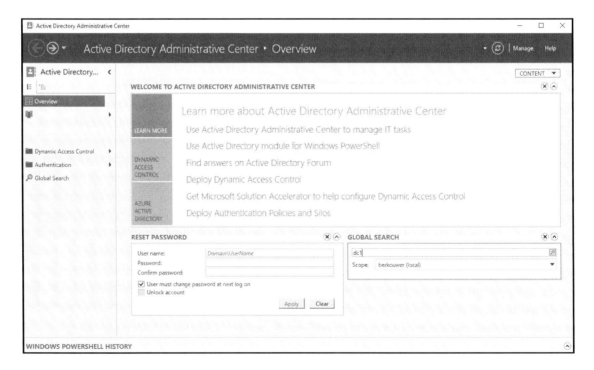

3. In the search results, locate the domain controller object.
4. Right-click it, and then click **Delete**.
5. Confirm you want to delete the domain controller.
6. Close the **Active Directory Administrative Center**.

To delete the computer object for the domain controller, alternatively, run the following PowerShell script:

```
Import-Module ActiveDirectory

Remove-ADComputer -Identity DC01
```

Deleting the SYSVOL replication membership

The domain controller was also a member of the replication group for the Active Directory SYSVOL.

Follow these steps to remove the domain controller:

1. Open the **Active Directory Administrative Center** (`dsac.exe`).
2. At the top of the left navigation pane, switch to **Tree view** from **List view**.
3. Expand the Active Directory domain.
4. Expand the **System** container.
5. Expand the **DFSR-Global Settings** container.
6. Expand the **Domain System Volume** container.
7. Expand the **Topology** container.

8. In the main window, right-click the object for the domain controller you want to delete from the **Topology** container:

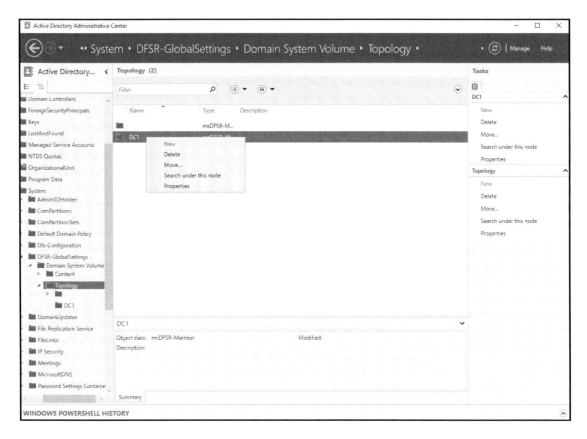

9. Select **Delete**.
10. In the **Delete Confirmation** popup, click **Yes** to acknowledge that you are sure you want to delete the **msDFSR-Member**.
11. Close the **Active Directory Administrative Center**.

Deleting the domain controller from Active Directory Sites and Services

To delete the domain controller from Active Directory Sites and Services, follow these steps:

1. Open **Active Directory Sites and Services** (`dssite.msc`).
2. The **Active Directory Sites and Services** window appears:

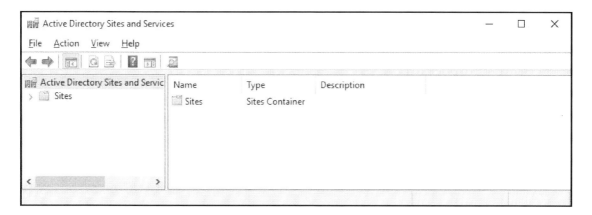

3. In the left navigation pane, expand **Sites**.
4. Expand the Active Directory site where the domain controller resides.
5. Expand the **Servers** node.
6. Right-click the object for the domain controller you want to delete from the **Servers** node, and select **Delete**.
7. In the **Active Directory Domain Services** popup, click **Yes** to acknowledge that you are sure you want to delete the server.
8. Close **Active Directory Sites and Services**.

Deleting an orphaned domain

Follow these steps to perform a metadata cleanup:

1. Open **Command Prompt** (`cmd.exe`) with an account that is a member of the **Enterprise Admins** group, on a domain controller that is of good standing. A domain controller that hasn't experienced any replication challenges throughout its lifetime might be your best choice. Also, note that performing the following actions on the domain controller holding the Domain Naming Master FSMO Role is preferred.

2. Run the following command to start the NTDS utility in interactive mode:

   ```
   ntdsutil.exe
   ```

3. Type the following command in interactive mode to start the metadata cleanup:

   ```
   metadata cleanup
   ```

4. Type the following commands to specify the current domain controller as the server on which to make the changes, as it is the Domain Naming Master:

   ```
   connections
   connect to server localhost
   quit
   ```

5. Type the following command to list the Active Directory domains in the Active Directory forest to select as the domain to remove:

   ```
   select operation target
   list domains
   ```

6. This outputs a list of domain in the forest, denoted by an identifier. Note down the identifier for the orphaned domain you want to remove

7. Type the following command in interactive mode to select the domain to remove:

   ```
   select domain <ID>
   ```

8. Type the following command to exit the operation target selection context:

   ```
   quit
   ```

9. Type the following command to remove the domain:

   ```
   remove selected domain
   ```

10. Type the following command in interactive mode to exit the metadata cleanup context and then the NTDS utility itself:

    ```
    quit
    quit
    ```

11. Close the Command Prompt window.

See also

To seize the FSMO roles, see the *Managing FSMO roles* recipe of `Chapter 3`, *Managing Active Directory Roles and Features.*

To configure domain controllers as global catalog servers, see the *Managing global catalogs* recipe of `Chapter 3`, *Managing Active Directory Roles and Features.*

Inventory domain controllers

It's a good thing to know all of the domain controllers throughout an Active Directory domain. This activity doesn't just show the management burden for Active Directory administrators; it also allows them to make smart choices, especially when the environment is breached.

 Although it's not recommended practice, administrators may place domain controllers outside the domain controller OU. In that case, simply checking the computer accounts in that OU will not provide a 100% view of the domain controller in use.

How to do it...

There are two ways to get a good overview of the domain controllers in an Active Directory domain:

- Using Active Directory Users and Computers to inventory domain controllers
- Using the Active Directory module for Windows PowerShell to inventory domain controllers

Using Active Directory Users and Computers to inventory domain controllers

Active Directory Users and Computers allows for querying the entire Active Directory domain for either **Writable Domain Controllers** and **Read-only Domain Controllers** in the following way:

1. Open **Active Directory Users and Computers**, (`dsa.msc`).
2. In the left navigation pane, right-click the target domain name for which you want to inventory the domain controllers.
3. Select **Find**.
4. In the **Find** drop-down box, select **Computers**.
5. In the **Role** drop-down box, select **Writable Domain Controllers** or **Read-Only Domain Controllers**.
6. Click **Find Now**.

The list of domain controllers for the domain is now shown in the search results pane.

Using the Active Directory module for Windows PowerShell to inventory domain controllers

Using the Active Directory Module for Windows PowerShell to inventory domain controllers is even easier.

Simply use the following PowerShell script:

```
Import-Module ActiveDirectory

Get-ADDomainController | Select Name
```

If you want more information on the domain controllers within the current domain, simply add the characteristics you would like to see after the `Select` statement. For instance, you can add `IPv4Address`, `IsGlobalCatalog`, `isReadOnly`, `OperatingSystem` and `Site` for good measure. If you're looking for a smart layout simply append `| Format-Table`. If you want to get the information straight to your clipboard so you can paste it in a report or anywhere else, append `| clip`.

Decommissioning a compromised read-only domain controller

One of the benefits of deploying read-only domain controllers is their ability to recover quickly from an information security breach.

Since only the passwords for a subset of users is cached on the read-only domain controller when these users signed on through the read-only domain controller and the passwords for really sensitive accounts weren't allowed to be cached on the read-only domain controller, the impact of a stolen read-only domain controller is small, compared to a fully-writable domain controller.

How to do it...

To render the read-only domain controller useless to an attacker or thief, perform these steps:

1. Open **Active Directory Users and Computers** (`dsa.msc`).
2. In the left navigation pane, expand the domain name.
3. In the left navigation pane, expand the **Domain Controllers** OU.
4. Right-click the compromised read-only domain controller and select **Delete**.
5. On the **Deleting Active Directory Domain Controller** screen, select the **Reset all passwords for user accounts that were cached on this read-only domain controller** option.
6. Since the persons associated with the user accounts will be forced to have their passwords reset by service desk personnel, it's recommended practice to also check **Export the list of accounts that were cached on this read-only domain controller to this file:** and to specify a file. This way, the service desk may proactively approach affected colleagues.
7. Click **Delete**.

How it works...

Each read-only domain controller caches the hashes of the passwords for users signing in through the read-only domain controller. For this functionality, the read-only domain controller contacts a writable domain controller. However, when a user account is denied to have their passwords cached, the password is not cached. For accounts for which the passwords have been cached, the best remedy is to reset these passwords.

Every Kerberos ticket that is given to devices or user accounts is encrypted using the separate `krbtgt` account for the read-only domain controller. These tickets are bound to the read-only domain controller. When the read-only domain controller is removed from the Active Directory domain, these Kerberos tickets become useless.

3
Managing Active Directory Roles and Features

Creating domain controllers is fun, but leveraging all of them is key to implementing a responsive and highly-available Active Directory. Therefore, we'll focus on the differences between domain controllers in terms of **Flexible Single Master Operations (FSMO)** roles and global catalog configuration. There's a reason why the following quote, inspired by George Orwell's Animal Farm, is popular among Active Directory admins:

> *"All domain controllers are equal, but some domain controllers are more equal than others."*

The following recipes will be covered in this chapter:

- Querying FSMO role placement
- Transferring FSMO roles
- Seizing FSMO roles
- Configuring the Primary Domain Controller emulator to synchronize time with a reliable source
- Managing time synchronization for virtual domain controllers
- Managing global catalogs

Before we begin with the recipes, we will look at FSMO roles and practices.

About FSMO roles

Active Directory uses the multi-master model, where domain controllers are all able to respond to client requests. When comparing to the old Windows NT 4 server-style **Primary Domain Controller** (PDC) and **Backup Domain Controller** (BDC) models, where BDCs were read-only until switched to become the only PDC, this model offers many benefits.

However, some tasks within Active Directory don't work well with the multi-master model. When designing Active Directory, Microsoft created five roles outside of the model, labeled FSMO roles, to prevent conflicting updates.

These roles can be flexibly assigned to domain controllers and seized when a domain controller holding the role fails. These roles offer single master operations within the scope of the roles. Hence the name FSMO role.

In every Active Directory environment there are five roles with two different scopes:

Role	Scope
Domain Naming Master	Active Directory forest
Schema Master	Active Directory forest
Primary Domain Controller emulator (PDCe)	Active Directory domain
RID Master	Active Directory domain
Infrastructure Master	Active Directory domain

In an environment with multiple domains in a forest, the FSMO roles with the domain scope will be present for each domain, where the two FSMO roles for the forest would only be represented once.

The roles for each of these FSMO roles can best be described as the following:

- **Domain Naming Master**: The domain controller holding the Domain Naming Master FSMO role is responsible for changes to the forest-wide domain namespaces. The domain controller with this FSMO role is the only domain controller that can add and remove domains to and from the forest.
- **Schema Master**: The domain controller holding the Schema Master FSMO role is responsible for changes to the schema partition. The domain controller with this FSMO role is the only domain controller that can make changes to the Active Directory schema. It is the source of authority for replicating schema changes.
- **PDCe**: The domain controller acting as the PDCe has many responsibilities in the Active Directory domain. It is the authority for time synchronization, replicating password changes, and resolving authentication errors due to recently changed passwords through PDC chaining.

- **RID Master**: The domain controller holding the RID Master FSMO role is responsible for handing out pools of RIDs to all the other domain controllers in the domain (and itself). These identifiers are used to create SIDs by appending to the domain SID namespace. Because SIDs are used to authorize access to resources, it is important to not hand out the same RID to multiple accounts. Before a domain controller reaches the end of its RID Pool, it asks the domain controller holding the RID Master FSMO role for a new RID Pool. By default, RID Pools contain 500 RIDs.
- **Infrastructure Master**: The domain controller holding the Infrastructure Master FSMO role is responsible for updating objects in cross-domain object references.

When the Active Directory Recycle Bin optional feature is enabled, every domain controller becomes responsible for updating cross-domain object references. In this case, the Infrastructure Master FSMO role can be neglected, including all the advice for placement considerations for global catalog servers.

Recommended practices for FSMO roles

Microsoft has published the following recommendations as part of Knowledge Base article 223346 (`https://support.microsoft.com/en-us/help/223346`):

- Place the schema master on the PDCe of the forest root domain.
- Place the domain naming master on the forest root PDCe.
- Place the PDCe on your best hardware in a reliable hub site that contains replica domain controllers in the same Active Directory site and domain.
- Place the RID master on the domain PDCe in the same domain.

For a single domain in a single forest with the Active Directory Recycle Bin optional feature enabled, this means that all five FSMO roles can best be placed on one domain controller.

For an Active Directory forest with multiple domains, it means the forest-wide Schema Master and Domain Naming Master FSMO roles can best be combined with the PDCe and RID Master roles for the forest-root domain on one domain controller. For every other domain, the PDCe and RID Master roles are to be placed on a domain controller per domain. Whether or not the Infrastructure Master FSMO role plays any part depends on the Active Directory Recycle Bin.

This might not be the situation in every Active Directory environment, indicating the need to manage the FSMO roles.

Querying FSMO role placement

Follow this recipe to find out which domain controllers run FSMO roles.

Getting ready

To query FSMO roles, you'll need to be signed in with an account that is a member of the Enterprise Admins group.

How to do it...

To locate the domain controllers running the FSMO roles, run the following command on any domain-joined device, member server, or domain controller:

```
netdom.exe query fsmo
```

Or, use the following PowerShell commands on a domain-joined system that has the Active Directory Module for Windows PowerShell installed:

```
Import-Module ActiveDirectory

Get-ADForest | Format-List DomainNamingMaster,SchemaMaster

Get-ADDomain | Format-List InfrastructureMaster,PDCEmulator,RIDMaster
```

How it works...

Domain controllers hold FSMO roles. Each FSMO role is automatically assigned to one domain controller. This information is stored in the Active Directory database. The information for the domain controller holding the Schema Master and the information for the domain controller holding the Domain Naming Master is stored at the forest level. The information for the domain controllers holding the other roles is stored at the domain level.

Transferring FSMO roles

Use this recipe to transfer FSMO roles between domain controllers.

Getting ready

When both the domain controller holding a FSMO role and the domain controller you intend to transfer the FSMO role to are both online, functioning and replicating perfectly, you can transfer FSMO roles without problems. If you can't transfer successfully you can seize the FSMO roles.

To transfer the Schema Master and/or Domain Naming Master FSMO roles, you'll need to be signed in with an account that is a member of the Enterprise Admins group. To transfer the other FSMO roles, you'll need to be signed in with an account that is a member of the Domain Admins group.

How to do it...

You can transfer FSMO roles using one of the following:

Tool	FSMO role
Active Directory Users and Computers MMC snap-in (`dsa.msc`)	RID Master PDC emulator Infrastructure Master
Active Directory Domains and Trusts MMC snap-in (`domain.msc`)	Domain Naming Master
Active Directory schema MMC snap-in	Schema Master

Alternatively, you can use the `ntdsutil.exe` command-line tool or the `Move-ADDirectoryServerOperationMasterRole` PowerShell cmdlet from the Active Directory Module for Windows PowerShell.

Transferring FSMO roles using the MMC snap-ins

To transfer the Domain Naming Master FSMO role, follow these steps while on a domain controller in the root forest domain, signed in with an account that is a member of the Enterprise Admins group:

1. Open **Active Directory Domains and Trusts** (`domain.msc`).
2. In the left navigation pane, right-click **Active Directory Domains and Trusts** and select **Change Active Directory Domain Controller**.
3. Select the domain controller you want to transfer the Domain Naming Master FSMO role to from the list of domain controllers.

4. Click **OK** when you're done.
5. In the left navigation pane, right-click **Active Directory Domains and Trusts** and select **Operation Master**.
6. Click **Change**.
7. Click **Yes** to answer the question **Are you sure you want to transfer the operations master role to a different computer?** in the **Active Directory Domains and Trusts** popup window.
8. Click **OK** to acknowledge that **The operations master was successfully transferred** in the second **Active Directory Domains and Trusts** popup window.
9. Click **Close** to close the **Operations Master** window.
10. Close **Active Directory Domains and Trusts**.

To transfer the Domain Naming Master FSMO role, follow these steps while on a domain controller in the root forest domain, signed in with an account that is a member of the Enterprise Admins group:

1. Open an elevated **Command Prompt** (cmd.exe).
2. Register the schmmgmt.dll library on the **Command Prompt** (cmd.exe) with the following command:

```
regsvr32.exe schmmgmt.dll
```

3. Click **OK** in the **RegSvr32** popup screen stating DllRegisterServer in schmmgmt.dll succeeded.
4. On the **Command Prompt** (cmd.exe), run the following command to start the **Microsoft Management Console (MMC)**:

```
mmc.exe
```

5. In the MMC screen, open the **File** menu from the task bar.
6. Click **Add/Remove Snap-in** in the **File** menu.
7. In the **Add or Remove Snap-ins** screen, in the right list of **Available Snap-ins**, select **Active Directory Schema**.
8. Click **Add >** to add the snap-in to the list of **Selected snap-ins**.
9. Click **OK** to close the **Add or Remove Snap-ins** screen.
10. In the left navigation pane, right-click **Active Directory Schema** and select **Change Active Directory Domain Controller.**
11. Select the domain controller you want to transfer the Schema Master FSMO role to, from the list of domain controllers.

12. Click **OK** when done.
13. Click **OK** in the **Active Directory Schema** popup to acknowledge that the **Active Directory Schema snap-in is not connected to the schema operations master. You will not be able to perform any changes. Schema modifications can only be made on the schema FSMO holder.**
14. Right-click **Active Directory Schema** again and select **Operation Master** from the menu.
15. Click **Change**.
16. Click **Yes** to answer the question **Are you sure you want to change the Operations Master?** in the **Active Directory Schema** popup window.
17. Click **OK** to acknowledge that the Operations Master transferred successfully.
18. Click **Close** to close the **Operations Master** window.
19. Close the **Microsoft Management Console**. If the Active Directory schema is useful as an MMC snap-in, you can optionally save the console settings.

To transfer the RID Master, PDCe and Infrastructure Master FSMO roles, follow these steps on a domain controller, logged in with an account that is a member of the Domain Admins group:

1. Open **Active Directory Users and Computer**s (dsa.msc).
2. In the left navigation pane, right-click **Active Directory Users and Computers** and select **Change Active Directory Domain Controller....**
3. Select the domain controller you want to transfer the RID Master, PDC emulator, and/or Infrastructure Master FSMO roles to, from the list of domain controllers.
4. Click **OK** when done.
5. In the left navigation pane, right-click the domain name and select **Operation Masters**.
6. Select the appropriate tab for the FSMO role you intend to transfer and click **Change**.
7. Click **Yes** to answer the question **Are you sure you want to transfer the operations master role?** in the **Active Directory Domain Services** popup window.
8. Click **OK** to acknowledge that **The operations master was successfully transferred.** in the second **Active Directory Domain Services** popup window.
9. Repeat steps five through seven to transfer the other FSMO roles, if applicable.
10. Click **Close** to close the **Operations Master** window.
11. Close **Active Directory Users and Computers**.

Transferring FSMO roles using the ntdsutil command-line tool

To transfer FSMO roles using the `ntdsutil.exe` command-line tool, follow these steps:

1. Open **Command Prompt** (`cmd.exe`) with an account that is a member of the Enterprise Admins group on the domain controller that you intend to transfer the FSMO roles to.

2. Run the following command to start the NTDS utility in interactive mode:

   ```
   ntdsutil.exe
   ```

3. Type the following command in interactive mode to enter the FSMO maintenance context:

   ```
   roles
   ```

4. Type the following commands to specify the current domain controller as the server to transfer the FSMO roles to:

   ```
   connections
   connect to server localhost
   quit
   ```

5. Type the following command to transfer the Schema Master FSMO role:

   ```
   transfer schema master
   ```

6. Type the following command to transfer the FSMO role:

   ```
   transfer naming master
   ```

7. Type the following command to transfer the PDCe FSMO role:

   ```
   transfer PDC
   ```

8. Type the following command to transfer the RID Master FSMO role:

   ```
   transfer RID master
   ```

9. Type the following command to transfer the Infrastructure Master FSMO role:

   ```
   transfer infrastructure master
   ```

10. Type the following command to exit the FSMO maintenance context:

    ```
    quit
    ```

11. Type the following command in interactive mode to exit the NTDS utility:

    ```
    quit
    ```

12. Close the Command Prompt window.

Transferring FSMO roles using Windows PowerShell

To transfer FSMO roles using the `Move-ADDirectoryServerOperationMasterRole` PowerShell cmdlet from the Active Directory Module for Windows PowerShell, use (pieces of) the following script:

```
Import-Module ActiveDirectory

Move-ADDirectoryServerOperationMasterRole -Identity "DC01"
-OperationMasterRole SchemaMaster

Move-ADDirectoryServerOperationMasterRole -Identity "DC01"
-OperationMasterRole DomainNamingMaster

Move-ADDirectoryServerOperationMasterRole -Identity "DC01"
-OperationMasterRole PDCEmulator

Move-ADDirectoryServerOperationMasterRole -Identity "DC01"
-OperationMasterRole RIDMaster

Move-ADDirectoryServerOperationMasterRole -Identity "DC01"
-OperationMasterRole InfrastructureMaster
```

How it works...

To accommodate domain controller life cycles, FSMO roles need to be transferable between domain controllers, so domain controllers that are no longer needed can be decommissioned. FSMO roles are not automatically transferred when a domain controller is decommissioned.

Seizing FSMO roles

When the domain controller that holds a FSMO role is no longer available and there is no prospect that the domain controller will ever be restored, then transferring the FSMO role is no longer an option. In this case, seizing the FSMO role is the best way to go.

Getting ready

To seize the Schema Master and/or Domain Naming Master FSMO roles, you'll need to be signed in with an account that is a member of the Enterprise Admins group. To seize the other FSMO roles, you'll need to be signed in with an account that is a member of the Domain Admins group.

How to do it...

Seizing FSMO roles is not available in the GUI, but can be accomplished using the `ntdsutil.exe` command-line tool and the `Move-ADDirectoryServerOperationMasterRole` PowerShell cmdlet from the Active Directory Module for Windows PowerShell.

Seizing FSMO roles using the ntdsutil command-line tool

To transfer FSMO roles using the `ntdsutil.exe` command-line tool, follow these steps:

1. Open Command Prompt with an account that is a member of the Enterprise Admins group on the domain controller that you intend to seize the FSMO roles from.

2. Run the following command to start the NTDS utility in interactive mode:

   ```
   ntdsutil.exe
   ```

3. Type the following command in interactive mode to enter the FSMO maintenance context:

   ```
   roles
   ```

4. Type the following commands to specify the current domain controller as the server on which to seize the FSMO roles:

   ```
   connections
   connect to server localhost
   quit
   ```

5. Type the following command to seize the Schema Master FSMO role:

   ```
   seize schema master
   ```

6. Type the following command to seize the Domain Naming Master FSMO role:

   ```
   seize naming master
   ```

7. Type the following command to seize the PDCe FSMO role:

   ```
   seize PDC
   ```

8. Type the following command to seize the RID Master FSMO role:

   ```
   seize RID master
   ```

9. Type the following command to seize the Infrastructure Master FSMO role:

```
seize infrastructure master
```

10. Type the following command to exit the FSMO maintenance context:

```
quit
```

11. Type the following command in interactive mode to exit the NTDS utility:

```
quit
```

12. Close the Command Prompt window.

Seizing FSMO roles using Windows PowerShell

To seize FSMO roles using the `Move-ADDirectoryServerOperationMasterRole` PowerShell cmdlet from the Active Directory Module for Windows PowerShell, use (pieces of) the following script:

```
Import-Module ActiveDirectory

Move-ADDirectoryServerOperationMasterRole -Identity "DC01"
-OperationMasterRole SchemaMaster -Force

Move-ADDirectoryServerOperationMasterRole -Identity "DC01"
-OperationMasterRole DomainNamingMaster -Force

Move-ADDirectoryServerOperationMasterRole -Identity "DC01"
-OperationMasterRole PDCEmulator -Force

Move-ADDirectoryServerOperationMasterRole -Identity "DC01"
-OperationMasterRole RIDMaster -Force

Move-ADDirectoryServerOperationMasterRole -Identity "DC01"
-OperationMasterRole InfrastructureMaster -Force
```

How it works...

A situation may occur where, for whatever reason, a domain controller is no longer usable. In this case, the FSMO role needs to be seized on another domain controller to make sure the multi-master model is retained.

Configuring the Primary Domain Controller emulator to synchronize time with a reliable source

The domain controller holding the PDCe FSMO role in the forest root domain is the authoritative source for time in an Active Directory domain in the default time synchronization hierarchy.

Getting ready

Before a Windows Server installation can synchronize time, the **Network Time Protocol (NTP)** should be available. By default, NTP is allowed toward domain controllers through their Windows Firewalls. However, NTP traffic toward the internet might not be available.

When an organization has deployed a reliable time source within the network, with, for instance, a GPS-enabled network time appliance, than the IP address or the hostname for this appliance can be used to configure the domain controller holding the PDCe FSMO role to synchronize time with a reliable source.

In other scenarios, synchronizing time with a reliable source will depend on the availability of a reliable internet-based time source. In this case, my recommendation is to use a list of sources, some denoted as DNS names and others denoted as IPv4 or IPv6 addresses. This way, the domain controller holding the PDCe FSMO role can synchronize time, even in the case of missing DNS resolution.

For a list of available servers, refer to `http://support.ntp.org/bin/view/Servers/WebHome`.

UDP port `123` should be allowed from the domain controller to NTP servers on the internet, except for networking infrastructures, where dedicated NTP appliances are deployed and the domain controller holding the PDCe role synchronizes with these hosts.

How to do it...

Follow these steps to configure the domain controller holding the PDCe FSMO role to synchronize time with a reliable source:

1. Sign into the domain controller holding the PDCe FSMO role.
2. Start an elevated **Command Prompt** (cmd.exe) window.
3. Run the following command:

```
w32tm.exe /config /manualpeerlist:"europe.pool.ntp.org
time.nist.gov 192.43.244.18 193.67.79.202" /syncfromflags:manual
/reliable:yes /update

net.exe stop w32time && net.exe start w32time
```

4. Close the **Command Prompt** (cmd.exe) window.

How it works...

The first of the preceding commands instructs the Windows Time Service to synchronize time with the following sources:

- europe.pool.ntp.org
- time.nist.gov
- 192.43.244.18
- 193.67.79.202

A mix of both DNS names and IP addresses is recommended for the /manualpeerlist parameter to avoid time synchronization problems when DNS problems occur within the environment. Also, it hardens time synchronization from DNS poison attacks. However, the IP addresses should be checked regularly to make sure they're still time sources.

The second command stops and then starts the Windows Time Service on the domain controller to make the settings take effect.

Microsoft's recommendation is to have this domain controller synchronize its internal clock with an external time source, so other domain controllers can synchronize their clocks with its clock. The domain controller holding the PDCe FSMO role in additional domain throughout the forest can synchronize their clocks, so that eventually, other servers, networking appliances, and client devices can synchronize their clocks.

Under normal circumstances, time synchronization is not terribly important for Active Directory. For Kerberos authentications, a time difference of up to five minutes is acceptable. However, when domain controllers handle conflicts for multiple changes to the same object, the time stamp of the last change determines the state of the object.

Managing time synchronization for virtual domain controllers

Virtual domain controllers consists of Windows Server installations running as virtual machines on hypervisor platforms. The following two hypervisor platforms dominate the server virtualization scene today:

- VMware vSphere
- Microsoft Hyper-V

Getting ready

There are two methods to manage time synchronization for virtual domain controllers:

- For virtual domain controllers running on Hyper-V, make the hardware clock of the virtualization host work together with the clock of the virtual domain controller.
- For virtual domain controllers running on vSphere, make the clock of the virtual domain controller work independently from the hardware clock of the virtualization host.

How to do it...

Choose between the two methods:

- Managing time synchronization for virtual domain controllers running on VMware vSphere
- Managing time synchronization for virtual domain controllers running on Microsoft Hyper-V

Managing time synchronization for virtual domain controllers running on VMware vSphere

For virtual domain controllers running on VMware vSphere, change the following eight lines for the virtual machines in the **Advanced Configuration Options**:

```
tools.syncTime = "0"
 time.synchronize.continue = "0"
 time.synchronize.restore = "0"
 time.synchronize.resume.disk = "0"
 time.synchronize.shrink = "0"
 time.synchronize.tools.startup = "0"
 time.synchronize.tools.enable = "0"
 time.synchronize.resume.host = "0"
```

To add these settings across multiple virtual machines at once, use VMware vRealize Orchestrator.

Managing time synchronization for virtual domain controllers running on Microsoft Hyper-V

For virtual domain controllers running on Microsoft Hyper-V, take care of the following:

- Make sure that the virtual domain controllers synchronize their clocks with the internal clocks of the Hyper-V hosts.
- Ensure that the hardware clock on all Hyper-V hosts is correct.
- Configure reliable NTP sources on all Hyper-V hosts, or join the Hyper-V hosts to an Active Directory forest, where the domain controller holding the PDCe FSMO role correctly synchronizes time with a reliable source.

How it works...

For both these platforms, it is important to have the integration components/VMware Tools installed on the virtual domain controllers.

It's tempting to think that disabling the **Synchronize guest time with host** options in the integration components/VMware Tools keeps virtual domain controllers from synchronizing time with the virtualization host on which they run. Even if the option is disabled, a virtual domain controller will synchronize its time when you do the following:

- Suspend it, the next time you resume it.
- Migrate the virtual domain controller using vMotion or live migration.
- Take a snapshot.
- Restore to a snapshot.
- Shrink the virtual disk.
- Restart the VMware Tools service.
- Reboot the virtual domain controller.

When the virtual domain controller happens to run on a virtualization host with incorrect time settings, the domain controller picks up the wrong time and will share this wrong time with other servers, networking appliances, and client devices. When users rely on these servers or devices to access resources that have the correct time, the authentication to these resources might fail because of the time difference.

Managing global catalogs

Domain controllers with the additional global catalog role hold partial information on the most requested attributes for objects in Active Directory. With multiple global catalogs, the information is replicated between the global catalogs throughout the forest.

There are two tasks concerning global catalog servers:

- Enable a domain controller as a global catalog.
- Disable a domain controller as a global catalog.

Getting ready

Before enabling or disabling domain controllers as global catalog servers, the placement rules should be considered.

Global catalogs are of importance in environments with multiple domains. Except for Active Directory environments, in which the Active Directory Recycle Bin is enabled, the placement of global catalogs should be considered in close relation to the domain controller holding the Infrastructure Master FSMO role.

In environments where we consider the placement of global catalogs, either:

- All domain controllers should be configured to be global catalogs.
- The Infrastructure Master FSMO role should be hosted on a domain controller that is not configured as a global catalog.

In environments with Microsoft Exchange Server, sufficient global catalog servers should be configured to handle the Exchange Server address book lookups, both in the domain where the Exchange Organization lives, and in the domain where user accounts reside that access the services of the Exchange Server implementation.

To manage global catalogs, you'll need to be signed in with an account that is a member of the Domain Admins group.

How to do it...

Perform these steps to enable a domain controller to be configured as a global catalog server:

1. Open **Active Directory Sites and Services** (`dssite.msc`).
2. In the left navigation pane, expand **Sites**.
3. Expand the Active Directory site where the domain controller resides.
4. Expand the **Servers** node.
5. Expand the domain controller you want to enable as a global catalog.
6. Right-click the **NTDS Settings** node underneath the domain controller.
7. Select **Properties**.
8. On the **General** tab, check the option next to **Global Catalog**.
9. Click **OK**.
10. Close **Active Directory Sites and Services**.

In environments with Microsoft Exchange Server, reboot the domain controller after enabling it as a global catalog. Otherwise, the global catalog will not be functioning from the point of view of the Microsoft Exchange Server.

Perform these steps to disable a domain controller to be configured as a global catalog server:

1. Open **Active Directory Sites and Services** (`dssite.msc`).
2. In the left navigation pane, expand **Sites.**
3. Expand the Active Directory site where the domain controller resides.
4. Expand the **Servers** node.
5. Expand the Domain controller you want to enable as a global catalog.
6. Right-click the **NTDS Settings** node underneath the domain controller. Select **Properties**.
7. On the **General** tab, uncheck the option next to **Global Catalog**.
8. Click **OK**.
9. Close **Active Directory Sites and Services**.

How it works

Global catalog servers are used when you do the following:

- Perform forest-wide searches.
- Perform Exchange Server address book lookups.
- Log on in Active Directory forests that have multiple domains.

In these cases, the global catalog server responds to requests using TCP port 3268 (insecure) and TCP port 3269 (secure).

The preceding steps enable a domain controller to be a global catalog server.

4
Managing Containers and Organizational Units

A default Active Directory domain comes with default containers and a default **Organizational Unit** (**OU**). The default containers serve as default locations when you create objects, for instance, the Computers container, and for important objects, for example, the Builtin container. The default Domain Controllers OU serves as the location for domain controller objects.

The following containers are available by default:

- Builtin
- Computers
- ForeignSecurityPrincipals
- Keys
- LostAndFound
- Managed Service Accounts
- NTDS Quotas
- Program Data
- System
- TPM devices
- Users

In Active Directory users and computers (`dsa.msc`), some of these default containers are hidden from sight, unless you check the **Advanced Features** option in the **View** menu.

We can easily spot the default structure by using the Active Directory Administrative Center (`dsac.exe`) and Active Directory Users and Computers (`dsa.msc`), but it's not that hard using Windows PowerShell either. Simply type the following lines of PowerShell to get a list of the OUs in the Active Directory domain that you've signed in to:

```
Import-Module ActiveDirectory

Get-ADOrganizationalUnit -filter * | ft name
```

Containers and OUs don't have **security identifiers** (**SIDs**), so they can't be used as security principals to directly grant access to resources.

The configuration partition of the Active Directory database can get messy during the life cycle of the domain. As complexity is the archenemy of every admin, there needs to be a way to organize or even segregate objects.

This chapter serves up the following recipes:

- Creating an OU
- Deleting an OU
- Modifying an OU
- Delegating control of an OU
- Modifying the default location for new user and computer objects

Differences between OUs and containers

Before we get into the recipes, it's important for us to explore the differences between OUs and containers. OUs and containers play different roles and act differently in Active Directory.

Containers

Containers are created by default. Creating or deleting containers using the built-in tools is not supported. Containers don't support delegation or group policy as well. Creating an OU is not possible in a container.

OUs

OUs can be created and deleted by Active Directory admins. They support delegation of control, using the **Delegation of Control Wizard** and the built-in tools. Group policy objects and managers can be applied to OUs. OUs can be nested.

OUs versus Active Directory domains

One of the most heated discussions when setting up and/or extending Active Directory environments is to create OUs for departments, locations, and/or organizations. Please refer to the *Choosing between a new Domain or Forest* recipe in `Chapter 1`, *Optimizing Forests, Domains, and Trusts*, to make the best-informed decision.

Creating an OU

In this recipe, we will create an OU.

Getting ready

To create an OU, you'll need to be signed in with an account that is a member of the domain admin group or have delegated privileges to create OUs.

See the *Delegating Control of an OU* recipe in this chapter for more information on delegating control of an OU.

How to do it...

There are three ways to do it:

- Using the Active Directory Administrative Center
- Using the command line
- Using Windows PowerShell

Using the Active Directory Administrative Center

To create an OU using the Active Directory Administrative Center, follow these steps:

1. Open the **Active Directory Administrative Center** (`dsac.exe`).
2. In the left navigation pane, switch to tree view:

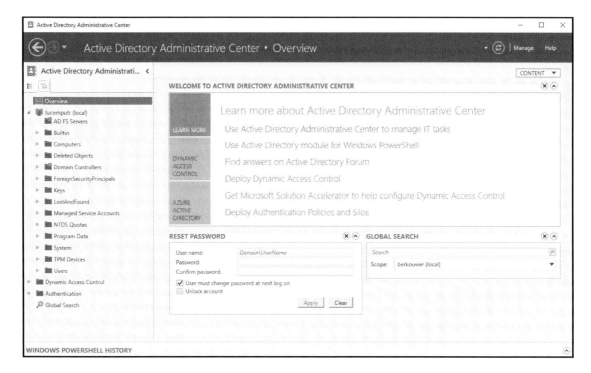

3. Expand the tree, if necessary, to locate the domain or OU you want to be the parent object.
4. Select the parent object for the new OU.
5. Right-click the parent object, select **New...**, and from the menu, select **Organizational Unit**. The **Create Organizational Unit** window appears:

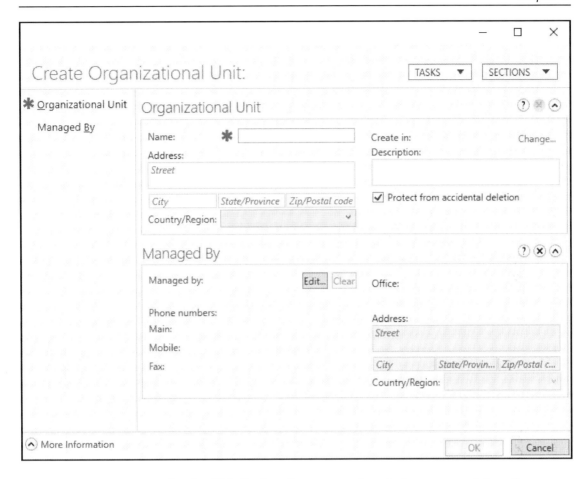

6. Enter a name for the OU. Optionally, enter a description or any of the other fields.
7. Click **OK** to create the OU.

Using the command line

Since Windows 2000 Server, `dsadd.exe`, a command-line tool, has been available to create objects, including OUs.

Run the following command line on a domain controller or any domain-joined Windows or Windows Server installation with the **Remote Server Administration Tools** (**RSAT**) for Active Directory Domain Services installed:

```
dsadd.exe ou "OU=Finance,DC=LucernPub,DC=com" -desc "Finance OU"
```

Using Windows PowerShell

The `New-ADOrganizationalUnit` PowerShell cmdlet is the most elaborate option to create OUs on Windows Server installations without the desktop experience and through automation of administrative tasks.

Use the following lines of PowerShell on a system with the Active Directory module for Windows PowerShell installed:

```
Import-Module ActiveDirectory

New-ADOrganizationalUnit "Finance" -Description "Finance OU"
```

How it works...

You can use the Active Directory Administrative Center, command line, and/or Windows PowerShell to create OUs. When you create them this way, OUs are automatically protected from accidental deletion.

Creating OUs using the Active Directory Administrative Center allows for more overview of the creation process, but is not very scalable. You wouldn't use it to create 1,000 OUs, for instance. The command line and Windows PowerShell are more suited for these scenarios. The PowerShell History Viewer feature might help you out when discovering the Windows PowerShell cmdlets to get the latter process going.

When you create an OU, the **Name** attribute is the only required attribute to specify.

There's more...

When you use the PowerShell example from this recipe, you can optionally use the `-ProtectedFromAccidentalDeletion $false` **parameter.**

Deleting an OU

Use this recipe to delete an OU.

Getting ready

To delete an OU, you'll need to be signed in with an account that is a member of the **Domain Admins** group or have delegated privileges to delete OUs.

OUs are protected from accidental deletion by default. When you try to delete an OU that is protected from accidental deletion, you'll get an **Access denied** error. In this case, uncheck the **Protected from Accidental Deletion** checkbox from the OU's properties.

 Unless you create OUs using `csvde.exe` or `ldifde.exe`, OUs are protected from accidental deletion by default.

How to do it...

There are three ways to do it:

- Using the Active Directory Administrative Center
- Using the command line
- Using Windows PowerShell

Using the Active Directory Administrative Center

To delete an OU, using the Active Directory Administrative Center, follow these steps:

1. Open the **Active Directory Administrative Center** (`dsac.exe`).
2. In the left navigation pane, switch to **tree view**.
3. Expand the tree, if necessary, to locate the OU you want to delete.
4. Select the OU.
5. Right-click the OU and click **Properties**.
6. Uncheck the **Protected from Accidental Deletion** checkbox.
7. Click **OK**.

8. Right-click the OU again. This time, click **Delete**.
   The **Delete Confirmation** window appears:

9. Click **Yes** to confirm.
10. If the OU contains child objects, click **Yes** again.

Using the command line

Since Windows 2000 Server, a command-line tool has been available to delete objects, including OUs: dsrm.exe.

Run the following command line on a domain controller or any domain-joined Windows or Windows Server installation with the RSAT for Active Directory Domain Services installed:

```
dsrm.exe "OU=Finance,DC=LucernPub,DC=com" -subtree
```

Using Windows PowerShell

The New-ADOrganizationalUnit PowerShell cmdlet is the most elaborate option to create OUs on Windows Server installations without the desktop experience and through automation of administrative tasks.

Use the following lines of PowerShell on a system with the Active Directory module for Windows PowerShell installed:

```
Import-Module ActiveDirectory

Remove-ADObject -Identity "OU=Finance,DC=LucernPub,DC=com"
 -Recursive -Confirm:$False
```

How it works...

As organizations change, so may the requirements on Active Directory. When an OU is no longer of use because it no longer holds any objects or the linked GPOs no longer apply or because the level of delegation and/or management is no longer needed, you can delete it.

Deleting containers using the built-in tools is not supported.

There's more...

When the Active Directory Recycle Bin is enabled in Active Directory, you can safely restore OUs and their child objects, if you need to.

Modifying an OU

After you've created an OU, you might find the need to change its properties.

Getting ready

To modify an OU, you'll need to be signed in with an account that is a member of the **Domain Admins** group or have delegated privileges to modify OUs.

How to do it...

There are three ways to do it:

- Using the Active Directory Administrative Center
- Using the command line
- Using Windows PowerShell

Using the Active Directory Administrative Center

To modify an OU using the Active Directory Administrative Center, follow these steps:

1. Open the **Active Directory Administrative Center** (`dsac.exe`).
2. In the left navigation pane, switch to the **tree view**.

3. Expand the tree, if necessary, to locate the OU you want to delete.
4. Select the OU.
5. Right-click the OU and click **Properties:**

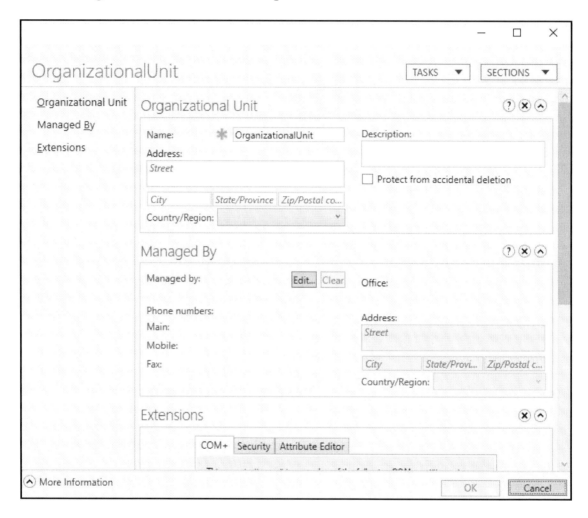

6. Change the properties you want to modify:
   - Modify the **Description.**
   - Modify the **Manager.**
   - Uncheck the **Protected from Accidental Deletion.**
7. Click **OK.**

Using the command line

Since Windows 2000 Server, a command-line tool has been available to modify objects, including OUs: `dsmod.exe`. Unfortunately, for OUs, it can only be used to change the description.

Run the following command line on a domain controller or any domain-joined Windows or Windows Server installation with the RSAT for Active Directory Domain Services installed:

```
dsmod.exe ou "OU=Finance,DC=LucernPub,DC=com" -desc "New description"
```

Using Windows PowerShell

The `Set-ADOrganizationalUnit` PowerShell cmdlet is the most elaborate option to modify OUs on Windows Server installations without the desktop experience and through automation of administrative tasks.

The following properties are easily accessible through the `Set-ADOrganizationalUnit` PowerShell cmdlet:

- `City`
- `Country`
- `Description`
- `DistinguishedName`
- `LinkedGroupPolicyObjects`
- `ManagedBy`
- `Name`
- `PostalCode`
- `State`
- `StreetAddress`

Simply use the following lines of PowerShell on a system with the Active Directory module for Windows PowerShell installed and hack away on the properties of the OU:

```
Import-Module ActiveDirectory

Set-ADOrganizationalUnit -Identity "OU=Finance,DC=LucernPub,DC=com" -
ManagedBy "CN=User,CN=Users,DC=LucernPub,DC=com"
```

How it works...

Modifying the properties of an OU means modifying its attributes in Active Directory.

A typical OU has a number of attributes:

- description
- gPLink
- gPOptions
- msDS-Approx-Immed-Subordinates
- managedBy
- ou

You can change these attributes to modify the OU.

There's more...

In PowerShell, it's not possible to change the distinguished name for an OU, as this would effectively move the OU. The process of moving OUs is different and requires the Move-ADObject PowerShell cmdlet.

Protection from accidental deletion is also not an attribute for an OU. Instead, the checkbox manifests itself as security permissions on the OU and the parent object.

See also

Modifying the gPLink and gPOptions attributes is covered in the *Linking group policy objects to an organizational unit* recipe of Chapter 10, *Securing Active Directory*.

Delegating control of an OU

In large Active Directory environments, the administrative burden may be high. Therefore, in environments with several teams of administrators and service desk personnel, delegation is needed. This way, for instance, service desk personnel may reset passwords, application administrators may change group memberships, and only true Active Directory admins may manage OUs.

Getting ready

To perform delegation of control, you'll need to be signed in with an account that is a member of the Domain Admins group or have full control privileges of the OUs you want to delegate control over.

How to do it...

There are two ways to delegate control over an OU:

- Using Active Directory Users and Computers
- Using the command line

Using Active Directory Users and Computers

By far, the easiest way to perform delegation of control is using the Delegation of Control Wizard from Active Directory Users and Computers (dsa.msc). Follow these steps:

1. Open **Active Directory Users and Computers** (dsa.msc):

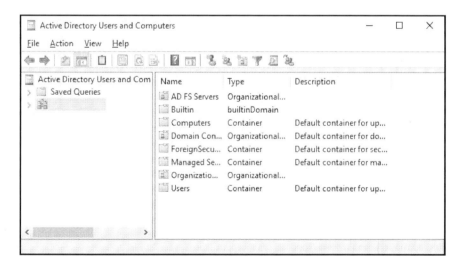

2. Right-click the OU you want to delegate control over, and select **Delegate control...** from the menu.

The Delegation of Control Wizard appears:

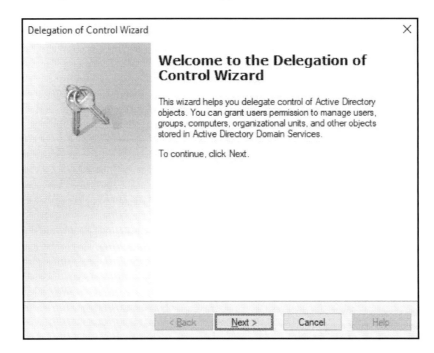

3. On the **Welcome to the Delegation of Control Wizard** screen, click **Next >.**

4. In the **Users or Group** screen, click the **Add...** button to select one or more users or groups to whom you want to delegate control.

5. In the **Select Users, Computers, or Groups** popup, select the groups you want to delegate to.

6. Click **OK** when done.

7. On the **Users or Group** screen, click **Next >** to continue to the next screen of the **Delegation of Control Wizard**:

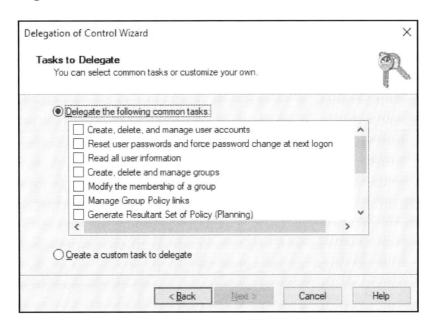

8. On the **Tasks to Delegate** screen, select the common task(s) you want to delegate from the list below **Delegate the following common tasks** or select the **Create a custom task to delegate** option to go at it from scratch.

 When you select **Create a custom task to delegate**, select the object(s) and action(s) on the **Active Directory Object Type** screen and the permissions on the **Permissions** screen.

9. On the **Completing the Delegation of Control Wizard** screen, click **Finish**.

The resulting delegation permissions (Access Control Entries or ACEs) can now be viewed on the **Security** tab of the properties of the OU.

Using the command line

Using `dsacls.exe`, you can delegate permissions from the command line. This is ideal for scripted deployments of predetermined permissions and for applying permissions on domain controllers running as Server Core installations.

In its most basic usage, `dsacls.exe` can be used to display permissions (using `/a`), deny permissions (using the `/d` parameter), and grant permissions (using `/g`). These permissions are set to an object, as denoted as a distinguished name for a group (or user, if you must). The permissions themselves take the form of generic permissions or specific permissions, all denoted by two letters, the so-called permission bits. The generic permissions are denoted as follows:

Permission bit	Permission
GR	Generic read
GE	Generic execute
GW	Generic write
GA	Generic all

The most popular specific permissions are denoted as follows:

Permission bit	Permission
SD	Delete
DT	Delete an object and all child objects
RC	Read security information
WD	Change security information
WO	Change owner information
CC	Create child object
DC	Delete child object
RP	Read property
WP	Write property

When you use the last four specific permissions, it's a best practice to also include the object type or attribute for which you want the permission to apply.

Use the following command line to delegate write permissions to a group for the mS-DS-ConsistencyGUID attribute for objects in the DC=Computers, DC=lucernpub, DC=com OU:

```
dsacls.exe "OU=Organizational Unit,DC=lucernpub,DC=com" /I:S /G
LucernPub\Group:RPWP;"ms-DS-ConsistencyGUID";user"
```

How it works...

There are two ways to delegate:

- Using the built-in groups
- Using delegation of control

Using the built-in groups

Using the built-in groups, such as Account Operators and Server Operators, is an easy and fast way to delegate administrative tasks in Active Directory. However, there are a number of things you need to be aware of:

- The built-in Account Operators group provides more permissions than are actually required in many organizations. While you might expect the members of this group to merely have permissions to reset passwords of non-admins, they can create, modify, and delete all objects, except members of the Domain Admins group, in all OUs except the Domain Controllers OU. They may not modify the group memberships for the Domain Admins group, but they may interactively sign in to Domain Controllers and have permissions to shut them down, by default.
- The built-in Server Operators group also grants permissions to interactively sign in to domain controllers. This might pose an unexpected security risk.

Using delegation of control

As an alternative to using the built-in groups, you can granularly delegate permissions per OU.

There are a couple of recommended practices to keep you and your colleagues from insanity:

- Build a delegation of control model and/or authorization matrix before performing delegation of control. This way, delegation settings can be continually documented, agreed upon, and transferred to other admins without adding unnecessary complexity.
- Always use groups when delegating permissions, not individual user or computer accounts. This way, giving permissions is a matter of (temporarily) adding a user account to a group, instead of going through the Delegation of Control Wizard each time. It also makes auditing *that* much easier.
- Try to avoid deny permissions to avoid complexity. Deny permissions take precedence over allowed and/or granted permissions.
- Use a hacker mindset. Always test the delegation settings for any unwanted effects.
- Use delegation of control of groups in combination with NTDS Quotas to prevent group administrators from creating over 1,000 groups, adding members to these groups, and performing a denial of service attack, because user accounts can't be used to sign in when they have over 1,023 group memberships.

See also

If you need help creating OUs, take a look at the *Creating an organizational unit* recipe of Chapter 3, *Managing Active Directory Roles and Features*.

Modifying the default location for new user and computer objects

When you join a device to the Active Directory domain or create a user object without context, these objects will be placed in default containers; devices end up in the Computers container. User objects end up in the Users container. You can change these locations to accommodate for processes, delegation, and group policy structure: when a computer object is placed in an OU different to the Computers container, it might get picked up by an IAM solution automatically, have proper settings deployed by group policy automatically, and be manageable by delegated service desk personnel automatically.

Getting ready

To modify the default location for new user objects and computer objects, the Active Directory environment needs to run the Windows Server 2003 domain functional level (DFL). If you try to modify the location in an Active Directory environment running the Windows 2000 Server DFL, you will receive the following error:

```
Error, unable to modify the wellKnownObjects attribute. Verify that the
domain functional level of the domain is at least Windows Server 2003:

Unwilling To Perform

Redirection was NOT successful.
```

 There is also a bug when you try to modify the default location for new user and computer objects on a domain controller running Windows Server 2008 in an Active Directory domain running the Windows Server 2008 DFL. The solution here is to install Service Pack 2, or run the commands from a domain controller running Windows Server 2008 R2 or a newer version of Windows Server.

Additionally, you need to be signed in interactively with a user object that is a member of the Domain Admins group on a domain controller. This action cannot be performed remotely from a management workstation or management server.

How to do it...

To modify the default location for new user and computer objects, we first need to create the OUs to which we want to redirect. I recommend creating two separate OUs to separate user objects from computer objects. Redirected Users OU and Redirected Computers OU would do nicely.

Then, on an elevated Command Prompt, run the following commands, replacing the values for your environment:

```
redirusr.exe "OU=Redirected Users OU,DC=LucernPub,DC=com"

redircmp.exe "OU=Redirected Computers OU,DC=LucernPub,DC=com"
```

If you ever need to change back, then the following two commands can be used:

```
redirusr.exe "CN=Users,DC=LucernPub,DC=com"

redircmp.exe "CN=Computers,DC=LucernPub,DC=com"
```

How it works...

Microsoft deliberately chose to put devices in the Computers container and user objects in the Users container, because containers can't have policies attached, so even if an Active Directory administrator messed up the directory, at least you should be able to join a device and sign in to it without having group policy objects applied from the container.

Active Directory admins can change the default locations for objects. Since this action has the potential to mess things up, Microsoft has decided to make this change available only on the command line, through two specific executables:

Executable	Purpose
Redircmp.exe	Redirect computer objects to a different OU or container
Redirusr.exe	Redirect user objects to a different OU or container

See also

If you need help creating OUs, take a look at the *Creating an organizational unit* recipe of Chapter 3, *Managing Active Directory Roles and Features*.

5
Managing Active Directory Sites and Troubleshooting Replication

When I first learned about Active Directory sites, the concept was explained to me as being locations of readily-available connectivity.

There's an easy analogy for it: islands. In island states, people live on islands, but not everything people need might be available on their island. Additionally, something on their island might break and there are only a few trade routes for goods and services.

In this analogy, the trade routes between geographical locations are the networking connections between Active Directory sites, the islands of readily-available connectivity. The island's roads are that readily-available connectivity: you can use them all you want, without additional cost.

 Connections with a bandwidth below 10 Mbit/second and unreliable connections are considered reasons to create Active Directory sites.

Not many organizations place the domain controllers that hold **Flexible Single Master Operations (FSMO)** roles in poorly-connected Active Directory sites. Many networking topologies for organizations feature a hub-and-spoke layout with a central location and several outlying locations with, optionally, further outlying locations.

This chapter serves up the following recipes:

- Creating a site
- Managing a site
- Managing subnets
- Creating a site link
- Managing a site link
- Modifying replication schedules
- Creating a site link bridge
- Managing bridgehead servers
- Managing the Inter-site Topology Generation and Knowledge Consistency Checker
- Managing Universal Group Membership caching
- Working with repadmin.exe
- Forcing replication
- Managing inbound and outbound replication
- Modify the tombstone lifetime period
- Managing strict replication consistency
- Upgrading SYSVOL replication from File Replication Service to Distributed File System Replication
- Checking for and remediating lingering objects

Before studying the recipes, we will look at a few points on Active Directory sites and recommendations.

What do Active Directory sites do?

Active Directory sites govern access and replication.

Active Directory's DClocator process allows for devices to find the nearest domain controller. By default, these would be the domain controllers in the current Active Directory site where the device resides. The way the device knows in which site it resides is derived from its IP address, which matches a subnet, as defined for the Active Directory site.

When there are no domain controllers in an Active Directory site, the site link costs define the nearest domain controller to DClocator. The domain controllers in the site connected with the lowest cost will be returned to the device.

Domain controllers in different Active Directory sites replicate partitions over the same Active Directory site links through bridgehead servers; these are domain controllers that take on the additional role of replicating over the site link to the bridgehead server on the other side, on top of replicating with the domain controller(s) within its site.

Replication over site links can be managed in terms of schedule and replication type.

The DNS and the **Distributed Filesystem (DFS)** are both Active Directory site-aware, in that they can provide access to the services closest to the end user. For instance, in a DFS setup with a file server on each location, the end user in a specific site would be redirected to the file server in their respective Active Directory site and have readily-available connectivity, while the file servers take care of any replication needed.

Recommendations

It is a recommended practice to design Active Directory sites following these rules of thumb:

- Create one Active Directory site per location. If the bandwidth between locations is above 10 Mbit/second and reliable, and you don't want to segment services or subnets, create one Active Directory site for these locations.
- Configure one Active Directory site link between two Active Directory sites.
- Configure a catch-all subnet, for instance a 10.0.0.0/8 subnet, in your main location and create subnets with smaller ranges, for instance 10.1.0.0/16 and 10.3.1.0/24 subnets, for other locations.
- Do not disable the Bridge all site links option for all IP-based site links and all SMTP-based site links.
- Do not enable the Ignore schedules option for all IP-based site links.
- Keep Bridge all site links enabled.
- Keep the ISTG enabled.
- Keep the KCC enabled.
- Keep Strict Replication Consistency enabled.
- Define a process where networking admins communicate changes in their environment to Active Directory admins, so they can optimize Active Directory to take advantage of these changes.
- Do not link Group Policy objects to Active Directory sites, if you can avoid it.

Let's look at the recipes for this chapter.

Creating a site

An Active Directory site definition tells Active Directory to treat the subnets, domain controllers, member servers, and domain-joined device as well-connected. Its Active Directory site link defines the connectivity to other Active Directory sites.

To define connectivity, two sites are needed. The **Default-First-Site-Name** is present in Active Directory, by default. As Active Directory admins add Active Directory sites, the relationships between the sites evolve to align the logical Active Directory topology with the physical topology of even the most complex environments.

Getting ready

To create an Active Directory site, you'll need to be signed in with an account that is a member of the Enterprise Admins group. That's because Active Directory sites are defined for an entire Active Directory forest in the **CN=Configuration** partition.

How to do it...

There are two ways to do it:

- Using Active Directory Sites and Services
- Using Windows PowerShell

Let's discuss the first method.

Using Active Directory Sites and Services

To create an Active Directory site using Active Directory Sites and Services, perform these steps:

1. Open **Active Directory Sites and Services** (`dssite.msc`).
2. In the left navigation pane, select the **Sites** node.
3. Right-click the **Sites** node and click **New Site...**.
4. The **New Object – Site** window appears.
5. Type a logical name for the Active Directory site in the **Name:** field.
6. When this is the first site you create, next to the **Default-First-Site-Name**, select the **DEFAULTIPSITELINK** link.

7. Click the **OK** button to create the Active Directory site.
The **Active Directory Domain Services** popup window appears:

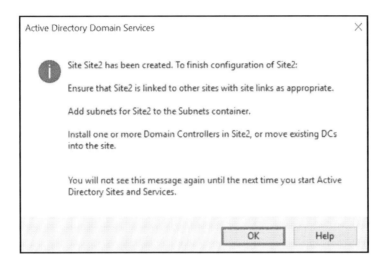

8. Click **OK** in the **Active Directory Domain Services** popup that notifies you of the additional actions to take to finish configuring the Active Directory site.

After you've performed the preceding steps, you can see the new Active Directory site in the left navigation pane, under the **Sites** node.

Using Windows PowerShell

To create an Active Directory site using the Active Directory module for Windows PowerShell, use the `New-ADReplicationSite` PowerShell cmdlet. An example of the simplest lines of PowerShell to achieve this goal looks like this:

```
Import-Module ActiveDirectory

New-ADReplicationSite -Name "Site2"
```

You can verify your change by listing the Active Directory sites:

```
Import-Module ActiveDirectory

Get-ADReplicationSite -Filter * | Select Name
```

See also

To make the right choice between creating an Active Directory site or an Active Directory domain, refer to the *Choosing between a new domain or forest* recipe in `Chapter 1`, *Optimizing Forests, Domains, and Trusts*.

To finish configuration of the Active Directory site, refer to the following recipes:

- *Managing subnets*
- *Creating a site link* or *Managing a site link*
- *Promoting a server to a domain controller* in `Chapter 2`, *Managing Domain Controllers*
- *Promoting a server to a read-only domain controller* in `Chapter 2`, *Managing Domain Controllers*

Managing a site

After creating an Active Directory site, you might find the need to manage it. You might want to do the following:

- Rename it
- Change its description
- Change its location
- Delete it
- Delegate control

Getting ready

To manage an Active Directory site, you'll need to be signed in with an account that is a member of the Enterprise Admins group or with an account that has been delegated permissions to manage the Active Directory site.

When your aim is to delete an Active Directory site, remove any domain controller for the site first by right-clicking the domain controller object(s) under the site node and selecting **Move**. Alternatively, demote the domain controller.

How to do it...

The manageable properties of an Active Directory site are stored in its attributes. The best way to change them is through Active Directory Sites and Services and/or the Active Directory module for Windows PowerShell.

Using Active Directory Sites and Services

To change the name of an Active Directory site, perform these steps:

1. Open **Active Directory Sites and Services** (`dssite.msc`).
2. In the left navigation pane, select the Active Directory site you want to manage.
3. Right-click the site name and select **Rename** from the menu.
4. Type the new name for the Active Directory site and press *Enter* when done.

To change the description of an Active Directory site, perform these steps:

1. Open **Active Directory Sites and Services** (`dssite.msc`).
2. In the left navigation pane, select the Active Directory site you want to manage.
3. Right-click the site name and select **Properties** from the menu.
4. On the **General** tab, type a description for the Active Directory site.
5. Press **OK** when done.

To change the location of an Active Directory site, perform these steps:

1. Open **Active Directory Sites and Services** (`dssite.msc`).
2. In the left navigation pane, select the Active Directory site you want to manage.
3. Right-click the site name and select **Properties** from the menu.
4. Navigate to the **Location** tab.
5. On the **Location** tab, type a location for the Active Directory site.
6. Press **OK** when done.

To delegate the manage Group Policy links permission of an Active Directory site, perform these steps:

1. Open **Active Directory Sites and Services** (`dssite.msc`).
2. In the left navigation pane, select the Active Directory site you want to manage.
3. Right-click the site name and select **Delegate Control...** from the menu. The **Delegation of Control Wizard** appears.
4. On the **Welcome to the Delegation of Control Wizard** screen, click **Next >**.

5. On the **Users or Groups** screen, click the **Add...** button and select the group(s) you want to delegate control for in the **Select Users**, **Computers or Groups** popup. Click **OK** when done.
6. Back on the **Users or Groups** screen, click **Next >**.
   You reach the **Tasks to Delegate** screen:

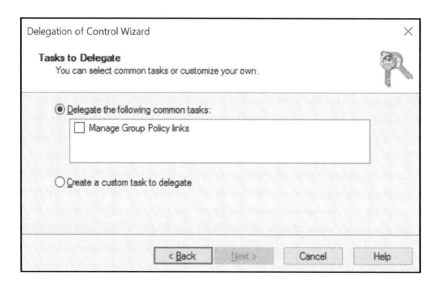

7. On the **Tasks to Delegate** screen, select the **Manage Group Policy links** task underneath **Delegate the following common tasks:**.
8. Click **Next >**.
9. On the **Completing the Delegation of Control Wizard** screen, click **Finish**.

To delete an Active Directory site, perform these steps:

1. Open **Active Directory Sites and Services** (`dssite.msc`).
2. In the left navigation pane, select the Active Directory site you want to delete.
3. Right-click the site name and select **Delete** from the menu.
4. In the **Active Directory Domain Services** popup, click **Yes** to answer the question **Are you sure you want to delete site** 'SiteName'**?**.

Do not delete the **Default-First-Site-Name** Active Directory site. Instead, rename it.

Using Windows PowerShell

Alternatively, Active Directory sites can be managed using the Active Directory module for Windows PowerShell.

Use the following lines of PowerShell to rename an Active Directory site:

```
Import-Module ActiveDirectory

Rename-ADObject -Identity "CN=Default-First-Site-
Name,CN=Sites,CN=Configuration,DC=Lucernpub,DC=com" -NewName "ADSite2"
```

Use the following lines of PowerShell to change the description of an Active Directory site:

```
Import-Module ActiveDirectory

Set-ADReplicationSite -Identity "CN=Default-First-Site-
Name,CN=Sites,CN=Configuration,DC=Lucernpub,DC=com" -Description "New
description here"
```

Use the following lines of PowerShell to change the location of an Active Directory site:

```
Import-Module ActiveDirectory

Set-ADReplicationSite "CN=Default-First-Site-
Name,CN=Sites,CN=Configuration,DC=Lucernpub,DC=com" -Location "New location
here"
```

How it works...

When you rename an Active Directory site, you change the common name of the object of the Active Directory site. While this is not a problem with most software, such as System Center Configuration Manager, your organization might get in trouble with software that references Active Directory sites by their names and not their GUIDs.

An Active Directory site's location might be a field you'd want to use to define the physical location and/or network type of an Active Directory site. This way, when there is a problem with the Active Directory site, admins might make their way to the root cause, the core problem, and/or physical location faster. In multi-domain environments, it might be useful to denote the domain for which the Active Directory site is in use. A perfect example for such an environment: using Airfield IATA code would be P ZRH LucernPub to denote a production Active Directory site for Lucern Publishing near Zurich Airport.

Before deleting an Active Directory site, make sure to move all domain controllers from that site to a different site. Don't worry about site links or subnets; these are not deleted when you delete an Active Directory site.

When you delegate control of an Active Directory site, you allow a group to manage Active Directory site Group Policy links through the `gPLink` attribute of an Active Directory site, out of the box, or any other granular task on any of the attributes you want to delegate.

See also

To finish configuration of the Active Directory site, refer to the following recipes:

- *Managing subnets*
- *Creating a site link* or *Managing a site link*

Managing subnets

Subnets define logical network segments to Active Directory. Based on the subnet, a device will contact the domain controllers in the right site. There might be domain controllers in the same site as the device, but depending on the costs of the site links, devices might also look for domain controllers in other sites.

Getting ready

To manage subnets, you'll need to be signed in with an account that is a member of the Enterprise Admins group.

How to do it...

Subnets can be created and deleted using Active Directory Sites and Services and/or the Active Directory module for Windows PowerShell.

Using Active Directory Sites and Services

To create a subnet, perform these steps:

1. Open **Active Directory Sites and Services** (`dssite.msc`).
2. In the left navigation pane, select the **Subnets** node.
3. Right-click the node's name and select **New Subnet...** from the menu.
4. Type the prefix for the subnet.
5. Optionally, select an Active Directory site for the subnet, for example, `10.5.15.0/24`.
6. Click **OK** when done.

To delete a subnet, perform these steps:

1. Open **Active Directory Sites and Services** (`dssite.msc`).
2. In the left navigation pane, expand the **Subnets** node.
3. Right-click the name of the subnet you want to delete and select **Delete** from the menu.
4. In the **Active Directory Domain Services** popup, click **Yes** to answer the question **Are you sure you want to delete the Subnet named** 'Subnet'?.

To change the description of a subnet, perform these steps:

1. Open **Active Directory Sites and Services** (`dssite.msc`).
2. In the left navigation pane, select the subnet you want to manage.
3. Right-click the subnet and select **Properties** from the menu.
4. On the **General** tab, type a description for the Active Directory subnet.
5. Press **OK** when done.

To change the site of a subnet, perform these steps:

1. Open **Active Directory Sites and Services** (`dssite.msc`).
2. In the left navigation pane, select the subnet you want to manage.
3. Right-click the subnet and select **Properties** from the menu.
4. Navigate to the **Location** tab.
5. On the **Location** tab, type a location for the Active Directory subnet.
6. Press **OK** when done.

To change the site of a subnet, perform these steps:

1. Open **Active Directory Sites and Services** (`dssite.msc`).
2. In the left navigation pane, select the subnet you want to manage.
3. Right-click the subnet and select **Properties** from the menu.
4. On the **General** tab, type the new network prefix for the Active Directory subnet.
5. Press **OK** when done.

To change the location of a subnet, perform these steps:

1. Open **Active Directory Sites and Services** (`dssite.msc`).
2. In the left navigation pane, select the subnet you want to manage.
3. Right-click the subnet and select **Properties** from the menu.
4. On the **General** tab, from the drop-down list of Active Directory sites, select one of the existing Active Directory sites, or select the empty entry in the list to remove the subnet from any Active Directory site.
5. Press **OK** when done.

Using Windows PowerShell

Use the following lines of PowerShell to create a subnet:

```
Import-Module ActiveDirectory

New-ADReplicationSubnet -Name 10.0.0.0/8 -Site Default-First-Site-Name
```

Use the following lines of PowerShell to delete a subnet:

```
Import-Module ActiveDirectory

Remove-ADReplicationSubnet -Identity 10.0.0.0/8
```

Use the following lines of PowerShell to change the description of a subnet:

```
Import-Module ActiveDirectory

Set-ADReplicationSubnet -Identity 10.0.0.0/8 -Description "New description here"
```

Use the following lines of PowerShell to change the location of a subnet:

```
Import-Module ActiveDirectory

Set-ADReplicationSubnet -Identity 10.0.0.0/8 -Location "New location here"
```

Use the following lines of PowerShell to change the site of a subnet:

```
Import-Module ActiveDirectory

Set-ADReplicationSubnet -Identity 10.0.0.0/8 -Site NewSiteName
```

How it works...

Based on the IP address for a device or member server or domain controller, it will determine the Active Directory site it needs to become a member of.

Subnets use the network prefix notation for network segments. This means the network IP address is noted, followed by the number of bits in the subnet mask. 10.0.0.0/8 denotes a network with IPv4 addresses starting with 10.0.0.1 throughout 10.255.255.254. 10.31.1.1/32 denotes the host with IPv4 address 10.31.1.1.

Subnets with less available IP addresses have precedence over larger subnets. This creates the ability to create a catch-all subnet at the main site and branch off smaller networks to outlying Active Directory sites.

Both IPv6 and IPv4 address ranges can be used with Active Directory subnets.

See also

To finish configuration of the Active Directory site, refer to the following recipes:

- *Creating a site* or *Managing a site*
- *Creating a site link* or *Managing a site link*

Creating a site link

Active Directory site links help domain controllers to find replication partners in other Active Directory sites.

Getting ready

To create an Active Directory site link, you'll need to be signed in with an account that is a member of the Enterprise Admins group.

To adhere to the recommended practices, be sure you have created two Active Directory sites already. Then, create a site link between exactly two Active Directory sites, for each combination. Only when the network topology is not fully routed, it might make sense to create an Active Directory site link with more than two sites.

While the naming of Active Directory objects should ideally adhere to the naming convention for the environment, a common practice is to name Active Directory site links for the two sites they connect separated by a hyphen.

How to do it...

There are two ways to do it:

- Using Active Directory Sites and Services
- Using Windows PowerShell

Using Active Directory Sites and Services

To create an Active Directory site link with default settings using **Active Directory Sites and Services**, perform these steps:

1. Open **Active Directory Sites and Services** (`dssite.msc`).
2. In the left navigation pane, expand the **Sites** node.
3. In the left navigation pane, expand the **Inter-Site Transports** node.
4. Right-click the **IP** node and click **New Site link...**.
5. The **New Object - Site** window appears.
6. Type a logical name for the Active Directory site link in the **Name:** field.
7. In the **Sites not in this site link** field, select two Active Directory sites for this Active Directory site link. Click **Add**.
8. Click the **OK** button to create the Active Directory site link.

After you've performed these steps, you can see the new Active Directory site link in the main pane, under the **Inter-Site Transports** node.

Using Windows PowerShell

To create an Active Directory site link using the Active Directory module for Windows PowerShell, use the `New-ADReplicationSiteLink` PowerShell cmdlet. An example of the simplest lines of PowerShell to achieve this goal looks like this:

```
Import-Module ActiveDirectory

New-ADReplicationSiteLink -Name "SiteLinkName" -SitesIncluded Site1,Site2
```

You can verify your change by listing the Active Directory sites:

```
Import-Module ActiveDirectory

Get-ADReplicationSiteLink -Filter * | Select Name
```

How it works...

Active Directory site links help domain controllers to find replication partners in other Active Directory sites. Additionally, when all domain controllers are unavailable in an Active Directory site, or no domain controllers were ever available, site links help devices to find the nearest domain controller.

In contrast to Active Directory sites, site links are not created by default. Active Directory site links need to be created manually.

There are two types of Active Directory site links:

- IP-based site links
- SMTP-based site links

IP-based site links are preferred, but when a networking connection is really low on bandwidth and is really unreliable, SMTP-based site links may offer better performance.

 SMTP-based site links do not require Microsoft Exchange Server or any other mail server functionality. Active Directory merely uses the same mail protocol.

See also

To finish configuration of the Active Directory site, refer to the following recipes:

- *Creating a site* or *Managing a site*
- *Creating a Subnet*
- *Managing a site link*

Managing a site link

After creating an Active Directory site link, you might find the need to manage it. You might want to do the following:

- Rename it
- Change its description
- Change its location
- Modify the sites that are part of the site link
- Delete it

Let's discuss each of these in the upcoming sections.

Getting ready

To manage an Active Directory site link, you'll need to be signed in with an account that is a member of the Enterprise Admins group.

How to do it...

Site links can be managed and deleted using Active Directory Sites and Services and/or the Active Directory module for Windows PowerShell.

Using Active Directory Sites and Services

To rename an Active Directory site link using **Active Directory Sites and Services**, perform these steps:

1. Open **Active Directory Sites and Services** (`dssite.msc`).
2. In the left navigation pane, expand the **Sites** node.
3. In the left navigation pane, expand the **Inter-Site Transports** node.
4. Select either **IP** or **SMTP**.
5. In the main pane, select the site link that you want to rename.
6. Right-click the site link and click **Rename** in the menu.
7. Type the new name for the Active Directory site link and press *Enter* when done.

To change the description for an Active Directory site link using Active Directory Sites and Services, perform these steps:

1. Open **Active Directory Sites and Services** (`dssite.msc`).
2. In the left navigation pane, expand the **Sites** node.
3. In the left navigation pane, expand the **Inter-Site Transports** node.
4. In the main pane, select the site link that you want to manage.
5. Right-click the site link and click **Properties** in the menu.
6. On the **General** tab, type the new description for the Active Directory site link.
7. Click **OK**.

To modify the sites that are part of the site link using **Active Directory Sites and Services**, perform these steps:

1. Open **Active Directory Sites and Services** (`dssite.msc`).
2. In the left navigation pane, expand the **Sites** node.
3. In the left navigation pane, expand the **Inter-Site Transports** node.
4. Select either **IP** or **SMTP**.
5. In the main pane, select the site link that you want to manage.
6. Right-click the site link and click **Properties** in the menu.
7. On the **General** tab, select the Active Directory sites to include to the Active Directory site link and/or exclude from the Active Directory site link.
8. Click **OK**.

To delete an Active Directory site link using **Active Directory Sites and Services**, perform these steps:

1. Open **Active Directory Sites and Services** (`dssite.msc`).
2. In the left navigation pane, expand the **Sites** node.
3. In the left navigation pane, expand the **Inter-Site Transports** node.
4. Select either **IP** or **SMTP**.
5. In the main pane, select the site link that you want to delete.
6. Right-click the site link and click **Delete** in the menu.
7. In the **Active Directory Domain Services** popup, click **Yes** to answer the question **Are you sure you want to delete the site link named** 'Sitelink'?.

Using Windows PowerShell

Alternatively, Active Directory site links can be managed and deleted using the Active Directory module for Windows PowerShell.

Use the following lines of PowerShell to rename an Active Directory site link:

```
Import-Module ActiveDirectory

Rename-ADObject -Identity "CN=DEFAULTIPSITELINK,CN=IP,CN=Inter-Site
Transports,CN=Sites,CN=Configuration,DC=Lucernpub,DC=com" -NewName
"NewADSiteLinkName"
```

Use the following lines of PowerShell to change the description of an Active Directory site link:

```
Import-Module ActiveDirectory

Set-ADReplicationSiteLink -Identity "DEFAULTIPSITELINK" -Description "New
description here"
```

Use the following lines of PowerShell to modify the sites that are part of the site link:

```
Import-Module ActiveDirectory

Set-ADReplicationSiteLink -Identity "DEFAULTIPSITELINK" -SitesIncluded
Site1,Site2
```

Use the following lines of PowerShell to delete a site link:

```
Import-Module ActiveDirectory

Remove-ADReplicationSiteLink -Identity "DEFAULTIPSITELINK"
```

See also

Take a look at the following recipes:

- *Modifying replication settings for an Active Directory site link*
- *Creating a site link bridge*

Modifying replication settings for an Active Directory site link

After creating Active Directory site links, you might find the need to change the following replication settings:

- Change the cost for an Active Directory site link.
- Change the replication schedule for an Active Directory site link.

Getting ready

To manage an Active Directory site link, you'll need to be signed in with an account that is a member of the Enterprise Admins group.

How to do it...

Replication settings for Active Directory site links can be managed using Active Directory Sites and Services and/or the Active Directory module for Windows PowerShell.

Using Active Directory Sites and Services

To modify the cost for an Active Directory site link using Active Directory Sites and Services, perform these steps:

1. Open **Active Directory Sites and Services** (`dssite.msc`).
2. In the left navigation pane, expand the **Sites** node.
3. In the left navigation pane, expand the **Inter-Site Transports** node.
4. Select either **IP** or **SMTP**.
5. In the main pane, select the site link that you want to manage.
6. Right-click the site link and click **Properties** in the menu.
7. On the **General** tab, in the **Cost:** field, enter the new cost for the site link.
8. Click **OK**.

To modify the replication interval using Active Directory Sites and Services, perform these steps:

1. Open **Active Directory Sites and Services** (`dssite.msc`).
2. In the left navigation pane, expand the **Sites** node.
3. In the left navigation pane, expand the **Inter-Site Transports** node.
4. Select either **IP** or **SMTP**.
5. In the main pane, select the site link that you want to manage.
6. Right-click the site link and click **Properties** in the menu.
7. On the **General** tab, in the **Replicate every** field, enter the new replication interval, specified in minutes.
8. Click **OK**.

To modify the replication schedule using Active Directory Sites and Services, perform these steps:

1. Open **Active Directory Sites and Services** (`dssite.msc`).
2. In the left navigation pane, expand the **Sites** node.
3. In the left navigation pane, expand the **Inter-Site Transports** node.
4. Select either **IP** or **SMTP**.
5. In the main pane, select the site link that you want to manage.
6. Right-click the site link and click **Properties** in the menu.

7. On the **General** tab, click the **Change Schedule...** button.
The **Schedule for** 'SitelinkName' appears:

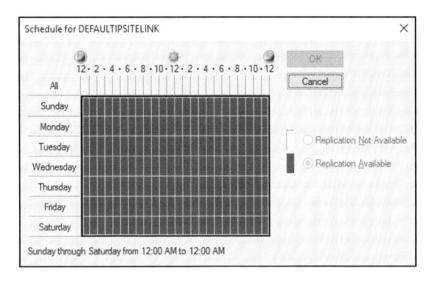

8. Exclude 60-minute time periods from the replication schedule.
9. Click **OK** when done.
10. Back in **Active Directory Sites and Services**, click **OK** to save the new replication schedule for the Active Directory site link.

Using Windows PowerShell

Alternatively, replication settings for Active Directory site links can be managed using the Active Directory module for Windows PowerShell.

Use the following lines of PowerShell to modify the cost for an Active Directory site link:

```
Import-Module ActiveDirectory

Set-ADReplicationSiteLink -Identity DEFAULTIPSITELINK -Cost 50
```

Use the following lines of PowerShell to modify the replication interval for an Active Directory site link to 30 minutes:

```
Import-Module ActiveDirectory

Set-ADReplicationSiteLink -Identity DEFAULTIPSITELINK
-ReplicationFrequencyInMinutes 30
```

The `-replicationschedule` **parameter for** `Set-ADReplicationSiteLink` allows for the most granular management of the replication schedule for an Active Directory Site link. Just like the graphical schedule tool, it can be used to specify the days of the week for the replication schedule. But in contrast to the graphical tool, it can be used to define the available or non-available replication times per minute.

Use the following lines of PowerShell to modify the replication schedule for an Active Directory site link by only allowing replication between 8:00 A.M and 5:00 P.M:

```
$replicationSchedule = New-Object -TypeName
System.DirectoryServices.ActiveDirectory.ActiveDirectorySchedule

$replicationSchedule.SetDailySchedule("Eight","Zero","Seventeen","Zero")

Import-Module ActiveDirectory

Set-ADReplicationSiteLink DEFAULTIPSITELINK -ReplicationSchedule
$replicationSchedule
```

 The default replication schedule is to allow replication Sunday through Saturday from 12:00 A.M. to 12:00 A.M. and is defined as `$null` in the `Get-ADReplicationSiteLink` and `Set-ADReplicationSiteLink` PowerShell cmdlets.

How it works...

This recipe details site link costs and site link replication schedules.

Site-link costs

The cost for an Active Directory site link defines the weight of the link. An Active Directory site link with a high cost tells domain controllers, member servers, and devices that the link is less preferable to use compared to an Active Directory site link with a lower cost.

The following factors that would cause a higher cost when designing the Active Directory site link layout:

- The available bandwidth for Active Directory traffic on the networking connection (the networking connection might be flooded with other traffic already)
- The reliability of the networking connection, in terms of unavailability, such as traffic loss or service level

In complex networking environments, where the ring, hub-and-spoke, and mesh topologies are used, end-to-end costs for traversing site links should also be taken into consideration.

The default cost of an Active Directory site link is 100.

Site-link replication schedules

As opposed to intra-site replication, inter-site replication, by default, uses a replication schedule. Instead of processing change notifications, domain controllers wait their scheduled replication time, based on an interval.

By default, domain controllers on each side of the site link replicate every 180 minutes and the site link's replication schedule is to allow replication Sunday through Saturday from 12:00 A.M. to 12:00 A.M.

See also

To change other properties of an Active Directory site link, take a look at the *Managing a site link* recipe.

Creating a site link bridge

For IP-based and SMTP-based Active Directory site links, an option exists to disable the **Bridge all site links** option. This option is enabled, by default, and defines the site links as transitive. This transitivity means that domain controllers, member servers, and devices may traverse site links to get from *site A* to *site C*, through *site B*, even though *site A* and *site C* are only connected with site links to *site B* and not with each other.

In complex networking environments, more granular control over replication and service discovery might be needed. In these scenarios, disabling site-link transitivity and manually defining site-link bridges might be the preferred method.

Getting ready

To create a site link bridge and disable the Bridge all site links option, you'll need to be signed in with an account that is a member of the Enterprise Admins group.

The Bridge all site links option needs to be disabled for all site links. Perform these actions while logged on with an account that is a member of the Enterprise Admins group:

1. Open **Active Directory Sites and Services** (`dssite.msc`).
2. In the left navigation pane, expand the **Sites** node.
3. In the left navigation pane, expand the **Inter-Site Transports** node.
4. Right-click the **IP** node and select **Properties** from the menu.
5. On the **General** tab, deselect the **Bridge all site links** option.
6. Click **OK**.

Repeat the last three steps for SMTP-based site links, if needed.

The Bridge all site links option can also be disabled using the Active Directory module for Windows PowerShell:

```
Import-Module ActiveDirectory

Set-ADObject "CN=IP,CN=Inter-Site
Transports,CN=Sites,CN=configuration,DC=lucernpub,DC=com" -Replace
@{Options=2}
```

How to do it...

You can take advantage of manually-created site link bridges after you disable the Bridge all site links option.

To create a site-link bridge using Active Directory Sites and Services, perform these steps:

1. Open **Active Directory Sites and Services** (`dssite.msc`).
2. In the left navigation pane, expand the **Sites** node.
3. In the left navigation pane, expand the **Inter-Site Transports** node.
4. Right-click the **IP** node and select **New Site Link Bridge...** from the menu. The **New Object-Site Link Bridge** appears.
5. Select site links from the list of site links underneath **Site links not in this site link bridge:**.
6. Click **Add >>** to add the site links to the list underneath **Site links in this site link bridge:**.
7. Click **OK**.

To create a site link bridge using the Active Directory module for Windows PowerShell, run the following lines of PowerShell:

```
Import-Module ActiveDirectory

New-ADReplicationSiteLinkBridge "SiteLinkBridgeName" -SiteLinksIncluded
SiteLink1,SiteLink2
```

The site links can be a DN or a name.

See also

To change properties of an Active Directory site link, take a look at the *Managing a site link* and *Modifying replication settings for a site link* recipes.

Managing bridgehead servers

Bridgehead servers are the domain controllers on each side of an Active Directory site link that take care of inter-site replication on behalf of all of the domain controllers in their respective sites.

Getting ready

To manage bridgehead servers, you'll need to be signed in with an account that is a member of the Enterprise Admins group.

How to do it...

Bridgehead servers can be set using Active Directory Sites and Services and/or the Active Directory module for Windows PowerShell.

Using Active Directory Sites and Services

To set a domain controller as the bridgehead server for the Active Directory site, using Active Directory Sites and Services, perform these steps:

1. Open **Active Directory Sites and Services** (dssite.msc).
2. In the left navigation pane, expand the **Sites** node.

3. In the left navigation pane, expand the **Servers** node.
4. In the left navigation pane, right-click the domain controller that you want to set as the bridgehead server and select **Properties** from the menu.
5. On the **General** tab, select **IP** and/or **SMTP** from the list under **Transports available for inter-site data transfer:**. Click **Add >>** to set the domain controller as the bridgehead servers for the selected transport(s) in the list underneath **This server is a preferred bridgehead server for the following transports:**.
6. Click **OK**.

Using Windows PowerShell

Run the following lines of PowerShell to set a domain controller as the bridgehead server for the IP transport for its Active Directory site:

```
Import-Module ActiveDirectory

Set-ADObject -Identity "CN=DC01,CN=Servers,CN=Default-First-Site-
Name,CN=Sites,CN=Configuration,DC=LucernPub,DC=com" -Add
@{bridgeHeadTransportList="CN=IP,CN=Inter-Site Transports,
CN=Sites,CN=Configuration,DC=LucernPub,DC=com"}
```

Run the following lines of PowerShell to set a domain controller as the bridgehead server for the SMTP transport for its Active Directory site:

```
Import-Module ActiveDirectory

Set-ADObject -Identity "CN=DC01,CN=Servers,CN=Default-First-Site-
Name,CN=Sites,CN=Configuration,DC=LucernPub,DC=com" -Add
@{bridgeHeadTransportList="CN=SMTP,CN=Inter-Site Transports,
CN=Sites,CN=Configuration,DC=LucernPub,DC=com"}
```

How it works...

By default, bridgehead servers are dynamically set to domain controllers by the **Knowledge Consistency Checker (KCC)**. However, bridgehead servers can also be set manually to accommodate even the most complex routing challenges in a networking environment.

When a domain controller is set as the bridgehead server for an Active Directory partition, but becomes unavailable, replication stops for that partition to the Active Directory site where the domain controller resides. Hence, you should configure at least two bridgehead servers per site when possible.

See also

To further manage Active Directory sites, refer to the following recipes:

- *Creating a site*
- *Managing subnets*
- *Creating a site link* or *Managing a site link*

Managing the Inter-site Topology Generation and Knowledge Consistency Checker

The **Inter-site Topology Generator** (**ISTG**) and the KCC play an important role in Active Directory replication.

Getting ready

To manage the ISTG and the KCC, you'll need to be signed in with an account that is a member of the Enterprise Admins group.

How to do it...

Moving the ISTG to another domain controller and disabling the KCC can be performed using Active Directory Sites and Services and/or the Active Directory module for Windows PowerShell.

Using Active Directory Sites and Services

To move the ISTG to a different domain controller using Active Directory Sites and Services, perform these steps:

1. Open **Active Directory Sites and Services** (`dssite.msc`).
2. In the left navigation pane, select the Active Directory site for which you want to manage the ISTG.
3. In the main pane, right-click the **NTDS Site Settings** node and select **Properties** from the menu.
4. Navigate to the **Attribute Editor** tab.
5. In the list of **Attributes:**, find and select the **interSiteTopologyGenerator** attribute:

6. Click **Edit**.
7. In the **Value** field, change the distinctive name of the domain controller to the distinguished name of the domain controller you want to set as the ISTG.

8. Click **OK** to set the new domain controller.
9. Click **OK** to close the **NTDS Settings Properties** window.

To disable the **KCC** and/or **ISTG** on an Active Directory site, follow these steps:

1. Open **Active Directory Sites and Services** (`dssite.msc`).
2. In the left navigation pane, select the Active Directory site for which you want to manage the **Knowledge Consistency Checker (KCC)** and/or **Inter-site Topology Generator (ISTG)**.
3. In the main pane, right-click the **NTDS Site Settings** node and select **Properties** from the menu.
4. Navigate to the **Attribute Editor** tab.
5. In the list of **Attributes:**, find and select the **Options** attribute. The options attribute is made up of bits, ranging from 0 to 4. When you enable a bit, you add the corresponding 2^x for the bit.
6. To disable the **Knowledge Consistency Checker (KCC)**, enable bit 4. Enter `16` as the value. To disable the **Inter-site Topology Generator (ISTG)**, enable bit 0. Enter `1` as the value. To disable the **Knowledge Consistency Checker (KCC)** and **Inter-site Topology Generator (ISTG)**, enable bits 0 and 4. Enter `17` as the value.
7. Click **OK** to close the **NTDS Settings Properties** window.

Using Windows PowerShell

Run the following lines of PowerShell to move the ISTG to a different domain controller using the Active Directory module for Windows PowerShell:

```
Import-Module ActiveDirectory

Set-ADObject -Identity "CN=NTDS Site Settings,CN=Default-First-Site-
Name,CN=Sites,CN=Configuration, DC=LucernPub,DC=com" -Replace
@{interSiteTopologyGenerator="CN=NTDS
Settings,CN=DC01,CN=Servers,CN=Default-First-Site-Name,
CN=Sites,CN=Configuration, DC=LucernPub,DC=com"}
```

Run the following lines of PowerShell to disable the KCC and/or the ISTG for an Active Directory site using the Active Directory module for Windows PowerShell:

```
Import-Module ActiveDirectory

Set-ADObject "CN=NTDS Site Settings,CN=Default-First-Site-
Name,CN=Sites,CN=Configuration,DC=LucernPub,DC=com" -Replace
@{Options="<Value>"}
```

Define the following value, depending on the outcome you desire:

Outcome	Value
Disable the KCC	16
Disable the ISTG	1
Disable the KCC and ISTG	17

How it works...

In every Active Directory site, one domain controller is dynamically assigned to the ISTG. Its role is to automatically create the inter-site connection objects between the bridgehead server in its respective Active Directory site and bridgehead servers in other Active Directory sites.

 While you can disable the ISTG and create inter-site connection objects manually, it is highly recommended to let the ISTG create the connection objects based on the Active Directory sites, Active Directory site links and bridgehead servers.

The KCC is a process that runs on all domain controllers within an Active Directory site to automatically create the intra-site connection objects between the domain controllers in the Active Directory site.

 While you can disable the KCC and create intra-site connection objects manually, it is highly recommended to let the KCC create the connection objects.

See also

To further manage Active Directory sites, refer to the following recipes:

- *Creating a site*
- *Managing subnets*
- *Creating a site link* or *Managing a site link*

Managing universal group membership caching

To avoid placing a global catalog in every Active Directory site and not requiring a global catalog server for every logon, you can use Universal Group Membership Caching.

Getting ready

To enable **Universal Group Membership Caching** for an Active Directory site, all domain controllers in the site will need to run Windows Server 2003, or a newer version of Windows Server.

To enable or disable Universal Group Membership Caching, you'll need to be signed in with an account that is a member of the Enterprise Admins group.

How to do it...

There are two ways to do it:

- Using Active Directory Sites and Services
- Using Windows PowerShell

Using Active Directory Sites and Services

To manage Universal Group Membership Caching for an Active Directory site using Active Directory Sites and Services, perform these steps:

1. Open **Active Directory Sites and Services** (`dssite.msc`).
2. In the left navigation pane, select the Active Directory site you want to manage Universal Group Membership Caching for.
3. In the main pane, right-click the **NTDS Site Settings** node and select **Properties** from the menu.
4. On the **General** tab, under **Universal Group Membership Caching**, select the option to **Enable Universal Group Membership Caching**.

5. Optionally, select a specific Active Directory site from the drop-down list to
    Refresh cache from:, or leave it <Default> to refresh the Universal Group
    Membership cache from the global catalog server(s) in the Active Directory site
    nearest to the Active Directory site you're managing Universal Group
    Membership Caching for.
6. Click **OK**.

To disable Universal Group Membership Caching, deselect the option to Enable Universal
Group Membership Caching.

Using Windows PowerShell

Run the following lines of PowerShell to enable Universal Group Membership Caching for
an Active Directory site:

```
Import-Module ActiveDirectory

Set-ADReplicationSite -Identity  Default-First-Site-Name
-UniversalGroupCachingEnabled $True
```

Run the following lines of PowerShell to disable Universal Group Membership Caching for
an Active Directory site:

```
Import-Module ActiveDirectory

Set-ADReplicationSite -Identity  Default-First-Site-Name
-UniversalGroupCachingEnabled $False
```

How it works...

In multi-domain and multi-forest environments, it is a common practice to use universal
groups to traverse Active Directory trusts. This is also why, in Microsoft Exchange Server, it
is recommended you create this type of groups for distribution lists, instead of domain local
groups or global groups.

However, for every logon, a global catalog server is required to enumerate the universal
groups the account is a member of. In multi-domain and multi-forest environments, global
catalog servers require more replication, and, therefore, replication bandwidth. Often, it is
far from ideal to place global catalogs in poorly-connected Active Directory sites.

To accommodate the scenario of a non-global catalog in an Active Directory site, but not require a global catalog for every logon, you can use Universal Group Membership Caching. Now, only the first logon in an Active Directory site requires contacting a global catalog. In the background, domain controllers will exchange the information needed with global catalog servers to keep the group memberships up-to-date throughout the Active Directory environment, every eight hours.

See also

Please refer to the *Managing global catalog servers* recipe from `Chapter 2`, *Managing Domain Controllers*, for more information on global catalogs and global catalog placement.

Working with repadmin.exe

In this recipe, we'll concentrate on `repadmin.exe` for troubleshooting Active Directory replication.

Getting ready

To work with `repadmin.exe`, sign in to a domain controller.

How to do it...

`repadmin.exe` has the following high-level commands:

`repadmin.exe /kcc`	Forces the KCC on the targeted domain controller to immediately recalculate its inbound replication topology
`repadmin.exe /prp`	Allows an admin to view or modify the **Password Replication Policy (PRP)** for Read-only Domain Controllers (RODCs)
`repadmin.exe /queue`	Displays inbound replication requests that the domain controller needs to issue to become consistent with its source replication partners
`repadmin.exe /replicate`	Triggers the immediate replication of the specified directory partition to the destination domain controller from the source domain controller

`repadmin.exe /replsingleobj`	Replicates a single object between any two domain controllers that have common directory partitions
`repadmin.exe /replsummary`	Quickly and concisely summarizes the replication state and relative health of an Active Directory forest
`repadmin.exe /rodcpwdrepl`	Triggers replication of passwords for the specified user(s) from the source domain controller to one or more RODCs
`repadmin.exe /showattr`	Displays the attributes of an object
`repadmin.exe /showbackup`	Displays the last time the domain controller(s) was backed up
`repadmin.exe /showobjmeta`	Displays the replication metadata for a specified object stored in Active Directory, such as attribute ID, version number, originating and local Update Sequence Number (USN), and originating server's GUID and data and time stamp
`repadmin.exe /showrepl`	Displays the replication status and when the specified domain controller last attempted to inbound replicate Active Directory partitions
`repadmin.exe /showutdvec`	Displays the highest committed Update Sequence Number (USN) that the targeted domain controller's copy of Active Directory shows as committed for itself and its transitive partners
`repadmin.exe /syncall`	Synchronizes a specified domain controller with all replication partners

Optionally, the following parameters can be used with `repadmin.exe` to specify the pre-Windows 2000 logon name for a user account that has permissions to perform operations in Active Directory:

`/u:`	DOMAIN\UserName
`/pw:`	Password for the user account

`userPrincipalName` logons are not supported with `repadmin.exe`.

How it works...

Active Directory sites, site links, site link bridges, subnets, replication schedules, and the ISTG, KCC, and Universal Group Membership Caching can make every Active Directory admin feel overwhelmed at first.

When troubleshooting replication in an environment with a lot of moving replication parts, the complexity of any environment hinders you from getting to the root cause.

Microsoft has offered three tools in the past to check replication:

- `Replmon.exe`
- `Repadmin.exe`
- The Active Directory Replication Status Tool

Unfortunately, the graphical `replmon.exe` tool, part of the Windows Server Support Tools, is no longer available for Windows Server 2008 and newer versions of Windows Server. The Active Directory Replication Status Tool moved from being an on-premises tool to a model with on-premises agents and a cloud-powered dashboard. As you can imagine, not many admins feel good about connecting their domain controllers to the internet.

See also

For more information, refer to the following recipe:

- *Forcing replication* recipe

Forcing replication

After troubleshooting failing networking connections, resetting Active Directory's replication topology, and/or removing domain controllers, there is a need to check proper replication.

As an admin, you can wait for intra-site replication to occur and for inter-site replication to trigger upon the replication schedules, but there's also a way to force replication.

The obvious choice to force replication is to use `repadmin.exe`.

Getting ready

To work with `repadmin.exe`, sign in to a domain controller.

How to do it...

Issue the following command on an elevated **Command Prompt** (`cmd.exe`) on any domain controller:

```
repadmin.exe /syncall /Aped
```

How it works...

This command will synchronize all partitions (`/A`), using push notifications (`/p`), in enterprise mode across Active Directory sites (`/e`) using distinguished names instead of DNS names (`/d`).

See also

Please refer to the *Working with repadmin.exe* recipe for more information on `repadmin.exe`.

Managing inbound and outbound replication

On a per-domain controller basis, an Active Directory admin can disable inbound and/or outbound replication. Later, inbound and/or outbound replication can be re-enabled.

The obvious choice for managing inbound and outbound replication is to use `repadmin.exe`.

Getting ready

To work with `repadmin.exe`, sign in to a domain controller.

How to do it...

Issue the following command on an elevated **Command Prompt** (cmd.exe) on the domain controller for which you want to disable inbound replication:

```
repadmin.exe /options DC01 +DISABLE_INBOUND_REPL
```

Issue the following command on an elevated **Command Prompt** (cmd.exe) on the domain controller for which you want to disable outbound replication:

```
repadmin.exe /options DC01 +DISABLE_OUTBOUND_REPL
```

Issue the following command on an elevated **Command Prompt** (cmd.exe) on the domain controller for which you want to re-enable inbound replication:

```
repadmin.exe /options DC01 -DISABLE_INBOUND_REPL
```

Issue the following command on an elevated **Command Prompt** (cmd.exe) on the domain controller for which you want to re-enable outbound replication:

```
repadmin.exe /options DC01 -DISABLE_OUTBOUND_REPL
```

How it works...

The preceding repadmin.exe commands use the options flag for the domain controller to enable and/or disable inbound and/or outbound replication.

There's more...

When the goal is to enable and/or disable inbound and/or outbound replication on all domain controllers throughout the environment, replace the name of the domain controller with *.

The option to disable outbound replication sounds like a fantastic way to perform schema updates and schema extensions on the domain controller that holds the Schema Master FSMO role, without the need to rebuild the entire Active Directory forest or bring back all domain controllers from backups. Alas, the domain controller checks whether outbound replication is enabled before attempting to extend or upgrade the Active Directory schema.

See also

The following recipes provide more information:

- *Extending the schema*
- *Working with repadmin.exe*
- *Forcing replication*

Modifying the tombstone lifetime period

When an object is deleted from Active Directory, it is not actually removed from the database, as this would hinder replication of the deletion. Instead, the object is tombstoned. This tombstone prevents the object from being usable (for logins, for example) and being visible in all, the common Active Directory tools. It also instructs the garbage collection process on each domain controller to remove the object from the database, once the tombstone lifetime period has expired.

Getting ready

To modify the tombstone lifetime period, you'll need to be signed in with an account that is a member of the Domain Admins group.

How to do it...

There are two ways to modify the tombstone lifetime period:

- Using ADSI Edit
- Using Windows PowerShell

Using ADSI Edit

Perform these steps to modify the tombstone lifetime period for an Active Directory domain using ADSI Edit:

1. Open **ADSI Edit** (`adsiedit.msc`).
2. In the left navigation pane, expand the **CN=Configuration** node.
3. In the left navigation pane, expand the **CN=Services** node.

4. In the left navigation pane, expand the **CN=Windows NT** node.
5. In the left navigation pane, right-click the **CN=Directory Service** node and select **Properties** from the menu.
6. In the list of attributes, scroll down to the `tombstoneLifetime` attribute.
7. Change the value for the `tombstoneLifetime` attribute and press **OK** when done.
8. Click **OK** to close the **CN=Directory Service Properties** window.
9. Close **ADSI Edit**.

Using Windows PowerShell

To modify the tombstone lifetime period to 180 days, run the following lines of PowerShell on a system with the Active Directory module for Windows PowerShell installed:

```
Import-Module ActiveDirectory

Set-ADObject "CN=Directory Service,CN=Windows
NT,CN=Services,CN=Configuration,DC=Lucernpub,DC=com" -Replace
@{"tombstoneLifetime"="180"}
```

How it works...

The tombstone lifetime period is set at the domain level and applies to all domain controllers in the Active Directory domain.

The tombstone lifetime period instructs the garbage collection process on each domain controller with the period to wait before removing objects from the database after receiving a delete update for an object and processing the update as a tombstone for the object.

The default tombstone lifetime period for an Active Directory domain that has been set up and run by domain controllers running Windows 2000 Server and Windows Server 2003 is 60 days. Active Directory domains that have begun their life run by domain controllers running Windows Server 2008, or newer versions of Windows Server, have a default tombstone lifetime period of 180 days.

See also

- *Checking for and remediating lingering objects*

Managing strict replication consistency

Strict replication consistency is a mechanism on domain controllers that prevents them from replicating with a replication partner when it suspects an object that is replicated in is a lingering object. Strict replication consistency is enabled, by default, but can be disabled.

Getting ready

To manage strict replication, sign into a domain controller with local administrative privileges.

How to do it...

To disable strict replication consistency on a domain controller, perform the following steps:

1. Open the Registry Editor (`regedit.exe`).
2. In the top address bar, type
   `HKLM\SYSTEM\CurrentControlSet\Services\NTDS \Parameters` or navigate there in the left navigation pane.
3. In the main pane, right-click an empty space and select **New** and then **DWORD Value** from the menu.
4. Name the new DWORD value `Strict Replication Consistency`.
5. Double-click the new **Strict Replication Consistency** value.
6. Enter 1 to disable strict replication consistency.
7. Click **OK**.
8. Reboot the domain controller.

To re-enable strict replication consistency on a domain controller, perform the following steps:

1. Open the Registry Editor (`regedit.exe`).
2. In the top address bar, type
   `HKLM\SYSTEM\CurrentControlSet\Services\NTDS \Parameters` or navigate there in the left navigation pane.

3. In the main pane, double-click the **Strict Replication Consistency** value.
4. Enter *0* to enable strict replication consistency.
5. Click **OK.**
6. Reboot the domain controller.

How it works...

When a domain controller suspects an object that is replicated in is a lingering object and strict replication consistency is enabled, the Domain Controller will stop replicating with the replication partner it suspects of outbound replication the suspected object.

Both inbound replication and outbound replication will be stopped to the specific domain controller.

A lingering object is an object that was tombstoned and then garbage-collected on all domain controllers, but after that point in time was reintroduced by a domain controller that was restored from a backup that was older than the tombstone lifetime period.

Strict replication consistency is a per-domain-controller setting and is enabled by default.

Upgrading SYSVOL replication from File Replication Service to Distributed File System Replication

Since Windows 2000 Server, Active Directory features the **System Volume (SYSVOL)**. This shared folder is replicated between all of the domain controllers in an Active Directory domain and contains commonly-accessed files such as Group Policy objects, logon scripts, and logoff scripts and can hold any file an Active Directory admin wants it to hold.

In legacy Active Directory environments, SYSVOL replication uses the **File Replication Service (FRS)**. This should be migrated to **Distributed File System Replication (DFSR)**.

Getting ready

The deprecation of FRS may or may not be a problem in your Active Directory environment.

If your Active Directory environment has ever featured Windows 2000 Server, Windows Server 2003, or Windows Server 2003 R2-based domain controllers, you have some work to do. Your domain controllers rely on FRS to replicate the contents of the SYSVOL shares between them, even when these domain controllers have long been decommissioned and/or replaced with Windows Server 2008, Windows Server 2008 R2, and/or Windows Server 2012-based domain controllers.

 There is a detailed guide available from Microsoft to help you with this task. This *SYSVOL Replication Migration Guide* details the same steps as this recipe to perform the migration from FRS to DFSR, but also features roll-back steps and a command-line reference for dfsrmig.exe.

To change the replication of the SYSVOL from FRS to DFSR, all domain controllers in the Active Directory domain need to run Windows Server 2008, or a newer version of Windows Server, and the Active Directory **Domain Functional Level** (**DFL**) needs to be Windows Server 2008, or a higher functional level.

Since the SYSVOL is replicated between domain controllers in Active Directory domains, sign into the domain controller that holds the **Primary Domain Controller emulator** (**PDCe**) FSMO role, using an account that is a member of the Domain Admins group.

How to do it...

There is only one command-line tool available to migrate from FRS replication to DFS Replication: dfsrmig.exe. This tool guides you through the following states:

The initial state

When you begin upgrading SYSVOL replication from FRS to DFSR, all domain controllers in the Active Directory domain will be in this state. They are ready to begin the migration.

To go from the initial state to the prepared state, use the following command on an elevated **Command Prompt** (cmd.exe):

```
dfsrmig.exe /setglobalstate 1
```

The domain controllers will be instructed to do the work to go to the next stage. Use the following command to inspect the process:

```
dfsrmig.exe /getmigrationstate
```

When the output of this command indicates that all domain controllers have successfully migrated to the **Prepared** global state, you're good to go with the next command to get your Active Directory domain toward the next state.

The prepared state

The prepared state configures the DFS Replication service to replicate a copy of the original SYSVOL. When all domain controllers reach the prepared state, DFSR is properly configured, and it has completed an initial synchronization. However, in the prepared state, the replication of SYSVOL still depends on FRS.

To go from the prepared state to the redirected state, use the following command on an elevated **Command Prompt** (cmd.exe):

```
dfsrmig.exe /setglobalstate 2
```

The domain controllers will be instructed to do the work to go to the next stage. Use the following command to inspect the process:

```
dfsrmig.exe /getmigrationstate
```

When the output of this command indicates that all domain controllers have successfully migrated to the **Redirected** global state, you're good to go with the next command to get your Active Directory domain toward the next state.

The redirected state

In the redirected state, the live SYSVOL share (mapped to the old SYSVOL folder that FRS replicates) is mapped to a new copy of the SYSVOL folder, replicated by the DFS Replication service. From this point onward, SYSVOL replication depends on DFS Replication, but the migration is not quite finished yet.

To go from the redirected state to the eliminated state, use the following command on an elevated **Command Prompt** (cmd.exe):

```
dfsrmig.exe /setglobalstate 3
```

The domain controllers will be instructed to do the work to go to the next stage. Use the following command to inspect the process:

```
dfsrmig.exe /getmigrationstate
```

When the output of this command indicates that all Domain Controllers have successfully migrated to the **Eliminated** global state, read on.

The eliminated state

At the end of the eliminated state, the FRS SYSVOL replica set and the old SYSVOL folder are deleted. Not only does SYSVOL replication depend on DFSR, all remnants of SYSVOL FRS replication are gone.

How it works...

Typically, the SYSVOL is replicated between domain controllers using Windows NT 4 Server's legacy FRS, unless the Active Directory domain was started on a domain controller running Windows Server 2008, or any newer version of Windows Server. In the latter case, the SYSVOL is replicated between domain controllers using the new and more robust Distributed File System Replication (DFSR).

Starting with Windows Server 2003 R2, Microsoft began deprecating the use of FRS. In Windows Server 2003 R2, the more efficient and robust DFS Replication service replaced FRS for replication of Distributed File System folders, but FRS was still used to replicate the SYSVOL folder on domain controllers.

DFSR uses a more efficient, scalable, and reliable file replication protocol than FRS. Therefore, it is much faster, especially when you make small changes to large files with **Remote Differential Compression** (**RDC**) enabled. DFSR, additionally, provides built-in health-monitoring tools for ease of monitoring deployments, solving one of the biggest headaches with SYSVOL replication in larger Active Directory environments.

Since Windows Server 2012, Microsoft no longer tests and supports Active Directory with FRS-based SYSVOL replication. Microsoft urges Active Directory admins to move from FRS to DFSR to replicate the SYSVOL between domain controllers.

See also

See the *Raising the domain functional level to Windows Server 2016* recipe from `Chapter 1`, *Optimizing Forests, Domains, and Trusts*, to raise the DFL if it's not Windows Server 2008 yet.

Checking for and remediating lingering objects

A lingering object is an object that was tombstoned and then garbage-collected on all domain controllers but, after that point in time, the object was reintroduced by a domain controller that was restored from a backup that was older than the tombstone lifetime period.

You can periodically check for them.

Getting ready

Sign in to the domain controller that holds the PDCe FSMO role, using an account that is a member of the Domain Admins group.

Next, find the `objectGUID` attribute of the domain controller. Use the following command on an elevated Command Prompt:

```
dsquery.exe * "CN=DC01,OU=Domain Controllers,DC=LucernPub,DC=com" -scope
base -attr objectguid
```

Replace `DC01` with the hostname of the domain controller.

We'll need the `objectGUID` attribute for the next commands.

How to do it...

Use the following command line on an elevated **Command Prompt** (`cmd.exe`) to scan for lingering objects:

```
repadmin.exe /removelingeringobjects <FQDN of Domain Controller with
suspected lingering objects> <objectGUID of Domain Controller with correct
data> <Distinguished Name of partition containing lingering objects>
```

```
/advisory_mode
```

Here's an example of this command line for Lucern Publishing to check for lingering objects between `DC01` and `DC02`:

```
repadmin.exe /removelingeringobjects DC02.LucernPub.com
de235686-7bc1-4412-941a4f6e7e248be1 DC=LucernPub,DC=com /advisory_mode
```

If the environment suffers from one or more lingering objects, events with Event ID 1946 will be logged for each lingering object in the Directory Services log on the domain controller with the lingering objects. The string of events with Event ID 1946 would be marked by an event with Event ID 1938, marking the start of the detection process and an event with Event ID 1942 containing the final detection summary.

The objects detected as lingering objects might be objects that were inadvertently deleted or mangled on a domain controller or objects that are, indeed, lingering objects on a domain controller.

 Check with business representatives, such as department managers, to find out whether the lingering objects are indeed lingering objects or otherwise mangled objects. Trust me, the last thing you want to do is delete the user account for the CFO's secretary or any other important person in the organization.

To remove the lingering objects detected by `repadmin.exe` in the previous command line, perform it again, but without the `/advisory_mode` switch.

How it works...

A lingering object usually exists on one domain controller and is not affected by Active Directory replication anymore, since all of the replication partners of the domain controller have the tombstone change as the last change for the object and delete the object from the database.

Lingering objects can be truly nasty. For instance, an Active Directory admin that was fired on the spot a couple of months ago might suddenly have access again, after another Active Directory admin may have restored a domain controller in an environment with a tombstone lifetime period of 60 days.

Active Directory admins might not be aware of lingering objects, unless they keep an eye out for unexpected Active Directory behavior. They don't need to be sharp-eyed to notice lingering objects, though.

See also

See the *Managing strict replication consistency* recipe to learn how to avoid lingering objects in the future.

6
Managing Active Directory Users

Users and groups are, undeniably, the bread and butter of Active Directory. When there is something wrong, missing, or absent in these two object types, service desk personnel will be the first to know, because colleagues will ring the number for help. On the other hand, when an error is in a colleague's personal interest, due to lingering privileges or absent identity and access management processes, don't expect a call.

It's imperative to get users right. It is estimated that 20% of all IT costs in any organization is related to password resets and account lockouts. As colleagues use their accounts for authentication, any hiccup will inevitably result in loss of productivity.

A best practice is to cooperate with the **Human Resources (HR)** department for user creation and user expiration. HR people know when a contract is (to be) terminated. This can help in setting up account expiration. They also know when a person is on maternity leave or takes a sabbatical. We wouldn't want to automatically delete the accounts of these people based on their apparent inactivity, right?

It's also important to get group memberships right. In most organizations, groups govern access to applications and roles and/or privileges within applications. Colleagues without the right privileges might not be productive. Colleagues with too many privileges might inadvertently take down the application, delete data, or have access to data they shouldn't have. These confidentiality, integrity, and availability issues can easily be avoided by revoking access through regular access reviews processes by application owners.

A recommended approach to delegation of control in Active Directory is to delegate privileges based on groups, not on individual accounts.

The following recipes will be covered in this chapter:

- Creating a user
- Deleting a user
- Modifying several users at once
- Moving a user
- Renaming a user
- Enabling and disabling a user
- Finding locked-out users
- Unlocking a user
- Managing userAccountControl
- Using account expiration

Let's jump into the recipes. Many recipes offer a couple of ways to achieve the same goal. While using Active Directory Users and Computers (`dsa.msc`) is still commonplace, some admins have discovered the benefits of using the Active Directory Administrative Center (`dsac.exe`) and its Windows PowerShell History Viewer to learn the underlying PowerShell cmdlets of their clicks. PowerShell can then be used to automate everything as efficiently as possible; for complex actions you have to perform three times or more, it's better to automate.

Creating a user

Use this recipe to create a user object.

Getting ready

To create a user account, you should sign into a domain controller or a member server and/or device with the **Remote Server Administration Tools** (**RSAT**) for Active Directory Domain Services installed.

Sign in with an account that is a member of the Domain Admins group or the Account Operators group or with an account that is delegated to create user objects in the domain or scope of the **Organizational Unit** (**OU**) where the user account is to be created.

How to do it...

There are four ways to create a user object:

- Using Active Directory Users and Computers
- Using the Active Directory Administrative Center
- Using command-line tools
- Using Windows PowerShell

Using Active Directory Users and Computers

To create a user using Active Directory Users and Computers, follow these steps:

1. Open **Active Directory Users and Computers** (`dsa.msc`).
2. In the left navigation pane, navigate to the OU or container where you want to create the user object.
3. Perform one of these actions to open the **New Object - User** screen:
   - From the taskbar, click the **New User** icon.
   - Right-click an empty space in the main window and select **New** and then **User** from the menu.
   - Right-click the OU or container in which you want to create a new user and select **New** and then **User** from the menu.
4. In the **New Object - User** screen, specify values for the following fields:
   1. Specify the **Full name**, by either typing the full name or by filling the **First name** and **Last name** fields.
   2. Specify the **User logon name** in the top field of the two available fields. This will create the `userPrincipalName` attribute (the combination of the two top fields) and the `sAMAccountName` attribute (the combination of the two bottom fields, referred to as the **Pre-Windows 2000** user log-on name in the user interface).
5. Click **Next >**.
6. In the second **New Object - User** screen, specify a **Password** and then confirm it in the second field.
7. Click **Next >** when done.
8. In the third **New Object - User** screen, click **Finish**.

Using the Active Directory Administrative Center

To create a user using the Active Directory Administrative Center, follow these steps:

1. Open the **Active Directory Administrative Center** (`dsac.exe`).
2. In the left navigation pane, right-click the domain name and select **New** and then **User** from the menu.
   The **Create User:** window appears:

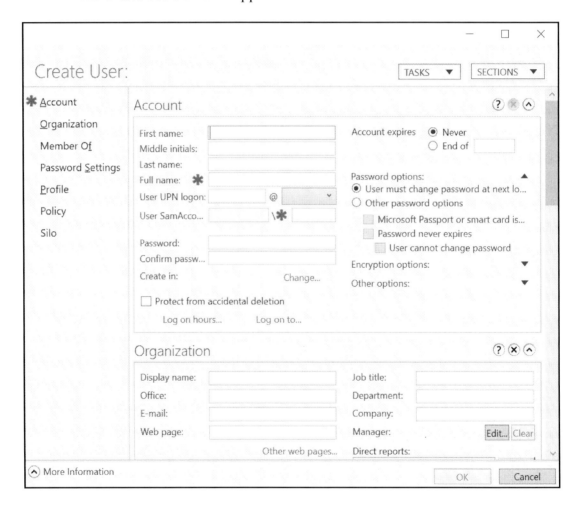

3. In the **Create User** screen, specify values for the following fields:
    1. Specify the **Full name**, by either typing the full name or by filling the **First name** and **Last name** fields.
    2. Specify the **User logon name** in the top field of the two available fields. This will create the userPrincipalName attribute (the combination of the two top fields) and the sAMAccountName attribute (the combination of the two bottom fields, referred to as the **Pre-Windows 2000** user logon name in the user interface).
4. Click **OK**.

Using command-line tools

Use the following command to create a user object in Active Directory:

```
dsadd.exe user "CN=User,CN=Users,DC=lucernpub,DC=com" -upn
user@lucernpub.com -fn "User's First Name" -ln "User's Last Name" -display
"User" -pwd "PasswordHere"
```

Using Windows PowerShell

Use the following lines of PowerShell on a system with the Active Directory module for Windows PowerShell installed:

```
Import-Module ActiveDirectory

New-ADUser -Name User -Path "CN=Users,DC=lucernpub,DC=com" -GivenName
"User's First Name" -Surname "User's Last Name" -sAMAccountName user
```

How it works...

When you create a user object, some fields are automatically populated and many settings are default settings, including the **User must change password at next logon** setting. These settings are recommended but can be changed after creating a user, either in the user interface or through commands.

A descriptive name for every user object is mandatory to make sure the user object can be identified in the graphical interface and in auditing scenarios. Many applications, including Microsoft Exchange Server, use the first, last, and/or full name to create their own default attributes and settings.

When you create a user object, the object consumes a **relative identifier** (**RID**) and **Distinguished Name Tag** (**DNT**) in the domain partition. The `Pre-Windows 2000 username` is usually the username people in the organization use to log on, but `userPrincipalName` can also be used in most scenarios. `userPrincipalName` is used when modern authentication protocols are utilized.

There's more...

All organizations create user accounts differently. Configuration steps may vary and may or may not include profile-, Microsoft Exchange Server-, Terminal Server-, or Office 365-specific steps. When additional steps are required, usually a work instruction is present. When there is none, the following steps might be a good basis for writing it yourself!

Deleting a user

Use this recipe to delete a previously created user object.

Getting ready

To delete a user account, you should sign in to a domain controller or a member server and/or device with the RSAT for Active Directory Domain Services installed.

Sign in with an account that is a member of the Domain Admins group or the Account Operators group or with an account that is delegated to delete user objects in the domain or scope of the OU where the user account is to be deleted.

How to do it...

There are four ways to delete a user object:

- Using Active Directory Users and Computers
- Using the Active Directory Administrative Center
- Using command-line tools
- Using Windows PowerShell

Using Active Directory Users and Computers

To delete a user using Active Directory Users and Computers, follow these steps:

1. Open **Active Directory Users and Computers** (dsa.msc).
2. In the **View** menu, enable **Advanced Features**.
3. In the left navigation pane, navigate to the OU or container where the user object that you intend to delete resides.
4. From the **Action** menu, select **Find**. In the **Name** field, type the name of the user object you intend to delete and press *Enter*. From the list of **Search results**, select the user object:

5. Right-click the user object and select **Properties** from the list.

6. Navigate to the **Object** tab:

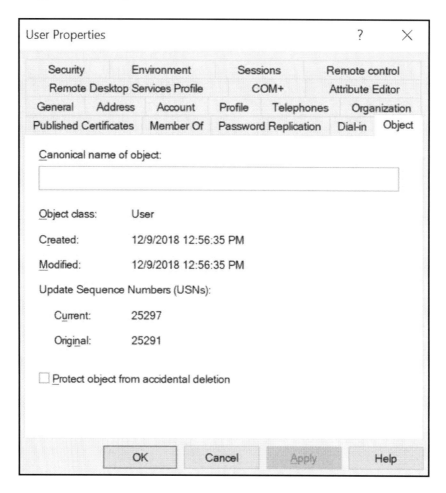

7. Disable **Protect object from accidental deletion** (optional).
8. Click **OK** to close the **Properties** window for the object.
9. Right-click the user object again. This time select **Delete** from the list.
10. Click **Yes** in the **Active Directory Domain Services** popup window to answer the question **Are you sure you want to delete the User named** 'user'?

Using the Active Directory Administrative Center

To delete a user using the Active Directory Administrative Center, follow these steps:

1. Open the **Active Directory Administrative Center** (`dsac.exe`).

2. Perform one of these series of actions:
   - In the left navigation pane, switch to **Tree** view. Navigate to the OU or container where the user object that you intend to delete resides. In the main pane, select the user object.
   - From the main pane menu, under **Global Search**, type the name of the user object you intend to delete and press *Enter*. From the list of **Global Search** results, select the user object.

3. Right-click the user object and select **Properties** from the list. The **User** window appears:

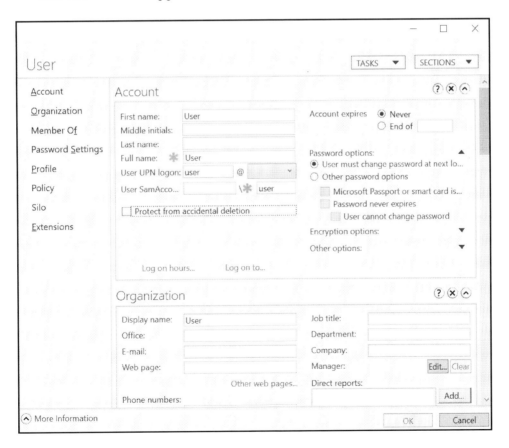

4. Disable **Protect object from accidental deletion** (optional).
5. Click **OK** to close the **Properties** window for the object.
6. Right-click the user object again. This time, select **Delete** from the list. The **Delete confirmation** popup window appears:

7. Click **Yes** in the **Delete Confirmation** popup window to answer the question **Are you sure you want to delete the User user?**

Using command-line tools

Use the following command to delete a user object in Active Directory:

```
dsrm.exe user "CN=User,CN=Users,DC=lucernpub,DC=com"
```

Using Windows PowerShell

Use the following lines of PowerShell on a system with the Active Directory module for Windows PowerShell installed:

```
Import-Module ActiveDirectory

Remove-ADUser -Identity "CN=User,CN=Users,DC=lucernpub,DC=com"
```

How it works...

When you delete a user object, the object no longer uses its RID, but the RID and the corresponding SID and DNT in the domain partition cannot be reused.

When you attempt to delete a user object that has the **Protect from accidental deletion** option enabled, you will not be able to delete the object. First, the option needs to be disabled.

Many organizations are wary of deleting user objects, because they fear their auditing systems may no longer be able to put a name to the RID or corresponding SID. Instead, most of them opt to disable user objects. Unfortunately, many admins forget to actually delete the object beyond the auditing retention period, getting stuck with numerous objects that take up space in the Active Directory database, making Active Directory more complex to manage.

When the **Active Directory Recycle Bin** is enabled, the deleted user object emerges in the **Deleted Objects** container.

See also

Refer to the following recipes for more information:

- The *Enabling the Active Directory Recycle Bin* recipe
- The *Enabling and disabling a user* recipe

Modifying several users at once

When creating user objects for a while, the need might arise to modify one attribute for all of the previously created user objects. Other scopes of user objects might also apply.

Modifying one user object is as simple as double-clicking on it in Active Directory Users and Computers or in the Active Directory Administrative Center. Modifying multiple objects at once is slightly different, and there are a couple of neat tricks you can use.

Getting ready

To modify user accounts, you should sign in to a domain controller or a member server and/or device with the RSAT for Active Directory Domain Services installed.

Sign in with an account that is a member of the Domain Admins group or the Account Operators group or with an account that is delegated to manage user objects in the domain or scope of the OU where the user objects reside.

How to do it...

There are three ways to modify user objects:

- Using Active Directory Users and Computers
- Using the Active Directory Administrative Center
- Using command-line tools

Using Active Directory Users and Computers

Active Directory Users and Computers is ideal when you have simple scopes for user objects to modify. Through its selection mechanisms, admins can easily select all of the users in an OU or container (by pressing *Ctrl + A*) or select all of the users whose names start with an *A*.

To modify multiple users using Active Directory Users and Computers, follow these steps:

1. Open **Active Directory Users and Computers** (`dsa.msc`).
2. In the left navigation pane, navigate to the OU or container where the user objects reside.
3. In the main pane, select the user objects by selecting them while holding down the *Shift* button.
4. Right-click the objects and select **Properties** from the menu.
5. Change the attribute or attributes that you want to modify.
6. Click **OK** when you have done this.

Using the Active Directory Administrative Center

The Active Directory Administrative Center allows for filters to filter out only the scope of user objects that you want to modify. Filters can be used on OUs and containers. Of course, the same method for selecting users as you would in Active Directory Users and Computers can be used.

To modify a selection of users using the Active Directory Administrative Center, follow these steps:

1. Open the **Active Directory Administrative Center** (`dsac.exe`).
2. In the left navigation pane, select the OU or container to use as the base scope for the filter.
3. In the main pane, expand the top bar.

4. Click the **Add criteria** button:

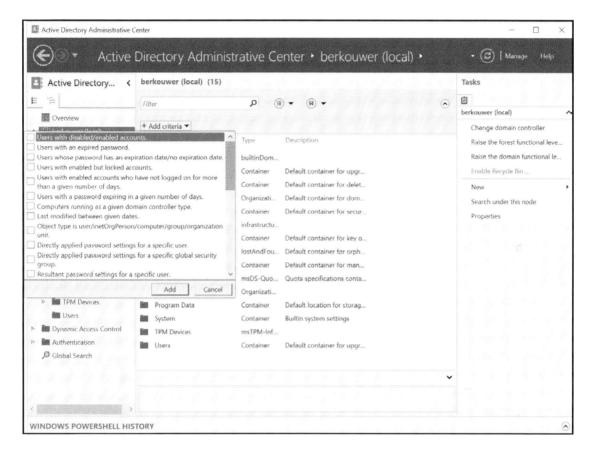

5. Add the criteria you want to use to select the user objects you want to modify at once. Use one or more of the built-in filters or scroll down to create a filter based on the user-friendly names of one or more attributes. Click **Add** to add the filter.

> When going the last route, you can use matches such as **starts with**, **equals**, **does not equal**, **is empty**, and **is not empty**.

6. In the **Search results** pane, select all the user objects that match the filter, by selecting one and then pressing *Ctrl + A*.

7. In the right task pane, click **Properties**.
   The **Multiple Users** window appears:

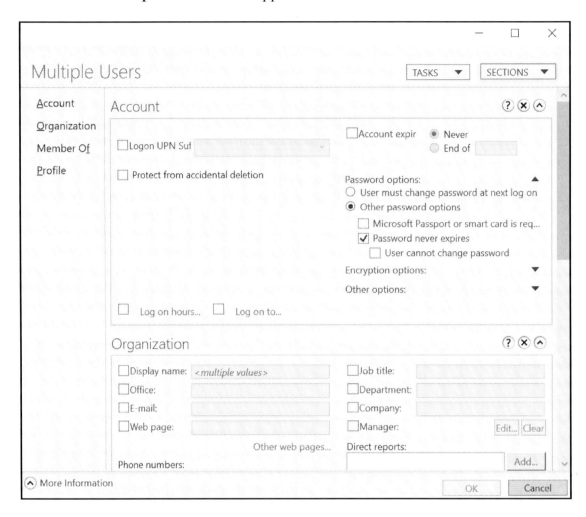

8. Change the attribute or attributes that you want to modify.
9. Click **OK** when you have done this.

Using Windows PowerShell

The Active Directory module for Windows PowerShell can be used to select multiple user objects as well. Modifications can then be applied to the scope of users using the piping mechanism in PowerShell. Since scoping in PowerShell is more advanced, this way is best used to modify multiple user objects throughout the Active Directory forest and/or to modify user objects, repeatedly.

As an example, use the following lines of PowerShell on a system with the **Active Directory module for Windows PowerShell** is installed to modify **Prevent from accidental deletion** for all of the user objects whose sAMAccountName starts with service_:

```
Import-Module ActiveDirectory

Get-ADUser -ldapfilter "(sAMAccountName=service_*)" |
Set-ADObject -ProtectedFromAccidentalDeletion $true
```

How it works...

Using filters, several user objects can be modified at once.

Not all attributes can be changed when multiple user objects are selected using Active Directory Users and Computers (dsa.msc) and the Active Directory Administrative Center (dsac.exe). Typical attributes include those that are unique to a user object, such as userPrincipalName, sAMAccountName, and securityIdentifier.

There's more...

When using the Active Directory Administrative Center (dsac.exe), the Windows PowerShell History feature can be used to find modifications on one user object from the user interface in PowerShell. This way, the modifications behind the | can be found easily. To enable the Windows PowerShell history pane, perform these actions:

1. Open the **Active Directory Administrative Center** (dsac.exe).
2. In the bottom bar, expand the **Windows PowerShell History** bar.

Moving a user

After creating a user, you might find that it should live in another OU or container. This recipe describes how to move a user object.

Getting ready

To move a user account, you should sign in to a domain controller or a member server and/or device with the RSAT for Active Directory Domain Services installed.

Sign in with an account that is a member of the Domain Admins group or the Account Operators group or with an account that is delegated to modify and delete user objects in the domain or scope of the OUs in scope for the user object move.

How to do it...

There are four ways to move a user object:

- Using Active Directory Users and Computers
- Using the Active Directory Administrative Center
- Using command-line tools
- Using Windows PowerShell

Using Active Directory Users and Computers

To move a user using Active Directory Users and Computers, follow these steps:

1. Open **Active Directory Users and Computers** (`dsa.msc`).
2. In the **View** menu, enable **Advanced Features**.
3. Perform one of these series of actions:
    - In the left navigation pane, navigate to the OU or container where the user object that you intend to delete resides. In the main pane, select the user object.
    - From the **Action** menu, select **Find...**. In the **Name** field, type the name of the user object you intend to move, and press *Enter*. From the list of **Search results:**, select the user object.
4. Right-click the user object and select **Properties** from the list.
5. Navigate to the **Object** tab.

6. Disable **Protect object from accidental deletion**.

7. Click **OK** to close the **Properties** window for the object.

8. Right-click the user object again. This time, select **Move...** from the list. The **Move** window appears:

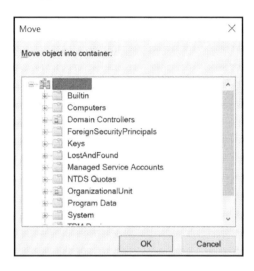

9. In the **Move** window, navigate to the OU or container where you want to move the user object to, and select it.

10. Click **OK** to move the object.

Using the Active Directory Administrative Center

To move a user using the Active Directory Administrative Center, follow these steps:

1. Open the **Active Directory Administrative Center** (`dsac.exe`).

2. Perform one of these series of actions:

   - In the left navigation pane, switch to **Tree** view. Navigate to the OU or container where the user object that you intend to move resides. In the main pane, select the user object.

   - From the main pane menu, under **Global Search**, type the name of the user object you intend to move, and press *Enter*. From the list of **Global Search** result, select the user object.

3. Right-click the user object and select **Properties** from the list.
4. Disable **Protect object from accidental deletion**.
5. Click **OK** to close the **Properties** window for the object.

6. Right-click the user object again. This time, select **Move…** from the list. The **Move** window appears:

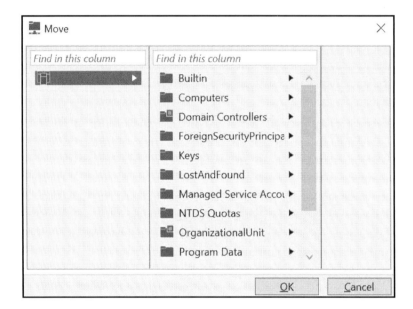

7. In the **Move** window, navigate to the OU or container where you want to move the user object to, and select it.
8. Click **OK** to move the object.

Using command-line tools

Use the following command to move a user object in Active Directory:

```
dsmove.exe "CN=User,CN=Users,DC=lucernpub,DC=com" -newparent
"OU=Organizational Unit,DC=lucernpub,DC=com"
```

Using Windows PowerShell

Use the following lines of PowerShell on a system with the Active Directory module for Windows PowerShell installed:

```
Import-Module ActiveDirectory

Move-ADObject -Identity:"CN=User,CN=Users,DC=lucernpub,DC=com"
-TargetPath:"OU=Organizational Unit,DC=lucernpub,DC=com"
```

How it works...

When you move a user object in Active Directory, it will effectively fall out of scope of the parent OU or container. This is why the user account that is used for this purpose must have (delegated) permissions to delete user objects in the original location of the user object. Also, the user object can not have the **Protect from accidental deletion** option enabled. This option needs to be disabled to avoid permissions errors.

Renaming a user

Use this recipe to rename a previously created user object.

Getting ready

To rename a user account, you should sign in to a domain controller or a member server and/or device with the RSAT for Active Directory Domain Services installed.

Sign in with an account that is a member of the Domain Admins group or the Account Operators group or with an account that is delegated to modify user objects in the domain or scope of the OU where the user account resides.

How to do it...

There are four ways to rename a user object:

- Using Active Directory Users and Computers
- Using the Active Directory Administrative Center
- Using command-line tools
- Using Windows PowerShell

Using Active Directory Users and Computers

To rename a user using Active Directory Users and Computers, follow these steps:

1. Open **Active Directory Users and Computers** (`dsa.msc`).
2. In the **View** menu, enable **Advanced Features**.

3. Perform one of these actions:
   - In the left navigation pane, navigate to the OU or container where the user object resides. In the main pane, select the user object.
   - From the **Action** menu, select **Find...**. In the **Name** field, type the name of the user object and press *Enter*. From the list of **Search results:**, select the user object.
4. Right-click the user object and select **Rename** from the list.
5. Type the new name for the user object and press *Enter*.

6. In the **Rename User** popup window, type new values for other attributes that you want subsequently renamed:

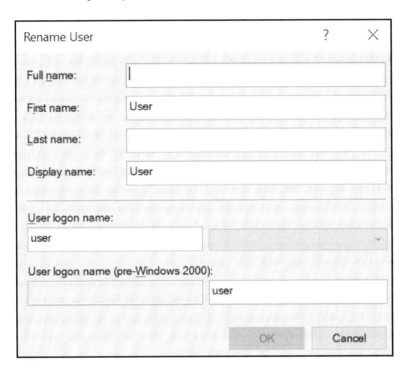

7. Click **OK**.

Using the Active Directory Administrative Center

To rename a user using the Active Directory Administrative Center, follow these steps:

1. Open the **Active Directory Administrative Center** (dsac.exe).
2. Perform one of these actions:
    - In the left navigation pane, switch to **Tree** view. Navigate to the OU or container where the user object resides. In the main pane, select the user object.
    - From the main pane menu, under **Global Search**, type the name of the user object, and press *Enter*. From the list of **Global Search** results, select the user object.

3. Right-click the user object and select **Properties** from the list.
4. In the **User** window, change one or more of the following fields for the user object:
    1. In the **Account** field:
        1. First name
        2. Last name
        3. Full name
        4. User UPN log-on
        5. User `SamAccountName` log-on
    2. In the **Organization** field, change the **Display Name**.

4. Click **OK**.

Using command-line tools

Use the following command to rename a user object in Active Directory:

```
dsmove.exe "CN=User,CN=Users,DC=lucernpub,DC=com" –NewName "User Account"
```

Using Windows PowerShell

Use the following lines of PowerShell on a system with the Active Directory module for Windows PowerShell installed:

```
Import-Module ActiveDirectory

Rename-ADObject –Identity "CN=User,CN=Users,DC=lucernpub,DC=com" –NewName "User Account"
```

How it works...

When you rename a user object, you change its **Canonical Name** (**CN**). When you perform this action using Active Directory Users and Computers (`dsa.msc`), a helpful popup helps you to change any other name-related attributes.

Even though you use the `dsmove.exe` command, when you rename a user object, the **Protect from accidental deletion** option does not come into effect, like when you move a user object. You will not need to disable this option first.

Enabling and disabling a user

When you want a person in your organization to no longer be able to log on interactively, you can disable the corresponding user object. Likewise, when a user object is disabled, you can opt to enable/re-enable. Use this recipe to perform both actions.

Getting ready

To enable or disable a user account, you should sign in to a domain controller or a member server and/or device with the RSAT for Active Directory Domain Services installed.

Sign in with an account that is a member of the Domain Admins group or the Account Operators group or with an account that is delegated to modify user objects in the domain or scope of the OU where the user account resides.

How to do it...

There are four ways to enable or disable a user object:

- Using Active Directory Users and Computers
- Using the Active Directory Administrative Center
- Using command-line tools
- Using Windows PowerShell

Using Active Directory Users and Computers

To enable or disable a user using Active Directory Users and Computers, follow these steps:

1. Open **Active Directory Users and Computers** (`dsa.msc`).
2. Perform one of these series of actions:
   - In the left navigation pane, navigate to the OU or container where the user object resides. In the main pane, select the user object.
   - From the **Action** menu, select **Find...**. In the **Name** field, type the name of the user object, and press *Enter*. From the list of **Search results:**, select the user object.
3. Right-click the user object and select **Enable account** or **Disable account** from the list.
4. In the **Active Directory Domain Services** popup window, dismiss the message that says **User Object has been disabled** or **User Object has been enabled** by clicking **OK**.

Using the Active Directory Administrative Center

To enable or disable a user using the Active Directory Administrative Center, follow these steps:

1. Open the **Active Directory Administrative Center** (`dsac.exe`).
2. Perform one of these series of actions:
   - In the left navigation pane, switch to **Tree** view. Navigate to the OU or container where the user object resides. In the main pane, select the user object.
   - From the main pane menu, under **Global Search**, type the name of the user object and press *Enter*. From the list of **Global Search** results, select the user object.
3. Right-click the user object and select **Properties** from the list.
4. In the top bar of the **User** window, click the **Tasks** button.

5. From the **Tasks** menu, select **Disable** or **Enable**.

6. Click **OK**:

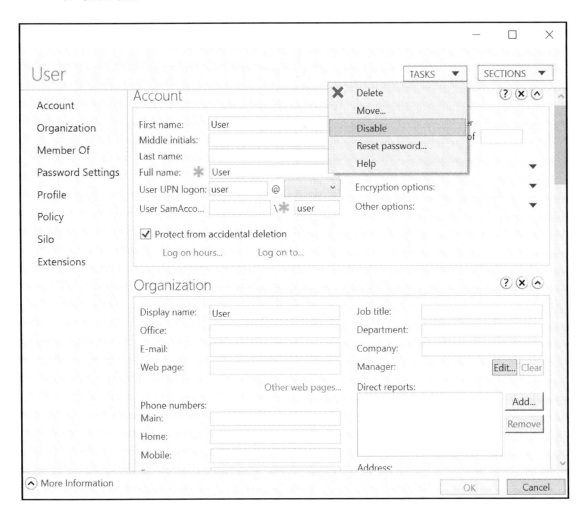

Using command-line tools

Use the following command to find locked-out user accounts in Active Directory:

```
dsmod.exe "CN=User,CN=Users,DC=lucernpub,DC=com" -disabled no
```

Use the following command to disable a user object in Active Directory:

```
dsmod.exe user "CN=User,CN=Users,DC=lucernpub,DC=com" -disabled yes
```

Using Windows PowerShell

Use the following lines of PowerShell on a system with the Active Directory module for Windows PowerShell installed to enable a user object:

```
Import-Module ActiveDirectory

Enable-ADAccount -Identity "CN=User,CN=Users,DC=lucernpub,DC=com"
```

Use the following lines of PowerShell on a system with the Active Directory module for Windows PowerShell installed to disable a user object:

```
Import-Module ActiveDirectory

Disable-ADAccount -Identity "CN=User,CN=Users,DC=lucernpub,DC=com"
```

How it works...

When a user object is disabled, it can no longer be used to log on interactively.

When an account is enabled, you can use the right-click menu in Active Directory Users and Computers or use the **Tasks** menu in the user object's properties in the Active Directory Administrative Center to disable it. When it's disabled, you can enable it in the same menus. The two menu options are not available at the same time.

There's more...

Even though interactive sign-ins are disabled when a user object is disabled, it can still be used for **Kerberos Constrained Delegation** (**KCD**) and other delegation scenarios that don't check whether a user object is disabled.

Finding locked-out users

User accounts may get locked-out. In this recipe, we will see how to find locked-out accounts.

Getting ready

To find locked-out user accounts, you should sign in to a domain controller or a member server and/or device with the RSAT for Active Directory Domain Services installed.

By default, any user object in Active Directory can be used to find locked-out accounts, as this kind of information is available to the **Everyone** group.

How to do it...

There are three ways to enable or disable a user object:

- Using the **Active Directory Administrative Center**
- Using command-line tools
- Using Windows PowerShell

Using the Active Directory Administrative Center

The Active Directory Administrative Center allows for filters to find out only locked-out user objects. Filters can be used on OUs and containers.

To find currently locked-out user objects using the Active Directory Administrative Center, follow these steps:

1. Open the **Active Directory Administrative Center** (`dsac.exe`).
2. In the left navigation pane, select the OU or container to use as the base scope for the filter.
3. In the main pane, expand the top bar.
4. Click the **Add criteria** button.

5. Select the **Users with enabled but locked accounts** criteria:

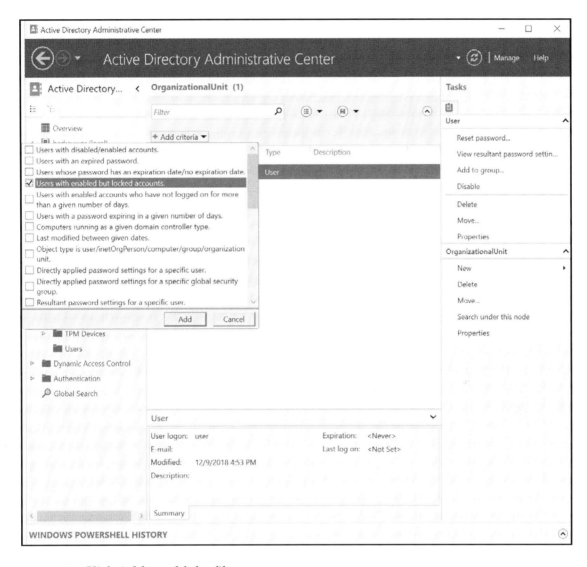

6. Click **Add** to add the filter.
7. The locked-out accounts will be displayed in the main pane.

Using Windows PowerShell

Use the following lines of PowerShell on a system with the Active Directory module for Windows PowerShell installed to find locked-out user accounts:

```
Import-Module ActiveDirectory

Search-ADAccount -LockedOut -UsersOnly | Format-Table Name,LockedOut
-AutoSize
```

How it works...

The Default Domain Policy contains password and account lockout policies. By default, the password part of these policies is enabled, but the lockout part is not. For some organizations, this makes sense. Other organizations might consider it a security best practice to enable account lockout, as these prevent brute force password attacks; when an attacker uses the maximum number of passwords within a certain amount of time, the user account is locked-out for an amount of time. All three metrics can be set in the lockout part of password and account lockout policies.

From Windows Server 2008 Active Directory onward, fine-grained password and account lockout policies can be used to set the metrics for a specific user account or specific groups.

For example, when an attacker of a clumsy colleague hits the maximum of five wrong passwords attempts in two minutes, the user object is locked out for 30 minutes.

See also

To unlock the user object(s) found in this recipe, see the *Unlocking a user* recipe.

Unlocking a user

In many organizations with account lock-out policies enabled, the number of passwords that can be mistyped is set to a high value, such as 50, and then the lock-out period is set to indefinitely. This way, a locked-out account hinders the productivity of the colleague, since he or she can't sign in until the account is unlocked. Manual unlocks need to be performed to enable the colleague to sign in again.

Getting ready

To modify user accounts, you should sign in to a domain controller or a member server and/or device with the RSAT for Active Directory Domain Services installed.

Sign in with an account that is a member of the Domain Admins group, the Account Operators group or with an account that is delegated to manage user objects in the domain or scope of the OU where the user object resides.

How to do it...

There are four ways to unlock a user object:

- Using Active Directory Users and Computers
- Using the Active Directory Administrative Center
- Using command-line tools
- Using Windows PowerShell

However, since finding locked-out accounts is not possible using Active Directory Users and Computers and working with the output of `unlock.exe` is troublesome, these two tools are not covered in this recipe.

Using the Active Directory Administrative Center

To unlock a user object using the Active Directory Administrative Center, follow these steps:

1. Open the **Active Directory Administrative Center** (`dsac.exe`).
2. In the left navigation pane, navigate to the OU or container where the user objects reside.

3. In the main pane, select the user object you want to unlock.
4. Right-click the object and select **Properties** from the menu. The **User window** appears:

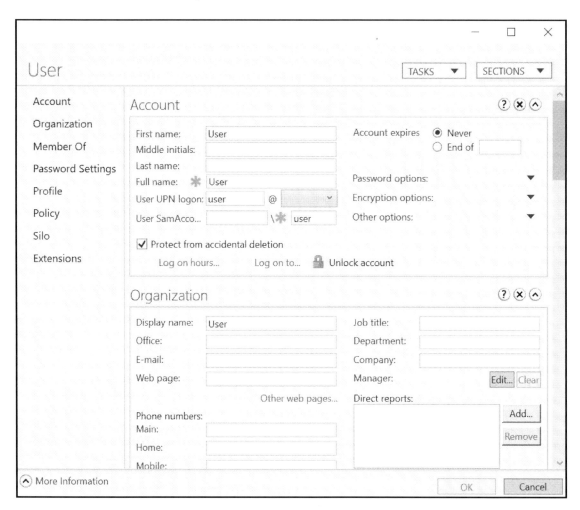

5. Click the **Unlock account** text.
6. Click **OK** when you have done this.

To unlock all locked-out accounts in a certain OU or container, combine the steps from the *Finding locked-out accounts* recipe with steps 4, 5, and 6.

Using Windows PowerShell

Use the following lines of PowerShell on a system with the Active Directory Module for Windows PowerShell installed to enable a user object:

```
Import-Module ActiveDirectory

Unlock-ADAccount -Identity "CN=User,CN=Users,DC=lucernpub,DC=com"
```

To unlock all locked-out accounts throughout the Active Directory domain, combine the commands from the *Finding locked-out accounts* recipe with the preceding lines in the following way:

```
Import-Module ActiveDirectory

Search-ADAccount -LockedOut -UsersOnly | Unlock-ADAccount
```

Managing userAccountControl

Many user objects' settings can be controlled using the userAccountControl attribute.

Getting ready

To set the userAccountControl attribute for users, you should sign in to a domain controller or a member server and/or device with the RSAT for Active Directory Domain Services installed.

Sign in with an account that is a member of the Domain Admins group.

How to do it...

userAccountControl can be managed in the following two ways:

- Reading the userAccountControl attribute
- Setting the userAccountControl attribute

Reading the userAccountControl attribute

There are three ways to read the `userAccountControl` attribute for users:

- Using Active Directory Users and Computers
- Using the Active Directory Administrative Center
- Using Windows PowerShell

Using Active Directory Users and Computers

To read the `userAccountControl` attribute for users using **Active Directory Users and Computers**, follow these steps:

1. Open **Active Directory Users and Computers** (`dsa.msc`).
2. In the **View** menu, enable **Advanced Features**.
3. Perform one of these series of actions:
     - In the left navigation pane, navigate to the OU or container where the user object resides.
     - In the main pane, select the user object.
     - From the **Action** menu, select **Find...**. In the **Name** field, type the name of the user object and press *Enter*. From the list of **Search results:**, select the user object.
4. Right-click the user object and select **Properties** from the list.
5. Navigate to the **Attribute Editor** tab.

6. In the list of **Attributes:**, scroll down until you reach the **userAccountControl** attribute:

7. Click **Cancel** to close the **Properties** window.

Using the Active Directory Administrative Center

To read the `userAccountControl` attribute for users using the **Active Directory Administrative Center**, follow these steps:

1. Open the **Active Directory Administrative Center** (`dsac.exe`).
2. Perform one of these series of actions:
   - In the left navigation pane, switch to **Tree** view. Navigate to the OU or container where the user object resides. In the main pane, select the user object.
   - From the main pane menu, under **Global Search**, type the name of the user object, and press *Enter*. From the list of **Global Search** results, select the user object.
3. Right-click the user object and select **Properties** from the list.
4. In the user properties window, click **Extensions** in the left navigation pane.
5. Navigate to the **Attribute Editor** tab.
6. In the list of **Attributes:**, scroll down until you reach the `userAccountControl` attribute:

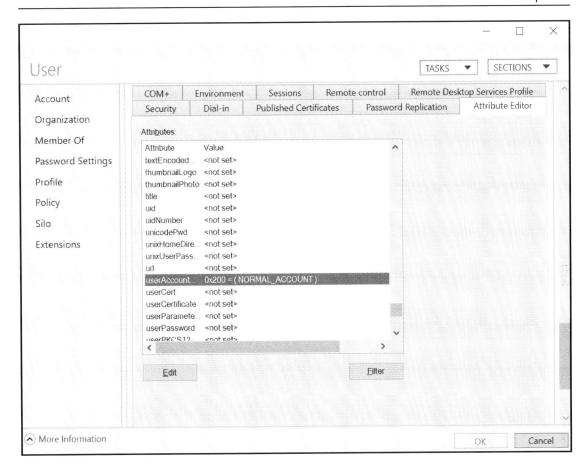

7. Click **Cancel** to close the **Properties** window.

Using Windows PowerShell

To read the `userAccountControl` attribute for a specific user object using Windows PowerShell, use the following lines of PowerShell on a system with the Active Directory module for Windows PowerShell:

```
Import-Module ActiveDirectory

Get-ADUser -Identity User -Properties userAccountControl | Format-Table
name,useraccountcontrol
```

To read the `userAccountControl` attribute for all users using Windows PowerShell, use the following lines of PowerShell on a system with the Active Directory module for Windows PowerShell:

```
Import-Module ActiveDirectory

Get-ADUser -Filter * -Properties userAccountControl | Format-Table
name,useraccountcontrol
```

Setting the userAccountControl attribute

There are two ways to set the `userAccountControl` attribute for users; follow these steps:

- Using ADSI Edit
- Using Windows PowerShell

Using ADSI Edit

To set the `userAccountControl` attribute for users using ADSI Edit, follow these steps:

1. Open **ADSI Edit** (`adsiedit.msc`).
2. Right-click the **ADSI Edit** text in the left navigation pane and select **Connect to...** from the menu.
3. Click **OK** to accept connecting to the **Default Naming Context**.
4. In the left navigation pane, expand the **Default Naming Context**.
5. In the left navigation pane, expand the distinctive name of the domain.
6. In the left navigation pane, expand the container or OU (structure) where the user object resides.
7. In the main pane, select the user object.
8. Next, right-click the user object and select **Properties** from the menu.
9. In the list of **Attributes**, scroll down to the **userAccountControl** attribute.
10. Select it.

11. Click the **Edit** button:

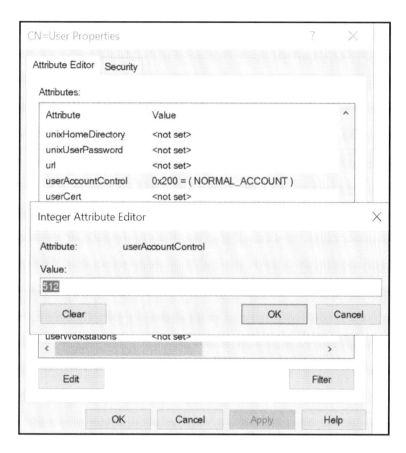

12. Type the new value for the object.
13. Click **OK** to save the new value.
14. Click **OK** to save the changes to the user object.

Using Windows PowerShell

To set the userAccountControl attribute for users using Windows PowerShell, use the following lines of PowerShell on a system with the Active Directory module for Windows PowerShell. Each of the following lines represents setting one of the bits in the userAccountControl attribute for user objects:

```
Import-Module ActiveDirectory
```

```
Set-ADAccountControl -Identity User -Enable $false

Set-ADAccountControl -Identity User -HomedirRequired $true

Set-ADAccountControl -Identity User -PasswordNotRequired $true

Set-ADAccountControl -Identity User -CannotChangePassword $true

Set-ADAccountControl -Identity User -AllowReversiblePasswordEncryption
$true

Set-ADAccountControl -Identity User -PasswordNeverExpires $true

Set-ADAccountControl -Identity User -MNSLogonAccount $true

Set-ADAccountControl -Identity User -TrustedForDelegation $true

Set-ADAccountControl -Identity User -AccountNotDelegated $true

Set-ADAccountControl -Identity User -UseDESKeyOnly $true

Set-ADAccountControl -Identity User -DoesNotRequirePreAuth $true

Set-ADAccountControl -Identity User -TrustedToAuthForDelegation $true
```

How it works...

Many individual settings and options for user accounts are stored for the object in the userAccountControl attribute. While administrators can set these options through the user interface, they can also be set by modifying the attribute itself.

Additionally, the userAccountControl attribute can also be used in scripts to find user objects with specific sets of values.

The userAccountControl attribute defines a lot of properties for any user and/or computer object. The value for this attribute is built up of bits; every value is a (combination of) 2^x value(s):

Name	Value	Value	Value	Description
SCRIPT	1	2^0	0x00000001	A log-on script is executed.
ACCOUNTDISABLE	2	2^1	0x00000002	The account is disabled.

HOMEDIR_REQUIRED	8	2^3	0x00000008	A home folder is required.
LOCKOUT	16	2^4	0x00000010	
PASSWD_NOTREQD	32	2^5	0x00000020	A password is not required.
PASSWD_CANT_CHANGE	64	2^6	0x00000040	The user cannot change the password.
ENCRYPTED_TEXT_PWD_ALLOWED	128	2^7	0x00000080	Store password using reversible encryption.
TEMP_DUPLICATE_ACCOUNT	256	2^8	0x00000100	This is an account for users whose primary account is in another domain.
NORMAL_ACCOUNT	512	2^9	0x00000200	This is a normal, enabled user account.
INTERDOMAIN_TRUST_ACCOUNT	2048	2^{11}	0x00000800	This is a permit to trust an account for a system domain that trusts other domains.
WORKSTATION_TRUST_ACCOUNT	4096	2^{12}	0x00001000	This is a normal computer account.
SERVER_TRUST_ACCOUNT	8192	2^{13}	0x00002000	This is a computer account for a domain controller.
DONT_EXPIRE_PASSWORD	65536	2^{16}	0x00010000	The password will not expire.
MNS_LOGON_ACCOUNT	131072	2^{17}	0x00020000	This is the **Majority Node Set (MNS)** logon account, used for clustering.
SMARTCARD_REQUIRED	262144	2^{18}	0x00040000	The user is forced to use a smartcard.

TRUSTED_FOR_DELEGATION	524288	2^{19}	0x00080000	The service account is trusted for Kerberos delegation.
NOT_DELEGATED	1048576	2^{20}	0x00100000	The user will not be delegated to a service even if the service account is set as trusted for Kerberos delegation.
USES_DES_KEY_ONLY	2097152	2^{21}	0x00200000	The user uses only **Data Encryption Standard (DES)** encryption.
DONT_REQ_PREAUTH	4194304	2^{22}	0x00400000	The user does not require Kerberos pre-authentication for log-on.
PASSWORD_EXPIRED	8388608	2^{23}	0x00800000	The user's password has expired.
TRUSTED_TO_AUTH_FOR_DELEGATION	16777216	2^{24}	0x01000000	The account is enabled for delegation.
PARTIAL_SECRETS_ACCOUNT	67108864	2^{26}	0x04000000	The account is a **Read-only Domain Controller (RODC)**.

Except for SCRIPT, LOCKOUT, TEMP_DUPLICATE_ACCOUNT, and PASSWORD_EXPIRED, all flags can be set on user objects by an administrator. NORMAL_ACCOUNT doesn't need to be set, as it is set, by default, on user objects.

SMARTCARD_REQUIRED isn't set this way, because it requires certificates and other prerequisites. It would make for an excellent Denial of Service attack vector if this flag could be set.

The INTERDOMAIN_TRUST_ACCOUNT, WORKSTATION_TRUST_ACCOUNT, SERVER_TRUST_ACCOUNT, and PARTIAL_SECRETS_ACCOUNT flags do not apply to user objects.

Using account expiration

User accounts can be set to automatically expire.

Getting ready

To set account expiration for a user account, you should sign in to a domain controller or a member server and/or device with the RSAT for Active Directory Domain Services installed.

Sign in with an account that is a member of the Domain Admins group or the Account Operators group or with an account that is delegated to modify user objects in the domain or scope of the OU where the user account resides.

How to do it...

There are four ways to do it:

- Using Active Directory Users and Computers
- Using the Active Directory Administrative Center
- Using command-line tools
- Using Windows PowerShell

The two graphical tools are useful for configuring account expiration on individual accounts, although the Active Directory Administrative Center can be used to retrieve the Windows PowerShell cmdlets through the Windows PowerShell History feature.

The command-line tool is particularly useful when you want to configure a time frame (in days) for the account to live on, instead of defining an end date.

Using Active Directory Users and Computers

To set account expiration a user using Active Directory Users and Computers, follow these steps:

1. Open **Active Directory Users and Computers** (`dsa.msc`).

2. Perform one of these series of actions:
   - In the left navigation pane, navigate to the OU or container where the user object resides. In the main pane, select the user object.
   - From the **Action** menu, select **Find…**. In the **Name** field, type the name of the user object and press *Enter*. From the list of **Search results:**, select the user object.

3. Right-click the user object and select **Properties** from the list.
4. Navigate to the **Account** tab:

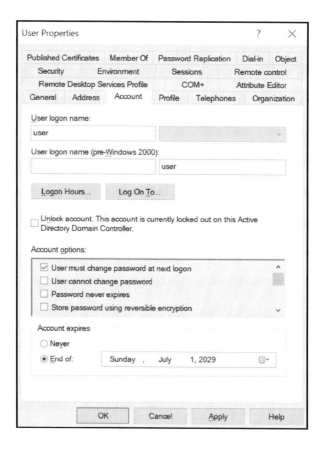

5. At the bottom of the tab, change the **Never** option for **Account expires:** to **End of:** by selecting the latter option.

6. Using the calendar icon to the right of the field, select the expiration date for the user account.

7. Click **OK** to save the settings and close the User Properties window.

Using the Active Directory Administrative Center

To set account expiration for a user using the Active Directory Administrative Center, follow these steps:

1. Open the **Active Directory Administrative Center** (`dsac.exe`).

2. Perform one of these series of actions:
    *   In the left navigation pane, switch to **Tree** view. Navigate to the OU or container where the user object resides. In the main pane, select the user object.
    *   From the main pane menu, under **Global Search**, type the name of the user object and press *Enter*. From the list of **Global Search** results, select the user object.

3. Right-click the user object and select **Properties** from the list.

4. In the top-right corner of the **Account** section, change the **Never** option for **Account expires:** to **End of:** by selecting the latter option:

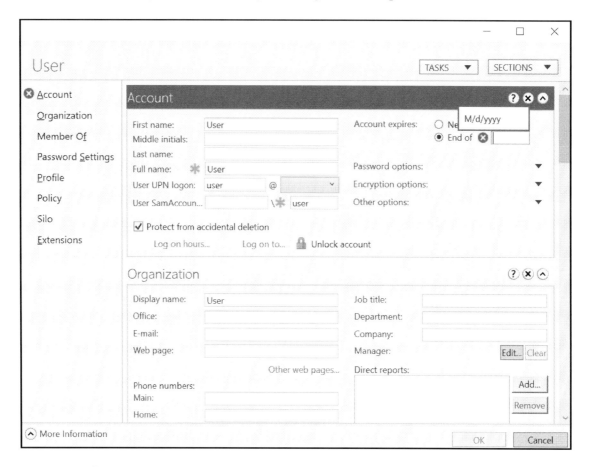

5. Type the date in the time format, specified for the operating system.
6. Click **OK** to save the settings and close the user properties window.

Using command-line tools

Use the following command to set the amount of days before an account expires in Active Directory:

```
dsmod.exe user "CN=User,CN=Users,DC=lucernpub,DC=com" -acctexpires 90
```

Using Windows PowerShell

Use the following lines of PowerShell on a system with the Active Directory module for Windows PowerShell installed to set account expiration for a user object:

```
Import-Module ActiveDirectory

Set-ADAccountExpiration -Identity "CN=User,OU=Organizational
Unit,DC=lucernpub,DC=com" -DateTime "03/01/2019 00:00:00"
```

How it works...

User objects can be configured with expiration dates. After this moment in time, the user object can no longer be used to authenticate, including when using KCD.

After the expiration date is set, it is stored in the `accountExpires` attribute. The 64-bit value stored for this attribute represents the number of 100-nanosecond intervals since January 1, 1601 (UTC).

Account expiration is a good way to fill in the gaps of missing communications between HR and IT in the joiners, movers, and leavers process for **Identity and Access Management (IAM)**.

In an organization where account expiration is used, the end date of the HR contract is used to ensure the user account automatically expires when the person would normally leave the organization. Of course, in some organizations, a couple of days are added to allow access to the expenses system and other services the organization offers to people leaving the organization.

There are some caveats, though. For external hires, who are normally hired based on project contracts, account expiration may be bothersome. Additionally, people who are on extended leave or travel beyond the end of their contract may be impacted too.

Managing Active Directory Groups

7

In typical Active Directory environments, groups govern access. Groups can be used as distribution lists, and/or in access control lists on file server shares and disks, for delegation in Active Directory itself, and to provide privileged access.

There are several built-in groups, such as the Domain Admins group and the Enterprise Admins group, which are used in many of the recipes throughout this book.

For several recipes in this chapter, multiple ways are shown that produce the same outcome. The Active Directory Users and Computers (dsa.msc) and the Active Directory Administrative Center (dsac.exe) tools provide graphical means to achieve your goals. The Active Directory Administrative Center, however, has an important trick up its sleeve; through its PowerShell History feature, it provides the ability to see the Windows PowerShell cmdlets behind the clicks. The PowerShell methods in this chapter and the additional hints from the Active Directory Administrative Center provide automation possibilities, while the Command Prompt commands provide a way to automate things on even the oldest of domain controllers.

The following recipes will be covered in this chapter:

- Creating a group
- Deleting a group
- Managing the direct members of a group
- Managing expiring group memberships
- Changing the scope or type of a group
- Viewing nested group memberships
- Finding empty groups

Creating a group

This recipe demonstrates how to create a group.

Getting ready

To create a group, you should sign in to a domain controller, a member server, and/or a device with the **Remote Server Administration Tools** (**RSAT**) for Active Directory Domain Services installed.

Sign in with an account that is a member of the Domain Admins group, the Account Operators group, or with an account that is delegated to create groups in the domain or in the scope of the **Organizational Unit** (**OU**), where the group is to be created.

How to do it...

There are four ways to create a group, as follows:

- Using Active Directory Users and Computers
- Using the Active Directory Administrative Center
- Using command-line tools
- Using Windows PowerShell

Using Active Directory Users and Computers

To create a group using Active Directory Users and Computers, perform the following steps:

1. Open **Active Directory Users and Computers** (`dsa.msc`).
2. In the left navigation pane, navigate to the OU or Container where you want to create the group object.
3. Perform one of the following actions to open the **New Object - Group** screen:
    - From the taskbar, click the **New Group** icon.
    - Right-click an empty space in the main window and select **New**; then, select **Group** from the menu.

- Right-click the OU or Container that you want to create a new group in and select **New**; then, select **Group** from the menu.

The **New Object - Group** screen appears:

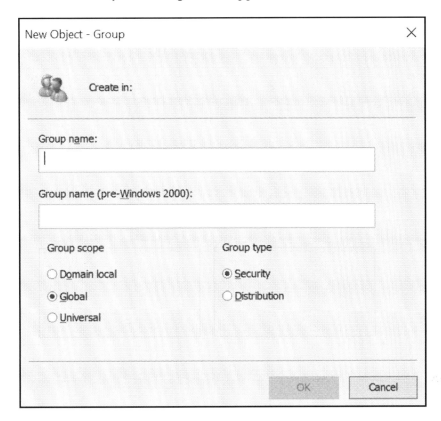

4. In the **New Object - Group** screen, specify values for the following fields:
    1. Specify the **Group Name**; the **pre-Windows 2000** group name will also be filled, based on the name of the group.
    2. Specify the **Group scope** or accept the default **Global** scope.
    3. Specify the **Group type** or accept the default **Security** type.
5. Click **OK** to create the group.

Using the Active Directory Administrative Center

To create a group using the Active Directory Administrative Center, perform the following steps:

1. Open the **Active Directory Administrative Center** (dsac.exe).

2. In the left navigation pane, right-click the domain name and select **New**; then, select **Group** from the menu.
   The **Create Group** screen appears:

3. In the **Create Group** screen, specify values for the following fields:
   1. Specify the **Group name**; the **Group (sAMAccountName) name** will also be filled, based on the name of the group.
   2. Specify the **Group scope** or accept the default **Global** scope.
   3. Specify the **Group type** or accept the default **Security** type.
4. Click **OK** to create the group.

Using command-line tools

Use the following command to create a group in Active Directory:

```
dsadd.exe group "CN=Group,OU=Organizational Unit,DC=lucernpub,DC=com"
```

Using Windows PowerShell

Use the following lines of PowerShell on a system with the Active Directory Module for Windows PowerShell installed:

```
Import-Module ActiveDirectory

New-ADGroup -GroupCategory Security -GroupScope Global -Name "Group" -Path "OU=Organizational Unit,DC=lucernpub,DC=com" -SamAccountName "Group"
```

When you create a group, some fields are automatically populated and many settings are in their default settings. These settings are recommended, but can be changed after creating a group, either in the user interface or through commands.

How it works...

This section details group scopes and group types.

Group scopes

There are three group scopes, as follows:

- Global groups
- Universal groups
- Domain local groups

When deciding what group to create, you might want to consider that global groups and universal groups can be nested into domain local groups and global groups can be nested into universal groups. Therefore, most organizations have opted to create global groups for departments, universal groups for distribution groups, groups that overarch Active Directory trusts, and domain local groups for access rights.

This way, the user accounts for people in a finance department can be made members of the finance global group. Then, this group can be nested into several domain local groups that provide read, modify, or full control of the finance department share. The finance universal group is used to send emails to, but it might also be used to access finance-related resources in other Active Directory domains, through the domain local groups in that Active Directory domain.

Group types

There are two group types, as follows:

- Distribution groups
- Security groups

Distribution groups do not have a **security identifier** (**SID**) and, therefore, can't be used to allow access to resources, except for resources within Microsoft Exchange Server. In comparison, security groups do have SIDs.

If required, you can convert a distribution group into a security group, and vice versa.

Deleting a group

You can use this recipe to delete a previously created group.

Getting ready

To delete a group, you should sign in to a domain controller, a member server, and/or a device with the RSAT for Active Directory Domain Services installed.

Sign in with an account that is a member of the Domain Admins group, the Account Operators group, or with an account that is delegated to delete groups in the domain or in the scope of the OU, where the group is to be deleted.

How to do it...

There are four ways to delete a group, as follows:

- Using Active Directory Users and Computers
- Using the Active Directory Administrative Center
- Using command-line tools
- Using Windows PowerShell

Using Active Directory Groups and Computers

To delete a group using Active Directory Groups and Computers, perform the following steps:

1. Open **Active Directory Users and Computers** (`dsa.msc`).
2. In the **View** menu, enable **Advanced Features**.
3. Perform one of these series of actions:
    - In the left navigation pane, navigate to the OU or container where the group that you intend to delete resides. Then, in the main menu pane, select the group.
    - From the **Action** menu, select **Find...**. In the **Name** field, type in the name of the group you intend to delete, and then press *Enter*. From the list of **Search results**, select the group.

4. Right-click the group and select **Properties** from the list.
   The **Group Properties** window appears:

5. Navigate to the **Object** tab.
6. Disable **Protect object from accidental deletion**.
7. Click **OK** to close the **Properties** window for the object.

8. Right-click the group again; this time, select **Delete** from the list.
9. Click **Yes** in the **Active Directory Domain Services** popup window to answer **Are you sure you want to delete the group named 'group'?**.

Using the Active Directory Administrative Center

To delete a group using the Active Directory Administrative Center, perform the following steps:

1. Open the **Active Directory Administrative Center** (`dsac.exe`).
2. Perform one of these series of actions:
   - In the left navigation pane, switch to the **Tree** view. Navigate to the OU or container where the group that you intend to delete resides. In the main menu pane, select the group.
   - From the main menu pane, under **Global Search**, type in the name of the group you intend to delete, and press *Enter*. From the list of **Global Search** results, select the group.
3. Right-click the group and select **Properties** from the list.
4. Disable **Protect object from accidental deletion**.
5. Click **OK** to close the **Properties** window for the object.
6. Right-click the group again; this time, select **Delete** from the list.
7. Click **Yes** in the **Delete confirmation** popup window to answer **Are you sure you want to delete the Group group?**.

Using command-line tools

Use the following command to delete a group in Active Directory:

```
dsrm.exe "CN=Group,OU=Organizational Unit,DC=lucernpub,DC=com"
```

Using Windows PowerShell

Use the following lines of PowerShell on a system with the Active Directory Module for Windows PowerShell installed:

```
Import-Module ActiveDirectory

Remove-ADObject -Identity "CN=Group,OU=Organizational
Unit,DC=lucernpub,DC=com"
```

How it works...

When you delete a security group, the object no longer uses its **relative identifier** (RID), but the RID and the corresponding SID and **Distinguished Name Tag** (DNT) in the domain partition also can't be reused.

When you attempt to delete a group that has the **Protect from accidental deletion** option enabled, you will not be able to delete the object—the option needs to be disabled first.

Managing the direct members of a group

You can use this recipe to manage the direct members of a group.

Getting ready

To manage a group, you should sign in to a domain controller, a member server, and/or a device with the RSAT for Active Directory Domain Services installed.

Sign in with an account that is a member of the Domain Admins group, the Account Operators group, or with an account that is delegated to manage groups in the domain or in the scope of the OU.

How to do it...

There are three ways to manage group memberships in Active Directory, as follows:

- Using Active Directory Users and Computers
- Using the Active Directory Administrative Center
- Using Windows PowerShell

Using Active Directory Groups and Computers

To manage group memberships for a user using Active Directory Groups and Computers, perform the following steps:

1. Open **Active Directory Users and Computers** (dsa.msc).

2. Perform one of these series of actions:
   - In the left navigation pane, navigate to the OU or container where the user that you intend to manage group memberships for resides. In the main menu pane, select the user.
   - From the **Action** menu, select **Find...**. In the **Name** field, type in the name of the user that you intend to manage group memberships for, and then press *Enter*. From the list of **Search results**, select the user.

3. Right-click the user object and select **Add to a group...** from the menu. The **Select Groups** window appears:

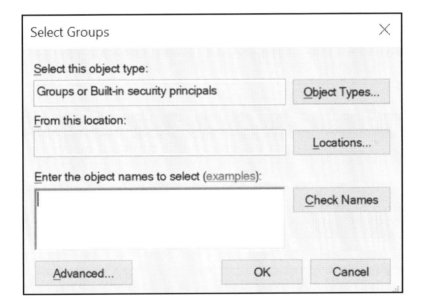

4. In the **Select Groups** window, type in the name of the group that you want to add the user account to, otherwise, click the **Advanced** button to search for the group.

5. Click **Check Names**.

6. Click **OK** to add the user to the group.

To manage group memberships for a group using Active Directory Groups and Computers, perform the following steps:

1. Open **Active Directory Users and Computers** (dsa.msc).
2. Perform one of these series of actions:
   - In the left navigation pane, navigate to the OU or container where the group that you intend to manage resides. In the main menu pane, select the group.
   - From the **Action** menu, select **Find...**. In the **Name** field, type in the name of the group that you intend to manage, and then press *Enter*. From the list of **Search results**, select the group.
3. Right-click the group and select **Properties** from the menu.
4. Navigate to the **Members** tab.
5. Perform one of the following actions:
   - In the **Group Properties** window, click **Add...** to add users, contacts, computers, service accounts, or groups to the group. In the **Select Users, Contacts, Computers, Service Accounts, or Groups** window, type in the name of the user account(s) that you want to add to the group, otherwise, click the **Advanced** button to search for the user account(s). Click **Check Names**, and then click **OK** to add the user to the group.
   - Select one or more user objects, contacts, computer objects, service accounts, or groups in the **Group Properties** window in the list of **Members**. Then, click **Remove** to remove the member(s) from the group. In the **Active Directory Domain Services** popup window, click **Yes** as the answer to **Do you want to remove the selected member(s) from the group?** in order to remove the selected member(s).
6. Click **OK** to close the **Group Properties** window and save the changes.

Using the Active Directory Administrative Center

To manage group memberships for a user using the Active Directory Administrative Center, perform the following steps:

1. Open the **Active Directory Administrative Center** (`dsac.exe`).

2. Perform one of these series of actions:
   - In the left navigation pane, switch to the **Tree** view. Navigate to the OU or container where the user object resides. In the main menu pane, select the user object.
   - From the main pane menu, under **Global Search**, type in the name of the user object, and then press *Enter*. From the list of **Global Search** results, select the user object.

3. Right-click the user object and select **Add to group...** from the list.

4. In the **Select Groups** window, type in the name of the group that you want to add the user account to or click the **Advanced** button to search for the group.

5. Click **Check Names**.

6. Click **OK** to add the user to the group.

To manage group memberships for a group using the Active Directory Administrative Center, perform the following steps:

1. Open the **Active Directory Administrative Center** (`dsac.exe`).

2. Perform one of these series of actions:
   - In the left navigation pane, switch to the **Tree** view. Navigate to the OU or container where the group resides. In the main menu pane, select the group.
   - From the main menu pane, under **Global Search**, type in the name of the group, and then press *Enter*. From the list of **Global Search** results, select the group.

3. Right-click the group and select **Properties** from the list.

4. In the left navigation pane, click **Members**, as shown in the following screenshot:

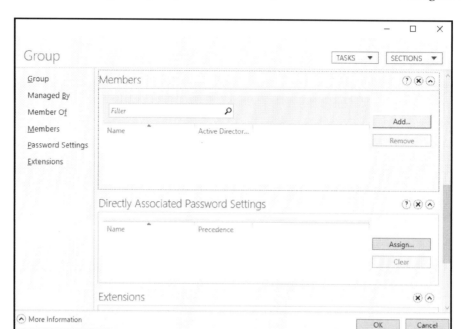

5. In the **Members** section, perform one of the following actions:
    - Click **Add...** to add users, contacts, computers, service accounts, or groups to the group. In the **Select Users, Contacts, Computers, Service Accounts, or Groups** window, type in the name of the user account(s) that you want to add to the group, otherwise, click the **Advanced** button to search for the user account(s). Click **Check Names**, and then click **OK** to add the user to the group.
    - Select one or more user objects, contacts, computer objects, service accounts, or groups in the **Group Properties** window in the list of **Members**. Click **Remove** to remove the member(s) from the group. In the **Active Directory Domain Services** popup window, click **Yes** as the answer to **Do you want to remove the selected member(s) from the group?** in order to remove the selected member(s).
6. Click **OK** to close the **Group Properties** window and save the changes.

Using Windows PowerShell

Use the following lines of PowerShell to remove a user from a group in Active Directory on a system with **Active Directory Module for Windows PowerShell** installed:

```
Import-Module ActiveDirectory

Remove-ADGroupMember -Identity "CN=Group,OU=Organizational
Unit,DC=lucernpub,DC=com" -Members "User"
```

How it works...

Groups can have members; members can be user accounts, contacts, computers, service accounts, and other groups. When a group is a member of another group, this is called group nesting.

Members are linked to the group through linked values; the SIDs for members are stored in the members attribute of the group object. The link values are replicated using link-value replication. This ensures that only changed links are replicated between domain controllers, instead of the entire members attribute, when the Windows Server 2003 **Forest Functional Level (FFL)** is used.

Managing expiring group memberships

Group memberships can alternatively be configured to expire.

Getting ready

To use the expiring group membership, the Active Directory FFL needs to be Windows Server 2012 R2, or a later version.

The optional **Privileged Access Management** feature needs to be enabled. This can be achieved using the following lines of PowerShell on a system with the Active Directory Module for Windows PowerShell installed:

```
Import-Module ActiveDirectory

Enable-ADOptionalFeature "Privileged Access Management Feature" -Scope
ForestOrConfigurationSet -Target lucernpub.com
```

To manage a group, you should sign in to a domain controller, a member server, and/or a device with the RSAT for Active Directory Domain Services installed.

Sign in with an account that is a member of the Domain Admins group, the Account Operators group, or with an account that is delegated to manage groups in the domain or in the scope of the OU.

How to do it...

This feature can only be leveraged using Windows PowerShell.

Normally, to add a group membership to a group, you'd use the following lines of PowerShell:

```
Import-Module ActiveDirectory

Add-ADGroupMember -Identity "CN=Group,OU=Organizational
Unit,DC=lucernpub,DC=com" -Members "User"
```

However, to create an expiring group membership to a group, use the following lines of PowerShell on a system with the **Active Directory Module for Windows PowerShell** installed:

```
Import-Module ActiveDirectory

Add-ADGroupMember -Identity "CN=Group,OU=Organizational
Unit,DC=lucernpub,DC=com" -Members "User" -MemberTimeToLive (New-TimeSpan -
Days 14)
```

To view the time-to-live for group memberships, use the following lines of PowerShell on a system with the **Active Directory Module for Windows PowerShell** installed:

```
Import-Module ActiveDirectory

Get-ADGroup "CN=Group,OU=Organizational Unit,DC=lucernpub,DC=com" -Property
member -ShowMemberTimeToLive
```

How it works...

Active Directory in Windows Server 2016 offers a new feature, that is, labeled **expiring links**. This feature configures links in link-value attributes, such as the `members` attribute, for a group with an optional time-to-live value. When the time is up, the link expires; if it is a group membership, then the membership disappears.

This feature can be used as a way to provide temporary group memberships.

Changing the scope or type of a group

You can use this recipe to change the scope and/or type of a group in Active Directory.

Getting ready

To manage a group, you should sign in to a domain controller, a member server, and/or a device with the RSAT for Active Directory Domain Services installed.

Sign in with an account that is a member of the Domain Admins group, the Account Operators group, or with an account that is delegated to manage groups in the domain or in the scope of the OU.

How to do it...

There are four ways to manage group memberships in Active Directory, as follows:

- Using Active Directory Groups and Computers
- Using the Active Directory Administrative Center
- Using the Active Directory command-line tools
- Using Windows PowerShell

Using Active Directory Groups and Computers

To change the scope or type for a group using Active Directory Groups and Computers, perform the following steps:

1. Open **Active Directory Users and Computers** (dsa.msc).
2. Perform one of these series of actions:
    *   In the left navigation pane, navigate to the OU or container where the group that you intend to manage resides. In the main menu pane, select the group.
    *   From the **Action** menu, select **Find....** In the **Name** field, type in the name of the group that you intend to manage, and then press *Enter*. From the list of **Search results**, select the group.
3. Right-click the group and select **Properties** from the menu.
    The **Group Properties** window appears:

4. Change the group scope in the **Group scope** field and/or change the group type in the **Group type** field.
5. Click **OK** to close the **Group Properties** window and save the changes.

Using the Active Directory Administrative Center

To change the scope or type for a group using the Active Directory Administrative Center, perform the following steps:

1. Open the **Active Directory Administrative Center** (`dsac.exe`).

2. Perform one of these series of actions:
   - In the left navigation pane, switch to the **Tree** view. Navigate to the OU or container where the group resides. In the main menu pane, select the group.
   - From the main menu pane, under **Global Search**, type in the name of the group, and then press *Enter*. From the list of **Global Search** results, select the group.

3. Right-click the group and select **Properties** from the list.
   The **Group** window appears:

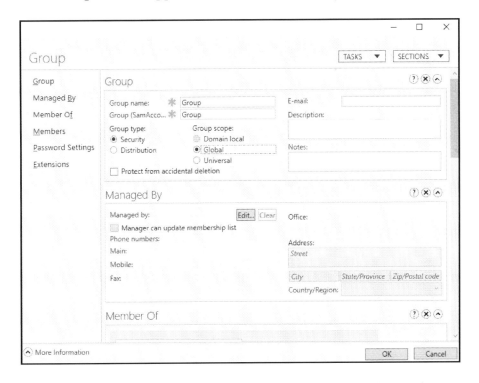

4. Change the group scope in the **Group scope** field and/or change the group type in the **Group type** field.

5. Click **OK** to close the **Group Properties** window and save the changes.

Using command-line tools

Use the following command to change the scope of a group in Active Directory to Global:

```
dsmod.exe group "CN=Group,OU=Organizational Unit,DC=lucernpub,DC=com"
-scope g
```

Use the following command to change the scope of a group in Active Directory to Universal:

```
dsmod.exe group "CN=Group,OU=Organizational Unit,DC=lucernpub,DC=com"
-scope u
```

Use the following command to change the scope of a group in Active Directory to Domain Local:

```
dsmod.exe group "CN=Group,OU=Organizational Unit,DC=lucernpub,DC=com"
-scope l
```

Use the following command to change the type of group in Active Directory from a distribution group to a security group:

```
dsmod.exe group "CN=Group,OU=Organizational Unit,DC=lucernpub,DC=com"
-secgrp yes
```

Use the following command to change the type of group in Active Directory from a security group to a distribution group:

```
dsmod.exe group "CN=Group,OU=Organizational Unit,DC=lucernpub,DC=com"
-secgrp no
```

Using Windows PowerShell

Use the following lines of PowerShell to change the scope of a group in Active Directory to global on a system with the Active Directory Module for Windows PowerShell installed:

```
Import-Module ActiveDirectory

Set-ADGroup -Identity "CN=Group,OU=Organizational Unit,DC=lucernpub,DC=com"
-GroupScope Global
```

Use the following lines of PowerShell to change the scope of a group in Active Directory to universal on a system with the Active Directory Module for Windows PowerShell installed:

```
Import-Module ActiveDirectory

Set-ADGroup -Identity "CN=Group,OU=Organizational Unit,DC=lucernpub,DC=com"
-GroupScope Universal
```

Use the following lines of PowerShell to change the scope of a group in Active Directory to domain local on a system with the Active Directory Module for Windows PowerShell installed:

```
Import-Module ActiveDirectory

Set-ADGroup -Identity "CN=Group,OU=Organizational Unit,DC=lucernpub,DC=com"
-GroupScope DomainLocal
```

Use the following lines of PowerShell to change the type of group in Active Directory from a distribution group to a security group on a system with the Active Directory Module for Windows PowerShell installed:

```
Import-Module ActiveDirectory

Set-ADGroup -Identity "CN=Group,OU=Organizational Unit,DC=lucernpub,DC=com"
-GroupCategory Security
```

Use the following lines in PowerShell to change the type of group in Active Directory from a security group to a distribution group on a system with the Active Directory Module for Windows PowerShell installed:

```
Import-Module ActiveDirectory

Set-ADGroup -Identity "CN=Group,OU=Organizational Unit,DC=lucernpub,DC=com"
-GroupCategory Distribution
```

How it works...

This section details group scopes and group types.

Group scopes

There are three group scopes, as follows:

- Global groups
- Universal groups
- Domain local groups

When deciding what group to create, you might want to consider that global groups and universal groups can be nested into domain local groups and global groups can be nested in universal groups. Therefore, most organizations have opted to create global groups for departments, universal groups for distribution groups, groups that overarch Active Directory trusts, and domain local groups for access rights.

This way, the user accounts for people in a finance department can be made members of the finance Global group. Then, this group can be nested into several domain Local groups that provide read, modify, or full control of the finance department share. The finance universal group is used to send emails, but it might also be used to access finance-related resources in other Active Directory domains, through the domain local groups in that Active Directory domain, you can change the group scope.

Group types

There are two group types, as follows:

- Distribution groups
- Security groups

Distribution groups do not have a SID and, therefore, can't be used to allow access to resources, except for resources within Microsoft Exchange Server. In comparison, security groups do have SIDs.

You can convert a distribution group into a security group, and vice versa.

Viewing nested group memberships

This recipe demonstrates how to enumerate all members of a group, even members in groups that are members of the group.

Getting ready

To view nested group memberships for a group, sign in to a domain controller, a member server, and/or a device with the RSAT for Active Directory Domain Services installed.

Sign in with an account that is a member of the Domain Admins group, the Account Operators group, or with an account that is delegated to manage groups in the domain or in the scope of the OU.

How to do it...

As an admin, you could click groups on the **Members** tab in the properties of a group and look at its members. When groups are heavily nested, though, this becomes tedious fast. A much better approach is to use Windows PowerShell.

Use the following lines of PowerShell to enumerate all group memberships in Active Directory for a group on a system with the Active Directory module for Windows PowerShell installed:

```
Import-Module ActiveDirectory

Get-ADGroupMember -Identity "CN=Group,OU=Organizational
Unit,DC=lucernpub,DC=com" -Recursive | Out-GridView
```

How it works...

The `Get-ADGroupMember` PowerShell cmdlet offers the `-recursive` switch to view the nested group memberships. When a user object has memberships through various other groups and/or direct memberships, the user object is only returned once.

To make the output readable and sortable, `Out-GridView` shows the output in a graphical user interface. This part can be omitted to show the results in the PowerShell window, or changed to output on the clipboard or CSV file.

Finding empty groups

This recipe demonstrates how to find groups without group members. Every object in Active Directory takes up resources. When a group is not used, it may be deleted to make room for other more important objects.

Getting ready

To view group memberships for a group, sign in to a domain controller, a member server, and/or a device with the RSAT for Active Directory Domain Services installed.

Sign in with an account that is a member of the Domain Admins group, the Account Operators group, or with an account that is delegated to manage groups in the domain or in the scope of the OU.

How to do it...

Use the following lines of PowerShell to find all groups without memberships in Active Directory on a system with the Active Directory module for Windows PowerShell installed:

```
Import-Module ActiveDirectory

Get-ADGroup -Filter * -Properties members | Where-Object {$_.Members.count
-eq 0}  | Out-GridView
```

How it works...

The `Get-ADGroup` PowerShell cmdlet is used to get the `members` attribute. Then, recursively, for each group the membership count is queried. If this count is zero, it means there are no group members; when this is the case, the group is returned.

To make the output readable and sortable, `Out-GridView` shows the output in a graphical user interface. This part can be omitted to show the results in the PowerShell window, or changed to output on the clipboard or CSV file.

8
Managing Active Directory Computers

Computer objects in Active Directory represent actual devices. When you join a device to an Active Directory domain, it shows up in the database. From there, you can manage it using Active Directory and Group Policy. Joining a computer to the domain can be done in several ways and it's good to keep certain scenarios in the back of your head when working with computer objects, such as the integrity of the secure channel and the default ability for any Active Directory user to join devices to the domain.

The following recipes will be covered in the chapter:

- Creating a computer
- Deleting a computer
- Joining a computer to the domain
- Renaming a computer
- Testing the secure channel for a computer
- Resetting a computer's secure channel
- Changing the default quota for creating computer objects

Creating a computer

In this recipe, we will create a computer object. This object can later be used to attach a device to when it is domain-joined.

Getting ready

To create a computer account, you need to sign in to a domain controller, a member server, and/or a device with the **Remote Server Administration Tools (RSAT)** for Active Directory Domain Services installed.

Sign in with an account that is a member of the Domain Admins group, the Account Operators group, or with an account that has delegated privileges to create computer objects in the domain or in the scope of the **Organizational Unit (OU)** where the computer account is created.

How to do it...

There are four ways to create a computer object:

- Using Active Directory Users and Computers
- Using the Active Directory Administrative Center
- Using command-line tools
- Using Windows PowerShell

Using Active Directory Users and Computers

To create a computer using Active Directory Users and Computers, follow these steps:

1. Open **Active Directory Users and Computers** (`dsa.msc`).
2. In the left navigation pane, navigate to the OU or container where you want to create the computer object.
3. Perform one of the following actions to open the **New Object – Computer** screen:
    - From the taskbar, click the **New Computer** icon.
    - Right-click an empty space in the main window and select **New**; then, select **Computer** from the menu.
    - Right-click the OU or container that you want to create a new computer in and select **New**; then, select **Computer** from the menu.

- The **New Object – Computer** screen appears:

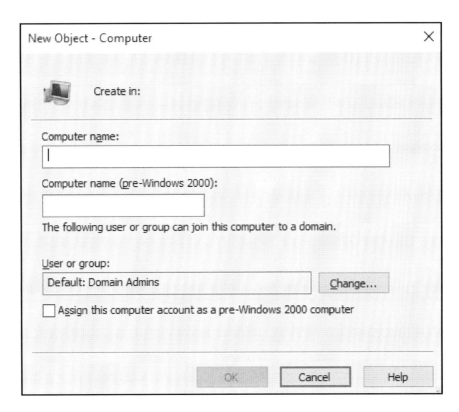

4. In the **New Object – Computer** screen, specify values for the following fields:
    1. Specify the **Computer name.**
    2. Change the **Computer name (pre-Windows 2000)** if you need it to be different from the automatically-generated value, based on the value of the **Computer name.**

5. Click **OK** when you are done.

Using the Active Directory Administrative Center

To create a computer using the Active Directory Administrative Center, follow these steps:

1. Open the **Active Directory Administrative Center** (dsac.exe).
2. In the left navigation pane, right-click the domain name and select **New**. Then, select **Computer** from the menu.
   The **Create Computer** screen appears:

3. In the **Create Computer** screen, specify values for the following fields:
   1. Specify the **Computer name.**
   2. Change the **Computer name (pre-Windows 2000)** if you need it to be different from the automatically-generated value, based on the value of the **Computer name.**

4. Click **OK**.

Using command-line tools

Use the following command to create a computer object in Active Directory:

```
dsadd.exe computer "CN=Computer,CN=Computers,DC=lucernpub,DC=com"
```

Using Windows PowerShell

Use the following lines of PowerShell on a system with the Active Directory module for Windows PowerShell installed:

```
Import-Module ActiveDirectory

New-ADComputer -Name "Computer" -sAMAccountName "Computer" -Path
"CN=Computers,DC=lucernpub,DC=com"
```

How it works...

When you create a computer object, an actual device can attach to it when it is domain-joined. This way, the location of the computer object, and any settings that you want the object to have, can be preconfigured. When a device is joined with the same hostname as the computer name, the computer object is attached too.

When the computer name is over 15 characters, the pre-Windows 2000 computer name is truncated to only use the first 15 characters, by default. It might be a good idea to change the computer name when the data that makes the computer object unique in the Active Directory context is part of the last part of the computer name. In this case, the first part of the computer name can be manually truncated to make room for the unique part.

A descriptive name for every computer object is useful to make sure that the computer object can be identified in the graphical interface and in auditing scenarios. Additionally, the **My Network locations** functionality on domain-joined Windows devices shows the description by default, rather than the hostname.

When you create a computer object, the object consumes a **relative identifier** (RID) and **Distinguished Name Tag** (DNT) in the domain partition.

There's more...

The Domain Admins group is assigned the right to attach an actual device to the computer object, but this can be changed to include any group in Active Directory.

When an organization scales up to multiple political entities with their own admin workforce, it might be a good idea to make sure that the computer objects for a certain entity can only be attached using the credentials given to the members of a specific group for that particular entity.

Deleting a computer

Follow the steps in this recipe to delete a previously-created computer object.

Getting ready

To delete a computer account, you should sign in to a domain controller, a member server, and/or a device with the RSAT for Active Directory Domain Services installed.

Sign in with an account that is a member of the Domain Admins group, the Account Operators group, or with an account that has delegated privileges to delete computer objects in the domain or in the scope of the OU where the computer account is to be deleted.

How to do it...

There are four ways to delete a computer object:

- Using Active Directory Users and Computers
- Using the Active Directory Administrative Center
- Using command-line tools
- Using Windows PowerShell

Using Active Directory Users and Computers

To delete a computer using Active Directory Users and Computers, follow these steps:

1. Open **Active Directory Users and Computers** (`dsa.msc`).
2. In the **View** menu, enable **Advanced Features.**
3. Perform one of these series of actions:
    1. In the left navigation pane, navigate to the OU or container where the computer object that you intend to delete resides. In the main menu pane, select the computer object.
    2. From the **Action** menu, select **Find**. In the **Name** field, type the name of the computer object that you intend to delete, and then press *Enter*. From the list of **Search results**, select the computer object.
4. Right-click the computer object and select **Properties** from the list.
5. Navigate to the **Object** tab.
6. Disable **Protect object from accidental deletion.**
7. Click **OK** to close the **Properties** window for the object.
8. Right-click the computer object again; this time, select **Delete** from the list. The **Active Directory Domain Services** popup window appears:

9. Click **Yes** in the **Active Directory Domain Services** popup window in order to answer the **Are you sure you want to delete the Computer named 'Computer'?** question.

Using the Active Directory Administrative Center

To delete a computer using the Active Directory Administrative Center, follow these steps:

1. Open the **Active Directory Administrative Center** (`dsac.exe`).
2. Perform one of these series of actions:
    - In the left navigation pane, switch to the **Tree** view. Navigate to the OU or container where the computer object that you intend to delete resides. In the main menu pane, select the computer object.
    - From the main menu pane, under **Global Search**, type the name of the computer object that you intend to delete, and then press *Enter*. From the list of **Global Search** results, select the computer object.
3. Right-click the computer object and select **Properties** from the list. The **Computer** properties window appears:

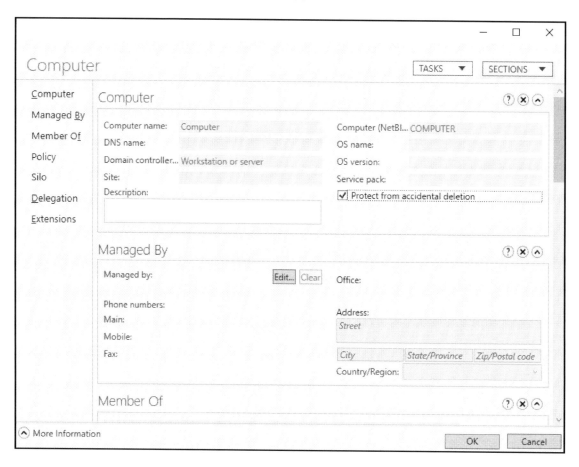

4. Disable **Protect object from accidental deletion.**
5. Click **OK** to close the **Properties** window for the object.
6. Right-click the computer object again; this time, select **Delete** from the list:

7. Click **Yes** in the **Delete Confirmation** popup window to answer the **Are you sure you want to delete the Computer Computer?** question.

Using command-line tools

Use the following command to delete a computer object in Active Directory:

```
dsrm.exe "CN=Computer,CN=Computers,DC=lucernpub,DC=com"
```

Using Windows PowerShell

Use the following lines of PowerShell on a system with the Active Directory module for Windows PowerShell installed:

```
Import-Module ActiveDirectory

Remove-ADComputer -Identity "CN=Computer,CN=Computers,DC=lucernpub,DC=com"
```

How it works...

When you delete a computer object, the object no longer uses its RID but the RID and the corresponding SID and DNT in the domain partition also can't be reused.

When you attempt to delete a computer object that has the **Protect from accidental deletion** option enabled, you will not be able to delete the object—the option needs to be disabled first.

When the Active Directory Recycle Bin is enabled, the deleted computer object emerges in the **Deleted Objects** container.

See also

- Refer to the *Enabling the Active Directory Recycle Bin* recipe in `Chapter 1`, *Optimizing Forests, Domains, and Trusts*.

Joining a computer to the domain

You can use this recipe to join a Windows-based computer to an Active Directory domain.

There are three ways to accomplish this:

- Attach a Windows-based device to a previously-created computer object.
- Join a Windows-based device to a domain using the GUI.
- Join a Windows-based device to a domain using Windows PowerShell.

Getting ready

In order to communicate with domain controllers, the device needs to be on the same logical networks as the domain controllers. You might also be able to join a device through a **virtual private network** (**VPN**) connection—when the required traffic is allowed through.

To find the domain controllers for the Active Directory domain, the device needs to be able to resolve the name of the Active Directory environment. Configuring devices with a DNS server address through **Dynamic Host Configuration Protocol** (**DHCP**) is the most convenient and, therefore, commonly used method, but this can also be achieved by adding the domain information to the hosts file.

When a device is joined to Azure Active Directory, the option to join Active Directory is not available, unless you configure a hybrid Azure Active Directory join with the domain-joined computer object as the source.

To attach a device to a previously-created computer object, you'll need the credentials for an account with the privileges to attach the device to the object. If you enter the credentials for an account without the proper group membership, attaching will fail.

How to do it...

To attach a Windows-based device to a previously-created computer object, simply create the object or have a person with a privileged account create it for you, and then join the device, using either of the following two methods.

Using the GUI

To join a Windows 10-based device to Active Directory, perform the following steps:

1. Press the **Start** flag and either click the cog in the left-side of the Start Menu to access **Settings**, or type `Settings` and click the **Settings** trusted Microsoft Store app from the results. Alternatively, press the *Start* button on your keyboard and the *X* key simultaneously, and select **Settings** from the context menu. The **Settings** trusted Microsoft Store app appears:

2. In the **Windows Settings** window, click **Accounts**.
3. In the left navigation pane, click **Access work or school**.
4. In the main menu pane, click **+ Connect**.
5. In the **Microsoft Account** window, click **Join this device to a local Active Directory domain** under **Alternative Options**.

6. In the **Join a Domain** window, type the DNS domain name or the NetBIOS name of the Active Directory environment. Then, click **Next**.

7. Type the credentials in the **Windows Security** popup message that asks to enter your domain account information to verify that you have permission to connect to the domain. Then, click **OK**.

8. In the **Restart your PC** window, click **Restart now** to restart the PC as a domain-joined device.

Using Windows PowerShell

To add a Windows-based device to an Active Directory domain, use the following lines of PowerShell:

```
Add-Computer -DomainName lucernpub.com -Credential LUCERNPUB\Administrator

Restart-Computer
```

How it works...

When a device is joined to Active Directory, it receives an RID through its corresponding computer object. The device has several permissions in Active Directory, including read permissions in the Active Directory **System Volume (SYSVOL)**.

By attaching a previously-created computer object, all the information for the device is already available to the device when communicating to the domain controllers. From the outset, this scenario looks as though it only has advantages.

One piece of information that is needed to attach to the computer object is the secret for the object. As the process needs to work for other operating systems too, the secret is straightforward; it is the NetBIOS name of the computer in all caps, followed by a dollar sign. This represents a disadvantage, because when a previously-created computer object is not used, its security principal can be misused. Therefore, be sure to have a process in place to clean up stale computer objects.

There's more...

The `Add-Computer` PowerShell cmdlet offers many more possibilities.

For instance, the `-NewName` parameter can be used to provide a new hostname for the device before joining it to the Active Directory domain. This way, you may avoid joining many `DESKTOP-XXXXXXX` devices to Active Directory, but can definitely avoid the reboot for renaming a device.

Another real gem is the `-OUPath` parameter, which can be used to specify the OU that the computer object is to be placed in. This is particularly useful when you only have privileges to add computer objects to certain OUs as a delegated admin.

When using Windows PowerShell to automate joining devices to Active Directory, you might want to add the `-Restart` parameter. When set, the device automatically restarts without leaving any time for unwanted actions by whoever is overseeing the joins.

See also

For more information refer the following recipes:

- The *Creating a computer*
- The *Deleting a computer*

Renaming a computer

You can use this recipe to rename a computer.

Getting ready

To rename a device's hostname, you'll need to log on to the device with administrative privileges and have the (delegated) privilege in Active Directory to change the corresponding computer object.

Additionally, the device needs to be on the same logical networks as at least one of the domain controllers. You might be able to rename a device when connected through a VPN connection—when the required traffic is allowed through.

How to do it...

There are three ways to change the hostname for a Windows 10-based device:

- Using the settings app
- Using the command line
- Using Windows PowerShell

Using the settings app

To rename a Windows 10-based device, perform the following steps:

1. Press the **Start** flag and either click the cog in the left-side of the Start Menu to access **Settings**, or type `Settings` and click the **Settings** trusted Microsoft Store app from the results. Alternatively, press *Start + X* on your keyboard and select **Settings** from the context menu.
2. In the **Settings** window, click **System**.
3. In the left navigation pane, click **About**.
4. In the main menu pane, click the **Rename this PC** button under **Device Specifications.**
   The **Rename your PC** window appears:

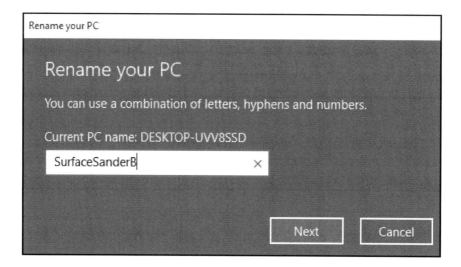

5. In the **Rename your PC** window, type the new hostname for the device. Then, click **Next**.

6. Click **Restart now**.

Using the command line

To rename a Windows 10-based device, issue the following command line on an elevated Command Prompt (cmd.exe):

```
netdom.exe renamecomputer localhost /newname NewComputerName /reboot
```

Using Windows PowerShell

To rename a Windows 10-based device, enter the following two lines of PowerShell:

```
Rename-Computer NewComputerName

Restart-Computer
```

How it works...

Even when a device is domain-joined, the built-in methods to rename the device work. Before the restart to rename the device's hostname, the name of the computer object is changed to match the hostname after restart

> When you rename the computer object for a device that is actively domain-joined, the domain trust is broken.

However, any custom NetBIOS name for the computer object becomes the default name, and is truncated to the first 15 characters when the hostname is longer than 15 characters.

There's more...

Using the command-line method, the credentials for the account with the (delegated) privilege in Active Directory to change the corresponding computer object can be specified. This way, you may avoid (temporarily) over-privileging a user account with privileges.

For netdom.exe, specify the additional /userd, /passwordd, /usero, and /passwordo parameters for the credentials for the privileged user accounts in Active Directory and the local administrator, respectively.

Testing the secure channel for a computer

You can use this recipe to test the secure channel for a domain-joined device.

Getting ready

To test the secure channel, the device needs to be on the same logical networks as at least one of the domain controllers. You might be able to rename a device when connected through a VPN connection—when the required traffic is allowed through.

When a specific domain controller is specified, make sure the Netlogon service is running.

How to do it...

There are two ways to test the secure channel for a Windows 10-based device:

- Using the command line
- Using Windows PowerShell

Using the command line

To test the secure channel, enter the following command line on an elevated Command Prompt (cmd.exe):

```
nltest.exe /server:DomainControllerName /sc_query:lucernpub.com
```

Using Windows PowerShell

To test the secure channel, use the following line of PowerShell:

```
Test-ComputerSecureChannel
```

How it works...

Domain-joined devices communicate to domain controllers using the secure channel. This way, these communications are protected using a secret. This secret is stored in Active Directory as an attribute to the computer object, and on the device as an LSA secret.

When these two values go out of sync, the device will no longer be able to authenticate and, thus, communicate with domain controllers.

While `nltest.exe` will provide information on the secure channel, `Test-ComputerSecureChannel` simply returns `False` or `True`. To gain more information from `Test-ComputerSecureChannel`, specify the `-Verbose` parameter.

See also

For more information refer the following recipe:

- The *Resetting a computer's secure channel*

Resetting a computer's secure channel

When you test a device's secure channel and it fails, the secure channel can be reset from the computer object using this recipe.

Getting ready

To reset a computer object's secret in the Active Directory object, privileges are needed to allow you to change the computer object. By default, Domain Admins and Account Operators have this privilege. When using the Windows PowerShell method on the device itself, an account is needed that has local administrative privileges on the device and the privileges mentioned previously.

To reset the secure channel, the device needs to be on the same logical networks as at least one of the domain controllers. You might be able to rename a device when connected through a VPN connection—when the required traffic is allowed through.

When a specific domain controller is specified, make sure the Netlogon service is running.

How to do it...

There are four ways to reset the secure channel for a domain-joined device:

- Using Active Directory Users and Computers
- Using the Active Directory Administrative Center

- Using the command line
- Using Windows PowerShell

Using Active Directory Users and Computers

To reset a computer object's secure channel using Active Directory Users and Computers, follow these steps:

1. Open **Active Directory Users and Computers** (`dsa.msc`).
2. Perform one of these series of actions:
   - In the left navigation pane, navigate to the OU or container where the computer object resides that you intend to reset. In the main menu pane, select the computer object.
   - From the **Action** menu, select **Find**. On the left-side of **Find** select **Computers** from the drop-down menu. In the **Name** field, type the name of the computer object that you intend to reset, and press *Enter*. From the list of **Search results**, select the object.
3. Right-click the computer object and select **Reset Account** from the menu. The **Active Directory Domain Services** popup window appears:

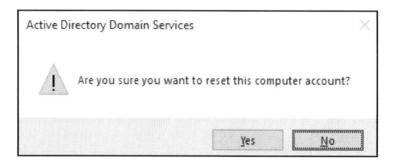

4. In the **Active Directory Domain Services** popup window, click **Yes** as the answer to the **Are you sure you want to reset this computer account?** question.
5. In the **Active Directory Domain Services** popup window, click **OK** to acknowledge that the account was reset.

Now log on to the device for which you reset the computer object and rejoin it to the domain.

Using the Active Directory Administrative Center

To reset a computer object's secure channel using the Active Directory Administrative Center snap-in, follow these steps:

1. Open the **Active Directory Administrative Center** (dsac.exe).
2. Perform one of these series of actions:
   - In the left navigation pane, switch to the **Tree** view. Navigate to the OU or container where the computer object resides that you intend to reset. In the main menu pane, select the computer object.
   - From the main menu pane, under **Global Search**, type the name of the computer object that you intend to reset, and press *Enter*. From the list of **Global Search** results, select the computer object.
3. Right-click the computer object and select **Reset account** from the list.
4. In the **Warning** popup window, click **Yes** as the answer to the **Are you sure you want to reset this computer account?** question.
5. In the **Reset Computer Account** popup window, click **OK** to acknowledge that the account was successfully reset.

Now log on to the device for which you reset the computer object and rejoin it to the domain.

Using the command line

To reset a computer object's secure channel, issue the following command line on an elevated Command Prompt (cmd.exe) on a domain controller:

```
dsmod.exe computer "CN=Computer,CN=Computers,DC=LucernPub,DC=com" -reset
```

Using Windows PowerShell

To reset the secure channel from a device that has its secure channel fail, issue the following line of PowerShell on the Windows device:

```
Test-ComputerSecureChannel -Repair
```

How it works...

By resetting the secure channel for a device, the secret that is stored in Active Directory as an attribute to the computer object and on the device as an LSA secret is changed at both sides.

Another way to reset the secure channel is to remove the device from the Active Directory domain, delete the corresponding computer object, and then rejoin the device to the domain. As this is more time-consuming and requires more effort, resetting the secure channel should be the preferred method.

Using Active Directory Users and Computers, the Active Directory Administrative Center, or the command line in this recipe, the secret in Active Directory is changed. After this change, the device will need to be rejoined to the domain. The PowerShell example in this recipe represents a way to perform the action on the Windows device itself.

Changing the default quota for creating computer objects

By default, every user object can be an owner of up to 10 computer objects. This means that every non-admin can join up to 10 devices to Active Directory. This recipe details how to change this number.

Getting ready

Changing the default quota for creating computer objects requires domain admin privileges.

How to do it...

There are two ways to change the default quota for creating computer objects:

- Using **Active Directory Service Interfaces (ADSI)** Edit
- Using Windows PowerShell

Using ADSI Edit

Follow these steps to change the default quota for creating computer objects:

1. Open **ADSI Edit** (`adsiedit.msc`)
2. In the left pane, right-click the **ADSI Edit** text and select **Connect to** from the menu.
   The **Connection Settings** window appears:

3. In the **Connection Settings** window, click the **Select a well known Naming Context** option and connect to **Default naming context.**
4. In the left navigation pane, expand **Default naming context.**
5. Right-click the domain name and select **Properties** from the menu.
6. On the **Attribute Editor** tab, scroll down to the **ms-DS-MachineAccountQuota** attribute and select it.

7. Click the **Edit** button.
   The **Integer Attribute Editor** window appears:

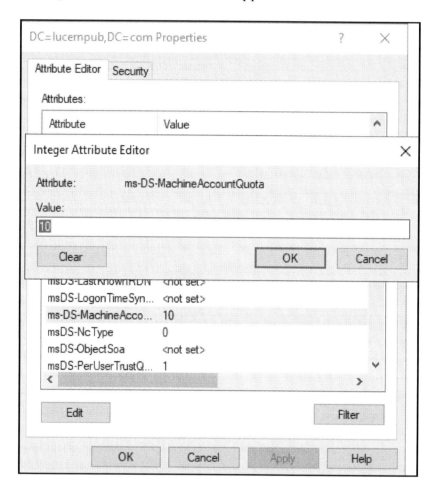

8. Type the new value for the attribute in the **Integer Attribute Editor** window.
9. Click **OK** to enter the new value, and then close the **Integer Attribute Editor** window.
10. Click **OK** to save the new value, and then close the **Properties** window.

Using Windows PowerShell

To change the default quota for creating computer objects, issue the following lines of PowerShell:

```
Import-Module ActiveDirectory

Set-ADDomain -Identity Lucernpub.com -Replace @{"ms-DS-
MachineAccountQuota"="Quota"}
```

How it works...

By default, every user object can be an owner of up to 10 computer objects. This means that every non-admin can join up to 10 devices to a domain. This behavior is governed by the `ms-DS-MachineAccountQuota` attribute per Active Directory domain.

When this attribute is changed to `0`, only user accounts with privileges to add computer objects to the domain are explicitly allowed to join devices to the domain. By default, members of the Domain Admins and Account Operators groups have these privileges, but these privileges can be specifically delegated.

Getting the Most Out of Group Policy

9

Group Policy allows administrators to manage one device, but also many thousands of devices and/or servers through a centralized management console. You can use it not only to secure domain-joined devices and make them more useful for end users, but also to make them look and feel identical as per your organization's standards. Of course, granularity in Group Policy objects offers the ability to just manage these settings for devices in an Active Directory domain, as for the Active Directory site (but please don't!) or per **Organizational Unit (OU)**, and beyond that using **Windows Management Instrumentation (WMI)** filters.

Group Policy has been around since the beginning of Active Directory in Windows 2000 Server. In the last two decades, Group Policy has seen many improvements, such as Group Policy preferences and many new settings corresponding to all the new client operating system possibilities.

Although currently considered archaic because of trends such as bring-your-own-device and solutions such as **mobile device management (MDM)** and **mobile application management (MAM)**, Group Policy should be considered an essential tool in every Active Directory admin's toolbox.

The following recipes will be covered in this chapter:

- Creating a Group Policy Object (GPO)
- Copying a GPO
- Deleting a GPO
- Modifying the settings of a GPO
- Assigning scripts
- Installing applications
- Linking a GPO to an OU

- Blocking inheritance of GPOs on an OU
- Enforcing the settings of a GPO link
- Applying security filters
- Creating and applying WMI Filters
- Configuring loopback processing
- Restoring a default GPO
- Creating a Group Policy Central Store

Creating a Group Policy Object (GPO)

This recipe shows you how to create a **Group Policy Object** (GPO).

Getting ready

To create a GPO, log into a system with the **Group Policy Management** Console installed with an account that is either of the following:

- A member of the Domain Admins group
- Delegated to create GPOs

 To use a Starter GPO or to link a GPO to an OU, additional permissions are needed besides the permission to create GPOs.

How to do it...

There are two ways to create a GPO:

- Using the Group Policy Management Console
- Using Windows PowerShell

Using the Group Policy Management Console

To create a Group Policy Object, perform the following steps:

1. Open the **Group Policy Management** Console (`gpmc.msc`).
2. In the left navigation pane, expand the **Forest** node.
3. Expand the **Domains** node, and then navigate to the domain where you want to create the GPO.
4. Expand the domain name and select the **Group Policy Objects** node:

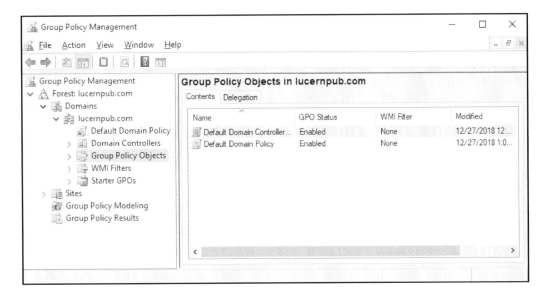

5. Right-click the **Group Policy Objects** node and select **New** from the menu.
6. In the **New GPO** popup window, enter the name of the GPO. Make sure that you don't select **Starter GPOs**.
7. Click **OK** to create the GPO.

You now have a GPO. However, it doesn't have any settings and it isn't linked—at least not yet.

Using Windows PowerShell

To create a GPO using Windows PowerShell, use the following lines of PowerShell:

```
Import-Module GroupPolicy

New-GPO -Name "New GPO Name"
```

How it works...

The Group Policy Management Console is the tool of choice to manage GPOs.

Regardless of the tool that's used, GPOs are created in the `Policies` container in Active Directory.

A GPO that is not linked to an OU, site, or domain does not have a justification and can be deleted without repercussions.

When creating one GPO, the graphical Group Policy Management Console is a great tool to use. When creating multiple GPOs or automating the process of creating GPOs, Windows PowerShell soon proves more efficient.

See also

To get things going with the GPO, refer to the *Linking a GPO to an OU* recipe.

Copying a GPO

This recipe shows you how to copy an existing GPO to a new GPO. This is useful when you have baked the perfect GPO, but want to adjust just a single setting to apply to legacy versions of the operating system or a test version of the same infrastructure in another OU.

Getting ready

To copy a GPO, log into a system with the Group Policy Management Console installed with an account that is either of the following:

- A member of the Domain Admins group
- Delegated to create GPOs

Additionally, the account should have at least read permissions on the Group Policy Object to be copied.

How to do it...

There are two ways to create a GPO:

- Using the Group Policy Management Console
- Using Windows PowerShell

Using the Group Policy Management Console

To create a GPO, perform the following steps:

1. Open the **Group Policy Management** Console (gpmc.msc).
2. In the left navigation pane, expand the **Forest** node.
3. Expand the **Domains** node, and then navigate to the domain where you want to copy a GPO.
4. Expand the domain name and then expand the **Group Policy Objects** node.
5. Locate the GPO that you want to copy.
6. Right-click the GPO and select **Copy** from the menu.
7. Right-click the **Group Policy Objects** node and select **Paste** from the menu. The **Copy GPO** popup window appears:

8. In the **Copy GPO** popup window, select **Preserve the existing permissions.** of the GPO or **Use the default permissions for new GPOs.**
9. In the **Copy** progress window, click **OK** to acknowledge that copying has succeeded.
10. The new GPO is now named **Copy of...**, referencing the source GPO name. Right-click the GPO in the left navigation menu and select **Rename** from the menu.

11. Enter the name of the GPO. Press *Enter* when done.

Using Windows PowerShell

To copy a GPO using Windows PowerShell, use the following lines of PowerShell:

```
Import-Module GroupPolicy

Copy-GPO -Sourcename "Existing GPO Name" -TargetName "New GPO Name"
```

How it works...

Copying a GPO is a sure way to create a GPO that is slightly different to an existing GPO. After copying a GPO, only the name is different when you choose to preserve the permissions.

If you didn't, your permissions on top of the default permissions would apply. The account that is used to copy the GPO would be the Group Policy owner.

There's more...

In a multi-domain Active Directory forest, copying a GPO between the Group Policy Objects node in one domain to the Group Policy Objects node in another domain is a sure way to keep settings identical across domains. It is especially useful in networking environments consisting of development, testing, acceptance, and production environments to stage GPOs.

Deleting a GPO

This recipe shows you how to delete a GPO . As part of this recipe, any GPO links that are present are first deleted to make sure that no stale references occur.

Getting ready

To delete a GPO, log into a system with the Group Policy Management Console installed with an account that is one:

- A member of the Domain Admins group
- The current owner of the GPO
- Delegated the **Edit settings, delete and modify security** permission on the GPO

How to do it...

There are two ways to delete a GPO:

- Using the Group Policy Management Console
- Using Windows PowerShell

Using the Group Policy Management Console

To delete a GPO, perform the following steps:

1. Open the **Group Policy Management** Console (gpmc.msc).
2. In the left navigation pane, expand the **Forest** node.
3. Expand the **Domains** node, and then navigate to the domain where you want to delete the GPO.
4. Expand the domain name, and then expand the **Group Policy Objects** node.
5. Locate the GPO that you want to delete.
6. Select the GPO.
7. In the main pane, on the **Scope** tab, check to see that the GPO is not linked to any GPO by inspecting the field for **The following sites, domains and OUs are linked to this GPO:**.
   If it's not empty, the GPO is still linked to OUs, sites, and/or domains. Remove these links by right-clicking them and selecting **Delete Link(s)** from the menu, before deleting the GPO.
8. In the left navigation pane, right-click the GPO and select **Delete** from the menu.
9. In the **Group Policy Management** popup window, click **OK** to answer the question **Do you want to delete this GPO and all links to it in this domain?**

This will not delete links in other domains.

Using Windows PowerShell

To delete a Group Policy Object using Windows PowerShell, use the following lines of PowerShell:

```
Import-Module GroupPolicy

Remove-GPO -Name "Existing GPO Name"
```

How it works...

When you delete a GPO, its links are not automatically deleted when the user account performing the delete does not have the permissions to manage the link. GPO links should be removed before deleting a GPO to avoid lingering GPO links.

See also

For more information, refer to the *Linking a GPO to an OU* recipe.

Modifying the settings of a GPO

This recipe shows how to modify settings in a Group Policy Object.

Getting ready

To manage settings in a GPO, log into a system with the Group Policy Management Console installed with an account that is one:

- A member of the Domain Admins group
- The current owner of the GPO
- Delegated the **Edit Settings** or **Edit settings, delete and modify security** permission on the GPO

How to do it...

Perform the following steps:

1. Open the **Group Policy Management** Console (gpmc.msc).
2. In the left navigation pane, expand the **Forest** node.
3. Expand the **Domains** node, and then navigate to the domain where you want to modify the GPO.
4. Expand the domain name and then expand the **Group Policy Objects** node.
5. Locate the GPO that you want to manage.
6. Select the GPO.
7. In the main pane, on the **Settings** tab, inspect the settings. Use the **show, hide,** and **show all** buttons to display the settings under their respective Group Policy setting nodes.
8. In the left navigation pane, right-click the GPO and select **Edit...** from the menu.
9. The **Group Policy Management Editor** (gpedit.msc) appears:

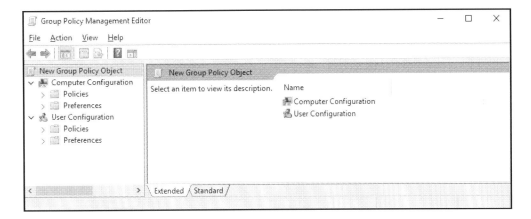

10. Edit the settings and/or preferences you want to edit in the **Group Policy Management Editor** window.
11. Close the **Group Policy Management Editor** window when you're done.

How it works...

When you manage the settings and/or preferences in a GPO, they become active immediately. There are slight delays due to replication and the Group Policy background refresh timeout (90 minutes by default, but with a 30-minute window of additional time, or 5 minutes for security settings).

Some settings and/or preference patterns cause GPOs to apply slowly. This might slow down device startups and user logons. Here are some tips:

- Please avoid configuring settings and policies in one GPO
- Please avoid setting **Computer Configuration** and **User Configuration** settings in one GPO, unless it's targeting Remote Desktop Session Hosts
- When you create a GPO with only **Computer Configuration**, disable **User Configuration** processing, and vice versa

Assigning scripts

This recipe you shows how to assign a logon script using Group Policies.

Getting ready

To manage settings for a GPO, log into a system with the Group Policy Management Console installed with an account that is one:

- A member of the Domain Admins group
- The current owner of the GPO
- Delegated the **Edit Settings** or **Edit settings, delete and modify security** permission on the GPO

How to do it...

Perform the following steps:

1. Open the **Group Policy Management** Console (`gpmc.msc`).
2. In the left navigation pane, expand the **Forest** node.
3. Expand the **Domains** node, and then navigate to the domain where you want to assign a logon script.

4. Expand the domain name and then expand the **Group Policy Objects** node.
5. Locate the GPO that you want to manage.
6. Select the GPO.
7. In the left navigation pane, right-click the GPO and select **Edit** from the menu. The **Group Policy Management Editor** (`gpedit.msc`) appears.
8. In the **Group Policy Management Editor** window, expand **User Configuration**, then **Policies** and **Windows Settings**.
9. Select **Scripts**.
10. In the main pane, right-click the **Logon** script and select **Properties** from the menu
11. In the **Logon** window, click the **Add...** button.
    The **Add a Script** popup window appears:

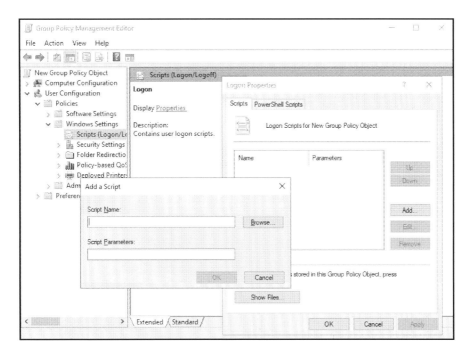

12. Type executable in the **Script Name:** field or browse to its location.
13. In the **Script Parameters:** field, type any optional script parameters.
14. Click **OK** to save the script settings.
15. Click **OK** to close the **Logon Properties** window.
16. Close the **Group Policy Management Editor** window.

How it works...

There are four types of script you can use with Group Policy:

- Logon scripts (**User Configuration**)
- Logoff scripts (**User Configuration**)
- Startup scripts (**Computer Configuration**)
- Shutdown scripts (**Computer Configuration**)

It is good practice to reference a script name in the Active Directory **System Volume** (**SYSVOL**). This way, unavailability of a server doesn't mean unavailability of the scripts you use to manage (part of) an environment. By default, when you type a script into the **Script Name** field, Group Policy assumes that the script is located in the `Scripts` folder in SYSVOL.

Installing applications

This recipe shows you how to install an application using Group Policy.

Getting ready

To manage settings for a Group Policy Object, log into a system with the **Group Policy Management** Console installed with an account that is one of the following:

- A member of the Domain Admins group
- The current owner of the Group Policy Object
- Delegated the **Edit Settings** or **Edit settings, delete and modify security** permission on the GPO

How to do it...

Perform the following steps:

1. Open the **Group Policy Management** Console (`gpmc.msc`).
2. In the left navigation pane, expand the **Forest** node.
3. Expand the **Domains** node, and then navigate to the domain where you want to install the application.

4. Expand the domain name and then expand the **Group Policy Objects** node.

5. Locate the GPO that you want to manage.

6. Select the GPO.

7. In the left navigation pane, right-click the GPO and select **Edit** from the menu. The **Group Policy Management Editor** (gpedit.msc) appears.

8. Expand **Computer Configuration** or **User Configuration**, depending on the kind of object you want to target the software installation to.

9. Expand the **Policies** node, and then the **Software Settings** node.

10. Right-click the **Software Installation** node and select **New** from the menu, and then **Package....**

11. In the **Open** screen, browse to the network share that has the package for the application as either an .msi or .zap file. Select the application and click **Open**. The **Deploy Software** popup screen appears:

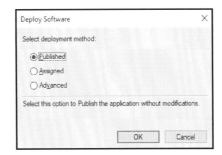

12. In the **Deploy Software** popup screen, select the deployment method.

13. Click **OK** to save the settings. The package will be listed with its version, its deployment state, and source path.

14. Close the **Group Policy Management Editor** window.

How it works...

Applications can be distributed to devices and user accounts using Group Policy. However, in medium and large-sized organizations, more advanced solutions are used, such as **System Center Configuration Manager** (**ConfigMgr**), because of the lack of advanced features, controls, and reporting in Group Policy.

To install an application package, point to the package on a shared folder, which is accessible to the objects you target the GPO to: Default share permissions are **Everyone – Full Control**, but default folders on Windows Servers are for **Users – Read**. When you deploy a package to devices, make sure that the UNC path is accessible to domain computers.

Assigned applications will deploy at logon (when this option is selected) or when a user clicks on the shortcut for the application or on a filetype associated with the application. Published applications (only available under **User Configuration**) will be installed when a user clicks on the shortcut for the application or on a filetype associated with the application, too. Published applications, however, can also be installed using **Apps and Features** on domain-joined devices.

Software installation settings are not processed when slow links are detected.

The **Advanced** button can be used to further specify settings for application installation, including but not limited to the presence of other application installations and versioning.

Linking a GPO to an OU

This recipe shows you how to link an existing GPO to an OU.

Getting ready

To link a GPO to an OU, log into a system with the Group Policy Management Console installed with an account that is one of the following:

- A member of the Domain Admins group
- The current owner of the GPO, and have the **Link GPOs** permission on the OU(s), Site(s), and/or Domain(s) where the Group Policy Object is to be linked
- Delegated the **Edit Settings** or **Edit settings, delete and modify security** permission on the GPO, and have the **Link GPOs** permission on the OUs, Site(s), and/or Domain(s) where the GPO is to be linked

How to do it...

Perform the following steps:

1. Open the **Group Policy Management** Console (gpmc.msc).
2. In the left navigation pane, expand the **Forest** node.
3. Expand the **Domains** node, and then navigate to the domain where you want to link the GPO.
4. Expand the domain name.
5. Navigate to the OU where you want to link an existing GPO.
6. Right-click the OU and select **Link an existing GPO...** from the menu:

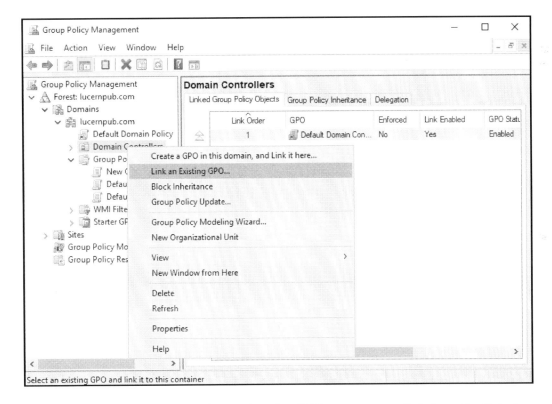

7. In the **Select GPO** window, select the GPO you want to link from the list of available **Group Policy objects:**.
8. Click **OK** to link the GPO.

How it works...

Without a link, a GPO is not applied to computer or user objects.

Despite the name Group Policy, GPOs cannot be linked to groups.

When a domain-joined device processes a Group Policy, it processes GPOs in this order:

- Locally defined Group Policy settings
- GPOs linked to sites
- GPOs linked to the domain the device resides in
- GPOs linked to the OUs in the OU structure down to the device object

When a user logs on, Group Policy is processed in the same order, except this time the domain and OU structure are defined by the location of the user object.

When there are overlapping settings in different GPOs linked in the preceding order, the last processed GPO with the setting wins.

When multiple GPOs are linked to the same OU, the GPO with the lowest link order wins, as the settings are applied in reverse sequence of the link order. Link order can best be seen as a priority when link enforcement and block inheritance don't come into play.

There's more...

Group Policy Objects can be linked to sites, domains, and an OU. It's a bad idea to link a GPO to a site due to the nature of intra-domain replication of GPOs.

Blocking inheritance of GPOs on an OU

This recipe shows you how to block inheritance of GPOs on an OU to circumvent GPOs in the OU structure applying settings.

Getting ready

To block inheritance of GPOs on an OU, log into a system with the Group Policy Management Console installed with an account that is any of the following:

- A member of the Domain Admins group
- The current owner of the GPO
- Delegated the **Edit Settings** or **Edit settings, delete and modify security** permission on the GPO

How to do it...

Perform the following steps:

1. Open the **Group Policy Management** Console (`gpmc.msc`).
2. In the left navigation pane, expand the **Forest** node.
3. Expand the **Domains** node.
4. Expand the domain name.
5. Navigate to the OU where you want to configure inheritance.
6. Right-click the OU and select **Block Inheritance** from the menu.

How it works...

The **Block Inheritance** and **Enforce** settings are two ways to manage how GPOs are processed.

In a situation where an OU structure, site, or domain governs settings through GPOs, and where these settings are unwanted, Group Policy inheritance can be managed. This way, any GPO will no longer be processed by computer objects and/or user objects in the OU that has inheritance blocked.

Managing inheritance is useful in environments where you want to strictly manage test environments. However, it does add complexity to the Group Policy infrastructure and may result in situations that are harder to troubleshoot.

Enforcing the settings of a GPO Link

This recipe shows you how to enforce a GPO link to make sure its settings always apply.

Getting ready

To enforce a GPO link, log into a system with the Group Policy Management Console installed with an account that is one of the following:

- A member of the Domain Admins group
- The current owner of the Group Policy Object
- Delegated the **Edit Settings** or **Edit settings, delete and modify security** permission on the GPO

How to do it...

Perform the following steps:

1. Open the **Group Policy Management** Console (`gpmc.msc`).
2. In the left navigation pane, expand the **Forest** node.
3. Expand the **Domains** node, and then navigate to the domain where you want to link the GPO.
4. Expand the domain name.
5. Navigate to the OU where you want to enforce the GPO link.
6. Expand the OU.
7. Right-click the GPO link you want to enforce and click **Enforced** in the menu to enable or disable it. A check mark indicates whether **Enforced** is enabled or not:

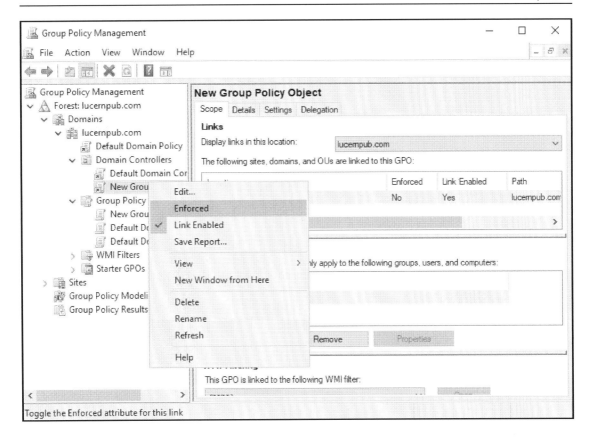

How it works...

The **Block Inheritance** and **Enforce** settings are two ways to manage how GPOs are processed.

In a complex environment where multiple conflicting GPOs may be applied, enforcing a GPO link ensures the GPO is processed and its settings are applied, regardless of Group Policy inheritance settings.

Applying security filters

Group Policy can be linked to OUs, but despite its name, not to groups. However, this recipe shows, how a security filter can be applied so that the GPO link only applies to members of a certain group.

Getting ready

To apply security filters on a GPO, log into a system with the Group Policy Management Console installed with an account that is one of the following:

- A member of the Domain Admins group
- The current owner of the Group Policy Object
- Delegated the **Edit Settings** or **Edit settings, delete and modify security** permission on the GPO

How to do it...

Perform the following steps:

1. Open the **Group Policy Management** Console (gpmc.msc).
2. In the left navigation pane, expand the **Forest** node.
3. Expand the **Domains** node, and then navigate to the domain where you want to apply security filters the GPO.
4. Expand the domain name and then expand the **Group Policy Objects** node.
5. Locate the Group Policy Object that you want to manage.
6. Select the Group Policy Object.
7. In the main pane, on the **Scope** tab, in the **Security Filtering** area, click the **Add...** button to add a group for security filtering.
8. In the **Select User, Computer or Group** window, type the name of a group and click the **Check Names** button.
9. Click **OK**. to add the group to **Security Filtering** for the GPO.
10. Select the default **Authenticated Users** entry and click the **Remove** button.
11. The **Group Policy Management** popup window appears:

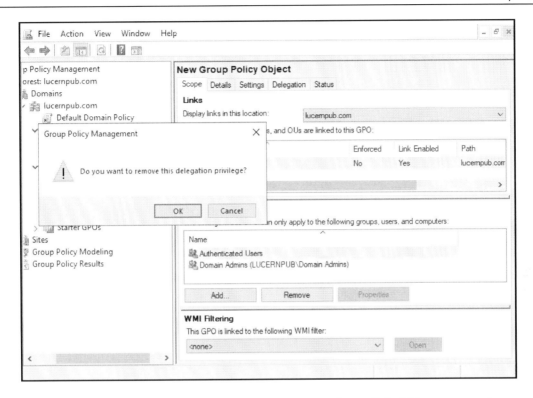

12. In the **Group Policy Management** popup window, click **OK** to answer the
    question **Do you want to remove this delegation privilege?.**

How it works...

By default, all Group Policy Objects have the **GpoApply** permission assigned to the
Authenticated Users group. This permission can be scoped down to a certain group by
removing the default permission and adding a scoped group. When the **GpoApply**
permission is absent, the settings in the GPO don't apply to each of its GPO links.

Since groups can be nested, security filtering can make Group Policy processing slow,
especially in multi-forest environments.

Creating and applying WMI Filters

This recipe shows you how to apply a WMI Filter so that GPOs only apply to certain domain-joined devices and systems.

Getting ready

To create WMI filters on a GPO, log into a system with the **Group Policy Management** Console installed with an account that is a member of the Domain Admins group.

To apply a WMI filter on a Group Policy Object, use an account that is either of the following:

- A member of the Domain Admins group
- Delegated the **Edit settings, delete and modify security** permission on the GPO

How to do it...

Perform the following steps:

1. Open the **Group Policy Management** Console (gpmc.msc).
2. In the left navigation pane, expand the **Forest** node.
3. Expand the **Domains** node, and then navigate to the domain where you want to apply WMI Filters.
4. Expand the domain name.
5. Right-click the **WMI Filters** node and select **New...** from the menu.
6. In the **New WMI Filter** window, enter a name for the new WMI Filter.
7. Optionally enter a description for the WMI Filter.
8. Click the **Add** button.
9. In the **WMI Query** window, select the WMI Namespace to target with the WMI Filter and enter the WMI Query:

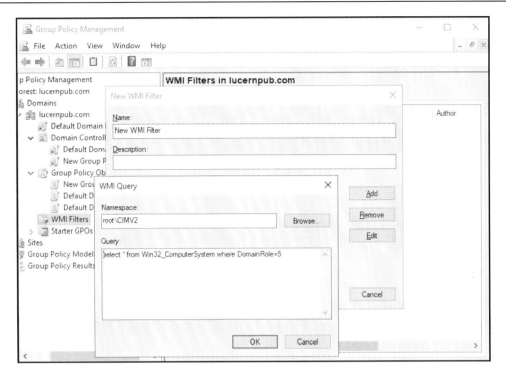

10. Click **OK** to save the WMI Query.
11. Click **Save** to create the WMI Filter.
12. In the left navigation pane, navigate to the **Group Policy Objects** node.
13. Select the GPO you want to apply the WMI Filter to.
14. In the main pane, on the **Scope** tab in the **WMI Filtering** area, select the WMI Filter.
15. In the **Group Policy Management** popup window, click **Yes** to answer the question **Would you like to change the WMI Filter to WMI Filter name?**.

How it works...

WMI filters can be used to target specific systems in the scope of the GPO throughout all its GPO links, based on the specifications of the device.

Only one WMI filter can be applied at one time for a GPO. Use WMI filters with caution, because they can seriously impact the performance of Group Policy processing.

There's more...

One of the perfect uses of WMI filters is a filter that targets only the domain controller holding the **Primary Domain Controller emulator (PDCe) Flexible Single Master Operations (FSMO)** role for a Group Policy that sets the Windows time service to synchronize time with a reliable external time source.

Configuring loopback processing

This recipe shows you how to configure Group Policy loopback processing.

Getting ready

To configure Group Policy loopback processing, log into a system with the Group Policy Management Console installed with an account that is one of the following:

- A member of the Domain Admins group
- The current owner of the Group Policy Object
- Delegated the **Edit Settings** or **Edit settings, delete and modify security** permission on the GPO

How to do it...

Perform the following steps:

1. Open the **Group Policy Management** Console (gpmc.msc).
2. In the left navigation pane, expand the **Forest** node.
3. Expand the **Domains** node, and then navigate to the domain where you want to create the GPO.
4. Expand the domain name and then expand the **Group Policy Objects** node.
5. Locate the GPO that you want to manage.
6. Select the GPO.
7. In the left navigation pane, right-click the GPO and select **Edit...** from the menu. The **Group Policy Management Editor** (gpedit.msc) appears.
8. In the **Group Policy Management Editor** window, expand **Computer Configuration**, **Policies**, then **Administrative Templates**, **System** and finally **Group Policy**.

9. In the main pane, locate the **Configure user Group Policy loopback processing mode** setting and double-click it.

The **Configure user Group Policy loopback processing mode** properties window appears:

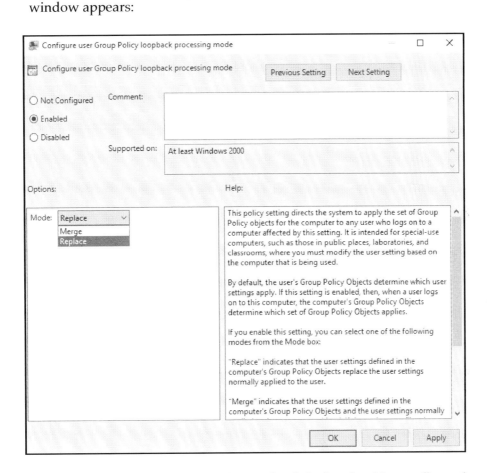

10. In the settings popup window, change the default value **Not configured** to **Enabled.**
11. From the **Mode** drop-down menu, select either **Merge** or **Replace** (default).
12. Click **OK** to save the setting.
13. Close the **Group Policy Management Editor** window.

How it works...

In Group Policy loopback processing mode, Group Policy processing is changed. In normal circumstances, the **Computer Configuration** parts of GPOs are processed by the computer object and the **User Configuration** parts of GPOs are processed for the user account. In loopback processing mode, though, Group Policy processing is different. It can be configured in two ways:

- **Merge mode**: In merge mode, any GPOs that are applicable to the user object will be processed first. The GPOs applicable to the computer object will be applied afterwards. This way, the user account will still correctly process any settings applicable to the account, but settings configured for the computer account override when there are conflicts.
- **Replace mode**: In replace mode, any GPOs that are applicable to the user object will not be processed. Only the settings in the GPOs applicable to the computer object will be applied.

Group Policy loopback processing mode is ideal for implementations of Remote Desktop Session Hosts and other Remote Desktop, Terminal Server, and **Virtual Desktop Infrastructure (VDI)** implementations.

Restoring a default GPO

This recipe shows you how to restore the default domain policy and the Default Domain Controller Policy to default settings.

Getting ready

To restore the Default Domain Policy and the Default Domain Controller Policy to default settings, log into a domain controller (a non-read-only domain controller) with an account that is a member of the Domain Admins group.

How to do it...

1. Use the following command to restore the default domain policy to its default settings on an elevated Command Prompt (cmd.exe):

```
dcgpofix.exe /target:Domain
```

2. Use the following command to restore the default domain controller policy to its default settings on an elevated Command Prompt (`cmd.exe`):

   dcgpofix.exe /target:DC

3. Use the following command to restore the **Default Domain Policy** and the **Default Domain Controller Policy** to its default settings on an elevated Command Prompt (`cmd.exe`):

   dcgpofix.exe /target:Both

How it works...

When you want to revert to the default settings for the **Default Domain Policy** and the **Default Domain Controller Policy**, or if you've deleted them, they can be easily restored using the `dcgpofix.exe` command-line utility.

There's more...

Since there have been changes to the Default Domain Policy and the Default Domain Controller Policy across versions of Windows Server and the Active Directory schema, `dcgpofix.exe` checks the schema version. If the schema level is different to the current domain controller operating system, `dcgpofix.exe` displays the following message:

    The Active Directory schema version for this domain and the version
    supported by this tool do not match. The GPO can be restored using the
    /ignoreschema command-line parameter. However, it is recommended that you
    try to obtain an updated version of this tool that might have an updated
    version of the Active Directory schema. Restoring a GPO with an incorrect
    schema might result in unpredictable behavior.

Creating the Group Policy Central Store

This recipe shows you how to configure the Group Policy Central Store in the SYSVOL to optimize Group Policy authoring and replication.

Getting ready

Implement or locate a default Windows client device with Microsoft Office and any other software that supports Group Policy management. Install language packs for the languages that are used by admins in your organization. Update this system with the latest available updates.

To create the Group Policy Central Store, log into a domain controller (a non-read-only domain controller) or access the SYSVOL over the network with an account that is a member of the Domain Admins group.

How to do it...

Perform the following steps:

1. Log on to the default Windows client device for your organization.
2. Open **File Explorer.**
3. Navigate to the Windows System location, typically `C:\Windows`.
4. Locate the `PolicyDefinitions` folder.
5. Right-click the `PolicyDefinitions` folder and select **Copy** from the menu.
6. Navigate the current **File Explorer** window to the Active Directory SYSVOL, for instance, `\\lucernpub.com\SYSVOL\lucernpub.com`.
7. In the SYSVOL, navigate to the `Policies` folder.
8. Right-click an empty space and select **Paste** from the menu.
9. Navigate to the `C:\Program Files (x86)\Microsoft Group Policy` folder, if it exists.
10. Copy the `PolicyDefinitions` folder in the latest version folder and paste it in the same location as step 7.

How it works...

Since Windows Server 2008 and Windows Vista, Group Policy settings in the **Administrative Templates** parts of GPOs are represented on the filesystem by the `*.admx` files and `*.adml` files. The first type of file defines the settings. The latter type of file provides language-dependent labels, so administrators using different languages can work together seamlessly.

Beyond the language benefit, the new filetypes also allow for a central store to store all Group Policy settings and language settings in the SYSVOL. This way, files for configured settings no longer have to be stored with each GPO in SYSVOL, but only once in SYSVOL. This optimizes Group Policy replication between domain controllers significantly.

There's more...

Creating the Group Policy Central Store requires a process that is revisited when new versions of software are introduced in the organization. Overwrite the `*.adml` and `*.admx` files with the newer versions.

10
Securing Active Directory

From a business perspective, Active Directory needs to be an available, confidential attribute store with absolute integrity. The security measures in this chapter detail how to achieve a higher level of confidentiality and integrity.

The following recipes will be covered in this chapter:

- Applying fine-grained password and account lockout policies
- Backing up and restoring GPOs
- Backing up and restoring the Active Directory database
- Working with Active Directory snapshots
- Managing the DSRM passwords on domain controllers
- Implementing LAPS
- Managing deleted objects
- Working with group Managed Service Accounts
- Configuring the advanced security audit policy
- Resetting the KRBTGT secret
- Using SCW to secure domain controllers
- Leveraging the Protected Users group
- Putting authentication policies and authentication policy silos to good use
- Configuring Extranet Smart Lockout

Applying fine-grained password and account lockout policies

Active Directory comes with a built-in password policy. Admins can configure stricter password policies and account lockout policies. This way, privileged accounts can be configured with more secure password and account lock-out settings. This recipe shows how.

Getting ready

To apply fine-grained password and account lockout policies, you should sign into a domain controller or a member server and/or device with the **Remote Server Administration Tools** (**RSAT**) for Active Directory Domain Services installed. Ideally, the domain controller or member server runs Windows Server 2012, or a newer version of Windows Server.

Sign in with an account that is a member of the Domain Admins group, or with an account that is delegated to fine-grained password and account lockout policies in the domain.

Fine-grained password and account lockout policies require the Windows Server 2008 **Domain Functional Level** (**DFL**), or a higher version of the DFL.

How to do it...

There are two ways to manage fine-grained password and account lockout policies:

- Using the Active Directory Administrative Center
- Using the Active Directory module for Windows PowerShell

Using the Active Directory Administrative Center

Follow these steps to create and apply a fine-grained password and account lock-out policy in the Active Directory Administrative Center:

1. Open the **Active Directory Administrative Center** (dsac.exe).
2. In the left navigation window, switch to **Tree view**.
3. Navigate to the **Password Settings Container** under the **System** container:

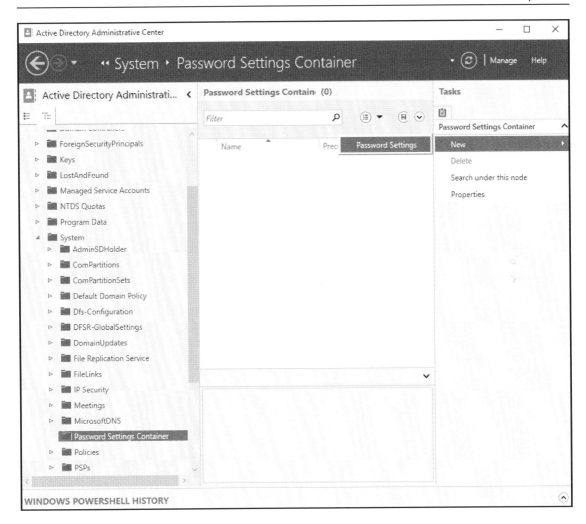

4. Right-click the **Password Settings Container** and select **New** and then **Password Settings** from the menu.
   The **Create Password Settings** screen appears.
5. In the **Create Password Settings** screen, in the **Password Settings** section, fill in values for the **Name** and **Precedence** fields.
6. Enable every setting that you want to apply to meet the requirements by selecting them.

There is no inheritance from other fine-grained password and account lockout policies. Only one policy applies to any user account. Define all the settings that you want to apply.

7. In the **Directly applies to** section, press the **Add...** button.
8. In the **Select Users or Groups** window, type the name of the user account(s) or groups you want to fine-grained password policy to directly apply to, or click the **Advanced** button to search for the user account(s) and/or groups.
9. Click **Check Names**.
10. Click **OK** to have the fine-grained password policy directly apply to the user(s) and/or group(s).
11. Click **OK** to create the fine-grained password and account lock-out policy.

Using the Active Directory Module for Windows PowerShell

To create a fine-grained password and account lock-out policy, use the following lines of PowerShell on a system with the Active Directory Module for Windows PowerShell installed:

```
Import-Module ActiveDirectory

New-ADFineGrainedPasswordPolicy PolicyName -ComplexityEnabled $true
-LockoutDuration "00:30:00" -LockoutObservationWindow "00:30:00"
-LockoutThreshold "5" -MaxPasswordAge "42.00:00:00" -MinPasswordAge
"7.00:00:00" -MinPasswordLength "15" -PasswordHistoryCount "21" -Precedence
"1" -ReversibleEncryptionEnabled $false -ProtectedFromAccidentalDeletion
$true
```

To apply a fine-grained password and account lock-out policy, use the following lines of PowerShell on a system with the Active Directory Module for Windows PowerShell installed:

```
Import-Module ActiveDirectory

Add-ADFineGrainedPasswordPolicySubject PolicyName -Subjects GroupName
```

How it works...

Active Directory comes with a built-in password policy. This is the password policy that is automatically set at the Active Directory domain level. This default policy does not enable account lock-out.

The password policy applies when the password is changed and when it is set by an admin. Account lockout policies observe bad password attempts. When a bad password is typed, it is added to the bad password count. When this count reaches the limit within the time specified as the observation period, the account is locked for the duration of the time-out period. Accounts can be locked indefinitely. In this case, accounts need to be unlocked by a person using their admin account or otherwise privileged account.

Admins can configure stricter password policies and also account lockout policies on the domain level, but they can also configure these policies granularly as follows:

- Per user account
- Per group

Only one password policy can apply. When multiple fine-grained password policies are applied, the policy applied to a user account directly applies. When a user account has memberships in multiple groups, the password policy with the lowest value for precedence is applied. All other password policies are ignored. The precedence value can be interpreted as a priority. Specifying unique precedence values for password policies is key to having the right policy applied.

In scenarios where lock-out is configured identically over all password policies, the maximum lifetime for the password makes for an excellent precedence value.

There's more...

When you're unsure which fine-grained password and account lock-out policy applies, look at the user account's **msDS-ResultantPSO** attribute. It exposes the reference to the password policy that is applied.

The `Get-ADUserResultantPasswordPolicy` PowerShell cmdlet can also be used for this purpose.

Backing up and restoring GPOs

The Group Policy Management Console does not offer to rollback changes in **Group Policy Objects (GPOs)**. However, when in the process of modifying a GPO, a step is added to create a backup of the GPOs, inadvertent settings can be rolled back by restoring a previous backup.

This recipe shows what that step would look like and how to restore a GPO.

Getting ready

You should sign into a domain controller or a member server and/or device with the RSAT for Active Directory Domain Services installed. Ideally, the domain controller or member server runs Windows Server 2012, or a newer version of Windows Server.

Sign in with an account that is a member of the Domain Admins group.

In contrast to the delegation of creating, linking, managing, editing, and reading GPOs, backing up and restoring GPOs cannot be delegated.

How to do it...

Follow these steps to back up GPOs:

1. Open the **Group Policy Management** Console (`gpmc.msc`).
2. In the left navigation pane, expand the forest, then the **Domains** node and then the domain for which you want to backup the GPOs.
3. Select the **Group Policy Objects** node and right-click it.
4. From the menu, select **Back Up All...**.
   The **Back Up Group Policy Object** window appears:

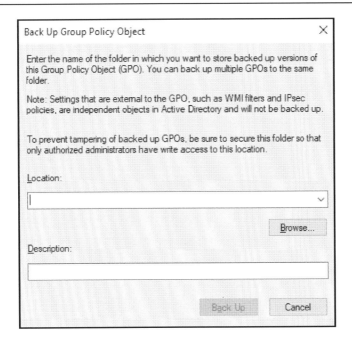

5. In the **Back Up Group Policy Object** window, for **Location:** provide a location to store the backups. Use the **Browse...** button to locate and/or create a folder for Group Policy backups.

6. Provide a description in the **Description:** field.

7. Click the **Back Up** button.

8. In the **Backup** window, review the statistics of the backup and click **OK** when done.

Follow these steps to restore inadvertent settings for a GPO:

1. Open the **Group Policy Management** Console (`gpmc.msc`).

2. In the left navigation pane, expand the forest, then the **Domains** node, and then the domain for which you want to restore a GPO.

3. Expand the **Group Policy Objects** node and locate the GPO you want to restore from a previous backup.

4. Select the GPO to restore.

5. Right-click the GPO and select **Restore from Backup** from the menu. The **Restore Group Policy Wizard** window appears:

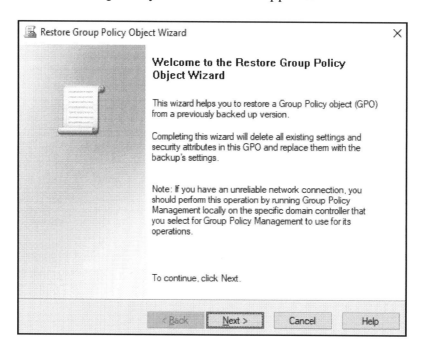

6. On the **Welcome to the Restore Group Policy Object Wizard** screen, Click **Next >**.

7. On the **Backup Location** screen, type the location of previous backups, or use the **Browse...** button to look it up. Click **Next >**.

8. On the **Source GPO** screen, select the GPO which you want to restore. Click **Next >**.

9. On the **Completing the Restore Group Policy Object Wizard screen,** click **Finish** to start restoration.

10. In the **Restore** window, review the outcome, and click **OK** when done.

Follow these steps to restore an inadvertently deleted GPO:

1. Open the **Group Policy Management** Console (`gpmc.msc`).

2. In the left navigation pane, expand the forest, then the **Domains** node and then the domain for which you want to restore a GPO.

3. Select the **Group Policy Objects** node and right-click it.

4. From the menu, select **Manage Backups...**.

5. Click the **Browse** button to navigate to the folder that contains the previous backups.

6. Select the GPO(s) that you want to restore from the backup.

7. Click **Restore** to start restoration.
   The **Group Policy Management** popup window appears:

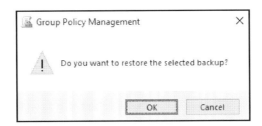

8. In the **Group Policy Management** popup window, click **OK**.

9. In the **Restore** window, review the outcome, and click **OK** when done.

How it works...

When you create backups of GPOs, the settings for these objects are stored in a backup file. Then, when inadvertent changes are made to these objects, they can be restored from the backup file.

Depending on the purpose of the GPO backup, the location to store the backups can be on the domain controller or in a remote location. Storing on a domain controller may be a good option for a fast restore test, duplicating group policies between Active Directory forests, or versioning. However, for true backups, always use a remote location.

Alternatively, you can implement the **Advanced Group Management Tool (AGPM)**.

There's more...

Backups for GPOs can only be restored in the same Active Directory forest. To recreate GPOs from one Active Directory forest to another, use the **Export** and **Import** functionality in the Group Policy Management Console.

Backing up and restoring Active Directory

To avoid the situation where Active Directory, the backbone of every Microsoft-oriented networking infrastructure, is irreversibly lost, Active Directory restores should be performed. Restores should be performed regularly in an isolated environment to make sure backups can be restored and procedures are up to date and known to admins.

This recipe shows how to create backups of Active Directory using Windows Backup.

Getting ready

To make a backup of a domain controller, sign into a domain controller with a user account that is a member of the Domain Admins group or of the Backup Operators group.

To restore a domain controller, you need to know the **Directory Services Restore Mode** (**DSRM**) password for the domain controller.

First off, the Windows Backup feature needs to be installed. Use the following PowerShell one-liner in an elevated PowerShell window to do so:

```
Install-WindowsFeature Windows-Server-Backup
```

To avoid any dependencies on Active Directory-integrated network and file access, make sure you back up to a dedicated (USB) hard drive for physical domain controllers or to a separate LUN in the virtualization fabric for virtual domain controllers. When working with USB hard disks, purchase at least two devices for off-site storage options and replacement upon failure scenarios.

How to do it...

Follow these steps to create backups of a domain controller:

1. Log on to the domain controller.
2. Plug in the dedicated hard drive or LUN to which you want to back up. Install drivers, if necessary.
3. Start **Server Manager** (`servermanager.exe`) if it doesn't start automatically by default.
4. From the **Tools** menu in the top grey bar, choose **Windows Server Backup**.
5. In the left navigation pane, select **Local Backup**.

6. In the action pane on the right side of **Windows Server Backup**, click **Backup Schedule...**.

The **Backup Schedule Wizard** window appears:

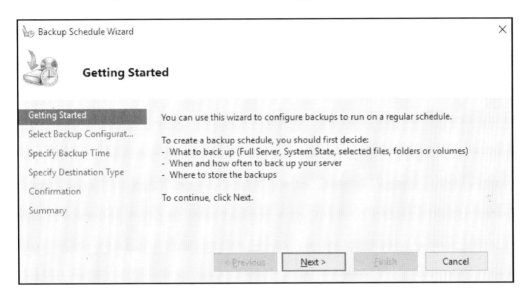

7. In the **Getting Started** screen, click **Next >**.

8. In the **Select Backup Configuration** screen, select **Full Server (recommended)**. Alternatively, select **Custom**, but in this case, always select the **System State** on the **Select Items for Backup** screen as part of the backup configuration if you want to be able to restore the domain controller functionality from the backups. Click **Next >**.

9. In the **Specify Backup Time** screen, select **Once a day**. Choose a time that is outside the typical opening hours or working day(s) in your organization. If you have other processes running out-of-hours, be sure not to collide with them. Click **Next >**.

10. In the **Specify Destination Type** screen, select **Back up to a hard disk that is dedicated for backups (recommended)**. Click **Next >**.

11. In the **Select Destination Disk** screen, select the removable disk to backup to and click **Next >**.

12. In the **Confirmation** screen, click **Finish**.

Windows Server Backup can also be used on the Command Prompt (cmd.exe). To create an instant System State Backup to a hard disk attached as F:\, use the following command on an elevated Command Prompt (cmd.exe):

```
wbadmin.exe start systemstatebackup --backuptarget:F:
```

Follow these steps to restore a backup of a domain controller:

1. Start the domain controller in DSRM.
2. Log on to the domain controller with the username **Administrator** and the DSRM password as the password.
3. Plug in the dedicated hard drive or LUN where you want to restore from.
4. Start **Server Manager** (servermanager.exe) if it doesn't start automatically by default.
5. From the **Tools** menu in the top grey bar, choose **Windows Server Backup**.
6. In the left navigation pane, select **Local Backup**.
7. In the action pane on the right side of **Windows Server Backup**, click **Recover....** The **Recovery Wizard** appears:

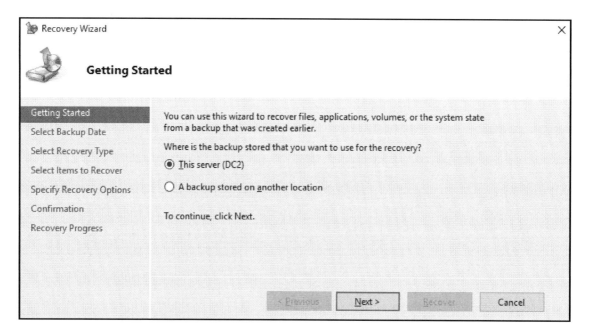

8. In the **Getting Started** screen, select the **This server (DC2)** option and click **Next >**.

9. In the **Select Backup Date** screen, select the backup to restore. Click **Next >**.

10. In the **Select Recovery Type** screen, select **System State** and click **Next >**.
You reach the **Select Location for System State Recovery** screen:

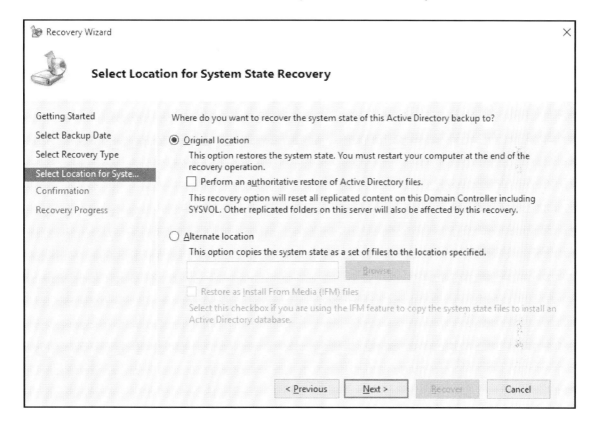

11. In the **Select Location for System State Recovery** screen, select **Original location** and click **Next >**.
Optionally, select the **Perform an authoritative restore of Active Directory files.** option.

12. In the **Confirmation** screen, click **Finish**.

13. After restoration, restart the domain controller normally.

Command Prompt (`cmd.exe`) is also available in this scenario; use the following command to get the backups on the hard disk connected as `F:\`:

```
wbadmin.exe get versions

wbadmin.exe start systemstaterecovery --version:04/26/2019-21:00
```

Add the `--AuthSysvol` parameter if you want to restore the domain controller authoritatively.

How it works...

By creating a backup of the system state, all the information to restore a domain controller is copied off the system and onto removable media. This way, when a domain controller becomes non-functional, the backup can be used to restore the functionality to a new Windows Server or to boot up from the backup media to restore the entire domain controller.

Windows Server Backup uses Volume Shadow Copies with the Active Directory VSS Writer to make a backup of the Active Directory files while they are in use. This way, there is no need to stop the Active Directory Domain Services service to make a consistent backup. In most third-party applications, this functionality is called **Application-consistent backups**.

Domain controllers can be restored authoritatively or non-authoritatively. When restored authoritatively, the restored domain controller will take the role of authoritative replication partner for Active Directory and SYSVOL replication; all domain controllers will assume that its version of the database and SYSVOL are the truth. When restoring non-authoritatively, the domain controller will report itself as a new Active Directory replication partner and replicate from other domain controllers, ignoring any changes it might have made before being restored.

The DSRM password for the domain controller is stored on the system and provides the ability to logon with a local administrator account when the Active Directory Domain Services service is not running. When the service runs on a domain controller, this password cannot be used. Document the password properly.

As modern malware attacks on environments feature invalidating backups, make sure to store backups for domain controller off the network, and ideally off-site.

Working with Active Directory snapshots

This recipe shows how to work with Active Directory snapshots as an alternative to having to restore entire backups for a domain controller to restore a couple of objects.

Getting ready

To work with snapshots for a domain controller, sign into a domain controller with a user account that is a member of the Domain Admins group or of the Backup Operators group.

How to do it...

1. To make a snapshot, type the following command in an elevated Command Prompt (cmd.exe) window:

   ```
   ntdsutil.exe "activate instance ntds" "snapshot" "create" q q
   ```

2. To view all snapshots, type the following command in an elevated Command Prompt (cmd.exe) window to get a numbered list of all available snapshots:

   ```
   ntdsutil.exe "activate instance ntds" "snapshot" "list all" q q
   ```

3. To mount a snapshot, type the following command in an elevated Command Prompt (cmd.exe) window, using the number of the snapshot you want to mount from the previous command:

   ```
   ntdsutil.exe "activate instance ntds" "snapshot" "mount GUID" q q
   ```

   The preceding command will output the folder where the database is mounted.

4. Run the following command to expose it as an LDAP Store:

   ```
   dsamain.exe -dpbath "Location from previous command" -ldapport
   PortNumber
   ```

Keep this command running for as long as you want the LDAP Server running.

To look up information, use the cmdlets in the Active Directory Module for Windows PowerShell. Specify the -Server parameter and type the hostname of the server, and the port number separated by a semi-colon, as follows:

```
Get-ADComputer -Identity * -Server Localhost:PortNumber
```

How it works...

Snapshots for Active Directory may be useful in scenarios where the organization has a need to compare information from a certain point in time (the time the snapshot was taken) with the information from another point in time (for instance: today).

Creating an Active Directory snapshot requires the Volume Shadow Copy functionality and a functional Active Directory VSS Writer. These features are available by default on Windows Server. However, if anything is not working, check them first.

There's more...

When you want to transfer information between a snapshot and the Active Directory, we can use tools like `ldifde.exe` and `csvde.exe`. There is no native tooling available to perform these kinds of actions.

Managing the DSRM passwords on domain controllers

This recipe shows how to manage the password to sign in to domain controllers when the Active Directory Domain Services service is not running.

Getting ready

To make a backup of a domain controller, sign into a domain controller with a user account that is a member of the Domain Admins group, the Backup Operators group, or the Server Operators group.

For the scenario where the DSRM Administrator password is automatically synchronized with an account in Active Directory, create a disabled user account with a strong password. Document the password in a password vault. Additionally, make sure all domain controllers run Windows Server 2008, or newer versions of Windows Server.

How to do it...

1. To manually reset the DSRM Administrator password on a domain controller, type the following command in an elevated Command Prompt (`cmd.exe`) window when the domain controller is running fine:

   ```
   ntdsutil.exe
   > set dsrm password
   > reset password on server null
   ```

2. Type or paste the password to use as the DSRM Administrator password:

   ```
   > quit
   > quit
   ```

3. To synchronize the DSRM Administrator password on a domain controller, type the following command in an elevated Command Prompt (`cmd.exe`) window, when the domain controller is running and replicating fine:

   ```
   ntdsutil.exe "set dsrm password" "sync from domain account
   DSRMDCXUser" quit quit
   ```

As there is no interaction needed with the preceding command and there are no passwords involved, this command line is suitable to be placed on one line and, therefore, suitable to be rolled out using Group Policy preferences.

How it works...

When the Active Directory Domain Service service is not running, or the domain controller is non-functional, you'll need a way to log on to the domain controller. As the Active Directory database is not available, a special password is maintained for the domain controller-local built-in Administrator account.

When a Windows Server-based member server is promoted to a domain controller, this password is configured as the DSRM Administrator password.

The password can be managed in two ways:

- The manual reset scenario
- The domain account password sync scenario

In the first scenario, the password is set manually per domain controller and then to be documented in a password vault.

In the second scenario, the domain controller is instructed to synchronize the password from a specific Active Directory account. This password is then set manually and then to be documented.

A recommended practice is to have different passwords for each domain controller and reset the passwords yearly.

Implementing LAPS

Microsoft's free **Local Administrator Password Solution** (**LAPS**) allows admins to periodically change the password for the local administrator password on domain-joined devices. This recipe shows how to implement and use it.

Getting ready

First, download LAPS from `http://aka.ms/LAPS`. Download the `*.msi` file that corresponds to the client operating system architecture(s) used in the organization. Most likely, this will be x64.

Make sure that all domain controllers in the environment run Windows Server 2003 with Service Pack 1 or a newer version of Windows Server.

If your organization places devices in the default Computers container, move the computer objects that you want to be part of LAPS from this container to an **Organizational Unit** (**OU**) dedicated to devices.

How to do it...

There are two sides to LAPS; implementing it and managing it.

Implementing LAPS

Implementing LAPS requires four steps:

Extending the schema

Follow these steps to extend the Active Directory schema with the LAPS extensions:

1. Sign into a domain controller or Windows Server-based management server that has .NET Framework 4.0 installed (or a newer version of the .NET Framework) with an account that is a member of the **Schema Administrators** group.
2. Double-click the MSI installer to install LAPS on the Windows Server.
3. Follow the instructions to install LAPS.
4. Open an elevated PowerShell window and type the following two lines of PowerShell to import the LAPS PowerShell module, and then to extend the Active Directory schema:

```
Import-Module AdmPwd.PS

Update-AdmPwdADSchema
```

Setting permissions

Next, we need to set permissions in Active Directory to enable devices to write to the new **mS-MCS-AdmPwd** and **mS-MCS-AdmPwdExpirationTime** attributes. Follow these steps:

1. Sign into the domain controller or Windows Server-based management server that has LAPS installed with an account that is a member of the **Domain Admins** group, or is delegated **Full Control** over the OU containing the devices in scope for LAPS (and its child OUs).

Open an elevated PowerShell window and type the following two lines of PowerShell to import the LAPS PowerShell module, and then to set the permissions on the OU with devices:

```
Import-Module AdmPwd.PS

Set-AdmPwdComputerSelfPermission -OrgUnit "OU ShortName"
```

Do not run the preceding PowerShell command on the entire directory, as it would include domain controllers, too. We don't want domain controllers to reset the built-in Administrator account every 30 days...

Creating the GPO to install the LAPS Client-side Extensions

As outlined in *Installing Applications* recipe, from `Chapter 9`, *Getting the Most Out of Group Policy*, follow these steps to install the LAPS **Client-side Extensions (CSEs)**:

1. Log into a system with the **Group Policy Management** Console (`gpmc.msc`) installed with an account that is either a member of the Domain Admins group, or the current owner of an existing GPO, or delegated the **Edit Settings** or **Edit settings, delete and modify security permission** on an existing GPO.
2. Open the **Group Policy Management** Console (`gpmc.msc`).
3. In the left pane, navigate to the **Group Policy objects** node.
4. Locate the Group Policy Object that you want to use and select it, or right-click the **Group Policy Objects** node and select **New** from the menu.
5. Right-click the Group Policy object and select **Edit...** from the menu.
   The Group Policy Management Editor window appears.
6. In the main pane of the Group Policy Management Editor window, expand the **Computer Configuration** node, then **Policies** and the **Software Settings** node.
7. Right-click the **Software Installation** node and select **New** from the menu, and then **Package...**.
8. In the **Open** screen, browse to the network share that has the LAPS MSI package. Select the application and click **Open**.
9. In the **Deploy Software** popup screen, select **Assigned**.
10. Click **OK** to save the settings. The package will be listed with its version, its deployment state and source path.
11. In the left navigation window, expand the **Administrative Templates** node and then the **LAPS** node.
12. Double-click the **Enable local admin password management** setting and enable it.
13. Click **OK**.
14. Double-click the **Do not allow password expiration time longer than required by policy** setting and enable it.
15. Click **OK**.
16. Close the **Group Policy Management Editor** window.

Linking the GPO to OUs with devices

As outlined in *Linking a GPO to an OU* recipe from `Chapter 9`, *Getting the Most Out of Group Policy*, follow these steps to link the GPO to OUs with devices in scope for LAPS:

1. Log into a system with the **Group Policy Management** Console feature installed with an account that is either a member of the Domain Admins group, or the current owner of the Group Policy Object, and have the **Link GPOs** permission on the OU(s), Site(s), and/or Domain(s) where the Group Policy Object is to be linked, or is delegated the **Edit Settings,** or **Edit settings, delete and modify security permission** on the GPO, and have the **Link GPOs** permission on the Organizational Unit(s) where the Group Policy Object is to be linked.
2. Open the **Group Policy Management** Console (`gpmc.msc`).
3. In the left navigation pane, navigate to the OU where you want to link the LAPS GPO.
4. Right-click the OU and select **Link an existing GPO...** from the menu.
5. In the **Select GPO** window, select the LAPS GPO.
6. Click **OK** to link the GPO.

Repeat steps 4-6 to link the LAPS GPO to all OUs that require the LAPS GPO. Take **Block Inheritance** into account for OUs by linking the LAPS GPO specifically to include all devices in its scope.

Managing passwords

After LAPS is implemented, the passwords in LAPS' Active Directory attributes can be viewed and managed. The LAPS UI is the preferred tool to manage passwords:

Viewing an administrator password

Follow these steps to view an administrator password:

1. Sign into the domain controller or Windows Server-based management server that has LAPS installed with an account that is a member of the **Enterprise Admins** group or the **Domain Admins** group.
2. Start the LAPS UI from the Start Menu of the Start Screen.
3. In the LAPS UI Window, enter a device name in the **ComputerName** field or use the **Search** button to search for a device.

4. The password is shown in the **Password** field, together with the moment the **Password expires**.

5. Press **Exit** to close the LAPS UI.

Resetting an Administrator password

Follow these steps to reset an administrator password:

1. Sign into the domain controller or Windows Server-based management server that has LAPS installed with an account that is a member of the **Enterprise Admins** group or the **Domain Admins** group.

2. Start the LAPS UI from the Start Menu of the Start Screen:

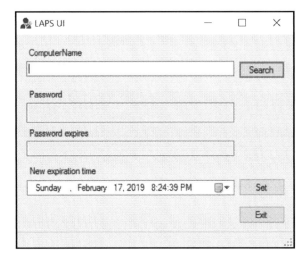

3. In the **LAPS UI** window, enter a device name in the **ComputerName** field or use the **Search** button to search for a device.

4. Press the **Set** button to immediately expire the password and have the LAPS CSE on the device communicate with Active Directory to set a new password and reset the **Password expires** timeframe.

5. Press **Exit** to close the **LAPS UI**.

How it works...

The Local Administrator Password Solution has three components:

- The LAPS GPO instructs domain-joined devices in scope with settings.
- The LAPS Client-side Extensions set and exchange clear-text passwords with Active Directory, based on the GPO.
- The LAPS attributes for computer objects in Active Directory store passwords and expiration timeframes for LAPS. Devices have SELF permissions to write to these attributes.

Passwords for local Administrator accounts are stored in clear-text in the LAPS attributes. The **Filtered Attribute Set (FAS)** protects these attributes from view. By default, only members of the Enterprise Admins and Domain Admins group have access to these attributes. The FAS relies on domain controllers running Windows Server 2003 Service Pack 1, or newer versions of Windows Server, to work reliably.

See also

Refer to the *Installing applications* recipe, in `Chapter 9`, *Getting the Most Out of Group Policy*.

Refer to the *Linking a GPO to an OU* recipe, in `Chapter 9`, *Getting the Most Out of Group Policy*.

Managing deleted objects

This recipe shows how to manage deleted objects in an Active Directory environment with the Active Directory Recycle Bin enabled.

Getting ready

To manage deleted objects, sign into a domain controller, a Windows Server-based management server with the RSAT for Active Directory Domain Services installed, or a Windows installation with the Remote Server Administration Tools installed with an account that is a member of the **Domain Admins** group.

How to do it...

There are two ways to manage deleted objects:

- Using the Active Directory Administrative Center
- Using Windows PowerShell

Using the Active Directory Administrative Center

To manage deleted objects using the Active Directory Administrative Center, perform these steps:

1. Open the **Active Directory Administrative Center** (dsac.exe).
2. In the left navigation pane, switch to **Tree view**.
3. Navigate to the **Deleted Objects** container.
4. Perform one of these actions:
   - When the object to restore is an Organizational Unit, expand the **Deleted Objects** container and select the OU to restore. Right-click it and select **Restore** from the menu.
   - When the object to restore is a user object, computer object, or group, select it in the main pane. Right-click it and select **Restore** from the menu.

Using Windows PowerShell

To view the deleted objects for a domain, use the following lines of PowerShell on a system with the Active Directory Module for Windows PowerShell installed:

```
Import-Module ActiveDirectory

Get-ADObject -ldapFilter:"(msDS-LastKnownRDN=*)" -IncludeDeletedObjects
```

To restore a deleted object, use the following lines of PowerShell on a system with the Active Directory Windows PowerShell Module installed:

```
Import-Module ActiveDirectory

Get-ADObject -Filter {displayName -eq "DisplayNameOfTheObject"} -IncludeDeletedObjects | Restore-ADObject
```

How it works...

When the Active Directory Recycle Bin is not enabled, objects that are deleted are tombstoned. This allows domain controllers to replicate the deletion. When the Active Directory Recycle Bin is enabled, deleted objects are not tombstoned immediately, but recycled first.

In this state, deleted objects are shown in the **Deleted Objects** container. Objects can be restored from this container to their original location or to a different container, including all their group memberships and other attributes.

There's more...

In the Active Directory Administrative Center, multiple objects can be selected in the main view by selecting them, or by using the *Shift* and *Ctrl* keys. Then, the selection can be used to restore multiple objects at once.

See also

For more information on the Active Directory Recycle Bin, look at *Enabling the Active Directory Recycle Bin* recipe from `Chapter 1`, *Optimizing Forests, Domains, and Trusts*.

Working with group Managed Service Accounts

This recipe shows how to work with **group Managed Service Accounts (gMSAs)**.

Getting ready

To create gMSAs, the Active Directory domain needs to have at least one domain controller running Windows Server 2012 or a newer version of Windows Server.

gMSAs can only be used to run services on domain-joined hosts running Windows Server 2012, or newer versions of Windows Server, or Windows 8, or newer versions of Windows. For the automatic password and **Service Principal Name (SPN)** management, the domain needs to run at least the Windows Server 2008 R2 **Domain Functional Level (DFL)**.

As gMSAs depend on the Key Distribution Service on domain controllers, prepare the forest by running the following lines of PowerShell on a system with the Active Directory module for Windows PowerShell:

```
Import-Module ActiveDirectory

Add-KdsRootKey -EffectiveImmediately
```

How to do it...

1. To create a gMSA, use the following lines of PowerShell on a system with the Active Directory Module for Windows PowerShell installed:

   ```
   Import-Module ActiveDirectory

   New-ADServiceAccount MSAName -DNSHostName
   DomainController.domain.tld
   -PrincipalsAllowedToRetrieveManagedPassword
   "CN=AppServer1,CN=Computers,DC=LucernPub,DC=com"
   ```

2. To install the gMSA on an application server so that it can be assigned to run a service, application, or application pool, use the following line of PowerShell:

   ```
   Install-ADServiceAccount -Identity MSAName
   ```

How it works...

Service accounts are notoriously hard for admins to get right. User objects are reused for this purpose and they are typically over-privileged, not secured enough, and admins rarely change the passwords for these accounts out of fear of breaking functionality.

Managed Service Accounts (MSAs) were introduced in Windows Server 2008 R2 to solve this problem. In Windows Server 2012, MSAs were superseded by gMSAs. Since then, when you create this type of object as an admin, you create a gMSA, by default.

The main difference between an MSA and a gMSA is that a gMSA can be used as a service account on more than one server, where an MSA is limited to one server.

gMSAs are `msDS-GroupManagedServiceAccount` objects. They are not based on user objects, but on computer objects. Just as with computer objects, they are prohibited from logging on interactively to systems, and automatically change their passwords every 30 days, by default. This makes them much more secure than service accounts based on user objects.

gMSAs use a password that is stored in the `msDS-ManagedPassword` attribute of the object. Only domain-joined servers that are listed in the `msDS-GroupMSAMembership` attribute are provided access to the attribute by the Key Distribution Service on domain controllers.

Although the line of PowerShell to create a gMSA specifies the Root Key to be effective immediately with the `-EffectiveImmediately` switch, you will actually have to wait 10 hours for it to become active. This ensures that there is ample time to replicate the information to other domain controllers.

There's more...

The interval that gMSAs use to change their passwords can be controlled using the `msDS-ManagedPasswordInterval` attribute. Even if password changes for computer objects has been turned off, gMSAs will continue to change their passwords. If the interval can be higher in your environment because strict regulations don't apply, set the attribute to a higher value (in days) when creating gMSAs.

Configuring the advanced security audit policy

This recipe shows how to configure the advanced security audit policy.

Getting ready

To configure the advanced security audit policy, sign into a domain controller with a user account that is a member of the Domain Admins group.

How to do it...

Follow these steps to configure the advanced security audit policy:

1. Open the **Group Policy Management** Console (`gpmc.msc`).
2. In the left pane, navigate to the **Domain Controllers** node for the domain in which you want to configure the advanced security audit policy.
3. Right-click the **Default Domain Controllers Policy** and select **Edit...** from the menu.
   The Group Policy Management Editor window opens.
4. In the left navigation window, expand the **Computer Configuration**, **Policies**, **Windows Settings**, **Security Settings**, **Advanced Audit Policy Configuration**, **Audit Policies**, and then **DS Access**:

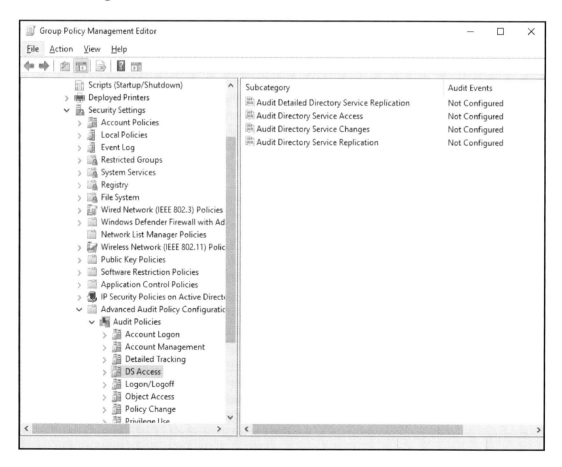

5. Double-click the **Audit Directory Service Changes** setting. The **Audit Directory Service Changes Properties** window opens.
6. Check the **Configure the following auditing events:**. Then, check to audit **Success** and/or **Failure** audit events.
7. Click **OK** to save the settings and close the **Audit Directory Service Changes Properties** screen.
8. Close the **Group Policy Management Editor** window.

How it works...

Microsoft introduced the advanced security audit policy in Active Directory in Windows Server 2008 R2. This feature offers more granular auditing options in 10 categories:

- Account Logon
- Account Management
- Detailed Tracking
- DS Access
- Logon/Logoff
- Object Access
- Policy Change
- Privilege Use
- System
- Global Object Access Auditing

For each of these categories, several auditing options are available. When these are enabled, additional entries are added to Event Viewer with the source **Microsoft Windows security auditing**.

A recommended practice is to copy auditing events from event viewer logs on the domain controller to a centralized **Security Incident and Event Management** (**SIEM**) solution.

Resetting the KRBTGT secret

This recipe shows how to reset the password of the KRBTGT account.

Getting ready

To reset the password for the KRBTGT account, sign into a domain controller with a user account that is a member of the Domain Admins group.

How to do it...

Perform the following lines of PowerShell:

```
Import-Module ActiveDirectory

Set-ADAccountPassword -Identity (Get-ADUser krbtgt).DistinguishedName
-Reset -NewPassword (ConvertTo-SecureString "Rand0mCompl3xP@ssw0rd!"
-AsPlainText -Force)
```

How it works...

Each Active Directory domain in a multi-domain environment has its own KRBTGT account used by all fully-writable domain controllers. Each read-only domain controller has its own **KRBTGT_*** account.

The password hash for the KRBTGT account is used as the secret to encrypt all Kerberos tickets.

The password for KRBTGT is set during the creation of an Active Directory domain. Microsoft only automatically reset the secret on the KRBTGT account for Active Directory domains when the Domain Functional Level was upgraded to Windows Server 2008.

A malicious person would not just be able to read all Kerberos authentication traffic. When a malicious person wants to attain a foothold in an Active Directory, the most common way to do so is by forging tickets, as in a *golden ticket attack*. As ticket control in Active Directory is client-side, malicious people may (re)use forged Kerberos tickets for as long as 10 years.

The only way to lock out malicious persons using forged Kerberos tickets is to reset the password for KRBTGT with different values. However, the process for signing tickets is designed to handle these password changes without locking out legitimate use. Any ticket that has been signed before the password change will use the fallback method provided for the TGT lifetime. This lifetime, by default, is 7 days.

Replication convergence may take time throughout a large Active Directory environment. Therefore, the password for KRBTGT needs to be reset twice with an interval in between.

Microsoft's recommendation is to reset the password for KRBTGT twice per year.

There's more...

Microsoft offers a script on the TechNet Gallery to automate the processes of generating complex passwords, changing the password, and checking for proper replication: `https://gallery.technet.microsoft.com/Reset-the-krbtgt-account-581a9e51`

Using SCW to secure domain controllers

This recipe shows how to secure domain controllers running older versions of Windows Server, using the Windows Server **Security Configuration Wizard** (**SCW**) and Group Policy.

Getting ready

To secure domain controllers using SCW, sign into a domain controller with a user account that is a member of the Domain Admins group.

The Security Configuration Wizard was removed from Windows Server 2016 and is not present in Windows Server versions since this version. Features are secured by default. This recipe applies to full installations of the following Windows Server versions:

- Windows Server 2008
- Windows Server 2008 R2
- Windows Server 2012
- Windows Server 2012 R2.

How to do it

Securing domain controllers using the Windows Server **Security Configuration Wizard** (**SCW**) and Group Policy consists of two steps:

1. Secure a representative domain controller using SCW.
2. Roll out the security settings to all domain controllers using Group Policy.

Secure a representative domain controller using SCW

Follow these steps to secure one of your domain controllers using SCW:

 Follow these steps on a domain controller in a test environment to test the settings in the context of routine administration processes before rolling the settings out to all production domain controllers.

1. Open **Server Manager** (`servermanager.exe`).
2. From the **Tools** menu in the top grey pane, select **Security Configuration Wizard**.
3. On the **Welcome** screen, click **Next**.
4. On the **Configuration Action** screen, select **Create a new security policy** option.
5. Click **Next**.
6. On the **Select Server** screen, select the local server. Click **Next >**.
7. On the **Role-based Service Configuration** screen, click **Next >**.
8. On the **Select Server Roles** screen, click **Next >**.
9. On the **Select Server Features** screen, click **Next >**.
10. On the **Select Administration and Other Options** screen, click **Next >**.
11. On the **Select Additional Services** screen, click **Next >**.
12. On the **Handling Unspecified Services** screen, select the **Disable the service** option and click **Next >**.
13. On the **Confirm Service Changes** screen, click **Next >**.
14. On the **Network Security** screen, click **Next >**.
15. On the **Network Security Rules** screen, click **Next >**.
16. On the **Registry Settings** screen, click **Next >**.
17. On the **Require SMB Security Signatures** screen, check the properties of the Windows Server. These properties determine the SMB signing settings.
18. Click **Next >**.

19. On the **Require LDAP Signing** screen, select the **Windows 2000 Service Pack 3 or later** option.
20. Click **Next >**.
21. On the **Outbound Authentication Methods** screen, check the **Domain Accounts** option.
22. Click **Next >**.
23. On the **Outbound Authentication using Domain Accounts** screen, select both options to require NTLM version 2.
24. Click **Next >**.
25. On the **Inbound Authentication Methods** screen, deselect all options unless your environment contains devices running Windows XP.
26. Click **Next >**.
27. On the **Registry Settings Summary** screen, click **Next >**.
28. On the **Auditing Policy** screen, click **Next >**.
29. On the **System Auditing Policy** screen, select the **Audit successful and unsuccessful activities**.
30. Click **Next >**.
31. On the **Audit Policy Summary** screen, click **Next >**.
32. On the **Save Security Policy** screen, click **Save**.
33. Save the file with its `.xml` extension.
34. On the **Apply Security Policy** screen, click **Next >**.
35. On the **Application Complete** screen, click **Finish**.

Roll-out the security settings to all domain controllers using Group Policy

Run the following command line on an elevated Command Prompt (`cmd.exe`) to convert the settings file into a Group Policy Object:

```
scwcmd.exe transform /p:"C:\Windows\security\msscw\Policies\test.xml"
/g:"Domain Controller Security Settings"
```

The preceding command creates the Group Policy with the name **Domain Controller Security Settings**.

Next, link the new Group Policy object to the **Domain Controllers** Organizational Unit (OU), using the following steps:

1. Open the **Group Policy Management** Console (`gpmc.msc`).
2. In the left navigation pane, expand the **Forest** node.
3. Expand the **Domains** node, and then navigate to the domain where you want to link the GPO.
4. Expand the domain name.
5. Navigate to the **Domain Controllers** OU.
6. Right-click the OU and select **Link an existing GPO...** from the menu.
7. In the **Select GPO** window, select the GPO you want to link from the list of available **Group Policy objects:**.
8. Click **OK** to link the GPO.

How it works...

The Windows Server Security Configuration Wizard guides admins through the following settings:

- Permitted Server Roles and Server Features
- Permitted remote access
- Permitted services
- SMB and LDAP settings
- Auditing settings

This way, the wizard allows for straightforward management of these settings.

While the settings can be applied on a per-domain controller basis, a Group Policy can be applied with the settings, after the file is converted to a GPO using `scwcmd.exe`. After that, the GPO can be linked to the **Domain Controllers** OU to apply the settings to all domain controllers.

Leveraging the Protected Users group

This recipe shows how the Protected Users group can be used to protect privileged and sensitive accounts.

Getting ready

To use the Protected Users group, make sure the domain runs the Windows Server 2012 R2 DFL, or a newer version of the level. Also, be aware that the protections offered by the Protected Users group only apply when accounts that are members of the group are used on devices running Windows 8.1 or newer, Server 2012 R2 or newer.

To manage the Protected Users group, sign into a domain controller or a member server and/or device with the RSAT for Active Directory Domain Services installed. Sign in with an account that is a member of the Domain Admins group, the Account Operators group or with an account that is delegated to manage groups in the domain or in the scope of the OU.

How to do it...

There are three ways to manage group memberships in Active Directory:

- Using Active Directory Users and Computers
- Using the Active Directory Administrative Center
- Using Windows PowerShell

Using Active Directory Users and Computers

Follow these steps to add user accounts to the **Protected Users** group using Active Directory Users and Computers:

1. Open **Active Directory Users and Computers** (dsa.msc).
2. From the **Action** menu, select **Find...**. In the **Name** field, type the **Protected Users**, and press *Enter*. From the list of **Search results:** select the group.
3. Right-click the group and select **Properties** from the menu.
   The **Protected Users Properties** window will now appear.
4. Navigate to the **Members** tab.
5. Click **Add...** to add users, contacts, computers, service accounts or groups to the group.

6. In the **Select Users, Contacts, Computers, Service Accounts, or Groups** window, type the name of the user account(s) you want to add to the group, or click the **Advanced** button to search for the user account(s).

7. Click **Check Names**:

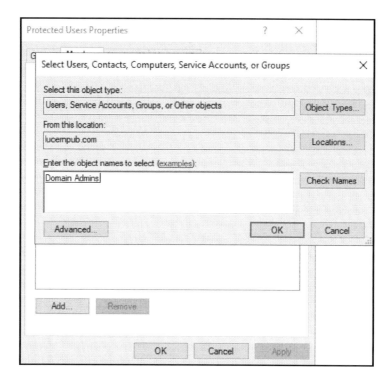

8. Click **OK** to add the user, contact, computer, service account, or group to the **Protected Users** group.

9. Click **OK** to close the **Protected Users Properties** window and save the changes.

Using the Active Directory Administrative Center

Follow these steps to add user accounts to the **Protected Users** group using the Active Directory Administrative Center:

1. Open the **Active Directory Administrative Center** (dsac.exe).

2. From the main pane menu, under **Global Search**, type the name of the group, and press *Enter*.

3. From the list of **Global Search** results, select the group.

4. Right-click the group and select **Properties** from the list.
5. In the left navigation pane, click **Members**.
6. Click **Add...** to add users, contacts, computers, service accounts, or groups to the group.
7. In the **Select Users, Contacts, Computers, Service Accounts, or Groups** window, type the name of the user account(s) you want to add to the group, or click the **Advanced** button to search for the user account(s).
8. Click **Check Names**.
9. Click **OK** to add the user to the group.
10. Click **OK** to close the **Group Properties** window and save the changes.

Using Windows PowerShell

Use the following lines of PowerShell to add a user to the **Protected Users** group in Active Directory on a system with the Active Directory Module for Windows PowerShell installed:

```
Import-Module ActiveDirectory

Add-ADGroupMember -Identity "CN=Protected
Users,CN=Users,DC=lucernpub,DC=com" -Members "User"
```

How it works...

The **Protected Users** group is a new feature in Active Directory in Windows Server 2016. Accounts that are members of the group lose the ability to do the following:

- Use cached logons.
- Use outdated authentication protocols, such as NTLM, Digest Authentication, and CredSSP.
- Use weak encryption algorithms, such as DES and RC4, for Kerberos pre-authentication.
- Be delegated as part of both **Kerberos Constrained Delegation** (**KCD**) and Kerberos unconstrained delegation.
- Use and renew their Kerberos **Ticket Granting Ticket** (**TGT**) for longer than 240 minutes, compared to the default 10-hour validity and 7-day renewal periods.

The preceding protections are non-configurable.

The Protected Users group is ideal for privileged and sensitive user accounts, such as members of the Domain Users group. Don't add service accounts, MSAs, gMSAs, or computer objects as members to the Protected Users group, as it may break their functionality.

Putting authentication policies and authentication policy silos to good use

This recipe shows how to use Authentication Policies and Authentication Policy Silos.

Getting ready

To use Authentication Policies and Authentication Policy Silos, make sure the domain runs the Windows Server 2012 R2 DFL, or a newer version of the level. Also, be aware that the protections offered by the Authentication Policies and Authentication Policy Silos only apply when accounts that are members of the group are used on devices running Windows 8.1 or newer versions of Windows or Windows Server 2012 R2 or newer versions of Windows Server.

To manage Authentication Policies and Authentication Policy Silos, sign into a domain controller or a member server and/or device with the RSAT for Active Directory Domain Services installed. Sign in with an account that is a member of the **Domain Admins** group.

How to do it...

Putting Authentication Policies and Authentication Policy Silos to good use consists of five steps:

- Enable domain controller support for claims.
- Enable compound claims on devices in scope for an authentication policy.
- Create an Authentication Policy.
- Create an Authentication Policy Silo.
- Assign the Authentication Policy Silo.

Enable domain controller support for claims

Follow these steps to enable domain controller support for claims:

1. Open the **Group Policy Management** Console (gpmc.msc).
2. In the left navigation pane, expand the **Forest** node.
3. Expand the **Domains** node, and then navigate to the domain where you want to enable compound claims on devices.
4. Expand the domain name.
5. Right-click the **Group Policy Objects** node and select **New** from the menu.
6. In the **New GPO** popup window, enter the name of the Group Policy Object. Make sure you don't select a Starter GPO.
7. Click **OK** to create the GPO.
8. Expand the **Group Policy Objects** node.
9. Locate the Group Policy Object that you want to manage.
10. Select the Group Policy Object.
11. In the left navigation pane, right-click the GPO and select **Edit** from the menu. The Group Policy Management Editor (gpedit.msc) appears.
12. In the Group Policy Management Editor window, expand **Computer Configuration**, then **Policies, Windows Administrative Settings**, and **System**.
13. Select **KDC**.
14. In the main pane, right-click the **KDC support for claims, compound authentication, and Kerberos armoring** setting and select **Properties** from the menu.

15. Click **Enabled**, as shown in the following screenshot:

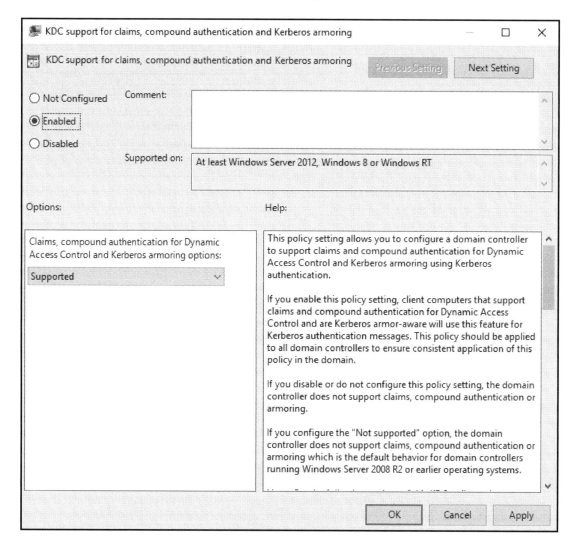

16. Click **OK** to close the Group Policy Management Editor window.
17. Link this Group Policy to the **Domain Controllers** Organizational Unit (OU) by right-clicking the OU in the left pane and selecting **Link an existing OU** from the menu.
18. In the **Select GPO** window, select the GPO you want to link from the list of available **Group Policy objects:**.
19. Click **OK** to link the GPO.

Enable compound claims on devices in scope for an authentication policy

Follow these steps to enable compound claims on devices in scope for an authentication policy:

1. Create another Group Policy by repeating previous steps 5-7, and start editing it by repeating steps 8-11 from the previous list of steps.
2. In the Group Policy Management Editor window, expand **Computer Configuration**, then **Policies, Windows Administrative Settings**, and **System**.
3. Select **Kerberos**.
4. In the main pane, right-click the **Kerberos client support for claims, compound authentication, and Kerberos armoring** setting and select **Properties** from the menu.
5. Click **Enabled:**

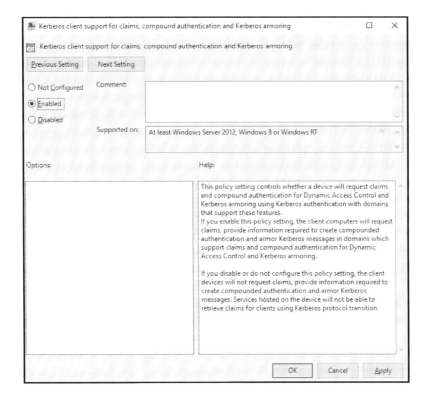

6. Click **OK** to close the Group Policy Management Editor window.
7. Link the second Group Policy to the Organizational Unit(s) with devices in scope, or to the domain by repeating steps 17-19 from the previous list of steps.

To restrict administrators from using certain devices, do not apply the preceding Group Policy object to the Organizational Unit(s) containing these devices.

Create an Authentication Policy

Follow these steps to create an Authentication Policy:

1. Open the **Active Directory Administrative Center** (`dsac.exe`).
2. In the left navigation window, switch to **Tree view**.
3. In the left navigation pane, click **Authentication**.
4. In the main pane select the **Authentication Policies** node.
5. In the **Tasks** pane to the right, click **New** under **Authentication Policies**.
6. Select **Authentication Policy** from the menu.
   The **Create Authentication Policy** screen appears:

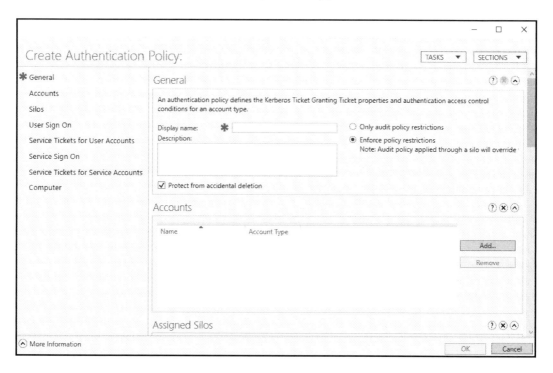

7. Provide a name for the authentication policy in the **Display name:** field.

8. Optionally, you can also provide a **Description:**.

9. In the left navigation pane, click **User Sign On**.

10. Select the settings you want to configure, such as the **Specify a Ticket Granting Ticket lifetime for user accounts.** option. Then, select a value between 45 and 2147483647 (2^{31}-1)for the **Ticket-Granting-Ticket Lifetime (minutes):** to limit the lifetime for the TGT for objects in scope for this Authentication Policy.

11. Click **OK** to close the **Create Authentication Policy** window and save its settings.

Create an Authentication Policy Silo

Follow these steps to create an Authentication Policy Silo:

1. Open the **Active Directory Administrative Center** (dsac.exe).

2. In the left navigation pane, click **Authentication**.

3. In the main pane select the **Authentication Policy Silos** node.

4. In the **Tasks** pane to the right, click **New** under **Authentication Policy Silos**. The **Create Authentication Policy Silo** window appears:

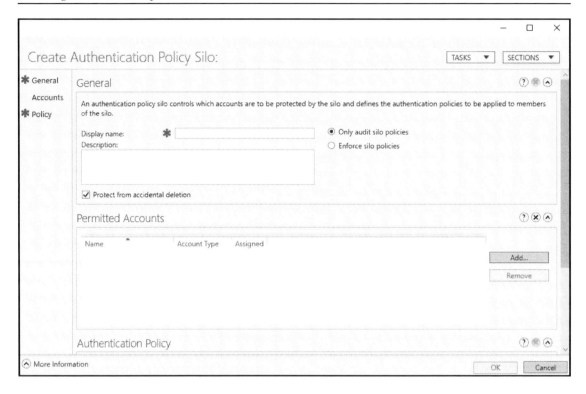

5. Provide a name for the authentication policy silo in the **Display name:** field.

6. Optionally, you can also provide a **Description:**.

7. As the behavior for this authentication policy silo, select **Enforce silo policies**.

8. In the left navigation pane, select **Accounts**.

9. In the list of **Permitted Accounts:**, add the accounts for which you want the policy silo to apply. Use the **Add...** button to add accounts.

10. In the left navigation pane, select **Policy**.

11. Select the **Use a single policy for all principals that belong to this authentication policy silo** option.

12. In the **authentication policy that applies to all accounts in this silo:** field, select the Authentication Policy you created in the previous steps from the drop-down list.

13. Click **OK** to close the **Create Authentication Policy Silo** window and save its settings.

Assign the Authentication Policy Silo

Follow these steps to assign the Authentication Policy Silo:

1. Open the **Active Directory Administrative Center** (`dsac.exe`).
2. In the left navigation pane, click **Authentication**.
3. Under the **Authentication Policy Silos** node, select the Authentication Policy Silo you created earlier.
4. Right-click it and select **Properties** from the menu.
5. In the left pane click **Permitted Accounts**.
6. Double-click the first item in the **Permitted Accounts:** list to open its properties. The properties window for the account will now open.
7. In the left pane, click **Silo**.
8. In the **Authentication Policy Silo** section, select the **Assign Authentication Policy Silo** option. Use the drop-down list for **Authentication Policy Silo:** to select the Authentication Policy silo created earlier.
9. Click **OK** to save the Authentication Policy Silo DN in the object's **msDS-AssignedAuthNPolicySilo** attribute.
10. Repeat steps 5-8 for all other accounts in the list of **Permitted Accounts:**.
11. Click **OK** to close the **Create Authentication Policy Silo** window.

How it works...

Using Authentication Policies and Authentication Policy Silos is a perfect way to set the scene for Microsoft's *Privileged Access Workstation* strategy to prevent people from signing in with their privileged account to devices other than their secure ones. This way, lateral movement toward admin (cached) credentials is hugely limited, benefiting the overall security posture of the organization.

Authentication Policies define policies, but do not assign these policies to accounts. Authentication Policy Silos assign policies to accounts. An Authentication Policy can be assigned through many Authentication Policy Silos, as the policies need to be the same, but for different audiences of accounts.

When a person tries to log on with an account that is governed by an Authentication Policy on a device that does not support claims, compound authentication, and Kerberos armoring, signing into the device will be prohibited with the following error:

```
Your account is configured to prevent you from using this PC. Please try
another PC.
```

Configuring Extranet Smart Lock-out

This recipe shows how to configure Extranet Smart Lock-out on an **Active Directory Federation Services** (**AD FS**) farm running Windows Server 2016, or a newer version of Windows Server.

Getting ready

When using AD FS on Windows Server, make sure at least the June 2018 Cumulative update for Windows Server 2016 (KB4284880 (https://support.microsoft.com/en-us/help/4284880/windows-10-update-kb4284880), OS build 14393.2312), is installed on all AD FS servers in the AD FS farm.

Sign in with an account that is an AD FS Administrator. By default, members of the **Domain Admins** group have the required permissions. Sign into the primary AD FS server when the AD FS farm is using the **Windows Internal Database** (**WID**) as its replication model, or any AD FS server when the AD FS farm leverages SQL Server as its configuration database.

How to do it...

To enable Extranet Smart Account Lock-out for an AD FS farm running SQL Server, run the following lines of PowerShell to update the AD FS Artifact Store:

 These three lines of PowerShell do not need to be run on AD FS farms using Windows Internal Database.

```
$cred = Get-Credential

Import-Module ADFS

Update-AdfsArtifactDatabasePermission -Credential $cred
```

To enable Extranet Smart Account Lock-out for an AD FS farm, run the following lines of PowerShell:

```
Import-Module ADFS

Set-AdfsProperties -ExtranetLockoutThreshold 10
```

```
Set-AdfsProperties -ExtranetObservationWindow (New-Timespan -minutes 5)

Set-AdfsProperties -EnableExtranetLockout $true

Set-AdfsProperties -ExtranetLockoutMode AdfsSmartLockoutEnforce

Restart-Service adfssrv
```

How it works...

When adding AD FS to an environment running Active Directory, the last thing you want is for AD FS to have a negative impact on the overall information security of the environment.

AD FS adds Extranet Lockout to the Active Directory (fine-grained) password and account lock-out policies to prevent malicious persons from locking out accounts with incorrect password attempts from the internet. However, when the AD FS Extranet Lockout threshold is reached, the account cannot be used for the period of the AD FS Extranet Lockout duration to authentication to AD FS-integrated resources (while authenticating to other resources will work without a hitch).

To prevent this latter scenario, enable Extranet Smart Lockout. With this feature enabled, IP addresses for successful authentications by users are logged as familiar IPs in the **AccountActivity** table for the account. For this IP address, the regular AD FS threshold still applies and each legitimate user may still lock himself or herself out, like always.

The difference occurs, when authentications start to fail for the account from unfamiliar IP addresses. The failed authentication count for that IP address is incremented, and when the lock-out threshold is reached, authentication attempts from that specific unfamiliar IP address are locked out. However, legitimate users do not experience any lock-outs from their familiar IP addresses.

Microsoft recommends using more strict lock-out settings for AD FS (Smart Account Lock-out) than for Active Directory (fine-grained) password and account lock-out policies to make sure AD FS authentication attempts to do not lock out accounts in Active Directory itself.

11
Managing Federation

Active Directory Domain Services (AD DS) has been around for 20 years. Its interactions are based on protocols, such as NTLM and Kerberos, that Microsoft has invented and/or expanded on. In fact, these protocols originated before some companies were even connected to the internet era; they were intended for safe networks. However, today, there's a need for open protocols, which are usable on all networks, allowing for interactions without technology boundaries. **Active Directory Federation Services (AD FS)** allows for these interactions.

AD FS was initially purposed for organization-to-organization collaboration without a need to set up and maintain AD trusts. Recently, it gained traction as the common way to implement single sign-on between AD DS on-premises and Azure AD.

The following recipes will be covered in this chapter:

- Choosing the right AD FS farm deployment method
- Installing the AD FS server role
- Setting up an AD FS farm with Windows Internal Database
- Setting up an AD FS farm with SQL Server
- Adding additional AD FS servers to an AD FS farm
- Removing AD FS servers from an AD FS farm
- Decommissioning an AD FS farm
- Creating a Relying Party Trust (RPT)
- Deleting an RPT
- Configuring branding
- Setting up a Web Application Proxy
- Decommissioning a Web Application Proxy

Choosing the right AD FS farm deployment method

Before implementing AD FS, it's useful to have a plan for configuring it so that it integrates with the existing networking infrastructure, strategy, and intended use in the organization. Use this recipe to make the right choices.

Getting ready

Before choosing the right AD FS farm deployment method, it's a good idea to get to know the organization. For example, its size and its intended use of AD FS will set the requirements for the number of AD FS servers that you will need. Its network layout may determine the available bandwidth between the datacenters and the AD FS servers in these datacenters.

Many organizations are consolidating SQL Server installations to more centralized SQL Server clusters and Always On Availability groups. All three models are supported by the AD FS database(s), but some caveats do exist.

In organizations, it's normal to have preferences in terms of Windows Server operating system versions. Due to licensing constraints, organizations may want to stick with Windows Server 2012 R2 for AD FS. It is important that you are aware of these preferences.

Create an inventory of the applications that the organization wants to make available through AD FS. Depending on the applications that you want to make available through AD FS authentication, features such as Artifact Resolution might be required.

How to do it...

If the organization employs fewer than 1,500 people, and/or if fewer than 1,500 people use the AD FS farm at peak moments, then the organization only needs one single AD FS server to meet the required capacity.

When more capacity or redundancy is required, a choice has to be made.

When deploying an AD FS farm on Windows Server 2016 (or a later version), you will need to deploy a SQL Server Cluster or SQL Server Always On Availability group to host the AD FS database under the following circumstances:

- When more than 30 SQL Servers are required
- When AD FS Management should be performed on any AD FS server
- When the advanced AD FS features (such as Artifact Resolution and Token Replay Detection) are required
- When the organization prefers SQL Server to host the database

Otherwise, deploy the AD FS farm with **Windows Internal Database** (**WID**), replicating between the primary AD FS server and the other AD FS servers.

How it works...

There are three types of AD FS deployments, as follows:

- A single AD FS server using the WID
- Using the WID on each AD FS server in the farm, replicating through SQL Server replication
- Using a SQL Server

A single AD FS server using WID offers a cost-effective AD FS solution but no redundancy, and capacity for approximately 1,500 concurrent sessions at peak moments.

When deploying multiple AD FS servers, these servers need a way to exchange the AD FS farm information.

The WID deployment model can scale up to 30 servers in the latest versions of Windows Server, but in previous versions, it couldn't scale that far:

Windows Server version	WID scale limit
Windows Server 2008 Windows Server 2008 R2 Windows Server 2012 Windows Server 2012 R2	5 AD FS servers
Windows Server 2016 Windows Server 2019	30 AD FS servers

The preceding scale limit only applies to AD FS servers, and not to AD FS Proxies or Web Application Proxies attached to the AD FS farm.

The first common downside of the WID deployment model is that there is a primary AD FS server that is in charge of (or has authority over) the AD FS farm information. This means that AD FS can only be managed from the primary server in the WID deployment model.

The second common downside is that, in the WID deployment model, each AD FS server needs to be able to communicate to the primary AD FS server in order to replicate the AD FS farm information in the AD FS configuration database.

In comparison, the SQL Server deployment model doesn't suffer from these downsides. As long as the SQL Server implementation is capable of handling the requests from the AD FS farm in a timely fashion, the AD FS farm can continue to scale out.

When using a SQL Server for the AD FS farm information, an AD FS Artifact Store is created next to the AD FS configuration database. This second database is used for the AD FS Artifact Resolution feature. Some eIDAS implementations and other applications require this functionality.

Token Replay Detection is another AD FS feature that is only available when using a SQL Server for the AD FS farm information. When token replay detection is a hard requirement from a security point of view, stick with the SQL Server deployment model.

Unfortunately, as the SQL Server deployment model leverages a SQL Server, licensing fees may apply for both the SQL Server installation and SQL Server CALs. This makes SQL Server deployment a costly implementation model.

There's more...

After deploying an AD FS farm with WIDs, it's still possible to switch to the SQL Server deployment model.

See also

For more information, you can refer to the following recipes:

- *Setting up an AD FS farm with Windows Internal Database*
- *Setting up an AD FS farm with SQL Server*

Installing the AD FS server role

In this recipe, you will learn how to install the AD FS server role.

Getting ready

Log on with local administrator privileges to a domain-joined Windows Server installation that you intend to use as an AD FS server for your organization.

How to do it...

To install the AD FS server role using the wizard, perform these steps:

1. Open **Server Manager** (`servermanager.exe`).
2. In the gray top bar of **Server Manager**, click **Manage**.
3. Select **Add Roles and Features** from the menu.
   The **Add Roles and Features Wizard** window appears.
4. On the **Before You Begin** screen, click **Next >**.
5. On the **Select installation type** screen, select **Role-based or feature-based installation**. Then, click **Next >**.
6. On the **Select destination server** screen, select the local Windows Server installation from the server pool list. Click **Next >** when you are done.
7. On the **Select server roles** screen, select the **Active Directory Federation Services** role from the list of available roles. Then, click **Next >**.

8. On the **Select features** screen, click **Next >**.
   You reach the **Active Directory Federation Services (AD FS)** screen:

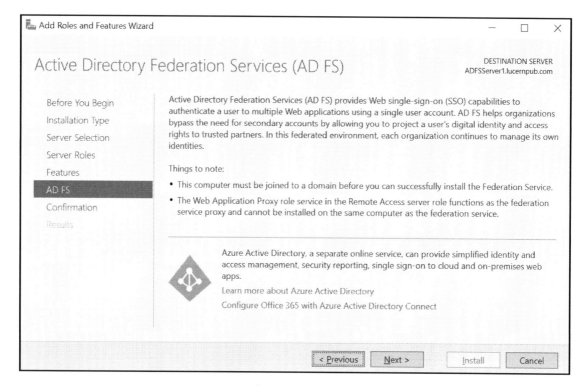

9. On the **Active Directory Federation Services (AD FS)** screen, click **Next >**.
10. On the **Confirm installation selections** screen, click **Install**.
11. When the configuration of the **Active Directory Federation Services** server role is done, click **Close**.

You can also perform this task using PowerShell. Use the following lines of PowerShell to install the AD FS server role in an elevated window:

```
Install-WindowsFeature ADFS-Federation -IncludeManagementTools
```

How it works...

The AD FS server role adds the necessary files to configure a Windows Server as an AD FS server as part of an AD FS farm.

Its management tools include the AD FS Module for Windows PowerShell and the AD FS Management tools. Unfortunately, these tools cannot be used remotely.

Setting up an AD FS farm with Windows Internal Database

In this recipe, you will learn how to set up an AD FS farm with WID.

Getting ready

In the organization, make sure that there is consensus on the name for the AD FS farm.

Additionally, make sure that a TLS certificate is available for the AD FS farm name, or request one from a **certification authority** (**CA**). Install the certificate in the personal certificate store for the local machine.

In order to create an AD FS farm, make sure that a domain-joined Windows Server installation is available to commission as an AD FS server and has the AD FS server role installed. Additionally, make sure the AD FS farm name is resolvable to this machine in the appropriate **Domain Name System** (**DNS**) zones.

How to do it...

Setting up an AD FS farm with Windows Internal Database consists of the following steps:

1. Configuring AD FS
2. Checking the proper AD FS configuration

Configuring AD FS

To configure AD FS using the **graphical user interface** (**GUI**), perform these steps while signed in with a user account that is a member of the Domain Admins group:

1. Open **Server Manager** (`servermanager.exe`).
2. In the gray top bar of **Server Manager**, click the warning sign to see the list of warnings and alerts.

3. Select the **Post-deployment Configuration** for the AD FS server role and click the link to **Configure the federation service on this server**.
The **Active Directory Federation Services Configuration Wizard** appears.

4. On the **Welcome** screen, select **Create the first federation server in a federation server farm** and click **Next >**.

5. On the **Connect to Active Directory Domain Services** screen, click **Next >** as you are already signed in to an account that has administrative privileges.
You reach the **Specify Service Properties** screen:

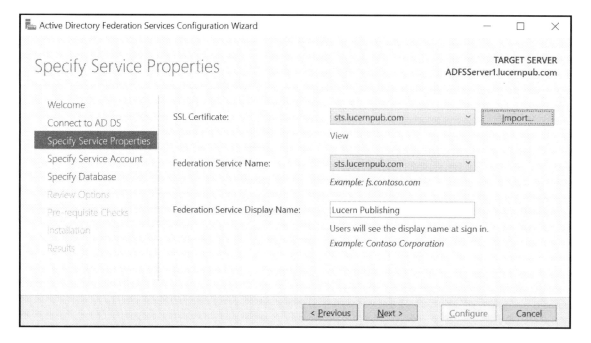

6. On the **Specify Service Properties** screen, select the installed TLS certificate from the drop-down list. Next, type the **Federation Service Name**, for instance, `sts.lucernpub.com`. Then, type the **Federation Service Display Name**, for instance, `Lucern Publishing`. Click **Next >** when you are done.

7. On the **Specify Service Account** screen, select the **Create a Group Managed Service Account** option and type the account name for the **group Managed Service Account (gMSA)**, for instance, `ADFSgMSA`. Then, click **Next >**.

8. On the **Specify Configuration Database** page, acknowledge the default option to **Create a database on this server using Windows Internal Database** by clicking **Next >**.
9. On the **Review Options** screen, click **Next >**.
10. On the **Prerequisite Checks** screen, click **Configure**.
11. On the **Results** screen, click **Close**.

Finally, restart the server.

Alternatively, use the following lines of PowerShell on a system with the AD FS Management tools and the AD Module for Windows PowerShell installed, while logged on with an account that is a member of the Domain Admins group:

```
New-ADServiceAccount -Name ADFSgMSA -DNSHostName DC01.lucernpub.com
$ADFSFarmName = "sts.lucernpub.com"

$Thumb = (Get-ChildItem -path cert:\LocalMachine\My | Where-Object
{$_.Subject -match $ADFSFarmName}).Thumbprint

Install-AdfsFarm -CertificateThumbprint $thumb -FederationServiceName
$ADFSFarmName -GroupServiceAccountIdentifier lucernpub.com\ADFSgMSA$

Restart-Computer
```

Change the values for the domain controller, the AD FS farm name, and the domain name in the preceding lines of PowerShell.

> As the gMSA's object type originates from the computer object type, make sure to add $ at the end of the object name in the script.

Checking the proper AD FS configuration

After configuring AD FS, the following URLs should be accessible from a web browser:

- `https://ADFSFarmName/FederationMetadata/2007-06/FederationMetadata.xml`
- `http://ADFSFarmName/adfs/probe`

How it works...

An AD FS farm handles authentication requests only when it is addressed with its farm name. For instance, Lucern Publishing might choose `adfs.lucernpub.com` or `signin.lucernpub.com` as its farm name.

As AD FS exchanges traffic for authentication requests using only TLS, a certificate is required. This certificate may originate from a locally managed CA or from a public CA, but it must always be published with the AD FS farm name.

As AD FS offers more services than end user authentication requests when requesting a certificate, it might make sense to also include the following URLs for AD FS farms with AD FS servers running Windows Server 2012 R2 and newer versions of Windows Server:

- `certauth.adfsfarmname.domain.tld`
- `enterpriseregistration.domain.tld`

The certificate for AD FS must meet the following requirements:

- It uses a non-**Cryptographic Next Generation (CNG)**-generated private key.
- It uses SHA-2 as the hashing algorithm.
- It uses a 3,072-bit key length (or larger).

AD FS can use a user object dedicated as its service account or a gMSA. The latter option is the preferred option, because these accounts automatically change their password every 30 days, thereby adding additional security to the solution. However, gMSAs require at least one domain controller running Windows Server 2012 and the Windows Server 2008 **Forest Functional Level (FFL)**.

For the replication of the AD FS configuration database, the AD FS servers in the farm will communicate to the primary server every five minutes using TCP 80. Make sure that these networking ports are available between AD FS servers, on top of TCP 443 for authentication requests and the networking ports that Microsoft recommends between AD FS and domain controllers.

There's more...

Microsoft's recommendation is to install AD FS servers as Server Core installations, as these servers offer end user services and are at an increased risk of being compromised. The lines of PowerShell in this recipe can be used to configure the AD FS farm in this scenario.

While AD FS can be installed and configured on a domain controller and can coexist with other roles, this is not a recommended practice from a security point of view.

See also

For more specific setups of AD FS farms, take a look at the following recipes in this chapter:

- *Setting up an AD FS farm with SQL Server*
- *Adding additional AD FS servers to an AD FS farm*
- *Removing AD FS servers from an AD FS farm*

Setting up an AD FS farm with SQL Server

In this recipe, you will learn how to set up an AD FS farm with a SQL Server-based backend.

Getting ready

In the organization, make sure that there is consensus on the name for the AD FS farm.

Make sure a TLS certificate is available for the AD FS farm name, or request one from a CA. Install the certificate in the personal certificate store for the local machine.

In order to create an AD FS farm, make sure a domain-joined Windows Server installation is available to commission as an AD FS server. Additionally, make sure that the AD FS farm name is resolvable to this machine in the appropriate DNS zones.

For AD FS with SQL Server-based databases, have a SQL Server available on the network that is also resolvable through DNS and reachable by the proposed AD FS server(s).

Perform all the following steps with an account that has these specific permissions:

- Domain administrator privileges in AD through membership of the Domain Admins group
- Local administrator privileges on the Windows Server, which is intended as the first AD FS server (default to Domain Admins privileges when the server is domain-joined)
- **SysAdmin** (**sa**) privileges on the Microsoft SQL Server

How to do it...

In order to set up an AD FS farm with SQL Server, perform the following steps:

1. Create a gMSA.
2. Create the script.
3. Create the databases.
4. Install the AD FS server role.
5. Configure AD FS.

Creating a gMSA

To create a gMSA, use the following lines of PowerShell on a system with the Active Directory Module for Windows PowerShell installed, while signed in with a user account that is a member of the Domain Admins group:

```
Import-Module ActiveDirectory

New-ADServiceAccount ADFSgMSA -DNSHostName DC01.lucernpub.com
-PrincipalsAllowedToRetrieveManagedPassword ADFSServer1
```

Change the values for the gMSA, the domain controller, and the AD FS server name in the preceding lines of PowerShell.

Creating the script

With the AD FS server role installed, we can use the PowerShell cmdlet to create the SQL scripts to create the databases on the SQL Server backend.

Use the following lines of PowerShell to install the AD FS server role in an elevated window:

```
New-Item "C:\ADFSSQLScript" -Type Directory

Export-AdfsDeploymentSQLScript -DestinationFolder "C:\ADFSSQLScript"
-ServiceAccountName LUCERNPUB\ADFSgMSA$
```

Change the values for the folder and the gMSA in the preceding lines of PowerShell.

 As the gMSA's object type originates from the computer object type, make sure to add $ at the end of the object name in the script.

This will create two files in the specified folder, as follows:

- CreateDB.sql
- Set-Permissions.sql

Creating the databases

Copy both files to the SQL Server and then perform the following steps:

1. Open the **SQL Server Management Studio**.
2. From the **File** menu, click the **Open** option. Then, click **File** (*Ctrl + O*).
3. Browse to the CreateDB.sql script and open it.
4. From the **Query** menu, click the **Execute** (*F5*) option.
5. From the **File** menu, click the **Open** option. Then, click **File** (*Ctrl + O*) again.
6. This time, browse to the SetPermissions.sql script and open it.
7. From the **Query** menu, click the **Execute** (*F5*) option.

Configuring AD FS

To begin, we will look at how to configure AD FS:

1. Open **Server Manager** (servermanager.exe).
2. In the gray top bar of **Server Manager**, click the warning sign to see the list of warnings and alerts.

3. Select the **Post-deployment Configuration** for the AD FS server role and click the link to **Configure the federation service on this server**.
The **Active Directory Federation Services Configuration Wizard** appears.

4. On the **Welcome** screen, select **Create the first federation server in a federation server farm** and then click **Next >**.

5. On the **Connect to Active Directory Domain Services** screen, click **Next >** as you are already signed in to an account that has administrative privileges.

6. On the **Specify Service Properties** screen, select the installed TLS certificate from the drop-down list. Next, type in the **Federation Service Name**, for instance, `sts.lucernpub.com`. Then, type in the **Federation Service Display Name**, for instance, `Lucern Publishing`. Click **Next >** when you are done. You reach the **Specify Service Account** screen:

7. On the **Specify Service Account** screen, select the **Use an existing Group Managed Service Account** option.

8. Click the **Select...** button.
The **Select User or Service Account** popup window appears.

9. Type in the account name for the gMSA, for instance, `ADFSgMSA`, and then click **Check Names**. Click **OK** to select the gMSA and close the **Select User or Service Account** popup window.

10. Click **Next >**.

11. On the **Specify Configuration Database** screen, select the **Specify the location of a SQL Server database** option. Specify **Database Host Name**, and then either specify **Database Instance** or leave it blank to use the default instance. Click **Next >**.

12. On the **Confirm Overwrite** screen, select the **Overwrite existing AD FS configuration database data** option. Then, click **Next >**.

13. On the **Review Options** screen, click **Next >**.

14. On the **Prerequisite Checks** screen, click **Configure**.

15. On the **Results** screen, click **Close**.

Finally, restart the server.

Alternatively, you can use the following lines of PowerShell to the same effect:

```
$ADFSFarmName = "sts.lucernpub.com"

$Thumb = (Get-ChildItem -path cert:\LocalMachine\My | Where-Object
{$_.Subject -match $ADFSFarmName}).Thumbprint

Install-ADFSFarm -CertificateThumbPrint $thumb -
FederationServiceDisplayName "Lucern Publishing" -FederationServiceName
$ADFSFarmName -GroupServiceAccountIdentifier "LUCERNPUB\ADFSgMSA$" -
OverwriteConfiguration -SQLConnectionString "Data
Source=SQLSERVER;IntegratedSecurity=True"

Restart-Computer
```

Change the values for the AD FS farm name, description, gMSA, and the SQL Server to be used in the preceding lines of PowerShell.

Checking the proper AD FS configuration

After configuring AD FS, the following URLs should be accessible from a web browser:

- https://ADFSFarmName/FederationMetadata/2007-06/FederationMetadata.xml
- http://ADFSFarmName/adfs/probe

How it works...

Just as with setting up an AD FS farm with Windows Internal Database, the certificate plays an important role.

When using SQL Server, however, the service account becomes really important, because it is not only used to run the AD FS service on AD FS servers in the AD FS farm, but also to connect to the SQL Server backend.

The service account specified when using the script from `Export-AdfsDeploymentSQLScript` will be added as a login to the SQL Server installation and will be provided with privileges in the database.

The `CreateDB.sql` script creates two databases: the **AdfsConfigurationV4** database, which stores the AD FS farm settings, and the **AdfsArtifactStore** database, which is used for the AD FS Artifact Resolution.

There's more...

In some environments, complex SQL connection strings might be returned by a SQL admin in response to the AD FS SQL scripts. In these cases, it is wise to test the SQL connection string manually on the AD FS servers before implementation. You can use the following lines of PowerShell for this purpose:

```
$conn = New-Object System.Data.SqlClient.SqlConnection
$conn.ConnectionString = "Data Source=SQLSERVER:Port;Integrated
Security=True"
# If no error occurs here, then connection was successful.
$conn.Open();
$conn.Close();
```

See also

For a more specific way to set up an AS FS farm, take a look at the following recipes:

- *Setting up an AD FS farm with Windows Internal Database*
- *Adding additional AD FS servers to an AD FS farm*
- *Removing AD FS servers from an AD FS farm*

Adding additional AD FS servers to an AD FS farm

This recipe demonstrates how you can add additional AD FS servers to an AD FS farm.

Getting ready

After setting up the AD FS farm by implementing the first AD FS server, adding additional AD FS servers to the farm is straightforward.

However, before you begin, make sure of the following:

- The same TLS certificate used on the first AD FS server is available for the additional AD FS servers in the AD FS farm. Install the certificate in the personal certificate store for the local machine.
- The proposed AD FS server is a domain-joined Windows Server installation and you are logged on with a domain account that is a member of the Domain Admins group.
- The AD FS farm name is resolvable to this machine in the appropriate DNS zones.
- The primary AD FS server is reachable for AD FS farms using WID, and the SQL Server is available and reachable for AD FS farms using SQL Server as their backends.
- The AD FS server role is installed on the proposed AD FS server.

Sign in with a user account that is a member of the Domain Admins group.

How to do it...

Perform the following steps:

1. Open **Server Manager** (`servermanager.exe`).
2. In the gray top bar of **Server Manager**, click the warning sign to see the list of warnings and alerts.

3. Select the **Post-deployment Configuration** for the AD FS server role and click the link to **Configure the federation service on this server**.
The **Active Directory Federation Services Configuration Wizard** appears:

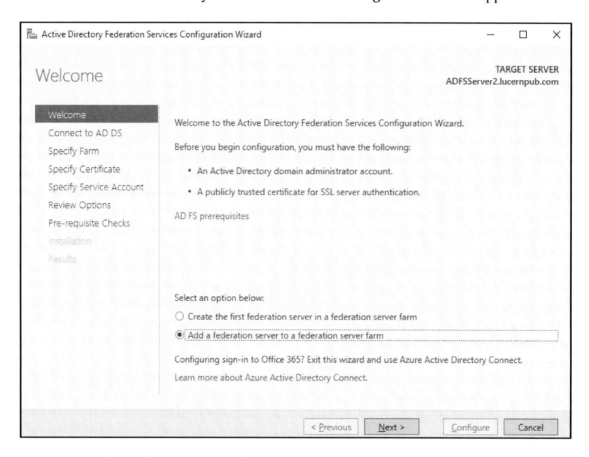

4. On the **Welcome** screen, select **Add a federation server to a federation server farm** and click **Next >**.
5. On the **Connect to Active Directory Domain Services** screen, click **Next >** as you are already signed in to an account that has administrative privileges.
6. On the **Specify Farm** screen, select **Specify the primary federation server in an existing farm using Windows Internal Database** by typing its DNS hostname, or select **Specify the database location for an existing farm using SQL Server**. Click **Next >** when you are done.

7. On the **Specify SLL Certificate** screen, select the installed TLS certificate from the drop-down list. Click **Next >** when you are done.

8. On the **Specify Service Account** screen, click the **Select...** button. The **Select User or Service Account** popup window appears.

9. Type in the account name for the gMSA, for instance, ADFSgMSA, and then click **Check Names**. Click **OK** to select the gMSA and close the **Select User or Service Account** popup window.

10. Click **Next >**.

11. On the **Review Options** screen, click **Next >**.

12. On the **Prerequisite Checks** screen, click **Configure**.

13. On the **Results** screen, click **Close**.

Finally, restart the server.

Use the following lines of PowerShell on a system with the **AD FS Management** tools (while logged on with an account that is a member of the Domain Admins group) to add an AD FS server to an AD FS farm using SQL Server for its database:

```
$ADFSFarmName = "sts.lucernpub.com"

$Thumb = (Get-ChildItem -path cert:\LocalMachine\My | Where-Object
{$_.Subject -match $ADFSFarmName}).Thumbprint

Add-AdfsFarmNode -CertificateThumbprint $thumb
-GroupServiceAccountIdentifier lucernpub.com\ADFSgMSA$ -SQLConnectionString
"Data Source=SQLSERVER;Integrated Security=True"

Restart-Computer
```

Change the values for the AD FS farm name, the gMSA, and the SQL Server to be used in the preceding lines of PowerShell.

How it works...

When an AD FS farm exists, AD FS servers can be added by specifying the primary AD FS server for the AD FS farms using WID, or the database specifics for the AD FS farms using SQL Server.

In an environment using WID, each AD FS server replicates the database from the primary AD FS server. Only this server has read/write access to the database. The AD FS Management tools can only be run on the primary server. The primary server is located through the DNS and the WID is replicated using TCP 80.

In an environment using SQL Server, each AD FS server communicates with the SQL Server for the database. Each server has read/write access to the database. The AD FS Management tools can be run on each AD FS server.

When multiple AD FS servers are added to an AD FS farm, make sure to use a load balancer solution to distribute authentication requests over the servers. Use the /adfs/probe endpoint to check if an AD FS server is up and running the load balancer.

See also

You can refer to these recipes for more information about setting up an AD FS farm:

- *Setting up an AD FS farm with Windows Internal Database*
- *Setting up an AD FS farm with SQL Server*

Removing AD FS servers from an AD FS farm

This recipe demonstrates how you can remove AD FS servers from an AD FS farm.

Getting ready

Sign in with a user account that is a member of the Domain Admins group.

How to do it...

Perform the following steps:

1. Open **Server Manager** (`servermanager.exe`).
2. From the gray top-banner, click **Manage**. From the menu, select **Remove Roles and Features**.
    The **Remove Roles and Features Wizard** appears.
3. On the **Before You Begin** screen, click **Next >**.
4. On the **Select destination server** screen, acknowledge the local server by clicking on **Next >**.
    You reach the **Remove server roles** screen:

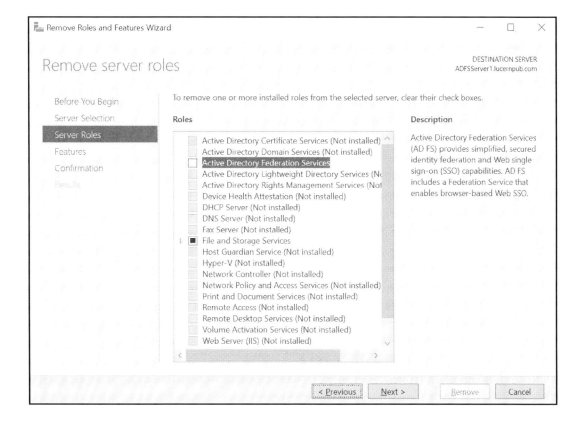

5. On the **Remove server roles** screen, deselect the **Active Directory Federation Services** role. Afterward, click **Next >**.

6. If the AD FS server is part of an AD FS farm running WID, then, on the **Remove features** screen, deselect the **Windows Internal Database** feature and click **Next >**. If the AD FS farm uses SQL Server, then simply click **Next >** the **Remove features** screen.

7. On the **Confirm removal selections** screen, click **Remove**.

8. When removal is done, click **Close** on the **Removal Progress** page.

Finally, restart the former AD FS server.

How it works...

For most Server Roles and Features in Windows Server, the decommissioning of the configured Windows Server installation occurs when the role or feature is removed.

When the AD FS role is removed from a server, it is automatically removed from the AD FS farm, and its AD FS role and its management tools are uninstalled. A restart is required to complete the removal.

Decommissioning AD FS by removing the server role does not remove other settings and infrastructure configurations, such as the TLS certificate, the service account from AD DS, domain membership of the server, and any memberships in the pools of load balancers. These items need to be removed or reconfigured manually afterward.

There's more...

When you decommission the last AD FS server in an AD FS farm, the farm is decommissioned. When you decommission an AD FS farm that leverages SQL Server, then also decommission the corresponding ADFSConfiguration and ArtifactStore databases and service account login on the SQL Server(s).

Creating a Relying Party Trust (RPT)

This recipe demonstrates how you can create an **Relying Party Trust** (RPT) in AD FS.

Getting ready

Log on to the AD FS server with an account that is a member of the Domain Admins group.

How to do it...

Perform these steps to create an RPT:

1. Open **AD FS Management** (`Microsoft.IdentityServer.msc`).
2. In the right-hand **Actions** pane or from the **Action** menu, follow the **Add Relying Party Trust...** link.
   The **Add Relying Party Trust Wizard** window appears:

3. On the **Welcome** screen, click **Claims aware** and then click **Start**.

4. Choose between these three options:
   - **Import data about the relying party published online or on a local network**:
     Type the **Federation metadata address (host name or URL)** in the required field.
   - **Import data about the relying party from a file**:
     Type the **Federation metadata file location** in the required field.
   - **Enter data about the relying party manually**
     For this RPT, the data will be typed manually.

5. Click **Next >**.

6. On the **Specify Display Name** screen, enter a **Display Name**. Then, click **Next >**.

7. On the **Configure Certificate** screen, optionally, select a token encryption certificate. Click **Browse...** and then select a certificate from a `.cer`, `.sst`, or `.p7b` file. Click **Open**, and then click **Next >**.

8. On the **Configure URL** screen, select the protocols for the RPT. Select the **Enable support for the WS-Federation Passive protocol** option and/or the **Enable support for SAML 2.0 Web SSO protocol** option and enter the required information. Then, click **Next >**.

9. On the **Configure Identifiers** screen, enter a **Relying party trust identifier**. Then, click **Next >**.

10. On the **Choose Access control Policy** screen, either accept the default **Permit Everyone** access control policy or select a different access control policy. Then, click **Next >**.

11. On the **Ready to Add Trust** screen, click **Next >**.

12. On the **Finish** screen, keep the **Configure claims issuance policy for this application** option enabled, and then click **Close**; the **Issuance Transform Rules** window for the RPT appears.

13. Click the **Add Rule...** button to add a claims issuance rule.

14. On the **Choose Rule Type** screen, select a **Claim rule template** from the drop-down list, and then click **Next >**.
    You are presented with the **Configure Rule** screen:

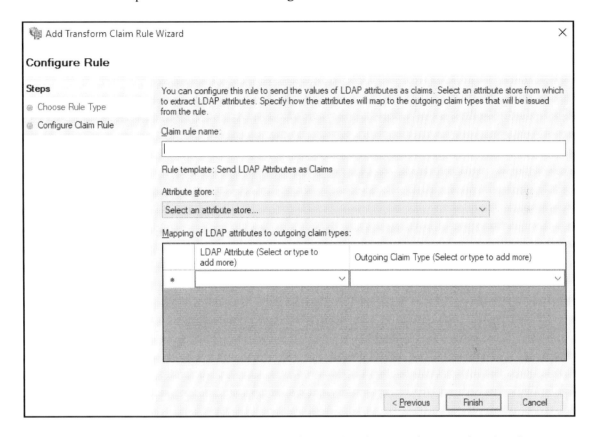

15. On the **Configure Rule** screen, configure the claims to be issued in the claim token for the RPT.
16. Click **Finish**.

How it works...

Without RPTs, an AD FS farm doesn't provide functionality. By adding one or more RPTs, an AD FS admin could unlock single sign-on access to the application.

An RPT adds a relationship between an application and the AD FS farm. In this relationship, the application trusts the claim tokens issued by the AD FS farm. When an authenticated user presents the claim token to the application, the application uses the content of the claim token to perform authentication and authorization.

The option to **Import data about the relying party published online or on a local network** should be your preferred option to add RPTs, as it adds the ability to monitor and, optionally, update the information for the RPT automatically.

Optionally, claim tokens can be encrypted. When a TLS certificate is exchanged between the administrator of the application and the AD FS administrator, the token encryption certificate can be configured on both sides and used to encrypt the claim tokens that are exchanged. This is useful to further protect the contents of the tokens beyond the default TLS connection that is used to exchange the claim tokens by the device of the end user.

In light of **General Data Protection Regulation (GDPR)**, applications tend to focus on the safe exchange of data and require encrypted claim tokens. The AD FS server encrypts the claim token with the private key of the certificate. The application decrypts the claim token with the public key of the certificate.

 When editing the claims issuance rules, do not type in the **Mapping of LDAP attributes to outgoing claim types** fields.

Deleting an RPT

This recipe demonstrates how you can delete an RPT in AD FS.

Getting ready

Log on to the AD FS server with an account that is a member of the Domain Admins group.

How to do it...

Perform these steps to delete an RPT:

1. Open **AD FS Management** (Microsoft.IdentityServer.msc).
2. In the left-hand navigation pane, under the **AD FS** node, expand the **Relying Party Trusts** node.
3. In the main menu pane, select the RPT that you want to delete.
4. In the right-hand **Actions** pane, click **Delete**, or right-click the RPT and select **Delete** from the menu:

5. In the **AD FS Management** popup window, click **Yes** as the answer to the **Are you sure you want to delete this item?** question.

How it works...

When an RPT is no longer needed, it can be removed from the AD FS farm. Without an RPT, end user access to the application will be lost.

Configuring branding

This recipe shows you how to apply your organization's branding to the AD FS login pages.

Getting ready

Ask the marketing team for your organization to produce the following files:

- One logo, ideally 280 pixels wide and 60 pixels high
- One big background picture, ideally 1,420 pixels wide and 1,200 pixels high, not exceeding 200 KB in size
- One disclaimer text

Place these files in a folder on the AD FS server, for instance, in the C:\Style folder.

Log on to the AD FS server with an account that is a member of the Domain Admins group.

How to do it...

Perform the following steps:

1. Open an elevated PowerShell window.
2. Use the following command to switch the appearance of the AD FS farm's login pages to the paginated experience with the centered user interface:

    ```
    Set-AdfsGlobalAuthenticationPolicy
    -EnablePaginatedAuthenticationPages $true
    ```

3. Use the following command to enable the /adfs/ls/idpinitiatedsignon.aspx page. This allows you to see the branding in action:

    ```
    Set-AdfsProperties -EnableIdpInitiatedSignonPage $True
    ```

Navigate to the page to see the default branding; it will resemble the following screenshot:

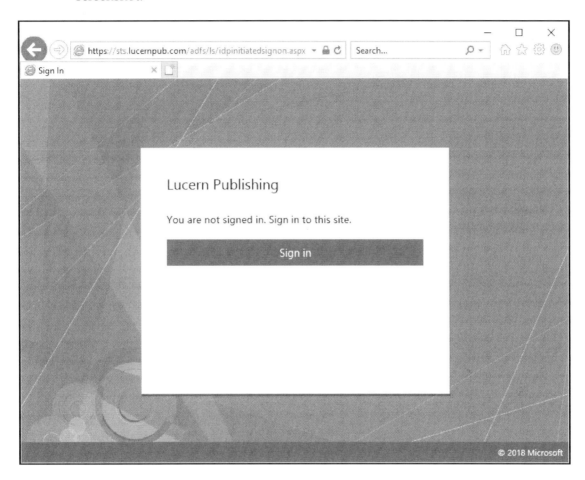

4. Perform the following command to create a custom theme:

```
New-AdfsWebTheme –Name custom –SourceName default
```

5. Perform the following command to change the AD FS farm name to the organization's logo:

```
Set-AdfsWebTheme –TargetName custom –Logo
@{path="C:\Style\logo.png"}
```

6. Perform the following command to change the background:

```
Set-AdfsWebTheme -TargetName custom -Illustration
@{path="C:\Style\background.jpg"}
```

7. Perform the following command to add the disclaimer text:

```
Set-AdfsGlobalWebContent -SignInPageDescriptionText "<p>By logging
on, you gain access to services. When using these services, rules
apply as stated in the protocol. Unauthorized access is
prohibited.</p>"
```

8. Perform the following command to switch from the default theme to the custom theme:

```
Set-AdfsWebConfig -ActiveThemeName custom
```

9. Navigate to the `/adfs/ls/idpinitiatedsignon.aspx` page to see the custom branding.
10. Perform the following command to disable the page:

```
Set-AdfsProperties -EnableIdpInitiatedSignonPage $False
```

How it works...

AD FS supports themes. By adding a custom theme, themes can be switched easily, allowing for quick roll-backs of botched functionality.

Starting with AD FS on Windows Server 2016, the `/adfs/ls/idpinitiatedsignon.aspx` page is no longer enabled by default. This adds to the information security, because the page can be used by malicious persons outside of the organization to discover RPTs.

If you are starting with AD FS on Windows Server 2019, then the paginated experience with the centered user interface is available by default. For Windows Server 2016, the experience needs to be downloaded from GitHub first.

Setting up a Web Application Proxy

This recipe shows you how to set up a Web Application Proxy in order to publish the AD FS farm on the internet.

Getting ready

After setting up the AD FS farm, you can add one or more Web Application Proxies to it.

Before you begin, make sure of the following:

- The same TLS certificate used on the AD FS servers in the AD FS farm is available on the intended Web Application Proxy. Install the certificate in the personal certificate store for the local machine.
- The AD FS farm name is resolvable to the AD FS servers for the Web Application Proxy.
- The AD FS farm name is resolvable to the Web Application Proxy from the internet.

How to do it...

Setting up a Web Application Proxy consists of the following steps:

1. Installing the Web Application Proxy feature
2. Configuring the Web Application Proxy
3. Checking the proper Web Application Proxy configuration

Log on with a local administrator account on the Web Application Proxy.

Installing the Web Application Proxy feature

Perform the following steps:

1. Open **Server Manager** (`servermanager.exe`).
2. In the gray top bar of **Server Manager**, click **Manage**.
3. Select **Add Roles and Features** from the menu.
   The **Add Roles and Features Wizard** window appears.
4. On the **Before You Begin** screen, click **Next >**.
5. On the **Select installation type** screen, select **Role-based or feature-based installation**. Afterward, click **Next >**.

6. On the **Select destination server** screen, select the local Windows Server installation from the server pool list. Click **Next >** when you are done.

7. On the **Select server roles** screen, select the **Remote Access** role from the list of available roles. Then, click **Next >**.

8. On the **Select features** screen, click **Next >**.

9. On the **Remote Access** screen, click **Next >**:

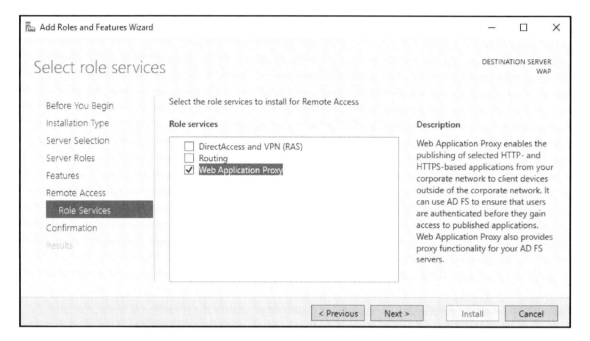

10. On the **Select role services** screen, select the **Web Application Proxy** feature. The **Add Roles and Features Wizard** popup appears.

11. Click **Add Features** to add the **Group Policy Management, RAS Connection Manager Administration Kit (CMAK)**, and **Remote Server Administration Tools** for Remote Access features.

12. Click **Next >**.

13. On the **Confirm installation selections** screen, click **Install**.

14. When the configuration of the **Active Directory Federation Services** server role is done, click **Close** to close **Add Roles and Features Wizard**.

This task can also be accomplished using Windows PowerShell. Use the following line of PowerShell to install the Web Application Proxy server role service in an elevated window:

```
Install-WindowsFeature Web-Application-Proxy -IncludeManagementTools
```

Configuring the Web Application Proxy

Perform the following steps:

1. Open **Server Manager** (`servermanager.exe`).
2. In the gray top bar of **Server Manager**, click the warning sign to see the list of warnings and alerts.
3. Select the **Post-deployment Configuration** for the Web Application Proxy server role service and then click the link to **Open the Web Application Proxy Wizard**. The **Web Application Proxy Configuration Wizard** appears.
4. On the **Welcome** screen, click **Next >**:

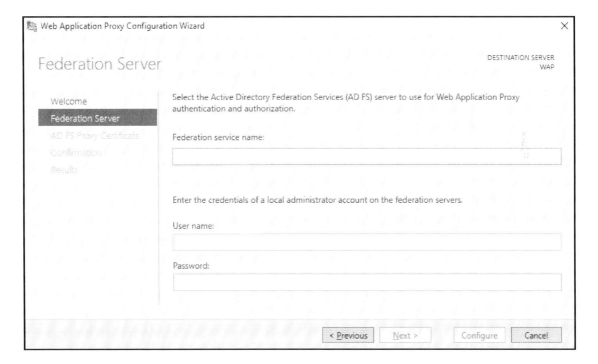

5. On the **Federation Server** screen, type the Federation service name, for instance, `sts.lucernpub.com`. Next, **Enter credentials of a local administrator account on the federation servers**. Click **Next >** when you are done.

6. On the **AD FS Proxy Certificate** screen, select the certificate to be used by the AD FS proxy from the drop-down list and, afterward, click **Next >**.

7. On the **Confirmation** screen, click **Configure**.

8. On the **Results** screen, click **Close**.

This task can also be accomplished using Windows PowerShell. Use the following lines of PowerShell in an elevated window:

```
$ADFSFarmName = "sts.lucernpub.com"

$Thumb = (Get-ChildItem -path cert:\LocalMachine\My | Where-Object
{$_.Subject -match $ADFSFarmName}).Thumbprint

Install-WebApplicationProxy -CertificateThumbprint $Thumb -
FederationServiceName $ADFSFarmName
```

Checking the proper Web Application Proxy configuration

After configuring the Web Application Proxy, the following URL should be accessible from the internet:

* `https://ADFSFarmName/FederationMetadata/2007-06/FederationMetad ata.xml`

How it works...

Web Application Proxies can be used to publish the AD FS farm on the internet safely. For authentication requests toward the AD FS farm from the internet, the Web Application Proxy functions as a reverse proxy for the AD FS servers, terminating the connection yet relaying the authentication requests to the AD FS servers.

When an authentication request comes in via a Web Application Proxy, the `insidecorporatenetwork` claim is set to false. This claim is leveraged in AD FS control access policies to distinguish between outside and inside clients. Using a configured MFA adapter, admins can require multifactor authentication for outside clients using the built-in access control policy.

Web Application Proxies have a certificate-based relationship with the AD FS farm. Using **MSADFS-PIP**, a certificate is obtained and automatically renewed using TCP 443 between the Web Application Proxy and AD FS servers only.

There's more...

By default, the `/adfs/probe` endpoint is not accessible on Web Application Proxies. This makes them hard to monitor as part of a load balancer's backend pool.

Enable Windows Firewall to allow traffic to the endpoint using the following line of PowerShell in an elevated Windows PowerShell window on the Web Application Proxy:

```
Import-Module NetSecurity

New-NetFirewallRule -Name Allow_HTTP -DisplayName "AD FS HTTP Services" -
Protocol HTTP -Profile Any -Action Allow
```

Decommissioning a Web Application Proxy

This recipe shows you how to decommission a Web Application Proxy.

Getting ready

Log on with a local administrator account on the Web Application Proxy.

How to do it...

Perform the following steps:

1. Open **Server Manager** (`servermanager.exe`).
2. In the gray top bar of **Server Manager**, click **Manage**.
3. Select **Remove Roles and Features** from the menu.
4. On the **Before You Begin** screen, click **Next >**.
5. On the **Select installation type** screen, click **Next >**.

6. On the **Remove server roles** screen, deselect the **Remote Access** role.
   The **Remove features that require Remote Access** popup window appears.

7. Click **Remove Features** to remove the Remote Server Administration Tools for Remote Access.

8. Click **Next >**.

9. On the **Remove features** screen, deselect the **Group Policy Management** feature and the **RAS Connection Manager Administration Kit (CMAK)** feature, unless these features are required for other functionality and you'd like to keep them.

10. Click **Next >**.
    The **Confirm removal selections** screen appears:

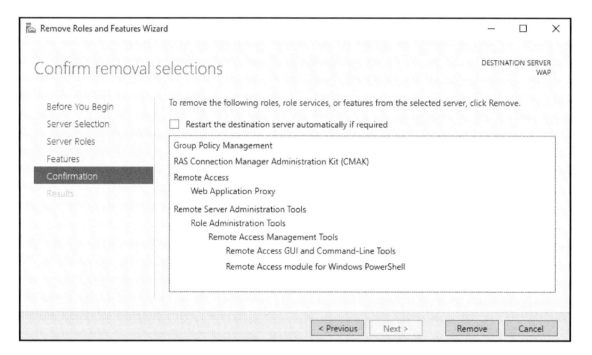

11. On the **Confirm removal selections** screen, click **Remove**.

12. On the **Removal progress** screen, click **Close**.

Finally, restart the server.

How it works...

For most **Server Roles** and **Features** in Windows Server, decommissioning of the configured Windows Server installation occurs when the role or feature is removed.

When the **Remote Access** role is removed from a server, the server stops functioning as a Web Application Proxy. A restart is required to complete the removal.

Decommissioning a Web Application Proxy by removing the **Server Role** service does not remove other settings and infrastructure configurations, such as the TLS certificate and any memberships in the pools of load balancers. These items need to be removed or reconfigured manually afterward.

12
Handling Authentication in a Hybrid World (AD FS, PHS, PTA, and 3SO)

Azure Active Directory is Microsoft's cloud-based identity and access management service. Organizations can register for an **Azure Active Directory** (**Azure AD**) tenant, where they can store and use the information on their identities.

Hybrid identity is Microsoft Marketing speak for connecting an on-premise Active Directory environment to Azure AD. When done correctly, the hybrid identity implementation allows end-users to authenticate to both on-premise and cloud-based applications, systems, and services:

- When accessing NTLM-, LDAP-, and Kerberos-integrated applications, systems, and services, the on-premise Active Directory takes care of authentication and authorization. These protocols are designed for safe networks and have been offering *single sign-on* for decades.
- When accessing cloud-based applications, systems and services, it is frowned upon to use the protocols for safe networks, or any other proprietary protocols. Instead, as an industry we've moved to a situation where we use open authentication protocols and interfaces, such as WS-Fed, SAML, Oauth2, OpenID Connect, and SCIM. Both AD FS and Azure AD offer these protocols and interfaces.

Hybrid identity consists of two distinct areas:

- Authentication
- Synchronization

This chapter discusses the first area in terms of AD FS, PHS, PTA, and 3SO. The area of synchronization is discussed in `Chapter 13`, *Handling Synchronization in a Hybrid World (Azure AD Connect)*.

The following recipes will be covered in this chapter:

- Choosing the right authentication method
- Verifying your DNS domain name
- Implementing Password Hash Sync with Azure AD Connect Express Settings
- Implementing Pass-through Authentication
- Implementing single sign-on to Office 365 using AD FS
- Managing AD FS with Azure AD Connect
- Implementing Azure Traffic Manager for AD FS geo-redundancy
- Migrating from AD FS to PTA for single sign-on to Office 365
- Making PTA (geo)redundant

Choosing the right authentication method

This recipe shows how to choose the right authentication method between Active Directory and Azure AD tenant.

Getting ready

To make a choice, you'll need to know the following characteristics of your organization:

- Is your organization OK with synchronizing secrets for end users to the (public) cloud?
- Does your organization already have a federation solution and use claims-based applications, either inside your organization, or cloud-based applications, systems, and/or services?
- Does your organization require smartcard- or certificate-based authentication to cloud applications, systems, and/or services, or does it rely on on-premise multi-factor authentication solutions?
- Is your organization's **Security Incident and Event Monitoring (SIEM)** solution cloud-aware?
- Do people in your organization use Internet Explorer and/or Edge, or other browsers as their default browsers?

How to do it...

Use the following flowchart to choose the right authentication method for your organization:

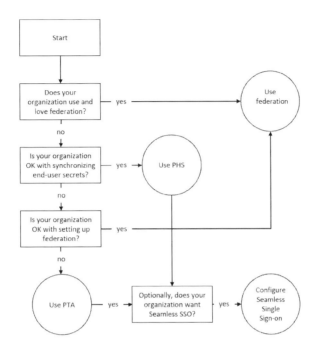

How it works...

In the following subsections, you'll find information and pros and cons for each of the authentication methods.

Active Directory Federation Services or PingFederate

Azure AD with **Active Directory Federation Services (AD FS)**, along with PingFederate, offers a claims-based trust between Azure AD and your organization's federation solution. It is the only solution today that offers certificate-based authentication and password expiry claims, and thus, notifications of expiring passwords when using Azure AD-integrated applications, services, and systems, such as Office 365. When AD FS or PingFederate is already in use within an organization, the knowledge and the processes are already in place to make connecting to Azure AD a success.

Since an AD FS implementation for Azure AD requires public connectivity for federation metadata exchange, using AD FS as the authentication method in a redundant setup requires at least five on-premise systems:

- Two AD FS servers
- Two Web Application Proxies in a perimeter network
- An Azure AD Connect installation

For organizations, additional training for personnel and the additional processes to keep AD FS optimized has proven too steep, unless organizations have already deployed AD FS or another federation solution, such as PingFederate.

Password Hash Sync

Azure AD with **Password Hash Sync** (PHS) is the default authentication method when using Azure AD Connect with default settings. While Microsoft labeled this scenario as Password Hash Sync (PHS), they've made sure that neither the password itself, nor the hash of the password that is stored for the user object in Active Directory, is synchronized to Azure AD. Rather, a hash of the hash of the password is synchronized.

This is the only scenario where Active Directory is not leveraged for actual authentications. Therefore, no authentication events for sign-ins to cloud applications appear in the Windows Event Log of domain controllers. When an SIEM solution is present within the networking infrastructure, make sure it also integrates with Azure AD to fetch the information there.

Pass-through authentication

Azure AD **Pass-through authentication** (PTA) enables organizations to continue to have a **Single Sign-on** (SSO) experience on their domain-joined devices, even those running Windows versions prior to Windows 10, and provides audit trail capabilities quite similar to AD FS, without the infrastructure overhead typically associated with implementing a highly available AD FS infrastructure. One or more PTA agents are installed within the network boundary.

These agents maintain outbound SSL connections to the Azure Service Bus. Azure AD places authentication requests on the service bus, where the PTA agents pick them up and process them against the on-premise domain controllers. Then, they put the signals for successful authentications back on the service bus for Azure AD to pick up.

Seamless Single Sign-on

When the optional **Enable single sign-on** setting is enabled in Azure AD Connect, next to PHS or PTA, it instructs Azure AD Connect to use Kerberos authentication using a specific computer object in the local Active Directory for this feature: `AzureADSSOACC`. This account is located in the default Computers container. The object creates two **Service Principal Names** (**SPNs**) defining the Azure Active Directory URLs. The credentials of the account are then shared by Azure AD Connect with Azure AD as the shared Kerberos secret to encrypt the interchanged Kerberos packets.

Using the SSO authentication method, persons authenticating to Azure AD on domain-joined devices talk Kerberos to Azure AD's authentication service, just like they would with an on-premise federation service, except this service runs in Microsoft's data centers.

Cloud-only

Of course, organizations can always choose to implement accounts manually in Azure AD that have no relationship to user accounts in Active Directory. These accounts authenticate to Azure AD's authentication service.

There's more...

The preceding authentication methods can be mixed and matched, but moving from one authentication method to another might not always yield the expected outcome: moving from **Password Hash Synchronization** (**PHS**) to PTA, for instance, does not clear previously synchronized hashes of password hashes.

Therefore, it's a good plan to start any hybrid identity journey by deciding what authentication method to use.

Verifying your DNS domain name

Any hybrid identity journey starts with verifying your DNS domain name in Azure AD. This recipe explains how to do this.

Getting ready

You'll need an Azure AD tenant for this recipe. If your organization doesn't have a tenant, sign up for one using `https://signup.microsoft.com/Signup?OfferId=B07A1127-DE83-4a6d-9F85-2C104BDAE8B4`.

The form provides a way to name the Azure AD tenant. This is a plus, because many other signup methods base the name of the tenant on the email address of the person signing up. The preceding link creates a non-expiring tenant with a 90-day Microsoft Office 365 E3 trial license. You specify an account with the Global administrator role during signup.

If your organization already has an Azure AD tenant, then use an account that has the Global administrator role assigned to it with this recipe.

How to do it...

Perform these steps in the Azure AD Tenant:

1. Navigate a browser to `https://portal.azure.com`.
2. Log in with an account in Azure Active Directory that has the **Global Administrator** role assigned.
3. Perform multi-factor authentication when prompted.

4. In the left navigation pane, click **Azure Active Directory**.
5. In the Azure AD pane, click **Custom domain names**:

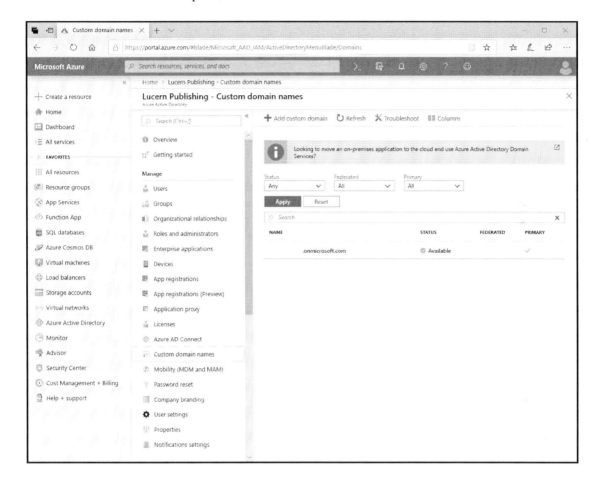

6. In the top bar, click **+ Add custom domain**.
   The **Custom domain name** blade appears on the right.
7. Enter the name of the DNS domain name that you want to federate.
8. Click the **Add domain** button at the bottom of the blade.
   You are then taken to the **Custom domain name** pane to verify the DNS name.
9. Use the information on this pane to create the DNS records that will prove you own the DNS domain.
10. After creating the records, click the **Verify** button at the bottom of the pane.

How it works...

Perform the steps in this recipe before you attempt to implement any of the following recipes. People in your organization might have already accepted invitations from people in Azure AD tenants to work together, for instance, in Power BI. These people already have Azure AD accounts based on their email addresses. After a DNS domain name is verified in Azure AD, these accounts come under the control of the Azure AD tenant.

When you first synchronize between Active Directory and Azure AD, these accounts are automatically reconfigured with the new authentication method. If you synchronize before scooping up these user objects, people might end up with two accounts, which defeats the purpose of SSO. If you synchronize without a verified DNS domain name, all user objects in Azure AD will be appended by the tenant name, for instance, lucernpub.onmicrosoft.com. The AD FS as an authentication method isn't even available without verifying a DNS domain name first.

If your organization's on-premise Active Directory does not utilize a publicly routable UPN suffix, for instance, `lucernpub.local`, perform these steps:

1. Decide on an appropriate DNS domain name for your organization.
   If your organization uses email, use the DNS domain name used for email purposes.
2. Register the DNS domain name if your organization does not own it on the internet.
3. Verify the DNS domain name in the Azure AD tenant by adding the required TXT or MX records in the public DNS zone for the DNS domain name.
4. Add the DNS domain name as a UPN suffix in Active Directory.
5. Change the userPrincipalName for each user object in the Active Directory to use the new DNS domain name as the new UPN suffix.

It is best practice to configure user objects with identical primary email addresses and `userPrincipalName` attribute. That way, when people in your organization are asked to identify as someone for your organization using a method that specifies the @-sign, it doesn't matter what they enter.

Implementing Password Hash Sync with Express Settings

This recipe shows how to configure Password Hash Sync as the authentication method toward Azure AD, using Azure AD Connect Express Settings.

This recipe assumes your organization already possesses an Active Directory domain and Azure AD tenant for which you know the credentials for an account that is a member of the Enterprise Admins group, and the credentials for an account that is assigned the Global administrator role, respectively.

Getting ready

Dedicate at least one domain-joined Windows Server system on the internal network as the host for Azure AD Connect for your organization. As this Windows Server will have a SQL Server Express database hosted on it, be sure not to combine this role with sensitive or overburdened hosts.

Make sure the accounts in the on-premise Active Directory are configured with a publicly routable `userPrincipalName` suffix, such as `lucernpub.com`. Make sure the DNS domain name(s) representing the UPN suffix(es) are owned by your organization on the internet and configured as verified DNS domain name(s) in your organization's Azure AD tenant.

Make sure that the Windows Server that will run Azure AD Connect is able to communicate to the internet without having to pass proxies and has the **Internet Explorer Enhanced Security Configuration (IE ESC)** turned off. If proxies need to be passed, take the appropriate measures by either making a proxy exception or configuring a proxy for Azure AD Connect in its configuration file. Download the latest version of Azure AD Connect from `http://aka.ms/aadconnect`.

Sign in as a local administrator on the Windows Server installation.

How to do it...

Perform these steps on the dedicated Windows Server installation that you want to use to configure Azure AD Connect with PTA:

1. Double-click `AzureADConnect.msi`.
2. On the **Welcome** screen, select the **I agree to the license terms and privacy notice.** option.

3. Click the **Next** button.
   You are presented with the **Express Settings** screen:

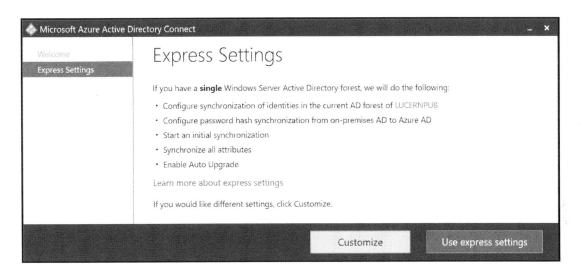

4. On the **Express Settings** screen, click the **Use express settings** button.
5. On the **Connect to Azure AD** screen, enter the credentials of an account in Azure AD that has been assigned the **Global administrator** role.
6. Click the **Next** button.
7. Optionally, perform multi-factor authentication, and/or elevate the account to **Global administrator** when using Azure AD **Privileged Identity Management (PIM)**.
8. On the **Connect to AD DS** screen, enter the credentials for an account that is a member of the **Enterprise Admins** group in your on-premise Active Directory.
9. Click the **Next** button.
10. On the **Azure AD Sign-in** screen, review the DNS domain names for the Azure AD tenant. Make sure those domains that your organization uses have been verified in Azure AD.
11. Click the **Next** button.
12. On the **Ready to configure** screen, click the **Install button**.
13. When the installation completes, click the **Exit** button.

How it works...

When you install and configure Azure AD Connect with **Express Settings**, the following configuration is performed:

- All user objects, groups, Windows 10-based computer objects, contacts, and InetOrgPerson objects in the Active Directory forest the Azure AD Connect installation belongs to are configured to be synchronized to Azure AD.
- All user objects and InetOrgPerson objects have hashes of their password hashes synchronized to Azure AD.
- Azure AD Connect's **Automatic Upgrade** feature is enabled.

Do not use **Express Settings** in the following situations:

- Your organization uses multiple Active Directory forests
- Your organization has over 100,000 objects, including groups and computer objects

Implementing Pass-through Authentication

This recipe shows how to configure Azure AD Connect with PTA and Seamless SSO.

Getting ready

To implement PTA, you'll need to sign in with an account that is a local administrator on the server dedicated to Azure AD Connect. As part of the following steps, you'll need to enter the credentials for these accounts:

- An account in Active Directory that is a member of the Enterprise Admins group
- An account in Azure Active Directory that has the Global administrator role assigned

Make sure the Windows Server running Azure AD Connect is able to communicate to the internet without having to pass proxies, is running Windows Server 2012 R2, or a newer version of Windows Server, and is domain-joined and has IE ESC turned off. If proxies need to be passed, take the appropriate measures, by either making a proxy exception or configuring a proxy for Azure AD Connect in its configuration file.

Make sure the accounts in the on-premise Active Directory are configured with a publicly routable `userPrincipalName` suffix, such as `lucernpub.com`. Make sure the DNS domain name(s) representing the UPN suffix(es) are owned by your organization on the internet and configured as verified DNS domain name(s) in your organization's Azure AD tenant.

The account in Active Directory that is a member of the Domain Admins group is also used to roll out the required Group Policy settings. It also works with an account that is delegated to create Group Policy Objects.

Download Azure AD Connect from `aka.ms/aadconnect`.

How to do it...

Configuring Azure AD Connect with PTA and Seamless SSO consists of the following high-level steps:

1. Adding the Azure AD Authentication Service to the intranet sites
2. Configuring Azure AD Connect

Adding the Azure AD Authentication Service to the intranet sites

Perform these steps to add the Azure AD Authentication service to Internet Explorer's and Edge's **Intranet Sites** list in a new Group Policy object that is targeted to the same Organizational Unit (OU) filtering scope as in Azure AD Connect:

1. Log into a system with the Group Policy Management Console feature installed.
2. Open the **Group Policy Management** Console (`gpmc.msc`).
3. In the left-hand pane, navigate to the **Group Policy objects** node.
4. Locate the Group Policy object that you want to use and select it, or right-click the **Group Policy Objects** node and select **New** from the menu.
5. Right-click the Group Policy object and select **Edit...** from the menu.
   The **Group Policy Management Editor** window appears.
6. In the left navigation pane, navigate to **User Configuration**, then **Policies**, then **Administrative Templates**, **Windows Components**, **Internet Explorer**, **Internet Control Panel**, and, lastly, **Security Page**.

7. In the main pane, select the **Site to Zone Assignment List** setting:

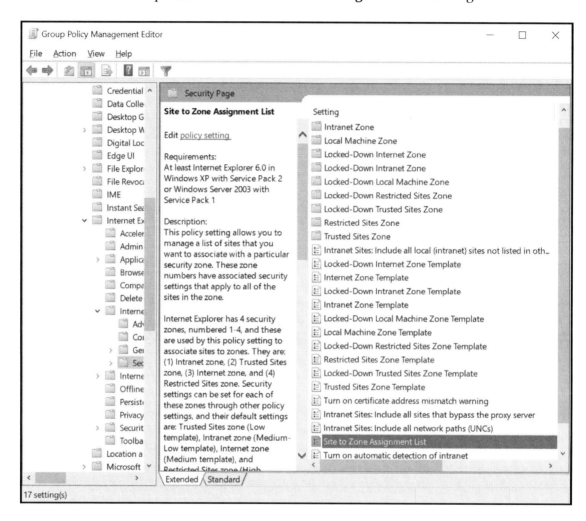

8. Double-click the **Site to Zone Assignment List** setting.
9. Select **Enabled**.
10. Click the **Show…** button.
11. In the **Value name** field, enter
    the `https://autologon.microsoftazuread-sso.com` URL.
12. In the **value** field, assign **1**, as this value corresponds to the **Intranet Sites** zone.
13. Click **OK**.
14. Click **OK** to close the Group Policy setting.

15. Close the **Group Policy Management Editor** window.
16. In the left navigation pane, navigate to the Organization Unit (OU) where you want to link the GPO.
17. Right-click the OU and select **Link an existing GPO...** from the menu.
18. In the **Select GPO** window, select the GPO.
19. Click **OK** to link the GPO.

Configuring Azure AD Connect

Perform these steps to configure Azure AD Connect:

1. Double-click AzureADConnect.msi.
2. On the **Welcome** screen, select the **I agree to the license terms and privacy notice.** option.
3. Click the **Next** button.
4. On the **Express Settings** screen, click the **Customize** button.
   You are presented with the **Install required components** screen:

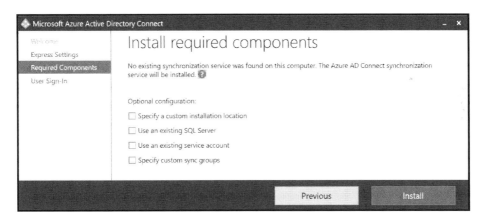

5. On the **Install required components** screen, click **Install**.
6. On the **User sign-in** screen, select the **Pass-through authentication** option and the **Enable single sign-on** option.
7. Click **Next**.
8. On the **Connect to Azure AD** screen, enter the credentials of an account in Azure AD that has been assigned the **Global administrator** role.

9. Click the **Next** button.

10. Optionally, perform multi-factor authentication, and/or elevate the account to **Global administrator** when using Azure AD Privileged Identity Management (PIM).

    You are presented with the **Connect your directories** screen:

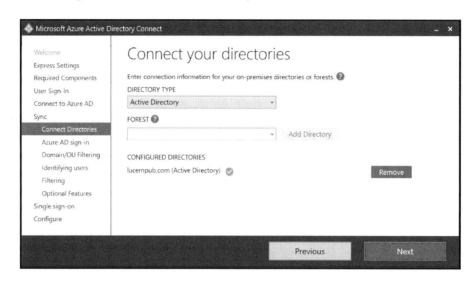

11. On the **Connect your directories** screen, click **Add directory**.
    The **AD forest account** pop-up window appears.

12. Sign in with an account that is a member of the Domain Admins group for the Active Directory domain in which PTA is configured, or an account that is a member of the Enterprise Admins group in the Active Directory forest that contains the domain in which PTA will be configured.

13. Click **OK**.

14. Back in the **Microsoft Azure Active Directory Connect** windows, click **Next**.

15. On the **Azure AD Sign-in configuration** screen, click **Next**.

16. On the **Domain and OU Filtering** screen, click **Next**.

17. On the **Uniquely identifying your users** screen, click **Next**.

18. On the **Filter users and devices** screen, click **Next**.

19. On the **Optional features** screen, click **Next**.

20. On the **Enable single sign-on** screen, click the **Enter credentials** button. A **Windows Security** popup appears to enter the credentials for the specified forest.

21. Enter the credentials of an account which is a member of the Domain Admins group for the Active Directory domain for which Seamless SSO will be configured, or an account that is a member of the Enterprise Admins group in the Active Directory forest, which contains the domain in which Seamless SSO will be configured.

22. Click **OK.**

23. Click **Next**.

24. Back in the **Microsoft Azure Active Directory Connect** windows, click **Next**. You are presented with the **Ready to configure** screen:

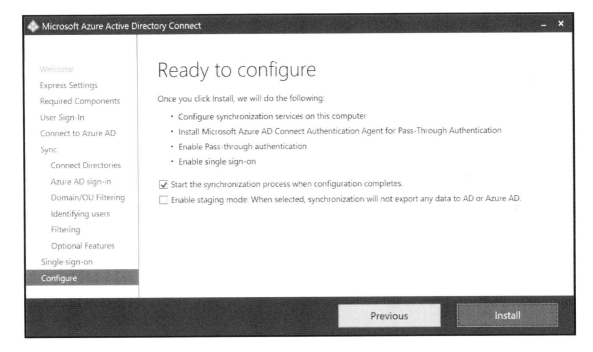

25. On the **Ready to configure** screen, click **Install**.

26. On the **Configuration complete** screen, click **Exit** to close the **Microsoft Azure Active Directory Connect** window and to start synchronization to Azure AD.

How it works...

When enabling PTA in Azure AD Connect, the Windows Server running Azure AD Connect gets the PTA agent installed.

To allow Seamless SSO, people using domain-joined devices need to communicate using Kerberos with the Azure AD Authentication Service with their domain accounts. Kerberos is **Windows Integrated Authentication (WIA)** in browser speak. WIA is not available by default for all websites in browsers for security reasons. The Azure AD Authentication Service needs to be added to the **Intranet Sites** list of Internet Explorer and Edge to allow WIA.

Mozilla Firefox does not automatically use Kerberos authentication. Each user that wants to use Firefox with the Seamless Sign-on feature needs to add the `https://autologon.microsoftazuread-sso.com` URL to **network.negotiate-auth.trusted-URI's** in Firefox's `about:config`. Google Chrome users can add `https://autologon.microsoftazuread-sso.com` to `AuthNegotiateDelegateWhitelist` or de `AuthServerWhitelist` settings for their browser.

There's more...

Install any additional PTA agents on additional Windows Server installations. Microsoft recommends that you have at least two additional PTA agents.

Implementing single sign-on to Office 365 using AD FS

This recipe shows how to configure an AD FS farm, consisting of one AD FS server and one publicly available Web Application Proxy, for SSO with Office 365.

Getting ready

While the recipes in `Chapter 11`, *Managing Federation*, show how to build an AD FS farm, for this recipe, we'll use the built-in capability of Azure AD Connect to configure two Windows Server 2019 installations as AD FS server and Web Application Proxy, respectively.

You'll need three domain-joined Windows Server installations, running Windows Server 2012 R2 or newer versions of Windows Server, for this recipe:

- One server for Azure AD Connect
- One AD FS server, which will use a Windows Internal Database to host the AD FS Configuration database
- One Web Application Proxy

The two Windows Server installations need to be resolvable and reachable on TCP port `5985` by the Windows Server you'll use for the Azure AD Connect installation.

To configure the AD FS farm, the following prerequisites need to be met:

- The AD FS farm name needs to be resolvable to the AD FS server in the internal DNS zone.
- The AD FS farm name needs to be resolvable to the Web Application Proxy in the public DNS zone.
- A publicly valid TLS certificate needs to be available for the AD FS farm name as a file in a password-protected `*.pfx` file, including the private key.

Make sure that the accounts in the on-premise Active Directory are configured with a publicly routable `userPrincipalName` suffix, such as `lucernpub.com`. Make sure the DNS domain name(s) representing the UPN suffix(es) are owned by your organization on the internet.

To connect Active Directory to Azure AD and to set up the AD FS farm, you'll need to sign in with an account that is a local administrator on the server dedicated to Azure AD Connect. As part of the following steps, you'll need to enter the credentials for these accounts:

- An account in Active Directory that is a member of the Enterprise Admins group
- An account in Azure Active Directory that has the Global administrator role assigned

Make sure that the Windows Server that will run Azure AD Connect is able to communicate to the internet without having to pass proxies and has IE ESC turned off. If proxies need to be passed, take the appropriate measures, by either making a proxy exception which configuring a proxy for Azure AD Connect in its configuration file.

How to do it...

Perform these steps on the Windows Server you dedicate to Azure AD Connect:

1. Double-click `AzureADConnect.msi`.
   The **Microsoft Azure Active Directory Connect** screen appears.
2. On the **Welcome** screen, select the **I agree to the license terms and privacy notice.** option.
3. Click the **Continue** button.
4. On the **Express Settings** screen, click the **Customize** button.
5. On the **Install required components** screen, click the **Install** button.
6. On the **User Sign-in** screen, select **Federation with AD FS** as the sign-in method.
7. Click **Next**.
8. On the **Connect to Azure AD** screen, enter the credentials of an account in Azure AD that has been assigned the global administrator role.
9. Click the **Next** button.
10. Optionally, perform multi-factor authentication, and/or elevate the account to **Global administrator** when using Azure AD Privileged Identity Management (PIM)

11. On the **Connect your directories** screen, click **Add directory**. The **AD forest account** pop-up window appears:

12. Make sure the **Create new AD account** option is selected.
13. Enter the credentials of an account that is a member of the **Enterprise Admins** group in the Active Directory forest you want to add.
14. Click **OK** when done.
15. Back in the **Microsoft Azure Active Directory Connect** screen, click **Next**.
16. On the **Azure AD sign-in configuration** screen, click **Next**.
17. On the **Domain and OU filtering** screen, click **Next**.
18. On the **Uniquely identifying your users** screen, click **Next**.
19. On the **Filter users and devices** screen, click **Next**.
20. On the **Optional features** screen, click **Next**.

21. On the **Domain administrator** screen, enter the credentials of an account that is a member of the Domain Admins group for the Active Directory domain in which AD FS will be deployed or configured, or an account that is a member of the Enterprise Admins group in the Active Directory forest that contains the domain in which AD FS server will be deployed or configured.

22. Click **Next**.
    You then reach the **AD FS farm** screen:

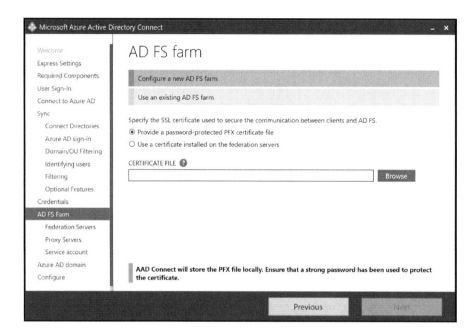

23. On the **AD FS farm** screen, select the **Configure a new AD FS farm** ribbon.

24. Make sure the **Provide a password-protected PFX certificate file** option is selected.

25. Click the **Browse** button.

26. Navigate to the file location of the certificate file and click **OK** when done to select it.
    The **Password** popup appears.

27. Enter the password for the PFX file.

28. Click **OK**.

29. Back in the **Microsoft Azure Active Directory Connect** screen, select the correct **Subject name** from the available subject names in the certificate.

30. Click **Next**.

31. On the **AD FS servers** screen, type the fully qualified domain name(s) of the domain-joined Windows Server(s) you dedicate as the AD FS server(s) in the AD FS farm. Click the **Add** button to add AD FS servers to the AD FS farm.

32. Click **Next**.

33. On the **Web application proxy servers** screen, type the fully qualified domain name(s) of the domain-joined Windows Server(s) you dedicate as the AD FS server(s) in the AD FS farm. Click the **Add** button to add AD FS servers to the AD FS farm.

34. Click **Next**.
    You reach the **AD FS service account** screen:

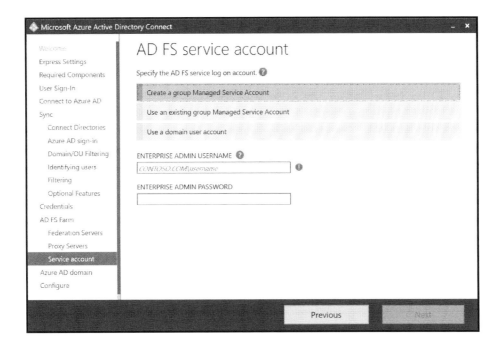

35. On the **AD FS service account** screen, select the **Create a group Managed Service Account** ribbon.

36. Specify the credentials of an account that is a member of the Enterprise Admins group in the Active Directory forest to create the group Managed Service Account (gMSA).

37. Click **Next**.

38. On the **Azure AD domain** screen, select the DNS domain name that is verified in Azure AD and represents the `userPrincipalName` suffix of the user objects in scope.

39. Click **Next**.

40. On the **Ready to configure** screen, click **Install**.
    After **Configuring**, the **Installation complete** screen appears.

41. On the **Installation complete** screen, click **Next** to continue to verify the federation settings.

42. On the **Verify federation connectivity**, ensure that both **I have created DNS A records or DNS AAAA records that allow clients to resolve my federation service from the intranet.** and **I have created DNS A records that allow clients to resolve my federation service from the extranet.** are selected.

43. Click **Verify**.

44. On the **Verify federation connectivity** screen, click **Exit** to close the **Microsoft Azure Active Directory Connect** window, and start off the initial synchronization to Azure AD.

How it works...

When the network ports for WMI Management (TCP 5985) are open between the proposed AD FS server and Web Application Proxy, Azure AD Connect is capable of configuring the hosts automatically with their role and the required configuration to federate with Azure Active Directory.

First, Azure AD Connect connects to the Azure AD tenant, using the credentials supplied for the Global administrator account. Then, the Active Directory forest is connected, using the credentials for the account that is a member of the Enterprise Admins group.

As AD FS is selected as the sign-in method, the Microsoft Azure AD Connect Configuration Wizard presents the flow to configure the AD FS farm consisting of one AD FS server and one Web Application Proxy.

The AD FS farm will be configured with the following:

- A **Windows Internal Database (WID)** to store and replicate the AD FS Configuration database
- A **group Managed Service Account (gMSA)** as the AD FS service account
- A **relying party trust (RPT)** between the AD FS farm and Azure Active Directory

After configuration, Azure AD Connect verifies name resolution for the AD FS farm, using both the internal and the public DNS zones.

There's more...

When using the recipes in `Chapter 11`, *Managing Federation*, an AD FS farm can be tailored to the specific needs of the organization. For instance, the Web Application Proxy can be stand-alone instead of domain-joined.

When reusing an existing AD FS farm with Azure AD Connect, specify **Use an existing AD FS farm** instead of **Configure a new AD FS farm** in *step 23*. Instead of setting up an AD FS farm, the ensuing steps would validate the AD FS farm and configure the relying party trust.

Managing AD FS with Azure AD Connect

This recipe explores the possibilities of managing an AD FS farm with Azure AD Connect.

Getting ready

For this recipe, you'll need the following:

- A properly configured AD FS farm, running Windows Server 2012 R2 or newer versions of Windows Server
- A properly configured Azure AD Connect installation, capable of communicating with the AD FS servers and Web Application Proxies in the AD FS farm using TCP 5985

Sign into the Windows Server installation with Azure AD Connect with an account that is a local administrator.

How to do it...

Perform these steps first:

1. Open the Azure AD Connect Configuration Wizard from the Start Menu or desktop.
2. In the **Welcome to Azure AD Connect** screen, click **Configure**.
3. In the **Additional tasks** screen, select the **Manage federation** ribbon.
4. Click **Next**.
   You are presented with the **Manage federation** screen:

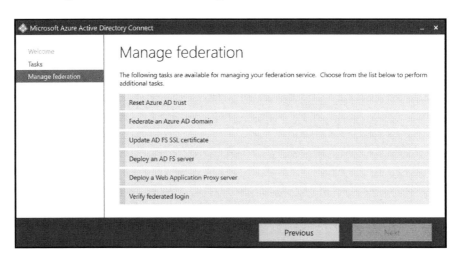

5. Choose between the available actions.

Perform these steps for each action shown in the following subsections.

Reset Azure AD trust

Perform these steps to reset the relying party trust between the AD FS farm and Azure AD:

1. Select the **Reset Azure AD trust** ribbon.
2. Click **Next**.
3. On the **Connect to Azure AD** screen, enter the credentials of an account in Azure AD that has been assigned the **Global administrator** role.
4. On the **Connect to AD FS** screen, enter the credentials for an account that is a member of the **Enterprise Admins** group.
   You are presented with the **Certificates** screen:

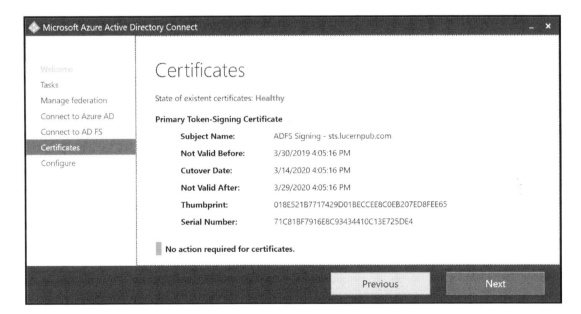

5. On the **Certificates** screen, click **Next**.
6. On the **Ready to Configure** screen, click **Configure**.
7. On the **Configuration complete** screen, click **Exit** to close the **Microsoft Azure Active Directory Connect** window and to restart synchronization to Azure AD.

Federate an Azure AD domain

Perform these steps to add a verified DNS domain name in Azure AD as a federated domain:

1. Select the **Federate an Azure AD domain** ribbon.
2. Click **Next**.
3. On the **Connect to Azure AD** screen, enter the credentials of an account in Azure AD that has been assigned the **Global administrator** role.
4. On the **Connect to AD FS** screen, enter the credentials for an account that is a member of the **Enterprise Admins** group.
5. On the **Azure AD Domain** screen, select the Azure AD domain to federate with the Azure AD Connect-managed AD FS farm.
6. Click **Next**.
7. On the **Ready to Configure** screen, click **Configure**.
8. On the **Configuration complete** screen, click **Exit** to close the **Microsoft Azure Active Directory Connect** window, and to restart synchronization to Azure AD.

Update the AD FS SSL certificate

Perform these steps to update the AD FS SSL certificate with a few simple clicks on all AD FS servers and Web Application Proxy servers in the Azure AD Connect-managed AD FS farm:

1. Select the **Update AD FS SSL certificate** ribbon.
2. Click **Next**.
3. On the **Connect to Azure AD** screen, enter the credentials of an account in Azure AD that has been assigned the **Global administrator** role.
4. On the **Connect to AD FS** screen, enter the credentials for an account that is a member of the **Enterprise Admins** group.
5. On the **AD FS servers** screen, check that all AD FS servers are present. Use the **Add** button to add missing AD FS servers. Use the **Remove** link next to the AD FS servers that are offline or no longer part of the AD FS farm.
    1. On the **Web Application Proxy servers** screen, check that all Web Application Proxies are present. Use the **Add** button to add missing Web Application Proxies. Use the **Remove** link next to Web Application Proxies that are offline or no longer part of the AD FS farm.
6. Click **Next**.

7. On the **SSL Certificate** screen, click the **Browse** button. Navigate to the file location of the certificate file and click **OK** when done to select it.
The **Certificate Password** popup appears.

8. Enter the password for the PFX file.

9. Click **OK**.

10. Click **Next**.

11. On the **Select servers for SSL certificate update** screen, check that all AD FS servers and Web Application Proxies that are connected to the AD FS farm are selected.

12. Click **Next**.

13. On the **Ready to Configure** screen, click **Configure**.
After configuration, the **Configuration complete** screen appears:

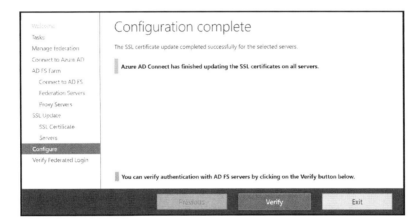

14. On the **Configuration complete** screen, click **Next** to continue to verify the federation settings.

15. On the **Verify federated login**, enter the credentials for a federated user account.

16. Click **Verify**.

17. On the **Verify federated login** screen, click **Exit** to close the **Microsoft Azure Active Directory Connect** window, and to restart synchronization to Azure AD.

Deploy an AD FS server

Perform these steps to add an additional AD FS server to the Azure AD Connect-managed AD FS farm:

1. Select the **Add an AD FS server** ribbon.
2. Click **Next**.
3. On the **Connect to Azure AD** screen, enter the credentials of an account in Azure AD that has been assigned the **Global administrator** role.
4. On the **Connect to AD FS** screen, enter the credentials for an account that is a member of the **Enterprise Admins** group.
   You then reach the **Specify SSL certificate** screen:

5. On the **Specify SSL certificate** screen, click the **Password** button.
   The **Password** popup appears.
6. Enter the password for the PFX file.
7. Click **OK**.
8. Back in the **Microsoft Azure Active Directory Connect** screen, select the correct **Subject name** from the available subject names in the certificate.
9. Click **Next**.

10. On the **AD FS Servers** screen, enter the server name or IP address of the domain-joined Windows Server installation to be added as an AD FS server to the AD FS farm.
11. Click **Add**.
12. Click **Next**.
13. On the **Ready to Configure** screen, click **Configure**.
14. On the **Configuration complete** screen, click **Next** to continue to verify the federation settings.
15. On the **Verify federation connectivity**, ensure that both **I have created DNS A records or DNS AAAA records that allow clients to resolve my federation service from the intranet.** and **I have created DNS A records that allow clients to resolve my federation service from the extranet.** are selected.
16. Click **Verify**.
17. On the **Verify federation connectivity** screen, click **Exit** to close the **Microsoft Azure Active Directory Connect** window and to restart synchronization to Azure AD.

Add a Web Application Proxy server

Perform these steps to add an additional Web Application Proxy server to the Azure AD Connect-managed AD FS farm:

1. Select the **Add a Web Application Proxy server** ribbon.
2. Click **Next**.
3. On the **Connect to Azure AD** screen, enter the credentials of an account in Azure AD that has been assigned the **Global administrator** role.
4. On the **Connect to AD FS** screen, enter the credentials for an account that is a member of the **Enterprise Admins** group.
5. On the **Specify SSL certificate** screen, click the **Password** button.
   The **Password** popup appears.
6. Enter the password for the PFX file.
7. Click **OK**.
8. Back in the **Microsoft Azure Active Directory Connect** screen, select the right **Subject name** from the available subject names in the certificate.
9. Click **Next**.

10. On the **Web Application Proxy Servers** screen, enter the server name or IP address of the domain-joined Windows Server installation to be added as a Web Application Proxy server to the AD FS farm.
11. Click **Add**.
12. Click **Next**.
13. On the **Ready to Configure** screen, click **Configure**.
14. On the **Configuration complete** screen, click **Next** to continue to verify the federation settings.
15. On the **Verify federation connectivity**, ensure that both **I have created DNS A records or DNS AAAA records that allow clients to resolve my federation service from the intranet.** and **I have created DNS A records that allow clients to resolve my federation service from the extranet.** are selected.
16. Click **Verify**.
17. On the **Verify federation connectivity** screen, click **Exit** to close the **Microsoft Azure Active Directory Connect** window and to restart synchronization to Azure AD.

Verify federated login

Perform these steps to verify federated logins:

1. Select the **Verify federated login** ribbon.
2. Click **Next**.
3. On the **Connect to Azure AD** screen, enter the credentials of an account in Azure AD that has been assigned the **Global administrator** role.
4. On the **Verify federated login screen**, enter the credentials for a federated user account.
5. Click **Verify**:

6. On the **Verify federated login** screen, click **Exit** to close the **Microsoft Azure Active Directory Connect** window and to restart synchronization to Azure AD.

How it works...

Azure AD Connect can help administrators to manage AD FS farms. For this functionality, the AD FS farm does not need to have been set up using the Azure AD Connect Configuration Wizard to be manageable with Azure AD Connect, as existing AD FS farms can also be on-boarded to Azure AD Connect by using the **Use an existing AD FS farm** option when configuring **Federation with AD FS** as the sign-in method for one or more UPN suffixes in Active Directory.

With all management actions, Azure AD Connect will configure the Azure AD synchronization connector and enable an Azure AD Connect deletion threshold. For all actions that concern the relying party trust with Azure AD in AD FS, the relying party trust information will be backed up first.

There's more...

Resetting the Relying Party Trust using Azure AD Connect after onboarding an existing AD FS farm is recommended, as the `Convert-MSOLDomainToFederated` PowerShell cmdlet in the **MSOnline** PowerShell module merely adds a handful of claims rules in AD FS for the "Office 365 Identity Platform" relying party trust. Using Azure AD Connect **Reset Azure AD trust** unlocks the full range of functionality, while providing a roll-back scenario through its backup.

Implementing Azure Traffic Manager for AD FS geo-redundancy

This recipe shows how to implement a geo-redundant AD FS deployment consisting of two AD FS servers and two Web Application Proxies, equally distributed over two geographically dispersed data centers.

Getting ready

For this recipe, we'll assume that an Active Directory domain exists with domain controllers in a networking environment consisting of two separate, geographically dispersed datacenters. Each data center is defined as an Active Directory site. The traffic required to allow Active Directory replication is allowed, as is TCP 80.

Follow the steps of *Installing the AD FS server role* recipe from Chapter 11, *Managing Federation*, to install the AD FS server role on two Windows Server installations, each running in a separate, geographically dispersed datacenter. Follow the steps of *Setting up an AD FS farm with WID* recipe from Chapter 11, *Managing Federation*, to set up an AD FS farm with WID on one of the two AD FS servers. Follow the steps of *Adding additional AD FS servers to an AD FS farm* recipe from Chapter 11, *Managing Federation*, to add the second AD FS server. Perform the steps of *Setting up a Web Application Proxy* recipe from Chapter 11, *Managing Federation*, to set up both Web Application Proxies.

Provide inbound access for both TCP 80 and TCP 443 to both Web Application Proxies, using separate IP addresses. Create DNS records for the public IP addresses of the two Web Application Proxies. For instance, when the AD FS farm URL is sts.lucernpub.com, dedicate sts1.lucernpub.com to the external IPv4 address of the first Web Application Proxy and sts2.lucernpub.com to the other.

How to do it...

Implementing geo-redundancy for AD FS consists of three steps:

1. Configuring the Web Application Proxies for probing
2. Configuring Azure Traffic Manager
3. Adding DNS records

Configuring the Web Application Proxies for probing

Run the following lines of PowerShell on each of the Web Application Proxies to configure them for probing:

```
Import-Module NetSecurity

New-NetFirewallRule -Name Allow_HTTP -DisplayName "AD FS HTTP Services" -
Protocol HTTP -Profile Any -Action Allow
```

Configuring Azure Traffic Manager

Perform these steps to configure Azure Traffic Manager:

1. Log onto the Microsoft Azure Portal at `https://portal.azure.com` with an account that has sufficient permissions to create a resource group or add resources to an existing resource group.
2. If the account is associated with multiple tenants, choose the right tenant by clicking on the name or email address of the account in the top right corner of the Azure portal. Select the tenant you want to use from the bottom of the context menu.
3. Click the big green plus sign in the left navigation menu to add products and services to your tenant.
4. In the **Search the Marketplace** field, search for **Traffic Manager Profile**, then select it.
   The **Traffic Manager Profile** blade appears. It contains information on what Traffic Manager does, information on its publisher, and help links.
5. Click the **Create** button on the bottom of the blade.
   The **Create Traffic Manager profile** blade appears.
6. Type and select the following information:
   1. Type the name of your Traffic Manager profile, for instance **LucernSTS**. This will be appended by `trafficmanager.net` to become the **Fully-qualified Domain Name (FQDN)** of the Traffic Manager profile.
   2. Select a **Routing method** from the drop-down list.
   3. Select a **Subscription** from the drop-down list.
   4. Create a new Azure Resource Manager (ARM) **Resource group**, or if you already have a resource group for Traffic Manager profiles and other load-balancing/high-availability resources in the subscription, reuse that, by selecting it from the drop-down list.
   5. Select a **Resource group location** from the drop-down list when you create a new Resource group, otherwise, continue with the next step.

7. Click **Create** on the bottom of the blade.
   You are redirected back to the Azure Portal dashboard and automatically taken into the configuration of your newly created Azure Traffic Manager profile:

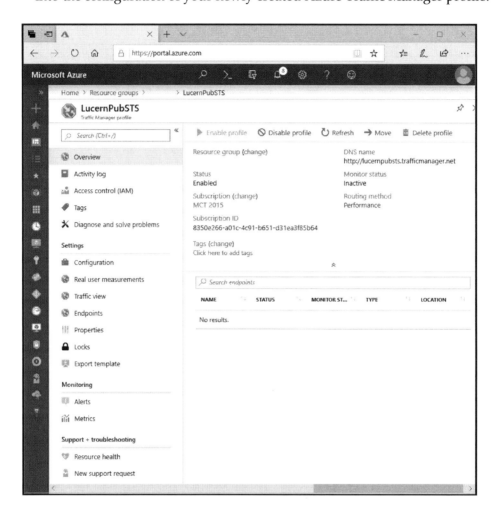

8. In the left navigation blade, click **Configuration** under **Settings**. The **Configuration** blade appears.
9. In the **Configuration** blade, click the **Path** field under **Endpoint monitor settings**. Change it to `/adfs/probe/`.
10. Click **Save** on the top of the blade.
11. In the left navigation blade, click **Endpoints**.
12. Follow the **+ Add** link on the top of the blade. The **Add endpoint** blade will then appear.
13. From the **Type** drop-down list, select **External endpoint**.
14. Type something meaningful as the name.
15. For the FQDN, enter the DNS name you assigned to the external IP address of the load balancer of Web Application Proxy in the location.
16. Select a **Location** from the drop-down list. This determines the end-user device locations to be directed to this endpoint.
17. Click **OK**.

Repeat steps 12 – 17 to add the endpoint for the other Web Application Proxy.

Adding DNS records

Next, add a DNS CNAME record for the AD FS farm name to the Azure Traffic Manager URL you choose the preceding in the external DNS zone. For instance, `sts.lucernpub.com` would point to `lucernpubsts.trafficmanager.net`.

How it works...

Azure Traffic Manager is an Azure-based user traffic load-balancing solution. It can direct user traffic between and/or to IP addresses associated with endpoints for Azure Virtual Machines, Azure (cloud and app) services, and on-premise networks. Traffic Manager uses DNS to direct client requests to the most appropriate endpoint in its configuration, based on the traffic routing method of your choice and the health of the endpoints. It provides automatic failover.

Traffic Manager offers failover, performance, geographic, or weighted routing methods for client requests originating from outside the organization. Active Directory sites would offer routing to the closest AD FS server inside the organization.

Azure Traffic Manager probes the `/adfs/probe/` URLs on the Web Application Proxies to determine whether the hosts are available to handle authentication requests. When Traffic Manager determines the endpoint is capable of handling authentication requests, it provides the endpoint's DNS address to the device based on the routing method. If the endpoint is deemed degraded or is offline, Azure Traffic Manager does not return its DNS name to the device.

There's more...

This method to make AD FS geo-redundant is very cost-efficient, as Azure Traffic Manager will merely consume a small amount of money for probing endpoints (per endpoint) and redirects (per million requests). However, it does not offer resilience for when an AD FS server is down, as the solution merely probes the Web Application Proxies.

Migrating from AD FS to Pass-through Authentication for single sign-on to Office 365

This recipe shows how to change the sign-in method from federation with AD FS to PTA and Seamless SSO

Getting ready

Make sure the organization has not implemented heavy customizations to the `onload.js` of the AD FS logon pages, uses smartcard- or certificate-based authentication to Office 365, or relies on on-premise multi-factor authentication solutions.

To configure the sign-in method within Azure AD Connect, you'll need to sign-in with an account that is a local administrator on the server dedicated to Azure AD Connect. As part of the following steps, you'll need to enter the credentials for these accounts:

- An account in Active Directory that is a member of the Enterprise Admins group
- An account in Azure Active Directory that has the Global Administrator role assigned

Make sure the Windows Server running Azure AD Connect is able to communicate to the internet without having to pass proxies and has IE ESC turned off.

The account in Active Directory that is a member of the **Domain Admins** group is also used to roll out the required Group Policy settings. It also works with an account that is delegated to create **Group Policy Objects** (**GPOs**).

How to do it...

Migrating from AD FS to PTA consists of the following high-level steps:

1. Adding the Azure AD Authentication Service to the intranet sites
2. Configuring Azure AD Connect
3. Checking domains in the Azure Portal
4. Disabling federation in Azure AD
5. Deleting the *Office 365 Identity Platform* relying party trust

Adding the Azure AD Authentication Service to the intranet sites

Perform these steps to add the Azure AD Authentication service to Internet Explorer's and Edge's **Intranet Sites** list in a new Group Policy object that is targeted to the same Organizational Unit (OU) filtering scope as in Azure AD Connect:

1. Log into a system with the Group Policy Management Console feature installed.
2. Open the **Group Policy Management** Console (gpmc.msc)
3. In the left pane, navigate to the **Group Policy objects** node.
4. Locate the Group Policy Object that you want to use and select it, or right-click the **Group Policy Objects** node and select **New** from the menu.
5. Right-click the Group Policy object and select **Edit...** from the menu.
   The **Group Policy Management Editor** window appears.

6. In the left navigation pane, navigate to **User Configuration**, then **Policies**, then **Administrative Templates**, **Windows Components**, **Internet Explorer**, **Internet Control Panel**, and, lastly, **Security Page**.
7. Double-click the **Site to Zone Assignment List** setting.
8. Select **Enabled**.
9. Click the **Show...** button.
   The **Show Contents** window appears:

10. In the **Value name** field, enter the `https://autologon.microsoftazuread-sso.com` URL.
11. In the **value** field, assign **1**, as this value corresponds to the **Intranet Sites** zone.
12. Click **OK**.
13. Click **OK** to close the Group Policy setting.
14. Close the **Group Policy Management Editor** window.
15. In the left navigation pane, navigate to the Organization Unit (OU) where you want to link the GPO.
16. Right-click the OU and select **Link an existing GPO...** from the menu.
17. In the **Select GPO** window, select the GPO.
18. Click **OK** to link the GPO.

Configuring Azure AD Connect

Perform these steps to configure Azure AD Connect:

1. Open the Azure AD Connect Configuration Wizard from the Start Menu or desktop.
2. In the **Welcome to Azure AD Connect** screen, click **Configure**.
3. In the **Additional tasks** screen, select the **Change user sign-in** ribbon.
4. Click **Next**.
5. On the **Connect to Azure AD** screen, enter the credentials of an account in Azure AD that has been assigned the **Global administrator** role.
6. Click **Next**.
   The **User sign-in** screen appears:

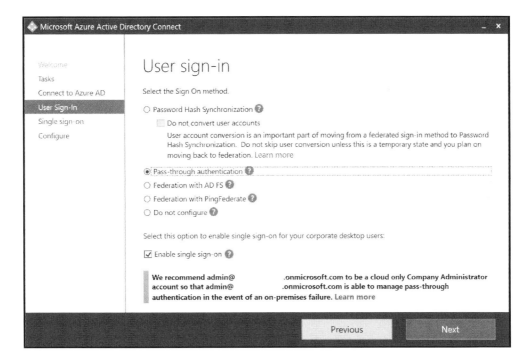

7. On the **User sign-in** screen, select the **Pass-through authentication** option. Additionally, you'll notice the **Enable single sign-on** option is automatically selected, too.
8. Click **Next**.

9. On the **Enable single sign-on** screen, click the **Enter credentials** button. A **Windows Security** popup appears for you to enter the credentials for the specified forest.

10. Enter the credentials of an account that is a member of the **Domain Admins** group for the Active Directory domain for which Seamless SSO will be configured, or an account that is a member of the **Enterprise Admins** group in the Active Directory forest, that contains the domain in which Seamless SSO will be configured.

11. Click **OK.**

12. Back in the **Microsoft Azure Active Directory Connect** windows, click **Next.** The **Ready to configure** screen appears:

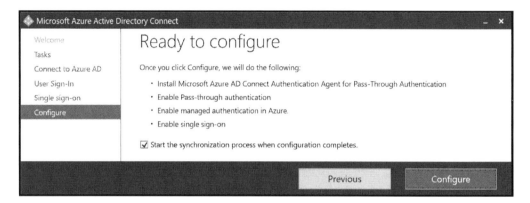

13. On the **Ready to configure** screen, click **Configure**.

14. On the **Configuration complete** screen, click **Exit** to close the **Microsoft Azure Active Directory Connect** window and to restart synchronization to Azure AD.

Checking domains in the Azure portal

Perform these steps to check whether all federated DNS domain names have successfully migrated to PTA:

1. Navigate a browser to `portal.azure.com`.
2. Log in with an account in Azure Active Directory that has the **Global administrator** role assigned.
3. Perform multi-factor authentication when prompted.
4. In the left navigation pane, click **Azure Active Directory**.
5. In the Azure AD pane, click **Azure AD Connect**.

6. In the main pane for Azure AD Connect, under **User sign-in**, you should see that 0 domains use **Federation**, that all custom DNS domain names use **Seamless single sign-on**, and that there is one **Pass-through Authentication** agent.

Disabling federation in Azure AD

Perform these steps, for each DNS domain name, to disable federation with AD FS on the Azure AD side:

1. Log on to the primary AD FS server in the AD FS farm with an account that is a member of the **Domain Admins** group for the Active Directory domain in which AD FS is configured, or an account that is a member of the **Enterprise Admins** group in the Active Directory forest, that contains the domain in which AD FS is configured.

2. Open an elevated Windows PowerShell window.

3. Type the following line of PowerShell to import the Microsoft Online (**MSOnline**) Windows PowerShell module:

```
Import-Module MSOnline
```

If this cmdlet fails, then install the module, using **Install-Module MSOnline**.

4. Type the following line of PowerShell to be presented a login prompt to Azure AD. Log in using an account that has the **Global administrator** role assigned:

```
Connect-MSOLService
```

5. Type the following line of PowerShell to convert a DNS domain name in Azure AD from **Federated** to **Managed**:

```
Set-MsolDomainAuthentication -Authentication Managed -DomainName
lucernpub.com
```

Repeat the preceding steps for each DNS domain name associated with the Azure AD tenant until the Azure portal reports that there are no more federated domain names for the Azure AD tenant. On the **Azure AD Connect** page in the Azure portal, next to **Federation**, it will display **Disabled**.

Deleting the Office 365 Identity Platform relying party trust

Perform these steps to disable federation on the AD FS side by deleting the **Office 365 Identity Platform** relying party trust:

1. Log on to the AD FS server with an account that is a member of the Domain Admins group.
2. Open **AD FS Management** (`Microsoft.IdentityServer.msc`).
3. In the left navigation pane, under the **AD FS** node, expand the **Relying Party Trusts** node.
4. In the main pane, select the **Office 365 Identity Platform** relying party trust.
5. In the right **Actions** pane, click **Delete**, or right-click the relying party trust and select **Delete** from the menu:

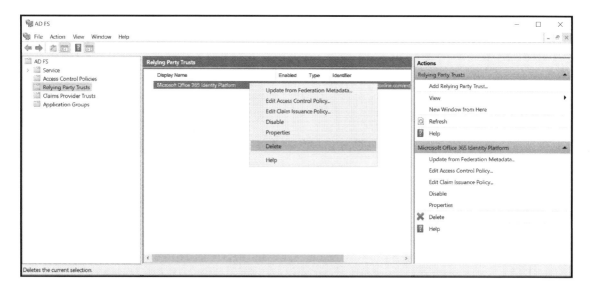

6. In the **AD FS Management** popup window, click **Yes** as the answer to the question **Are you sure you want to delete this item?**.

How it works...

PTA offers a sign-in method with less overhead. For organizations that adopted Office 365 early on, the migration from federation with Active Directory Federation Services as the authentication method to PTA with Seamless SSO as the authentication method is clear.

However, if your organization has heavy customizations in the `onload.js` file of the AD FS login pages, the Azure AD login pages might not fit your organization's needs. If your organization has implemented on-premise multi-factor authentication solutions, expand these solutions into Azure AD, migrate MFA settings for users to Azure AD or start over with Azure MFA to continue to have the same level of security going forward.

When enabling PTA in Azure AD Connect, the Windows Server running Azure AD Connect gets the PTA Agent installed. Install any additional PTA agents on additional Windows Server installations. Microsoft recommends that you have at least two additional PTA agents.

To allow Seamless SSO, people using domain-joined devices need to communicate to the Azure AD Authentication Service with their domain accounts using Kerberos. Kerberos, in browser-speak, is WIA. WIA is not available by default for all website in browser for security reasons. The Azure AD Authentication Service needs to be added to the **Intranet Sites** list of Internet Explorer and Edge to allow WIA.

 Mozilla Firefox does not automatically use Kerberos authentication. Each user that wants to use Firefox with the Seamless Sign-on feature needs to add the `https://autologon.microsoftazuread-sso.com` URL to **network.negotiate-auth.trusted-URI's** in Firefox's `about:config`. Google Chrome users can add `https://autologon.microsoftazuread-sso.com` to `AuthNegotiateDelegateWhitelist` or the `AuthServerWhitelist` settings for their browser.

Changing the user sign-in method in Azure AD Connect makes no changes to AD FS. Instead, the relying party trust between AD FS and Azure AD, aptly named *Office 365 Identity Platform,* needs to be deleted to properly clean up after migrating all DNS domain names from AD FS to PTA.

There's more...

When there are no more relying party trusts in AD FS, the AD FS farm can be decommissioned.

Follow these recipes to do so in `Chapter 11`, *Managing Federation*:

- *Decommissioning a Web Application Proxy*
- *Removing AD FS servers from an AD FS farm*

Making Pass-through Authentication (geo)redundant

This recipe shows how to install additional PTA Agents to make PTA (geo)redundant.

Getting ready

To register additional PTA Agents with Azure AD, you'll need to sign-in with an account that is a local administrator on the Windows Server installation you plan to run the PTA Agent on. As part of the following steps, you'll need to enter the credentials for these accounts:

- An account in Active Directory that is a member of the Enterprise Admins group
- An account in Azure Active Directory that has the Global administrator role assigned

Make sure the Windows Server running the additional PTA Agent is able to communicate to the internet without having to pass proxies, is running Windows Server 2012 R2, or a newer version of Windows Server, and has IE ESC turned off.

Download the PTA Agent from `aka.ms/getauthagent`.

How to do it...

Adding an additional PTA Agent consists of two steps:

1. Installing and configuring the PTA Agent
2. Checking proper installation and configuration

Installing and configuring the PTA Agent

Perform these steps on the additional PTA agent:

1. Double-click `AADConnectAuthAgentSetup.exe`:
   The **Microsoft Azure AD Connect Authentication Agent Package** window appears as follows:

2. Click **Install**.
   The **Sign in to your account** screen appears.
3. Enter the `userPrincipalName` of your account in Active Directory Domain Services that is a member of the **Enterprise Admins** group
4. Click **Next**.
5. Enter the password of your account and click **Sign in**.
6. Optionally, you can perform multi-factor authentication, and/or elevate the account to **Global administrator** when using Azure AD Privileged Identity Management (PIM)
7. Back in the **Microsoft Azure AD Connect Authentication Agent Package** window, click **Close**.

Checking proper installation and configuration

Perform these steps to check the installation and configuration of the PTA Agent in Azure AD:

1. Navigate a browser to `portal.azure.com`.
2. Log in with an account in Azure Active Directory that has the **Global administrator** role assigned.
3. Perform multi-factor authentication when prompted.
4. In the left navigation pane, click **Azure Active Directory**.
5. In the Azure AD pane, click **Azure AD Connect**.
   In the main pane for Azure AD Connect, under **user sign-in**, you should see two agents, **Enabled**. for **Pass-through authentication**.
6. Click the **Pass-through authentication** link:

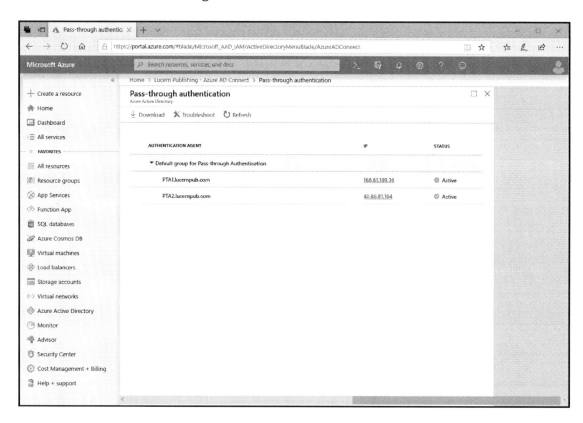

On the Pass-through authentication page, you should see your PTA agents with their IP address, indicating their outside IP addresses and their status. You should see green checks.

How it works...

By default, the Windows Server running Azure AD Connect, on which PTA was configured, acts as the first and only PTA Agent.

To make PTA (geo)redundant and make authentication for end-users not dependent on one Windows Server installation, PTA Agents can be added.

So, how many PTA Agents should you place? Microsoft recommends a minimum of three PTA Agents per tenant, depending on the number of user objects that use PTA. Each PTA agent is equipped with its own certificate, for which it uses the private key to decrypt authentication requests.

The Azure AD Authentication Service puts each authentication request on the Azure Service Bus, specifically encrypted for each of the registered PTA Agents. Registering unnecessary PTA Agents or PTA Agents that are across tremendously slow networking connections, therefore, might mean more authentication requests on the Azure Service Bus, and, thus, delays for end users authenticating using PTA.

13
Handling Synchronization in a Hybrid World (Azure AD Connect)

The previous chapter discussed authentication in a hybrid world and touched upon Azure AD Connect. This chapter provides in-depth recipes for Azure AD Connect, as it is both Microsoft's recommended synchronization tool, and the most used synchronization tool, used by 99% of all tenants worldwide.

The recipes in this chapter contain configuration items that are not available when **Express Settings** are used in Azure AD Connect. The **Customize** button is the key to the functionality outlined here.

The following recipes will be covered in this chapter:

- Choosing the right sourceAnchor
- Configuring staging mode
- Switching to a staging mode server
- Configuring Domain and OU filtering
- Configuring Azure AD app and attribute filtering
- Configuring MinSync
- Configuring Hybrid Azure AD Join
- Configuring Device writeback
- Configuring Password writeback
- Configuring Group writeback
- Changing the passwords for Azure AD Connect service accounts

Choosing the right sourceAnchor

This recipe shows how to choose the right **sourceAnchor** attribute for Azure AD Connect.

Getting ready

To make a choice, you'll need to know the following characteristics of your organization:

- Is your organization's current Active Directory environment a multi-forest environment?
- Is your organization currently consolidating Active Directory domains and/or planning to acquire other organizations and configure these organizations into the current hybrid identity environment in scope for synchronization by Azure AD Connect?
- Does your organization already have a federation solution and use claims-based applications, either inside your organization or cloud-based applications, systems, and/or services?
- Does your organization currently use or plan to use a third-party solution that leverages the **mS-DS-ConsistencyGUID** attribute?

How to do it...

Use the following flowchart to choose the right authentication method for your organization:

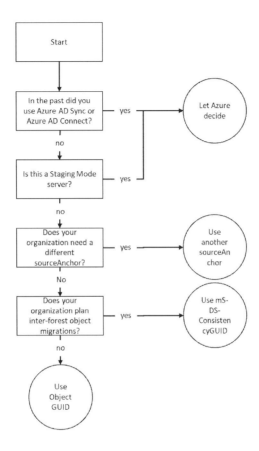

How it works...

In hybrid identity, where Active Directory and Azure AD work together, an attribute needs to be agreed upon to be the end-to-end identifier. In some synchronization solutions, this attribute is called the `ImmutableId`. In Azure AD Connect, it's called the `sourceAnchor`.

For synchronization purposes, this attribute needs to be immutable, meaning it doesn't change during the lifetime of an object, and unique. That's why an email address or surname make for bad `sourceAnchor` attributes: the email address might change when someone gets married. A surname might not be unique throughout the organization.

Beyond immutability and uniqueness, the attribute value for a `sourceAnchor` attribute must be fewer than 60 characters in length; must be either a string, integer, or binary; should not be case-sensitive and avoid values that may vary by case; and should be assigned when the object is created.

If you have a single forest on-premises, then the attribute you should use is `objectGUID`. If you foresee Active Directory migrations or consolidations, you should use `mS-DS-ConsistencyGUID`.

In Azure AD Connect, during initial configuration only, when **Customize** was chosen on the **Express Settings** screen, there are two options on the **Uniquely identifying your users** screen, as shown in the following screenshot:

- Let Azure manage the source anchor
- Choose a specific attribute

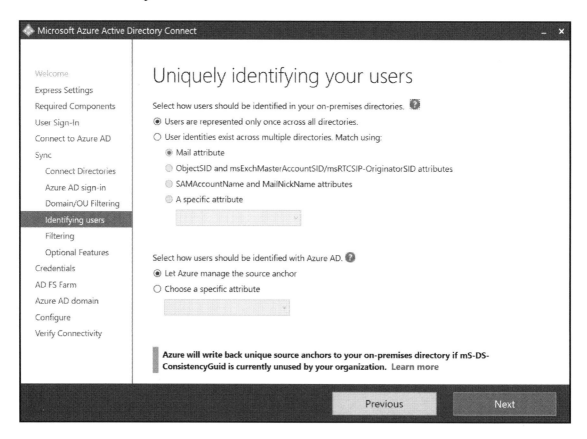

When you select the first option, Azure AD Connect scans the `mS-DS-ConsistencyGUID` attributes of objects in Active Directory using LDAP. When Azure AD Connect finds an object with the attribute filled, it will use `objectGUID`, unless a previous Azure AD Connect installation has specified in Azure AD that it used the `mS-DS-ConsistencyGUID` attribute as the `sourceAnchor` attribute.

In the first scenario, Azure AD Connect assumes another synchronization solution uses the attribute. In the second scenario, Azure AD Connect assumes the value was previously used by the same type of solution for the same purpose. When **Use Express Settings** was chosen on the **Express Settings** screen, the preceding logic always applies.

The `sourceAnchor` attribute value cannot be changed after the object has been created in Azure AD and the identity is synchronized. Therefore, Azure AD Connect only allows the `sourceAnchor` attribute to be set during initial installation.

If you need to change this setting, then you must uninstall and reinstall, except for switching from the `objectGUID` attribute to the `mS-DS-ConsistencyGUID` attribute using the **Configure Source Anchor** additional task:

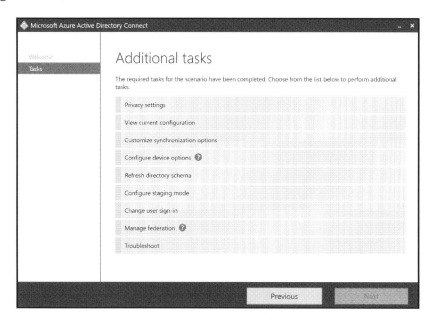

Any settings for the `sourceAnchor` need to be configured on Azure AD Connect installations in staging mode, too.

There's more...

The value stored in the `mS-DS-ConsistencyGUID` attribute is the Base64 representation of the `objectGUID` attribute.

When using **Customize** and creating your own Azure AD Connect service account, make sure the account is delegated to write the `mS-DS-ConsistencyGUID` attribute for user objects in scope.

Configuring staging mode

This recipe provides tips for configuring Azure AD Connect in staging mode.

Getting ready

To implement one or more staging mode servers, you'll need to meet the same requirements as when implementing the actively synchronizing Azure AD Connect installation. In short, these are the following:

- You sign in with an account that is a local administrator on the server
- You need to know the credentials for the following:
    - An account in Active Directory that is a member of the Enterprise Admins group
    - An account in Azure Active Directory that has the Global administrator role assigned
- You have to make sure that the following are true of the Windows Server:
    - Is able to communicate with the internet without having to pass proxies
    - Is running Windows Server 2012 R2, or a newer version of Windows Server
    - Is domain-joined
    - Has **Internet Explorer Enhanced Security Configuration (IE ESC)** turned off
- Download Azure AD Connect from `aka.ms/aadconnect`

How to do it...

Configure another Windows Server with Azure AD Connect. Perform identical steps to those you performed when configuring the actively synchronizing Azure AD Connect installation, with one exception. On the **Ready to Configure** screen, enable **Enable staging mode: When selected, synchronization will not export any data to AD or Azure AD**:

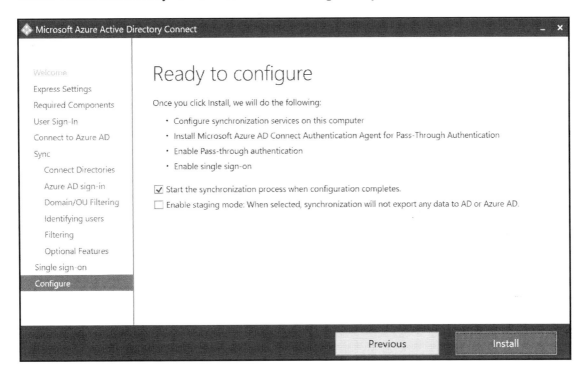

How it works...

Staging mode offers the ability to configure additional Azure AD Connect installations for an Azure AD tenant. To provide the same level of integrity for multiple Azure AD Connect installations as for a single Azure AD Connect installation, two processes occur:

- Only one Azure AD Connect installation is the actively synchronizing Azure AD Connect installation between Active Directory, its database and Azure AD.
- The other Azure AD Connect installations are only synchronizing changes into their databases, but not out to Active Directory or Azure AD.

Staging mode servers can be useful in the following scenarios:

- As cold standbys to the actively synchronizing Azure AD Connect installation.
- As a way to query the metaverse or create backups of the configuration, without impacting the performance of the actively synchronizing Azure AD Connect installation.
- As a way to perform life cycle management of Azure AD Connect.

There is one big downside to this approach: a lot of configuration changes need to be performed on each Azure AD Connect installation to retain the required level of integrity to achieve the preceding benefits. For each of the recipes in this chapter, a remark is made if a configuration change is needed on the actively synchronizing Azure AD Connect installation only, or also on all staging mode Azure AD Connect installations.

In staging mode, Azure AD Connect does not run exports. An Azure AD Connect installation in staging mode does have the ability to build the same database as the actively synchronizing Azure AD Connect installation, if both Azure AD Connect installations operate with identical configurations.

 It is important to configure the staging mode Azure AD Connect installation **identical** to the actively synchronizing Azure AD Connect installation. Using the Problem Steps Recorder (psr.exe) to record the actions when configuring Azure AD Connect can be helpful in this. The Azure AD Connect Configuration Documenter tool is useful to compare configurations.

The following items will be different between the actively synchronizing Azure AD Connect installation and staging mode Azure AD Connect installations:

- The service account
- The precise moment for the synchronization cycle within the default time frame

When configuring a staging mode server, there is no direct need to use the exact same accounts to connect to Azure AD or connect to Active Directory. As long as the account has the proper privileges, the staging mode server will work as expected. It will also not result in a difference in the configuration, as the accounts used to configure are not part of the configuration, but only part of the profile of an account used before to configure or reconfigure Azure AD Connect.

The service account will be different between the actively synchronizing Azure AD Connect installation and staging mode Azure AD Connect installations when you let Azure AD Connect create the account. If you manually create the service account, make sure each Azure AD Connect installation uses its own account to avoid reuse and lockouts.

When using a dedicated SQL Server on the network to store the Azure AD Connect configuration and metaverse, do not reuse the database between Azure AD Connect installations; each Azure AD Connect installation requires its own database.

 When you manually create the service accounts, delegate the appropriate permissions in Active Directory to a group and make your newly created service accounts members of the group. This avoids misconfiguration of individual accounts and adheres to Microsoft's recommended practices for Active Directory Delegation of Control.

See also

The Azure AD Connect Configuration Documenter can be used to compare Azure AD Connect configurations: `https://github.com/Microsoft/AADConnectConfigDocumenter`.

Switching to a staging mode server

This recipe shows how to switch the actively synchronizing Azure AD Connect installation and a staging mode installation.

Getting ready

Sign-in with an account that is a local administrator on the actively synchronizing Azure AD Connect installation and the staging mode installation that you want to switch.

As part of the switch, you'll need to enter the credentials for an account in Azure Active Directory that has the Global administrator role assigned.

How to do it...

To switch the actively synchronizing Azure AD Connect installation and a staging mode installation, perform these steps on the actively synchronizing Azure AD Connect installation, if this installation is still operable:

1. Open the **Azure AD Connect Configuration Wizard** from the Start Menu or desktop.
2. In the **Welcome to Azure AD Connect** screen, click **Configure**.
3. From the list of **Additional Tasks**, choose **Configure staging mode**.
4. Click **Next**.
5. On the **Connect to Azure AD** screen, sign in with an Azure AD-based account with **Global Administrator** or **Company Administrator** privileges. Perform multi-factor authentication and/or privileged identity management to connect.
6. On the **Configure Staging Mode** screen, select the **Enable staging mode** option.
7. Click **Next**.
8. On the **Ready to configure** screen, click **Configure**.
9. On the **Configuration complete** screen, click **Exit** to close the Microsoft Azure Active Directory Connect window:

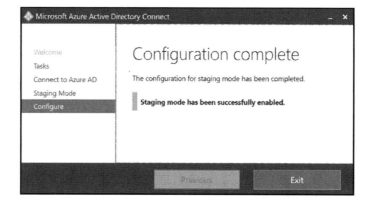

Perform these steps on the staging mode Azure AD Connect installation that you want to become the actively synchronizing Azure AD Connect installation:

1. Open the **Azure AD Connect Configuration Wizard** from the Start Menu or desktop.
2. In the **Welcome to Azure AD Connect** screen, click **Configure**.

3. From the list of **Additional Tasks**, choose **Configure staging mode**.
4. Click **Next**.
5. On the **Connect to Azure AD** screen, sign in with an Azure AD-based account with **Global administrator** or **Company administrator** privileges. Perform multi-factor authentication and/or privileged identity management to connect. You reach the **Configure stating mode** screen.
6. On the **Configure Staging Mode** screen, unselect the **Enable staging mode** option:

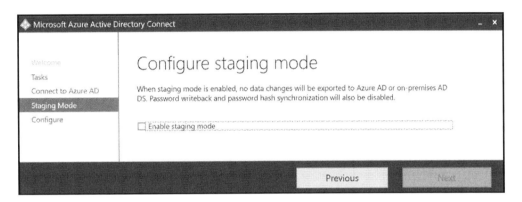

7. Click **Next**.
8. On the **Ready to configure** screen, click **Configure**.
9. On the **Configuration complete** screen, click **Exit** to close the **Microsoft Azure Active Directory Connect** window and to restart synchronization to Azure AD.

How it works...

There can only be one Azure AD Connect installation actively synchronizing to an Azure AD tenant. When the actively synchronizing installation fails, a staging mode server can be switched to being the actively synchronizing installation. The switch can also be predetermined in an Azure AD Connect life cycle management situation.

The first part of the switch is configuring the actively synchronizing Azure AD Connect installation as an additional staging mode server. After these steps, there is no actively synchronizing Azure AD Connect installation for the Azure AD tenant.

Don't wait too long to configure one of the Azure AD Connect installations to the actively synchronizing Azure AD Connect installations; synchronization cycles may be missed, resulting in out-of-date objects and attributes in Azure AD.

Configuring Domain and OU filtering

This recipe shows how to configure Domain and OU filtering in Azure AD Connect to filter the set of objects that is synchronized to Azure AD.

Getting ready

To configure the Domain and OU filtering functionality in Azure AD Connect, you'll need to know the following characteristics of your organization:

- In what domains, OUs, and containers are the end user for my organization stored?
- Where are the objects that the organization doesn't want synchronized to Azure AD?

To configure Domain and OU filtering within Azure AD Connect, you'll need to sign-in with an account that is a local administrator on the server dedicated to Azure AD Connect. As part of the following steps, you'll need to enter the credentials for these accounts:

- An account in Active Directory that is a member of the Enterprise Admins group
- An account in Azure Active Directory that has the Global administrator role assigned

How to do it...

Configuring Domain and OU filtering can be handled in two scenarios:

- When configuring Azure AD Connect initially
- When reconfiguring Azure AD Connect

Configuring Azure AD Connect initially

When initially configuring Azure AD Connect, make sure to click **Customize** on the **Express Settings** screen of Azure AD Connect. You'll encounter the **Domain and OU filtering** screen, regardless of configuring Azure AD Connect for Password Hash Synchronization, Pass-through Authentication, or federation:

1. Select **Sync selected domains and OUs** instead of the default **Sync all domains and OUs**.
2. Make the appropriate changes to the selection of domains, OUs, and containers:

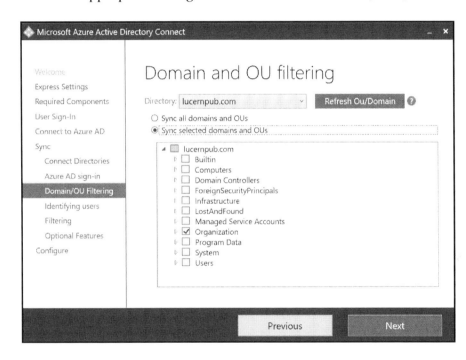

3. Click **Next** to continue configuring Azure AD Connect.

Reconfiguring Azure AD Connect

Perform these steps to reconfigure Azure AD Connect with Domain and OU filtering:

1. Open the **Azure AD Connect Configuration Wizard** from the Start Menu or desktop.
2. In the **Welcome to Azure AD Connect** screen, click **Configure**.

3. In the **Additional tasks** screen, select the **Customize synchronization options** ribbon:

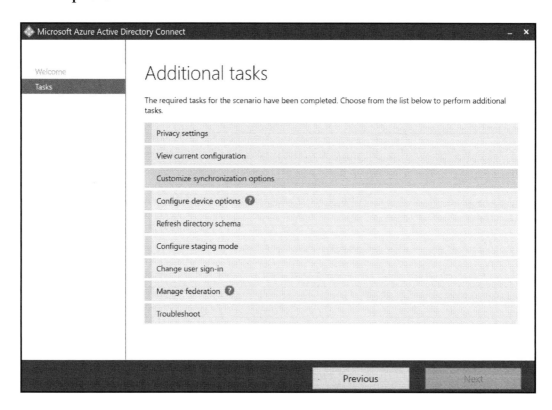

4. Click **Next**.
5. On the **Connect to Azure AD** screen, sign in with an Azure AD-based account with **Global administrator** or **Company administrator** privileges. Perform multi-factor authentication and/or privileged identity management to connect.
6. Click **Next**.
7. When you want to remove entire Active Directory forests from the scope of Azure AD Connect, remove them on the **Connect your directories** screen. Make sure to also remove or reconfigure any service account used by Azure AD Connect in that forest.
8. Click **Next**.
9. On the **Domain and OU filtering** screen, select **Sync selected domains and OUs** instead of the default **Sync all domains and OUs**, or when you are revisiting **Domain and OU filtering**, make sure the **Sync selected domains and OUs** option is selected.

10. Make the appropriate changes to the selection of domains, OUs, and containers.
11. Click **Next**.
12. On the **Optional features** screen, click **Next**.
13. On the **Ready to configure** screen, click **Configure**.
14. On the **Configuration complete** screen, click **Exit** to close the **Microsoft Azure Active Directory Connect** window and to restart synchronization to Azure AD.

How it works...

The Domain and OU Filtering screen presents the option to select and deselect Active Directory domains in a forest, OUs, and/or containers.

When you remove a forest, make sure to also remove or reconfigure any service account used by Azure AD Connect in that forest.

 There is a difference between unselecting a parent OU and selecting one or more of its child OUs, and selecting the parent OU, but unselecting one or more of its child OUs; in the latter scenario, new child OUs will be automatically in scope for synchronizing, while in the first scenario they will not.

When the objects that the organization doesn't want synchronized to Azure AD are located in OUs with objects that the organization wants synchronized, create new OUs.

When objects fall out of scope of Azure AD Connect, they will automatically be deleted in Azure AD. They will remain in the Azure AD Recycle Bin for 30 days. After these 30 days, they will be in the purge state for an additional 14 days. After this time period, the object is permanently gone.

Any setting for the scope of objects needs to be configured on Azure AD Connect installations in staging mode, too.

Configuring Azure AD app and attribute filtering

This recipe shows how to configure Azure AD app and attribute filtering in Azure AD Connect to filter the set of attributes for objects that are synchronized to Azure AD.

Getting ready

To configure the Azure AD app and attribute filtering functionality in Azure AD Connect, you'll need to know the following characteristics of your organization:

- What is the Office 365 functionality my organization is going to use?
- What attributes for my end users, groups, services, and devices am I allowed to synchronize to Azure AD in terms of regulatory compliance?

To configure the Azure AD app and attribute filtering within Azure AD Connect, you'll need to sign in with an account that is a local administrator on the server dedicated to Azure AD Connect. As part of the following steps, you'll need to enter the credentials for these accounts:

- An account in Active Directory that is a member of the Enterprise Admins group
- An account in Azure Active Directory that has the Global administrator role assigned

How to do it...

Configuring Azure AD app and attribute filtering can be handled in two scenarios:

- When configuring Azure AD Connect initially
- When reconfiguring Azure AD Connect

Configuring Azure AD Connect initially

When initially configuring Azure AD Connect, make sure to click **Customize** on the **Express Settings** screen of Azure AD Connect. You'll encounter the **Azure AD app and attribute filtering** screen, regardless of configuring Azure AD Connect for Password Hash Synchronization, Pass-through Authentication, or federation:

1. On the **Optional features** screen, select the **Azure AD app and attribute filtering** option:

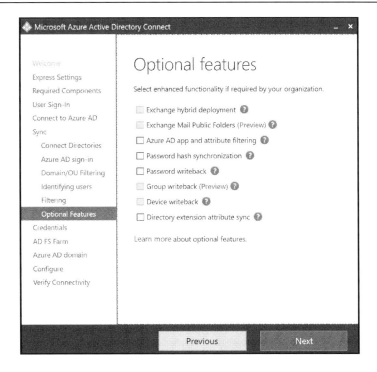

2. Click **Next**.
3. On the **Azure AD apps** screen, select the **I want to restrict the list of applications.** option.
   This will remove the grayed-out selections for **Office 365 ProPlus, Exchange Online, SharePoint Online, Lync Online, Azure RMS, Intune, Dynamics CRM,** and **3rd party application**.
4. Select at least one Azure AD app.
5. Click **Next**.
6. On the **Ready to configure** screen, click **Configure**.
7. On the **Configuration complete** screen, click **Exit** to close the **Microsoft Azure Active Directory Connect** window and to start the initial synchronization to Azure AD.

Reconfiguring Azure AD Connect

Perform these steps to reconfigure Azure AD Connect with **Azure AD app and attribute filtering**:

1. Open the Azure AD Connect Configuration Wizard from the Start Menu or desktop.
2. In the **Welcome to Azure AD Connect** screen, click **Configure**.
3. In the **Additional tasks** screen, select the **Customize synchronization options** ribbon.
4. Click **Next**.
5. On the **Connect to Azure AD** screen, sign in with an Azure AD-based account with **Global administrator** or **Company administrator** privileges. Perform multi-factor authentication and/or privileged identity management to connect.
6. On the **Connect your directories** screen, click **Next**.
7. On the **Domain and OU filtering** screen, click **Next**.
8. On the **Optional features** screen, select the **Azure AD app and attribute filtering** option.
9. Click **Next** to advance to the **Azure AD apps** screen:

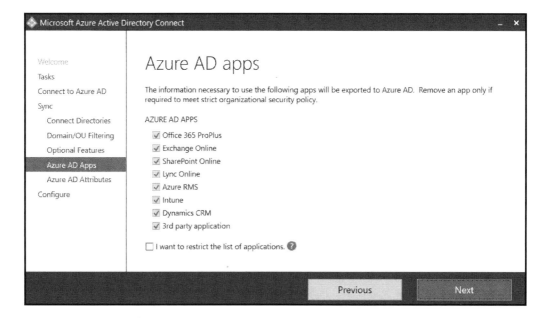

10. On the **Azure AD apps** screen, select the **I want to restrict the list of applications.** option.
    This will remove the grayed-out selections for **Office 365 ProPlus, Exchange Online, SharePoint Online, Lync Online, Azure RMS, Intune, Dynamics CRM,** and **3rd party application**.
11. Select at least one Azure AD app.
12. Click **Next**.
13. On the **Ready to configure** screen, click **Configure**.
14. On the **Configuration complete** screen, click **Exit** to close the **Microsoft Azure Active Directory Connect** window and to restart synchronization to Azure AD.

How it works...

Increasing regulations, including Europe's **General Data Protection Regulation (GDPR)**, force organizations to protect the privacy of people in technology. While it can be argued that synchronizing from Active Directory to Azure AD serves the same purposes in an employer-employee relationship, other organizations may have difficulties synchronizing over a hundred attributes for users, groups, contacts, and devices. Azure AD Connect offers the **Azure AD app and attribute filtering** functionality to address the needs of this latter kind of organization.

In contrast to stopping synchronization of objects using Domain and OU filtering, where the object eventually disappears, when organizations stop synchronizing certain attributes for objects using Azure AD app and attribute filtering, these attributes aren't (automatically) removed from Azure AD. When organizations want certain attributes to be cleared, the Azure AD Windows PowerShell module needs to be used, although some attributes, such as the ones where synchronized (and rehashed) password-hashes are stored, they lack of integrity of the values for these attributes, as they are no longer synchronized between the two platforms, might lead to problems later on, when the organization starts adopting additional services and/or applications, for which the old attribute values might lead to undesired behavior of the service and/or application or at least part of it.

The built-in CSV files act as templates for sets of attributes that Microsoft online services use. There are ready-to-use templates for organizations to deploy the Office 365 Professional Plus applications on users' devices, Exchange Online, and SharePoint Online, among others.

Any setting for the scope of attributes needs to be configured on Azure AD Connect installations in staging mode, too.

Using the **Azure AD app and attribute filtering** functionality does not result in unsupported synchronization rules.

Configuring MinSync

This recipe shows how to configure **Azure AD app and attribute filtering** in Azure AD Connect to minimize the number of attributes for user objects and groups that are synchronized to Azure AD.

Getting ready

To configure the **Azure AD app and attribute filtering** functionality towards MinSync in Azure AD Connect, you'll need to know the following characteristics of your organization:

- What is the Office 365 functionality my organization is going to use?
- What attributes for my end users, groups, services, and devices am I allowed to synchronize to Azure AD in terms of regulatory compliance?

To configure the Azure AD app and attribute filtering towards MinSync within Azure AD Connect, you'll need to sign in with an account that is a local administrator on the server dedicated to Azure AD Connect. As part of the following steps, you'll need to enter the credentials for these accounts:

- An account in Active Directory that is a member of the Enterprise Admins group
- An account in Azure Active Directory that has the Global administrator role assigned

How to do it...

Configuring **Azure AD app and attribute filtering** towards MinSync can be handled in two scenarios:

1. When configuring Azure AD Connect initially
2. When reconfiguring Azure AD Connect

Configuring Azure AD Connect initially

When initially configuring Azure AD Connect, make sure to click **Customize** on the **Express Settings** screen of Azure AD Connect. You'll encounter the **Azure AD app and attribute filtering** screen, regardless of configuring Azure AD Connect for Password Hash Synchronization, Pass-through Authentication, or federation:

1. On the **Optional features** screen, select the **Azure AD app and attribute filtering** option.
2. Click **Next**.
3. On the **Azure AD apps** screen, select the option **I want to restrict the list of applications**.
   This will remove the grayed-out selections for **Office 365 ProPlus, Exchange Online, SharePoint Online, Lync Online, Azure RMS, Intune, Dynamics CRM,** and **3rd party application**.
4. Select at least one Azure AD app. The **Office 365 ProPlus** app definition constitutes the option of least administrative effort here, as it seems to synchronize the minimum number of attributes of all listed apps.
5. Select the option **I want to further limit the attributes exported to Azure AD**.
6. Click **Next**.
7. For MinSync of user objects, unselect every attribute except for the `accountEnabled`, `sourceAnchor`, and `userPrincipalName` attributes. When groups are also in scope for Azure AD Connect, then the `cn`, `securityEnabled`, and `member` attributes also become essential and should be selected.
8. Click **Next**.
9. On the **Ready to configure** screen, click **Configure**.
10. On the **Configuration complete** screen, click **Exit** to close the **Microsoft Azure Active Directory Connect** window and to start the initial synchronization to Azure AD.

Reconfiguring Azure AD Connect

Perform these steps to reconfigure Azure AD Connect with **Azure AD app and attribute filtering** towards MinSync:

1. Open the Azure AD Connect Configuration Wizard from the Start Menu or desktop.
2. In the **Welcome to Azure AD Connect** screen, click **Configure**.
3. In the **Additional tasks** screen, select the **Customize synchronization options** ribbon.
4. Click **Next**.
5. On the **Connect to Azure AD** screen, sign in with an Azure AD-based account with **Global administrator** or **Company administrator** privileges. Perform multi-factor authentication and/or privileged identity management to connect.
6. On the **Connect your directories** screen, click **Next**.
7. On the **Domain and OU filtering** screen, click **Next**.
8. On the **Optional features** screen, select the **Azure AD app and attribute filtering** option.
9. Press **Next**.
10. On the **Azure AD apps** screen, select the option **I want to restrict the list of applications.** This will remove the grayed-out selections for **Office 365 ProPlus, Exchange Online, SharePoint Online, Lync Online, Azure RMS, Intune, Dynamics CRM**, and **3rd party application**.
11. Select at least one **Azure AD app**.
    The **Office 365 ProPlus** Azure AD app definition constitutes the option of least administrative effort here as it seems to synchronize the minimum number of attributes of the listed apps:

12. Select the **I want to further limit the attributes exported to Azure AD**.
13. For MinSync of user objects unselect every attribute except for
    the `accountEnabled`, `sourceAnchor`, and `userPrincipalName` attributes.
    When groups are also in scope for Azure AD Connect, then
    the `cn`, `securityEnabled`, and `member` attributes also become essential and
    should be selected:

14. Click **Next**.
15. On the **Ready to configure** screen, click **Configure**.
16. On the **Configuration complete** screen, click **Exit** to close the **Microsoft Azure Active Directory Connect** window and to restart synchronization to Azure AD.

How it works...

Beyond the Azure AD app and attribute filtering default functionality, MinSync offers a way to minimize the attributes synchronized in scope of Azure AD Connect.

Taking attributes out of scope for Azure AD Connect puts an organization on the path of having out-of-date attribute values for objects in Azure AD, as these attributes are no longer synchronized. However, not synchronizing attributes also means that some attributes, such as the first name, last name, and other attributes that end users can modify through the MyProfile interface remain empty. Some other attributes remain non-modifiable. When taking these attributes (back) into scope, these user-defined values will be overwritten by the attribute values stored in Active Directory.

The link **View the list of attributes as comma-separates values** offers the opportunity to view the set of attributes that the Azure AD App uses:

This file clearly indicates which attributes are mandatory and cannot be left out of synchronization in the `IsMandatory` column.

Any settings for the scope of attributes need to be configured on Azure AD Connect installations in staging mode, too.

Using the **Azure AD app and attribute filtering** functionality towards MinSync does not result in unsupported synchronization rules. However, it might result in unsupported use of Azure AD Apps.

Configuring Hybrid Azure AD Join

This recipe shows how to configure Hybrid Azure AD Join, to synchronize device properties for domain-joined devices from Active Directory to Azure AD.

Getting ready

To configure Hybrid Azure AD Join in Azure AD Connect, you'll need to know the following characteristics of your organization:

- What are the operating systems in use in the organization?
- What attributes for the devices am I allowed to synchronize?
- Which Azure AD Connect installation is the non-staging mode server? (Only applicable if the organization has multiple Azure AD Connect servers.)

To configure Hybrid Azure AD Join in Azure AD Connect, you'll need to sign-in with an account that is a local administrator on the server dedicated to Azure AD Connect. As part of following the steps, you'll need to enter the credentials for these accounts:

- An account in Active Directory that is a member of the Enterprise Admins group
- An account in Azure Active Directory that has the Global administrator role assigned

Azure AD Connect needs to be initially configured, although the chosen authentication method doesn't matter as Hybrid Azure AD Join works with PHS, PTA, and federation. PHS and PTA need to be configured in combination with Seamless Single Sign-on, when non-Windows 10 devices are to be Hybrid Azure AD Joined.

The Active Directory schema version needs to be Windows Server 2012 R2 (level 69), or higher.

To deploy the **Workplace Join for non-Windows 10 computers** package, download it from: `https://www.microsoft.com/en-us/download/details.aspx?id=53554`.

How to do it...

Configuring Hybrid Azure AD Join consists of these steps:

1. Adding the Azure AD Device Registration Service to the intranet sites
2. Distributing Workplace Join for non-Windows 10 computers
3. Setting the Group Policy to register for down-level Windows devices
4. Linking the Group Policy to the right Organizational Units
5. Configuring Hybrid Azure AD Join in Azure AD Connect

Steps 2 and 3 are only needed when the organization runs older versions of Windows, such as Windows 7 and Windows 8.1. The package needs to be deployed before the device is able to understand the Group Policy setting.

Adding the Azure AD Device Registration Service to the intranet sites

Perform these steps to add the Azure AD Authentication service to Internet Explorer's and Edge's **Intranet Sites** list in a new Group Policy object that is targeted to the same OU Filtering scope as in Azure AD Connect:

1. Log in to a system with the Group Policy Management Console feature installed.
2. Open the **Group Policy Management** Console (`gpmc.msc`).
3. In the left-hand pane, navigate to the **Group Policy objects** node.
4. Locate the Group Policy Object that you want to use and select it, or right-click the **Group Policy Objects** node and select **New** from the menu.
5. Right-click the Group Policy object and select **Edit...** from the menu. The Group Policy Management Editor window appears.
6. In the left-hand navigation pane, Navigate to **User Configuration**, then **Policies**, then **Administrative Templates**, **Windows Components**, **Internet Explorer**, **Internet Control Panel**, and, lastly, **Security Page**.
7. Double-click the **Site to Zone Assignment List** setting:

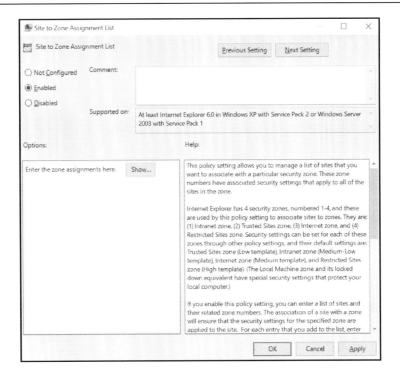

8. Select **Enabled**.

9. Click the **Show...** button.

10. In the **Value name** field, enter the URLs `https://device.login.microsoftonline.com` and `https://autologon.microsoftazuread-sso.com`.

11. In the **value** field, assign **1** to both URLs, as this value corresponds with the **Intranet Sites** zone.

12. Click **OK**.

13. Click **OK** to close the Group Policy setting.

14. Close the **Group Policy Management Editor** window.

15. In the left-hand navigation pane, navigate to the **Organization Unit (OU)** where you want to link the GPO.

16. Right-click the OU and select **Link an existing GPO...** from the menu.

17. In the **Select GPO** window, select the GPO.

18. Click **OK** to link the GPO.

Distributing Workplace Join for non-Windows 10 computers

Perform these steps:

1. Open the **Group Policy Management** Console (`gpmc.msc`).
2. In the left-hand navigation pane, expand the **Forest** node.
3. Expand the **Domains** node, and then navigate to the domain where you want to create the GPO.
4. Expand the domain name and then select the **Group Policy Objects** node.
5. Right-click the **Group Policy Objects** node and select **New** from the menu. The **New GPO** popup appears.
6. Enter a name for the new Group Policy object.
7. Click **OK**.
8. In the left-hand navigation pane, right-click the new GPO and select **Edit** from the menu. The **Group Policy Management Editor** (`gpedit.msc`) appears.
9. Expand **Computer Configuration**.
10. Expand the **Policies** node, and then the **Software Settings** node.
11. Right-click the **Software Installation** node and select **New** from the menu, and then **Package…**.
12. In the **Open** screen, browse to the network share that has the MSI or ZAP package for the application. Select the application and click **Open**.
13. In the **Deploy Software** popup screen, select **Assigned** as the deployment method.
14. Click **OK** to save the settings.

    The package will be listed with its version, its deployment state, and source path:

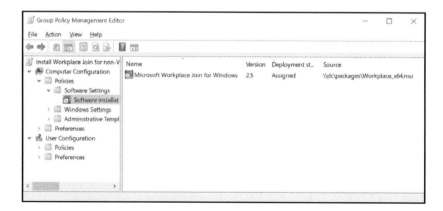

Setting the Group Policy to register for down-level Windows devices

The same Group Policy object can be reused to configure down-level Windows installations for Hybrid Azure AD Join, if only down-level Windows devices are present in the environment:

1. In the newly created Group Policy object, expand the **Administrative Templates** under **Policies** and **Computer Configuration**.
2. Expand the **Windows Components** node.
3. Expand the **Device Registration** node.
4. In the main pane, select the **Register domain-joined computers as devices** setting.
5. Right-click the setting and select **Edit** from the menu.
6. Select **Enabled**:

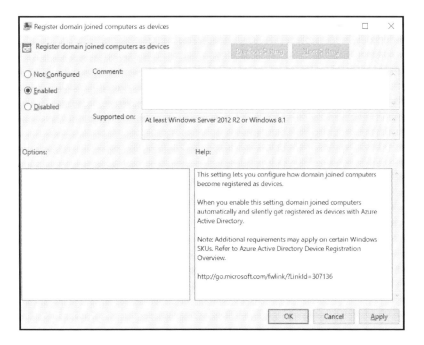

7. Click **OK**.

Link the Group Policy to the right Organizational Units

Link the newly created Group Policy object to the Organizational Units containing devices:

1. In the left-hand navigation pane of the Group Policy Management Console (gpmc.msc), navigate to the OU where you want to link an existing GPO.
2. Right-click the OU and select **Link an existing GPO...** from the menu.
3. In the **Select GPO** window, select the newly created GPO.
4. Click **OK** to link the GPO.

Configuring Hybrid Azure AD Join in Azure AD Connect

Perform these steps on the Windows Server running Azure AD Connect:

1. Open the Azure AD Connect Configuration Wizard from the Start Menu or desktop.
2. In the **Welcome to Azure AD Connect** screen, click **Configure**.
3. In the **Additional tasks** screen, select the **Configure device options** ribbon:

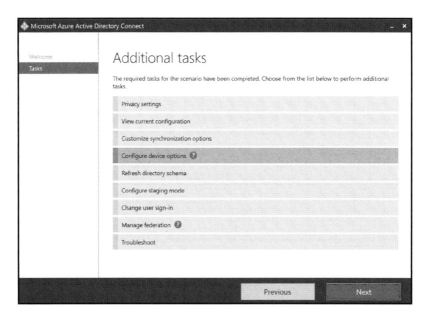

4. Click **Next**.
5. On the **Overview** screen, click **Next**.

6. On the **Connect to Azure AD** screen, sign in with an Azure AD-based account with **Global administrator** or **Company administrator** privileges. Perform multi-factor authentication and/or privileged identity management to connect.

7. On the **Device options** screen, select **Configure Hybrid Azure AD join**.

8. Click **Next**.

9. On the **SCP configuration** screen, select the Forest to configure Hybrid Azure AD Join for.

10. In the **Authentication Service** column, select **Azure Active Directory**.

11. Click the **Add** button in the **Enterprise Admin** column.
    The **Windows Security** popup window appears:

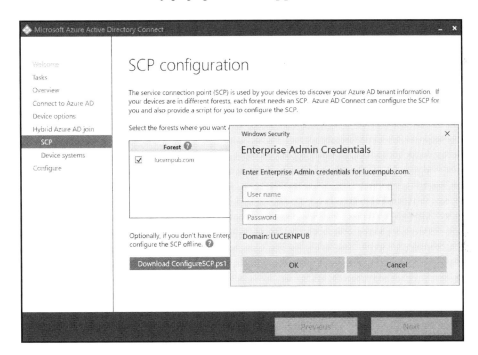

12. Enter the credentials for an account in Active Directory that is a member of the **Enterprise Admins** group.

13. Click **OK**.

14. Click **Next**.

15. On the **Device operating systems** screen, select the **Windows 10 or later domain-joined devices.** option.

16. If your organization is planning to also support Windows down-level domain-joined devices, select the **Supported Windows downlevel domain-joined devices.** option, too.
17. Click **Next**.
18. On the **Ready to configure** screen, click **Configure**.
19. On the **Configuration complete** screen, click **Exit** to close the **Microsoft Azure Active Directory Connect** window and to restart synchronization to Azure AD.

How it works...

Hybrid Azure AD Join leverages the domain-join bond a device has with Active Directory to create a device object in Azure AD. The device object is created and then attached to by the device, leveraging its TPM device as a secure enclave to store the private key for a certificate that seals the bond with Azure AD.

Active Directory on-premises is the source. Azure AD is the destination.

 After a device bonds with Azure AD, it no longer updates its data in Azure AD. For instance, if a device has its name changed or operating system upgraded. These changes aren't reflected in Azure AD. A **mobile device management** (**MDM**) solution, such as Microsoft Intune, is capable of offering this functionality.

Older versions of Windows, such as Windows 7 and Windows 8.1, require the Workplace Join for non-Windows 10 computers package. They also require a **Security Token Service** (**STS**). For this, configure Seamless Single Sign-on, when Password Hash Synchronization or Pass-through Authentication are used as an authentication method; the Azure AD Authentication Service will then be used as the STS. With **Active Directory Federation Services** (**AD FS**) as the authentication method, the AD FS servers act as STSs.

Older versions of Windows, and Windows 10 devices up to version 1607 require a Group Policy setting to start attaching to the device object in Azure AD. Newer versions of Windows 10 no longer require the Group Policy and will try attaching to their corresponding device objects unless the Group Policy setting is specifically configured as **Disabled**.

Older versions of Windows Server running the Group Policy Management Console or Windows Servers utilizing a non-up-to-date Centralized Policy Store might not show the **Register domain-joined computers as devices** setting, but instead show the **Register domain joined computer as device** setting. The label for the setting has been changed. This does not impact the effectiveness of the Group Policy.

Azure AD Join can also be configured in **System Center Configuration Manager** (**ConfigMgr**). The setting in ConfigMgr overrules the setting in any **Group Policy Object** (**GPO**).

Versions 1.1 of Azure AD Connect up to version 1.1.882.0 did not require configuration of Hybrid Azure AD Join; if a computer object in Active Directory was in scope of Azure AD Connect, device objects were created regardless.

In terms of Conditional Access, a Hybrid Azure AD-joined device constitutes a trusted device, just like compliant devices, that have earned their trust through health checks and enforced configuration settings by the organizations MDM solution. Many organizations choose to use more relaxed access policies for these types of devices, but the question is whether a domain-joined device is as trustworthy as a compliant device.

Hybrid Azure AD Join only needs to be configured on one Azure AD Connect installation. If you run multiple Azure AD Connect installations, perform the steps on the actively synchronizing Azure AD Connect installation (the non-staging mode server).

Configuring Device writeback

This recipe shows how to configure **Device writeback** in Azure AD Connect.

Getting ready

To configure **Device writeback** in Azure AD Connect, you'll need to know the following characteristics of your organization:

- In what forest are we going to write device objects? (Only applicable if your organization has multiple forests in scope for Azure AD Connect.)
- Which Azure AD Connect installation is the non-staging mode server? (Only applicable if your organization has multiple Azure AD Connect servers.)

The Device writeback functionality requires Azure AD Premium P1 licenses, or a Microsoft license that includes the P1 license, such as Azure AD Premium P2, EMS E3, EMS A3, Microsoft 365 E3, or Microsoft 365 Business licenses.

To configure Device writeback in Azure AD Connect, you'll need to sign in with a domain account that is configured as a local administrator on the server dedicated to Azure AD Connect. As part of the following steps, you'll need to enter the credentials for an account in Active Directory that is a member of the Enterprise Admins group

Azure AD Connect needs to be initially configured, although the chosen authentication method doesn't matter as Device writeback works with PHS, PTA, and federation.

The Active Directory schema version needs to be Windows Server 2012 R2 (level 69), or higher.

How to do it...

Perform these steps on the Windows Server running Azure AD Connect:

1. Open the Azure AD Connect Configuration Wizard from the start menu or desktop.
2. In the **Welcome to Azure AD Connect** screen, click **Configure**.
3. In the **Additional tasks** screen, select the **Configure device options** ribbon.
4. Click **Next**.
5. On the **Overview** screen, click **Next**.
6. On the **Connect to Azure AD** screen, sign in with an Azure AD-based account with **Global administrator** or **Company administrator** privileges. Perform multi-factor authentication and/or privileged identity management to connect.
7. On the **Device options** screen, select **Configure device writeback**.
8. Click **Next**.
9. On the **Writeback forest** screen, select the on-premises device writeback forest from the drop-down lists:

10. Click **Next**.
11. On the **Device container** screen, select the **I will provide Enterprise Admin credentials.** option and enter the credentials.
12. On the **Ready to configure** screen, click **Configure**.
13. On the **Configuration complete** screen, click **Exit** to close the **Microsoft Azure Active Directory Connect** window and to restart synchronization to Azure AD.

How it works...

Device writeback is an optional feature.

When people register their devices with Azure AD, their actions create device objects in Azure AD. In AD FS, these objects can be used in claims issuance rules. This way, when an Azure AD-joined device is used outside of one of your organization's locations, a claims issuance rule can be created to not require MFA, even though the device is outside and other outside users are still required to perform multi-factor authentication.

Azure AD is the source. Active Directory on-premises is the destination.

Device writeback does not support multi-domain and multi-forest topologies, as devices must be located in the same forest as the users. Admins can only define one domain to write back devices to.

When configuring Device writeback Azure AD Connect creates the **RegisteredDevices** container in the selected Active Directory domain to store the written-back devices.

The objects placed in the **RegisteredDevices** container are of the `mS-DS-Device` type. This type of object does not have an `objectSid` attribute and cannot be used on-premises other than in claims issuance rules in AD FS.

Device writeback only needs to be configured on one Azure AD Connect installation. If you run multiple Azure AD Connect installations, perform the steps on the actively synchronizing Azure AD Connect installation (the non-staging mode server). However, the service accounts for staging mode Azure AD Connect servers need to be configured with the same permissions as the service account of the actively synchronizing Azure AD Connect installation. The **I will configure it using the PowerShell script before continuing.** option on the **Device Container** results in a `CreateDeviceContainer.ps1` file with hints on how to configure the service account(s) of staging mode server(s):

```
$adConnectorAccount = "lucernpub.com\MSOL_9eee26c52012"
$registeredDevicesDN = "CN=RegisteredDevices,DC=lucernpub,DC=com"
$userAcl = $adConnectorAccount + ":GRGWCCDCSDDT"
 dsacls.exe $registeredDevicesDN /G $userAcl /I:T > $null
```

Configuring Password writeback

As an addition to the **Self-service Password Reset** and **Change Password** functionality in Azure AD, this recipe shows how to configure **Password writeback** in Azure AD Connect.

Getting ready

To configure the Password writeback functionality in Azure AD Connect, you'll need to know the following about your organization:

- Does my organization allow employees to reset their passwords from outside the organization?

To delegate permissions to the Azure AD Connect service accounts, sign in with an account that is a member of the Enterprise Admins group in the Active Directory forest for which you are configuring Password writeback to a Windows Server that has Active Directory Users and Computers (`dsa.msc`) installed or run Active Directory Users and Computers (`dsa.msc`) as the user.

To configure the Password writeback functionality within Azure AD Connect, sign in with an account that is a local administrator on the server dedicated to Azure AD Connect. As part of the following steps, you'll need to enter the credentials for these accounts:

- An account in Active Directory that is a member of the Enterprise Admins group
- An account in Azure Active Directory that has the Global administrator role assigned

The Password writeback functionality requires Azure AD Premium P1 licenses, or a Microsoft license that includes the P1 license, such as Azure AD Premium P2, EMS E3, EMS A3, Microsoft 365 E3, or Microsoft 365 Business licenses.

How to do it...

Configuring Password writeback consists of two steps:

1. Configuring the proper permissions for Azure AD Connect service accounts.
2. Configuring Azure AD Connect.

Configuring the proper permissions for Azure AD Connect service accounts

The first step to allow Password Writeback is to allow the service account(s) for the Azure AD Connect installations in your organization to write back the passwords to user objects in scope.

Perform these steps to create a group, make the Azure AD Connect service account(s) members of the group, and delegate the permissions to the group:

1. Open **Active Directory Users and Computers** (dsa.msc).
2. From the **View** menu, turn on **Advanced features**:

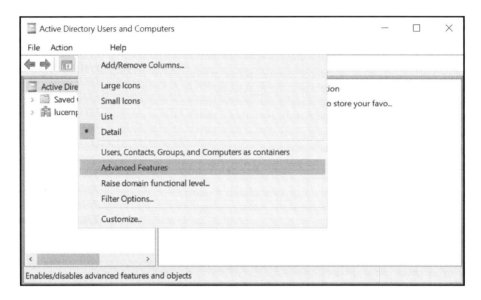

3. From the taskbar, click the **New Group** icon.
4. In the **New Object - Group** screen, specify values for the following fields:
    1. Specify the **Group Name**. The **pre-Windows 2000** group name will also be filled, based on the name of the group.
    2. Specify the Group scope or accept the default **Global** scope.
    3. Specify the Group type or accept the default **Security** type.
5. Click **OK** when done to create the group.
6. In the left-hand navigation pane, navigate to the Users container, or navigate to the OU where you placed or moved the Azure AD Connect service account(s) to.
7. In the main pane, select the service account(s).
8. Right-click the user object and select **Add to a group...** from the menu.
9. In the **Select Groups** window, type the name of the group you want to add the user account to, or click the **Advanced** button to search for the group.
10. Click **Check Names**.

11. Click **OK** to add the user to the group.

12. In the left-hand navigation pane, right-click the object that represents the root of the domain and select **Properties** from the menu.
    The *domainname* **Properties** window appears.

13. Navigate to the **Security tab**.

14. Click the **Advanced** button. The **Advanced Security Settings for** *domainname* window appears.

15. From the **Permissions** tab, select **Add**. The **Permission Entry for** *domainname* window appears:

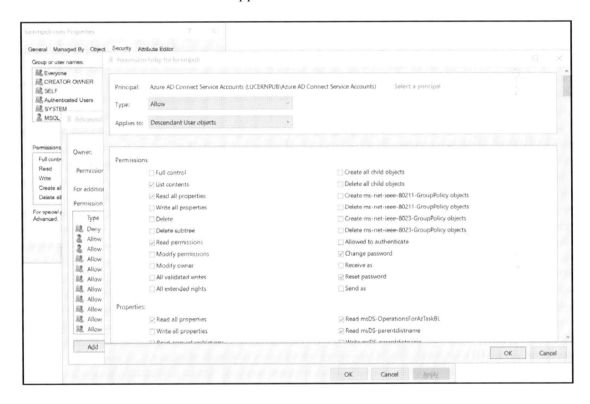

16. Pick the previously created group as the **Principal:**.
17. In the **Applies to** drop-down list, select **Descendant User objects**.
18. Under **Permissions**, select the following:
    - **Change password**
    - **Reset password**

19. Under **Properties**, select the following:
    - **Write lockoutTime**
    - **Write pwdLastSet**
20. Click **OK** three times to apply the changes and close the three windows.

Repeat the steps for all Active Directory domains in scope for Azure AD Connect.

Configuring Azure AD Connect

Configuring the **Password writeback** functionality can be handled in two scenarios:

1. When configuring Azure AD Connect initially.
2. When reconfiguring Azure AD Connect.

Configuring Azure AD Connect initially

When initially configuring Azure AD Connect, make sure to click **Customize** on the **Express Settings** screen of Azure AD Connect. You'll encounter the **Optional Features** screen, regardless of configuring Azure AD Connect for Password Hash Synchronization, Pass-through Authentication, or federation:

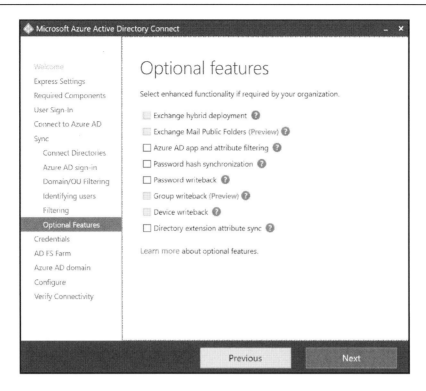

1. On the **Optional features** screen, select the **Password writeback** option.
2. Press **Next**.
3. On the **Ready to configure** screen, click **Configure**.
4. On the **Configuration complete** screen, click **Exit** to close the **Microsoft Azure Active Directory Connect** window and to start the initial synchronization to Azure AD.

Reconfiguring Azure AD Connect

Perform these steps to reconfigure Azure AD Connect with **Password writeback**:

1. Open the Azure AD Connect Configuration Wizard from the Start Menu or desktop.
2. In the **Welcome to Azure AD Connect** screen, click **Configure**.
3. In the **Additional tasks** screen, select the **Customize synchronization options** ribbon.
4. Click **Next**.

5. On the **Connect to Azure AD** screen, sign in with an Azure AD-based account with **Global administrator** or **Company administrator** privileges. Perform multi-factor authentication and/or privileged identity management to connect.

6. On the **Connect your directories** screen, click **Next**.

7. On the **Domain and OU filtering** screen, click **Next**.

8. On the **Optional features** screen, select the **Password writeback** option:

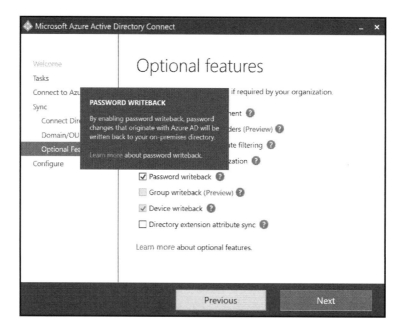

9. Press **Next**.

10. On the **Ready to configure** screen, click **Configure**.

11. On the **Configuration complete** screen, click **Exit** to close the **Microsoft Azure Active Directory Connect** window and to restart synchronization to Azure AD.

How it works...

Password writeback is an optional feature.

The Password writeback functionality in Azure AD Connect offers add-on functionality to the Self-service Password Reset and Change Password functionality in Azure AD for organizations that use both Active Directory and Azure AD in a Hybrid Identity setup.

When **Password writeback** is not enabled in Azure AD Connect or when their account is not in scope for Azure AD Connect, people that use the **Self-service Password Reset** functionality or the **Change Password** functionality in either their MyProfile or their Office 365 experience receive an error that passwords can't be changed right now.

With Password writeback, Azure AD places password reset requests on the Azure Service Bus, for Azure AD Connect to pick up. Azure AD Connect executes a password reset request, followed by a password change request against the on-premises domain controller that holds the **Primary Domain Controller emulator (PDCe) Flexible Single Master Operations (FSMO)** role, and signals the result back to Azure AD, by placing it on the same Azure Service Bus. For Password changes, only a password change request is processed in the preceding process.

This way, all password and account lock-out policies apply to self-service password reset requests and change password requests.

Password writeback only needs to be configured on one Azure AD Connect installation. If you run multiple Azure AD Connect installations, perform the steps on the actively synchronizing Azure AD Connect installation (the non-staging mode server). As this recipe shows how to create a group to delegate the permissions for service accounts, make sure any service accounts for new additional staging mode Azure AD Connect servers are also added to the group, going forward.

Configuring Group writeback

This recipe shows how to enable **Group writeback** in Azure AD Connect.

Getting ready

To configure Group writeback in Azure AD Connect, you'll need to know the following characteristics of your organization:

- In what **Organizational Unit (OU)** are we going to write back group objects?
- Which accepted domain name will be appended to the Office 365 groups? (Only applicable if your organization has multiple DNS domain names and accepted domains.)

The Group writeback functionality requires Azure AD Premium P1 licenses, or a Microsoft license that includes the P1 license, such as Azure AD Premium P2, EMS E3, EMS A3, Microsoft 365 E3, or Microsoft 365 Business licenses.

To configure Group writeback in Azure AD Connect, you'll need to sign in with an account that is a local administrator on the server dedicated to Azure AD Connect. As part of the following steps, you'll need to enter the credentials for an account in Active Directory that is a member of the Enterprise Admins group

Azure AD Connect needs to be initially configured, although the chosen authentication method doesn't matter, as **Group writeback** works with PHS, PTA, and federation. The **Exchange Hybrid** option needs to have already been selected.

If your organization needs the groups written back to an OU that doesn't exist yet, create it.

Make sure the Azure AD PowerShell Module is installed on the Windows Server running Azure AD Connect. Install the module if it's not installed yet, or upgrade the installed module to the latest version with the following line of PowerShell:

```
Install-Module AzureAD
```

How to do it...

Configuring Group writeback consists of three steps:

1. Creating the Organizational Unit where groups are to be written back.
2. Configuring Azure AD Connect.
3. Configuring the proper permissions for Azure AD Connect service accounts.

Creating the Organizational Unit where groups are to be written back

Perform these steps:

1. Open the **Active Directory Administrative Center** (dsac.exe).
2. In the left-hand navigation pane, switch to **Tree view**.
3. Expand the tree, if necessary, to locate the domain or Organizational Unit you want to be the parent object.

4. Select the parent object for the new Organizational Unit.

5. Right-click the parent object, select **New…**, and from the menu select **Organizational Unit**.

6. Enter a name for the Organizational Unit. Optionally, enter a description or fill in any of the other fields:

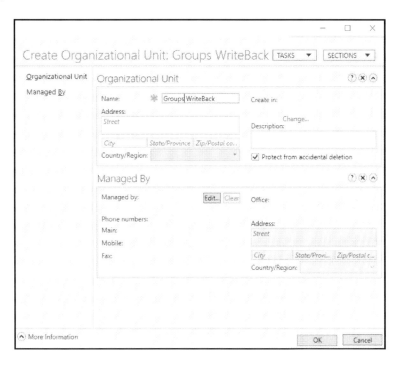

7. Click **OK** to create the Organizational Unit.

Configuring Azure AD Connect

Configuring the **Group writeback** functionality can be handled in two scenarios:

1. When configuring Azure AD Connect initially.

2. When reconfiguring Azure AD Connect.

Configuring Azure AD Connect initially

When initially configuring Azure AD Connect, make sure to click **Customize** on the **Express Settings** screen of Azure AD Connect. You'll encounter the **Optional Features** screen, regardless of configuring Azure AD Connect for Password Hash Synchronization, Pass-through Authentication, or federation:

1. On the **Optional features** screen, select the **Group writeback** option.
2. Press **Next**.
3. On the **Writeback** screen, select an Active Directory OU to store the group objects that will be written back:

4. Click **Next**.
5. On the **Ready to configure** screen, click **Configure**.
6. On the **Configuration complete** screen, click **Exit** to close the **Microsoft Azure. Active Directory Connect** window and to start the initial synchronization to Azure AD.

Reconfiguring Azure AD Connect

Perform these steps to reconfigure Azure AD Connect with **Group writeback**:

1. Open the Azure AD Connect Configuration Wizard from the Start Menu or desktop.
2. In the **Welcome to Azure AD Connect** screen, click **Configure**.
3. In the **Additional tasks** screen, select the **Customize synchronization options** ribbon.
4. Click **Next**.
5. On the **Connect to Azure AD** screen, sign in with an Azure AD-based account with **Global administrator** or **Company administrator** privileges.
   Perform multi-factor authentication and/or privileged identity management to connect.
6. On the **Connect your directories** screen, click **Next**.
7. On the **Domain and OU filtering** screen, click **Next**.
8. On the **Optional features** screen, select the **Group writeback** option:

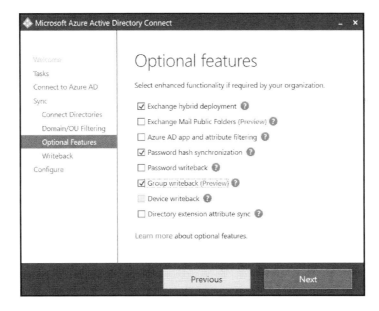

9. Click **Next**.
10. On the **Writeback** screen, select an Active Directory OU to store the group objects that will be written back.
11. Click **Next**.
12. On the **Ready to configure** screen, click **Configure**.
13. On the **Configuration complete** screen, click **Exit** to close the **Microsoft Azure Active Directory Connect** window and to restart synchronization to Azure AD.

Configuring the proper permissions for Azure AD Connect service accounts

The first step to allow **Group writeback** is to allow the service accounts for the Azure AD Connect installations in your organization to write back the groups.

Perform the following lines of PowerShell on an Azure AD Connect installation in your organization:

```
Import-Module AzureAD

Import-Module "C:\Program Files\Microsoft Azure Active Directory
Connect\AdPrep\AdSyncPrep.psm1"

Initialize-ADSyncGroupWriteBack -ADConnectorAccount "LUCERNPUB\MSOL_*" -
GroupWriteBackContainerDN "OU=Written Back,OU=Groups,DC=Lucernpub,DC=com"
```

Replace the values for the service account and the OUs distinguished name.

How it works...

Group writeback is an optional feature.

The Group writeback functionality in Azure AD Connect offers add-on functionality to the Office 365 Group functionality in Azure AD for organizations that use both Active Directory and Azure AD in a Hybrid Exchange setup.

When Group writeback is enabled, Office 365 groups are written back to Active Directory as distribution groups. This way, people in your organization with mailboxes on on-premises Exchange Server 2013 Cumulative Update 8 and newer versions of Exchange Server can send email messages to these groups and receive email messages from these groups.

If an Active Directory forest does not have its schema extended with the Exchange Server schema extensions, it is not eligible for Group writeback and the option will be grayed out in Azure AD Connect.

Exchange Servers in your organization need to run the following version of Exchange Server as a minimum:

- Exchange Server 2013 Cumulative Update 8
- Exchange Server 2016 Cumulative Update 1

Changing the passwords for Azure AD Connects service accounts

This recipe shows how to manually change the passwords for your Azure AD Connect service account(s).

Getting ready

To reconfigure Azure AD Connect, you'll need to sign in with an account that is a local administrator on the server dedicated to Azure AD Connect. As part of the following steps, you'll need to enter the credentials for these accounts:

- An account in Azure Active Directory that has the Global administrator role assigned
- An account in Active Directory that is a member of the Domain Admins group, for each of the domains in which Seamless Single Sign-on is configured (only applicable when Seamless Single Sign-on is configured)

Azure AD Connect needs to be initially configured.

Make sure the Azure AD PowerShell Module is installed on the Windows Server running Azure AD Connect. Install the module if it's not installed yet, or upgrade the installed module to the latest version with the following line of PowerShell:

```
Install-Module AzureAD
```

How to do it...

Perform the following steps to change the passwords for Azure AD Connects service accounts:

1. The service account connecting to Active Directory.
2. The service account connecting to Azure AD.
3. The computer account for Seamless Single Sign-on.

Managing the service account connecting to Active Directory

Perform these steps to change the password for the service account that connects to the on-premises Active Directory:

1. Open Azure AD Connects **Synchronization Service** from the Start Menu.
   The Synchronization Service Manager window appears.
2. Go to the **Connectors** tab.
3. Select an **AD Connector**.
4. From the **Actions** menu, select **Properties**.
   The **Connect to Active Directory Forest** popup window appears.
5. In the popup window, enter the new password for the service account.
6. Click **OK**.
7. Close the **Synchronization Service Manager** window.
8. Open **Services** (services.msc).
9. Select the **Azure AD Connect Synchronization Service**.
10. Right-click the service and select **Restart** from the menu.
11. Close the **Services** window.

Perform the preceding steps for all AD Connectors in Azure AD Connect to reset all their passwords. Perform the preceding steps on all Azure AD Connect installations.

Managing the service account connecting to Azure AD

Perform the following steps to change the password for the service account that connects to Azure AD:

1. Perform the following lines of PowerShell:

```
Import-Module ADSync

Add-ADSyncAADServiceAccount
```

2. A popup window appears.
3. Provide the credentials of an account that has the **Global administrator** role assigned to it.
4. Optionally, perform multi-factor authentication, and/or elevate the account to **Global administrator** when using Azure AD **Privileged Identity Management (PIM)**.

Perform the preceding steps on all Azure AD Connect installations.

Managing the computer account for Seamless Single Sign-on

Perform the following steps to change the password for the **AzureADSSOACC** computer account:

1. Perform the following lines of PowerShell:

```
Import-Module AzureAD

Import-Module "C:\Program Files\Microsoft Azure Active Directory
Connect\AzureADSSO.psd1"

New-AzureADSSOAuthenticationContext
```

2. A popup window appears.
3. Provide the credentials of an account that has the **Global administrator** role assigned to it.
4. Click **OK**.
5. Optionally, perform multi-factor authentication, and/or elevate the account to **Global administrator** when using Azure AD PIM.

6. Perform the following line of PowerShell in the same PowerShell session as the preceding lines:

```
Get-AzureADSSOStatus | ConvertFrom-Json
```

The preceding command shows the domains where Seamless Single Sign-on is configured. This provides a list of domains to change the password in.

7. Perform the following line of PowerShell in the same PowerShell session as the preceding lines:

```
$cred = Get-Credentials
```

8. A popup window appears.
9. Enter the credentials of an account that is a member of the **Domain Admins** group in the Active Directory forest. The Active Directory domain to reset the password for the **AzureADSSOACC** computer object in is derived from the account information.
10. Click **OK**.
11. Perform the following line of PowerShell in the same PowerShell session as the preceding lines:

```
Update-AzureADSSOForest -onPremCredentials $cred
```

The preceding command updates the Kerberos decryption key for the **AzureADSSOACC** computer object and updates the information in Azure AD.

Perform steps 6–9 for each of the domains from the output of step 5.

How it works...

Microsoft recommends changing the passwords for service accounts at least every year. This makes it hard for attackers to gain and maintain a foothold in your organization's systems.

The service account running the Azure AD Connect service

By default, Azure AD Connect runs with a **Virtual Service Account** (**VSA**). This account does not need have a password, so it doesn't need changing. Optionally, during the initial installation of Azure AD Connect, a **group Managed Service Account** (**gMSA**) can be configured to run Azure AD Connect. gMSAs change their passwords every 30 days, by default.

The service account connecting to Active Directory

The service account to connect to Active Directory is stored for the Active Directory **Management Agent (MA)**. After you successfully change the password for the service account (and thus pass the password requirements), change the account password in the configuration for the management agent in the Synchronization Service Manager.

The service account connecting to Azure AD

The service account to connect to Azure AD is stored for the Azure AD MA. Azure AD Connect does not let you create a password for the service account itself but offers a Windows PowerShell cmdlet to take care of everything for you.

The computer account for Seamless Single Sign-on

When the optional **Enable single sign-on** setting is enabled in Azure AD Connect, it instructs Azure AD Connect to use Kerberos authentication using a specific computer object in the local Active Directory for this feature: **AzureADSSOACC**. This account is located in the default Computers container.

As the password for this account is also stored in Azure AD for the Azure AD Authentication services to be able to decrypt the Kerberos packages, it requires a little more work to reset. Azure AD Connect offers a couple of Windows PowerShell cmdlets to take care of it.

14
Hardening Azure AD

Azure Active Directory (Azure AD) is a Microsoft cloud-based **Identity and Access Management (IAM)** solution. Over the years, many features have been added to the platform to address the needs of its millions of customers worldwide. Many of these features were security features that weren't turned on, by default. For newer Azure AD tenants, some of the security features are turned on, by default.

This chapter shows you how to configure an Azure AD tenant with features to increase its confidentiality, integrity, and availability. Some of these features and functionalities might hinder productivity, so you might not want to introduce them or communicate them first.

The recipes in this chapter start with recipes any admin can apply to harden any Azure AD tenant. Then, recipes are covered that require Azure AD Premium P1 licenses. At the end of the chapter, two recipes require Azure AD Premium P2 licenses.

The following recipes will be covered in this chapter:

- Setting the contact information
- Preventing non-privileged users from accessing the Azure portal
- Viewing all privileged users in Azure AD
- Preventing users from registering or consenting to apps
- Preventing users from inviting guests
- Configuring whitelisting and blacklisting for Azure AD B2B
- Configuring Azure AD Join and Azure AD Registration
- Configuring Intune auto-enrollment upon Azure AD Join
- Configuring baseline policies
- Configuring Conditional Access

- Accessing Azure AD Connect Health
- Configuring Azure AD Connect Health for AD FS
- Configuring Azure AD Connect Health for AD DS
- Configuring Azure AD Privileged Identity Management
- Configuring Azure AD Identity Protection

 We have gone to great lengths to make sure that the contents of this chapter are as future-proof as possible. However, as Azure AD is a cloud service, screen texts, panes, blades, and functionality in this chapter may change between the time of writing and when you read it, but the strategy and direction of Microsoft will still hold true.

Setting the contact information

This recipe shows you how to set the contact information for the tenant.

Getting ready

To complete this recipe, you'll need to sign into the Azure AD tenant with an account that has the Global administrator role assigned to it.

In a large organization, find out who the contact is for privacy. When you work in a team, create a distribution list to receive important updates for the Azure AD tenant.

How to do it...

Perform these steps to set the contact information:

1. Navigate your browser to `https://portal.azure.com`.
2. Sign in with an account in Azure Active Directory that has the Global administrator role assigned.
3. Perform multi-factor authentication when prompted.
4. In the left-hand navigation pane, click **Azure Active Directory**.
5. In the **Azure Active Directory** pane, click **Properties**:

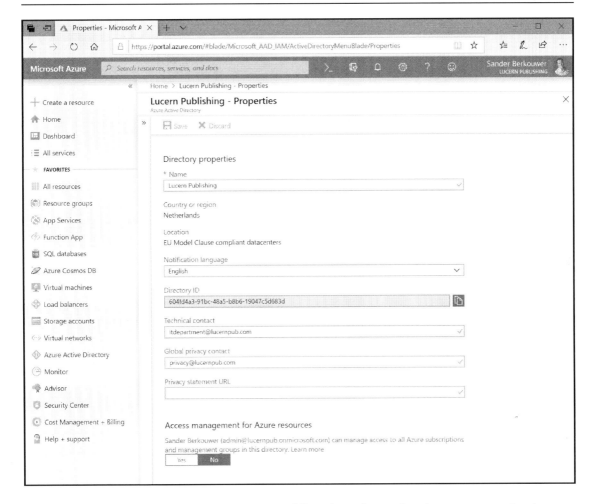

6. In the **Directory properties** pane, fill in the information for your organization.
7. Click **Save** at the top of the **Directory properties** pane.

How it works...

Azure AD tenants experience hostile takeovers; attackers brute-force passwords for users or reuse leaked credentials and then make their way to privileged accounts to take over the tenant. The percentage of tenants that experience this problem is tiny, but the scale of Azure means it happens to a couple of thousand tenants per day. When Microsoft detects this situation, they contact the owner of the tenant to help them regain control. However, for a lot of tenants the contact information is not provided or it's out of date.

The information for the **Technical contact** on the **Directory properties** pane is only used for these purposes. The information for the **Global privacy contact** and **Privacy statement URL** are accessible from the Azure AD sign-in experience.

The **Directory properties** is the only place in the Azure portal where the directory ID is exposed.

Preventing non-privileged users from accessing the Azure portal

This recipe shows you how to restrict access to the Azure portal for non-privileged users to make it only available to privileged users.

Getting ready

To complete this recipe, you'll need to sign into the Azure AD tenant with an account that has the Global administrator role assigned to it.

How to do it...

Perform these steps to restrict access to non-privileged users to the Azure AD Portal:

1. Navigate your browser to `https://portal.azure.com`.
2. Sign in with an account in Azure Active Directory that has the **Global administrator** role assigned.
3. Perform multi-factor authentication when prompted.
4. In the left-hand navigation pane, click **Azure Active Directory**.
5. In the **Azure Active Directory** pane, click **User settings**:

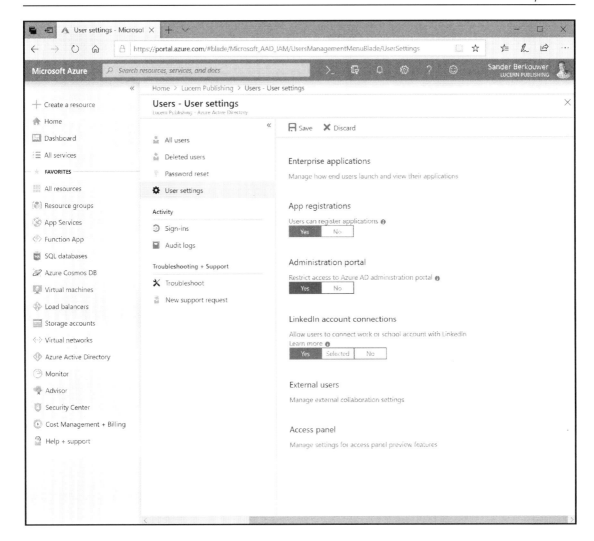

6. In the **User settings** pane, select **Yes** to **Restrict access to Azure AD administration portal**.

7. Click **Save** at the top of the pane.

How it works...

In Active Directory, by default, any user can access the contents of the directory to look up objects. Password(hashe)s are off limits, of course. Some organizations have limited this default access.

As many organizations synchronize user objects from Active Directory to Azure AD, many Azure AD tenants contain personal data for people inside organizations. By default, anyone can log in to the Azure portal with any browser and view the list of users, including many of their attributes, except, of course, passwords or password hashes. Because Azure AD is a cloud-based resource, by default anyone may access this information from any location. This is the big difference with Active Directory: looking up objects in Azure AD doesn't require a connection to an internal network, whereas Active Directory does.

For regulatory compliance with the **General Data Protection Regulation (GDPR)** and other privacy regulations, organizations may want to restrict the Azure AD administration portal experience.

By changing the default **No** value to **Yes** for **Restrict access to Azure AD administration portal**, it restricts all non-privileged users from accessing any Azure AD data in the administration portal but does not restrict such access using PowerShell or another client, such as Visual Studio.

Privileges in Azure AD are defined by roles.

Viewing all privileged users in Azure AD

This recipe shows two ways to view all privileged users in Azure AD.

Getting ready

To complete this recipe, you'll need to sign into the Azure AD tenant with an account that has the Global administrator role assigned to it.

When using the PowerShell method, install the AzureAD Windows PowerShell module first. Use the following line of PowerShell on a Windows or Windows Server system that runs Windows PowerShell 5.0 or higher in an elevated Windows PowerShell window:

```
Install-Module AzureAD
```

Press **Yes** twice.

To update the AzureAD Windows PowerShell Module, run the preceding line of PowerShell again.

How to do it...

You can view all privileged users in Azure AD in two ways:

- Using the Azure AD PowerShell
- Using the Azure Cloud Shell

Using the Azure AD PowerShell

Execute the following lines of PowerShell on the device where you installed the AzureAD
Windows PowerShell module:

```
Import-Module AzureAD
Connect-AzureAD
$_usersinroles = @()
Get-AzureADDirectoryRole | foreach {
    $_objectid = $_.ObjectId; $rolename = $_.Displayname
    $_usersinroles += Get-AzureADDirectoryRoleMember -ObjectId `
    $_objectid | select @{name='RoleName';expression={$rolename}},`
    displayname,UserPrincipalName,UserType
}
$_usersinroles"
```

Using the Azure Cloud Shell

Perform the following steps:

1. Navigate your browser to https://portal.azure.com.
2. Log in with an account in Azure Active Directory that has the **Global administrator** role assigned.
3. Perform multi-factor authentication when prompted.

4. In the top bar of the Azure portal, click the **Cloud Shell** icon, next to search. The Azure Cloud Shell appears underneath the Azure portal as part of the browser:

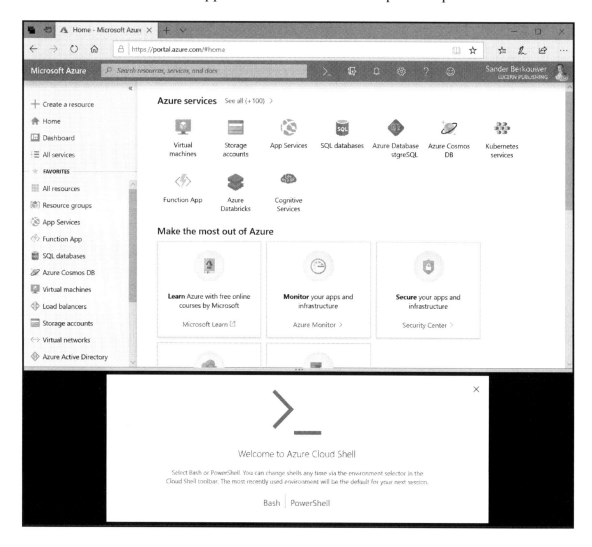

If this is your first time using Azure Cloud Shell, select **PowerShell** instead of **Bash**. You can change shells any time via the environment selector in the Cloud Shell toolbar. The most recently used environment will be the default for your next session.

5. Execute the following lines of PowerShell:

```
$_usersinroles = @()
Get-AzureADDirectoryRole | foreach {
    $_objectid = $_.ObjectId; $rolename = $_.Displayname
    $_usersinroles += Get-AzureADDirectoryRoleMember -ObjectId `
    $_objectid | select @{name='RoleName';expression={$rolename}}, `
    displayname,UserPrincipalName,UserType
}
$_usersinroles"
```

6. After consuming and/or copying the information, close the Azure Cloud Shell.

How it works...

While the Azure AD Portal, today, provides information on the roles and their members, which is a complete overview of all privileged users.

The lines of PowerShell in this recipe show this information. The first line creates an array. Then, each role is cycled through for members, who are then added to the array. The last line of PowerShell displays the contents of the array.

The Azure Cloud Shell is an ideal way to run PowerShell on systems that don't run or may not run PowerShell 5.0 or newer, or take advantage of .NET Framework. Since running the Azure Cloud Shell requires both access to Azure AD and Azure storage, it is not usable for Azure AD tenants that merely exist as Identity stores for Office 365.

Preventing users from registering or consenting to apps

This recipe shows how to prevent users from consenting to apps.

Getting ready

To complete this recipe, you'll need to sign into the Azure AD tenant with an account that has the Global administrator role assigned to it.

How to do it...

Perform these steps to prevent users consenting to apps:

1. Navigate your browser to `https://portal.azure.com`.
2. Sign in with an account in Azure Active Directory that has the **Global administrator** role assigned.
3. Perform multi-factor authentication when prompted.
4. In the left-hand navigation pane, click **Azure Active Directory**.
5. In the **Azure Active Directory** pane, click **User settings**:

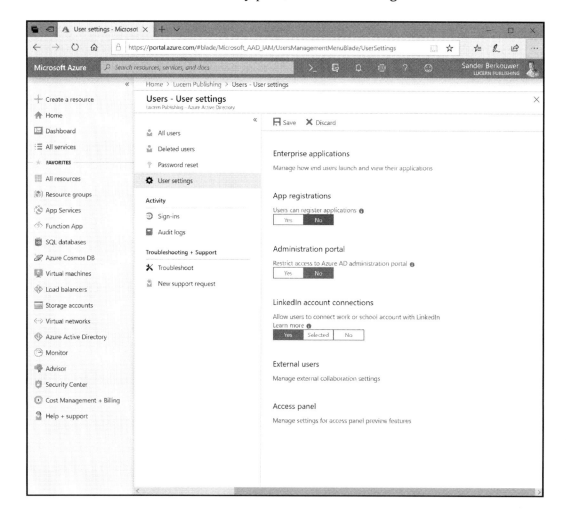

6. In the **User settings** pane, select **No** to **Users can register applications**.
7. Click **Save** at the top of the pane.
8. In the left-hand navigation pane, click **Azure Active Directory**.
9. In the **Azure Active Directory** pane, select **Enterprise Applications**.
10. In the **Enterprise applications** pane, click **User Settings**:

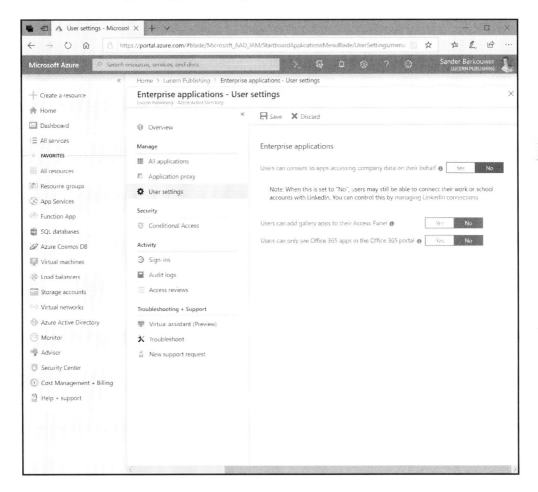

11. In the **Enterprise applications - User settings** pane, select **No** to **Users can consent to apps accessing company data on their behalf**. Note that the **Users can add gallery apps to their Access Panel** and **Users can only see Office 365 apps in the Office 365 portal** options are set to **No** by default.
12. Click **Save** at the top of the pane.

How it works...

By default, users of an Azure AD tenant can consent to any application they want to use with their Azure AD account. For admins, this might be an unwanted scenario, because they might want to do the following:

- Provide admin consent to certain applications, so end users don't have to.
- Lock down the Azure AD tenant by only allowing applications through admin consent.
- Avoid application sprawl in the Azure AD tenant.

To prevent user consenting to apps and other ways to add apps, the Azure AD tenant should be turned off in two locations inside the Azure Active Directory portal pages. The first option prevents users from registering custom-developed applications for use with the Azure AD tenant. The second option prevents users from consenting to third-party multi-tenant applications that access user data in the organization's tenant.

When turned off, the administrative overhead of Azure AD increases. This should be considered, especially in large environments. Application management may be delegated to people in the Application Administrator role.

There's more...

Consent labels are part of the app manifest. A rogue developer could trick one or more of your colleagues into consenting to serious permissions while presenting them as harmless permissions.

Preventing users from inviting guests

This recipe shows how to prevent people in the Azure AD tenant from inviting guests through Azure AD **Business to Business (B2B)**.

Getting ready

To complete this recipe, you'll need to sign into the Azure AD tenant with an account that has the Global administrator role assigned to it.

How to do it...

Perform these steps to prevent users from inviting guests:

1. Navigate your browser to `https://portal.azure.com`.
2. Sign in with an account in Azure Active Directory that has the **Global administrator** role assigned.
3. Perform multi-factor authentication when prompted.
4. In the left-hand navigation pane, click **Azure Active Directory**.
5. In the **Azure Active Directory** pane, click **User settings**.
6. Follow the link to **Manage external collaboration settings**:

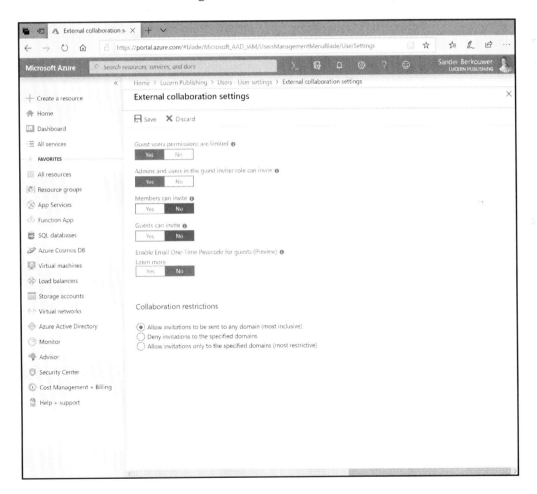

7. In the **External collaboration settings** pane, select **No** to **Members can invite** and **Guests can invite**.
8. Click **Save** at the top of the pane.

How it works...

People in your organization can invite other people outside of your organization to collaborate in Azure AD-integrated cloud applications, services, and systems.

When the people outside your organization successfully redeem the invitation, they appear as **Guest** objects instead of **Member** objects.

There's more...

When the Azure AD tenant already contains guests, selecting **Yes** to the **Guest user permissions are limited** option is a smart decision.

See also

For more information on how to take control of the Azure AD accounts that may have been created by your colleagues redeeming invitations, see the *Verifying your DNS domain name* recipe from `Chapter 12`, *Handling Authentication in a Hybrid World (AD FS, PHS, PTA, and 3SO)*.

To allow guest invites but limit the organizations to which invitations can be sent, see the *Configuring whitelisting or blacklisting for Azure B2B* recipe.

Configuring whitelisting or blacklisting for Azure AD B2B

This recipe shows how to configure whitelisting or blacklisting for DNS domain names for Azure AD B2B.

Getting ready

To complete this recipe, you'll need to sign into the Azure AD tenant with an account that has the Global administrator role assigned to it.

How to do it...

Perform these steps to configure whitelisting or blacklisting for Azure AD B2B:

1. Navigate your browser to `https://portal.azure.com`.
2. Sign in with an account in Azure Active Directory that has the **Global administrator** role assigned.
3. Perform multi-factor authentication when prompted.
4. In the left-hand navigation pane, click **Azure Active Directory**.
5. In the Azure Active Directory pane, click **User settings**.
6. Follow the link to **Manage external collaboration settings**.
7. In the **External collaboration settings** pane, under **Collaboration restrictions**, select either the **Deny invitations to the specified domains** or the **Allow invitations only to the specified domains (most restrictive)** option.

8. Type the DNS domain name(s) to blacklist (with the **Deny invitations to the specified domains** option selected) or to whitelist (with the **Allow invitations only to the specified domains (most restrictive)** option selected):

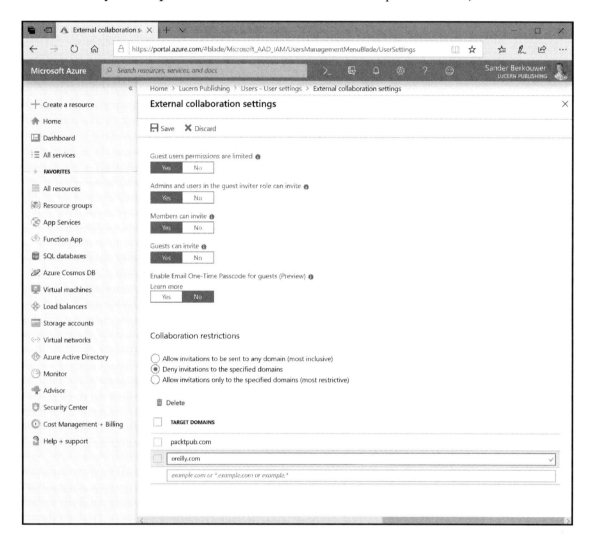

9. Click **Save** at the top of the pane.

How it works...

Not collaborating might not be an option for every organization.

When the organization wants to collaborate with organizations through Azure AD B2B, blacklisting can be used to make sure people in your organization cannot invite people in certain non-approved organizations. For this functionality, use the **Deny invitations to the specified domains** option. Invitations to email addresses with the DNS domain names specified will not be sent and logged.

When the organization wants to collaborate with organizations through Azure AD B2B, blacklisting can be used to make sure people in your organization can only invite people in approved organizations. For this functionality, use the **Allow invitations only to the specified domains (most restrictive)** option. Invitations to email addresses with other DNS domain names will not be sent and logged.

Whitelisting trumps blacklisting and, therefore, is the most restrictive option, but also the best option in terms of information security.

Configuring Azure AD Join and Azure AD Registration

This recipe shows how to limit the Azure AD Join and Azure AD Registration features for your organization, configuring additional cloud device administrators and allowing Enterprise State Roaming.

Getting ready

To complete this recipe, you'll need to sign into the Azure AD tenant with an account that has the Global administrator role assigned to it.

Configuring additional accounts with local administrator privileges on Azure AD-joined devices and enabling Enterprise State Roaming requires Azure AD Premium P1 licenses, or Microsoft licenses that include the P1 license, such as Azure AD Premium P2, EMS E3, EMS A3, Microsoft 365 E3, or Microsoft 365 Business licenses.

How to do it...

Configuring the Azure AD Join and Azure AD Registration features consists of these four distinct configuration changes:

1. Limiting who can join Azure AD devices.
2. Limiting who can register Azure AD devices.
3. Configuring additional administrators, next to Azure AD accounts with the **Cloud device administrator** role assigned to them (Azure AD Premium-only).
4. Enabling Enterprise State Roaming (Azure AD Premium-only).

Limiting who can join Azure AD devices

Perform these steps to limit the Azure AD Join feature for your organization:

1. Navigate your browser to `https://portal.azure.com`.
2. Sign in with an account in Azure Active Directory that has the **Global administrator** role assigned.
3. Perform multi-factor authentication when prompted.
4. In the left-hand navigation pane, click **Azure Active Directory**.
5. In the **Azure Active Directory** pane, click **Devices**.
6. In the **Devices** pane, click **Device settings**.
7. Select **Selected** or **None** instead of **All** for the **Users may join devices to Azure AD** option.
8. When we select **Selected**:
    1. Specify a group or multiple accounts that are allowed to join Azure AD devices by clicking the **No member selected** text. The **Members allowed to join devices** pane appears.
    2. Click **+ Add members**.
    3. The **Add members** blade appears. Select or search for members to add.
    4. Click **Select** at the bottom of the blade.

5. Click **OK** in the **Members allowed to join devices** pane:

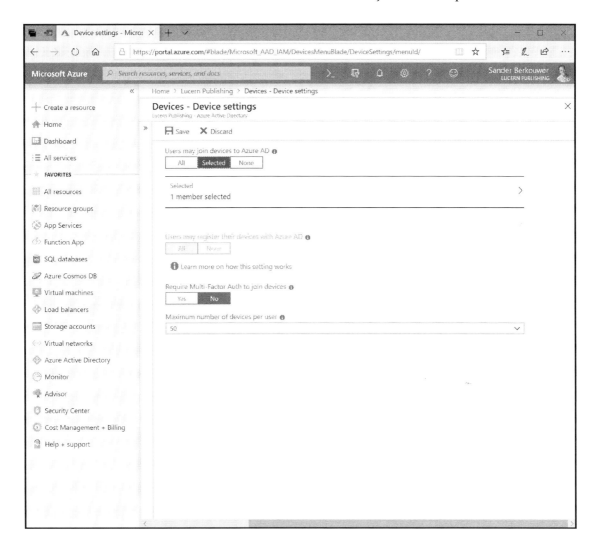

9. Click **Save** at the top of the **Devices - Device settings** pane.

Limiting who can register Azure AD devices

Perform these steps to limit who can register Azure AD devices:

1. Navigate your browser to `https://portal.azure.com`.
2. Sign in with an account in Azure Active Directory that has the **Global administrator** role assigned.
3. Perform multi-factor authentication when prompted.
4. In the left-hand navigation pane, click **Azure Active Directory**.
5. In the **Azure Active Directory** pane, click **Devices**.
6. In the **Devices** pane, click **Device settings**.
7. Select **None** instead of **All** for the **Users may register their devices with Azure AD** option:

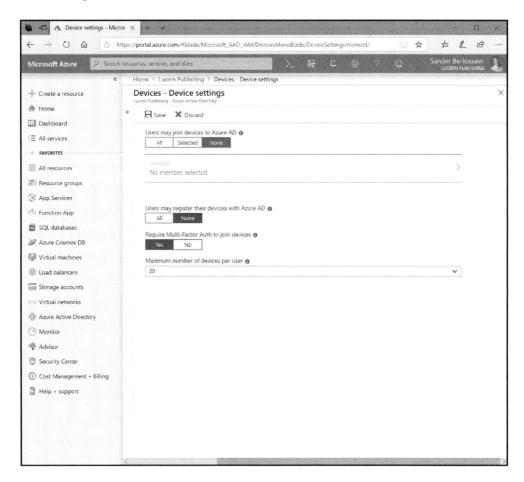

8. When the **Users may register their devices with Azure AD** option is grayed-out, Azure AD Registration is required for other features. If this is not the case, it's a recommended practice to select **Yes** for **Require Multi-Factor Auth to join devices**.

9. Click **Save** at the top of the **Devices - Device settings** pane.

Configuring additional administrators

Perform these steps to configure additional administrators, next to Azure AD accounts with the **Cloud device administrator** role assigned to them:

1. Navigate your browser to `https://portal.azure.com`.
2. Sign in with an account in Azure Active Directory that has the **Global administrator** role assigned.
3. Perform multi-factor authentication when prompted.
4. In the left-hand navigation pane, click **Azure Active Directory**.
5. In the **Azure Active Directory** pane, click **Devices**.
6. In the **Devices** pane, click **Device settings**.
7. With Azure AD Premium licenses assigned, the **Additional local administrators on Azure AD joined devices** option is available. Change it from **None** to **Selected**.

8. Click the **No member selected** text.
   The **Local administrators on devices** pane appears:

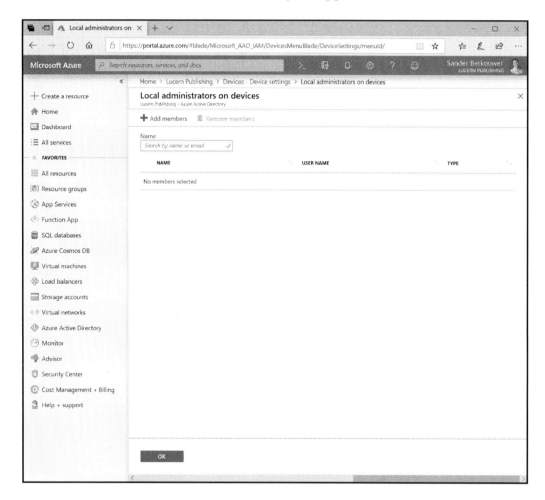

9. Click **+ Add members**.
10. The **Add members** blade appears. Select or search for members to add. Note that accounts with the **Global administrator** and **Cloud device administrator** roles are grayed out.
11. Click **Select** at the bottom of the blade.
12. Click **OK** on the **Local administrators on devices** pane.
13. Click **Save** at the top of the **Devices - Device settings** pane.

Enabling Enterprise State Roaming

Perform these steps to enable Enterprise State Roaming:

1. Navigate your browser to `https://portal.azure.com`.
2. Sign in with an account in Azure Active Directory that has the **Global administrator** role assigned.
3. Perform multi-factor authentication when prompted.
4. In the left-hand navigation pane, click **Azure Active Directory**.
5. In the **Azure Active Directory** pane, click **Devices**.
6. With the Azure AD Premium licenses assigned, **Enterprise State Roaming** is available in the **Devices** pane. Click it.
7. Change **Users may sync settings and app data across devices** from **None** to **All** or **Selected**:

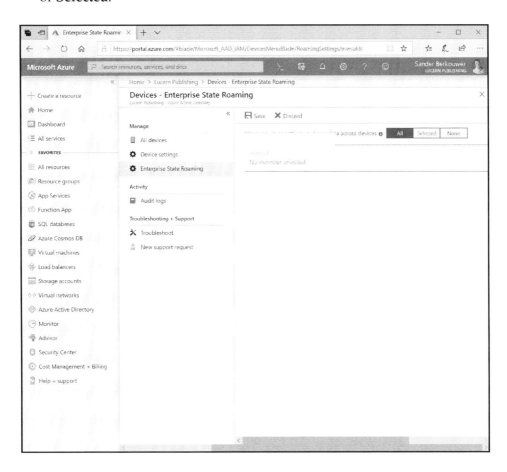

8. When we select **Selected**:
   1. Specify a group or multiple accounts that are allowed to join Azure AD devices by clicking the **No member selected** text. The **Members allowed to sync settings and app data** pane appears.
   2. Click **+ Add members**.
   3. The **Add members** blade appears. Select or search for members to add.
   4. Click **Select** at the bottom of the blade.
   5. Click **OK** on the **Members allowed to sync settings and app data** pane.
9. Click **Save** at the top of the **Devices - Enterprise State Roaming** pane.

How it works...

Out of the box, Windows 10 allows people to join the Azure AD device, marking it as an organizational device in Azure AD. End users who perform this action, by default, gain the same benefits as people using domain-joined devices, in terms of Single Sign-On to Azure AD-integrated cloud applications and being able to sign into other Azure AD-joined devices. With an Azure AD Premium license assigned, they can even benefit from Enterprise State Roaming for their settings.

When a device is domain-joined, it cannot be Azure AD-joined by the end user, because the Azure AD Join feature is considered a bring-your-own-device feature.

Android and iOS-based devices don't offer the Azure AD Join capability, but these devices can be registered with Azure AD to gain the same benefits as Azure AD-joined and domain-joined devices.

When you have either **Enrollment with Microsoft Intune** or **Device Management for Office 365** turned on, the **Users may register their devices with Azure AD** option is grayed-out. In these cases, devices use the Azure AD device registration service for compliance. Do not select **Yes** for **Require Multi-Factor Auth to join devices** in this case, as it may negatively impact automatic registrations.

By default, the **Cloud device administrators** are local administrators on Azure AD-joined devices. Azure AD accounts that are added using the **Additional local administrators on Azure AD joined devices** option gain the same local privileges.

Enterprise State Roaming is a Windows 10 feature that securely synchronizes user settings and application settings data to Azure. When people enabled with this feature switch from one Azure AD-joined device to another Azure AD-joined device, they retain their settings across these devices. By using Group Policy and **Mobile Device Management** (**MDM**) solutions, such Intune, admins can manage settings for synchronization.

See also

To Hybrid Azure AD Join devices to Azure AD, based on their domain-join status, see the *Configuring Hybrid Azure AD Join* recipe from `Chapter 13`, *Handling Synchronization in a Hybrid World (Azure AD Connect)*.

Configuring Intune auto-enrollment upon Azure AD Join

This recipe shows how to configure automatic enrollment into Microsoft Intune for MDM and **Mobile Application Management** (**MAM**) upon Azure AD Join.

Getting ready

To complete this recipe, you'll need to sign into the Azure AD tenant with an account that has the Global administrator role assigned to it.

A MDM solution, such as Microsoft Intune, needs to be configured for the Azure AD tenant. This recipe shows how to configure auto-enrollment for Intune, but when the URLs for the MDM solution are known, the default URLs can be replaced to meet your organization's needs.

How to do it...

Perform these steps to configure Intune auto-enrollment upon Azure AD Join:

1. Navigate your browser to `https://portal.azure.com`.
2. Sign in with an account in Azure Active Directory that has the **Global administrator** role assigned.
3. Perform multi-factor authentication when prompted.

4. In the left-hand navigation pane, click **Azure Active Directory**.
5. In the **Azure Active Directory** pane, click **Mobility (MDM and MAM)**.
6. In the **Mobility (MDM and MAM)** pane, click **Microsoft Intune**:

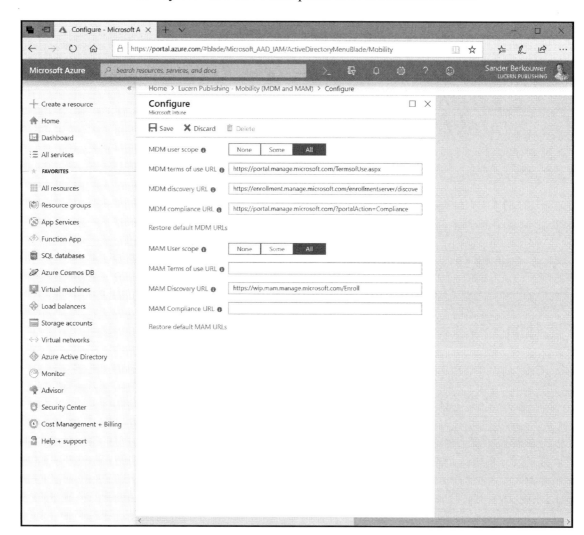

7. On the **Configure** pane, select **All** for the **MDM User Scope** option.
8. Select **All** for the **MAM User Scope** option.
9. Click **Save** at the top of the **Configure** pane.

How it works...

MDM and MAM are modern endpoint-management solutions that manage devices regardless of their operating system or location. MDM manages settings for complete devices, whereas MAM manages settings for applications on these devices, such as Outlook. A device can be MDM-managed and MAM-managed but does not need to be both to work.

When Intune-enrollment is configured, both Azure AD-joined devices and Hybrid Azure AD-joined devices are in scope.

Configuring baseline policies

Azure AD offers baseline policies to manage baselines for important security settings in the tenant. This recipe shows how to configure them, using the example of enabling the **Baseline Policy: Require MFA for admins**.

Getting ready

To complete this recipe, you'll need to sign into the Azure AD tenant with an account that has the Global administrator role assigned to it.

How to do it...

Perform these steps to configure the **Baseline Policy: Require MFA for admins**:

1. Navigate your browser to `https://portal.azure.com`.
2. Sign in with an account in Azure Active Directory that has the **Global administrator** role assigned.
3. Perform multi-factor authentication when prompted.
4. In the left-hand navigation pane, click **Azure Active Directory**.

5. In the **Azure Active Directory** pane, click **Conditional Access**:

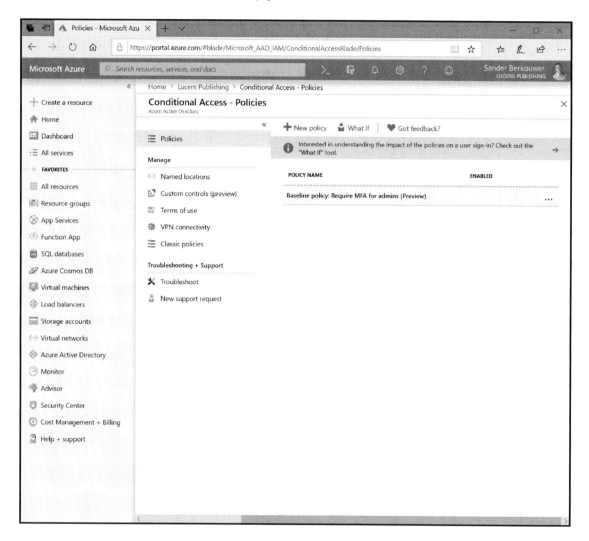

6. In the main pane of the **Conditional Access - Policies** pane, click the **Baseline Policy: Require MFA for admins**.
7. In the **Baseline Policy: Require MFA for admins** pane, select the **Use policy immediately** option.
8. Click **Save** at the bottom of the pane.

How it works...

The Conditional Access functionality in Azure Active Directory requires Azure AD Premium P1 licenses. However, some policies are important enough to fall outside the scope of this license requirement. Microsoft calls these policies **Baseline policies**.

The **Baseline policy: Require MFA for admins** is an important policy, because **multi-factor authentication** (**MFA**) reduces the risk of hostile takeovers for an Azure AD account by 99.9%.

The **Baseline policy: Require MFA for admins** requires Azure AD accounts that have the **Global administrator**, **SharePoint administrator**, **Exchange administrator**, **Conditional Access administrator** and/or **Security administrator** role to perform multi-factor authentication for every sign-in. For some applications, services and scripts get mangled by this baseline policy. If this is the case, exclude the account that runs these applications, services, and/or scripts from the policy, but make sure sufficient security measures are taken to prevent hostile takeovers of this account and communicate to the vendor or supplier of the applications, service, and/or scripts that this needs fixing.

Configuring Conditional Access

This recipe shows how to Configure Conditional Access. As three example policies, we will configure the following:

- All users can access an Azure AD-integrated application only when they perform multi-factor authentication.
- All users can access any Azure AD-integrated applications only when they use a Hybrid Azure AD-joined device when they are visiting sensitive countries on business trips.
- All users are not able to use legacy authentication.

Getting ready

To complete this recipe, you'll need to sign into the Azure AD tenant with an account that has the Global administrator role or Conditional access administrator role assigned to it.

The Conditional Access functionality requires Azure AD Premium P1 licenses, or Microsoft licenses that include the P1 license, such as Azure AD Premium P2, EMS E3, EMS A3, Microsoft 365 E3, or Microsoft 365 Business licenses.

How to do it...

Perform these steps to configure Conditional Access to allow all users to access an Azure AD-integrated application only when they perform multi-factor authentication:

1. Navigate your browser to `https://portal.azure.com`.
2. Sign in with an account in Azure Active Directory that has the **Global administrator** role or the **Conditional access administrator** role assigned.
3. Perform multi-factor authentication when prompted.
4. In the left-hand navigation pane, click **Azure Active Directory**.
5. In the **Azure Active Directory** pane, click **Conditional Access**.
6. In the main pane of the **Conditional Access - Policies** pane, click **+ New policy**. The **New** pane appears:

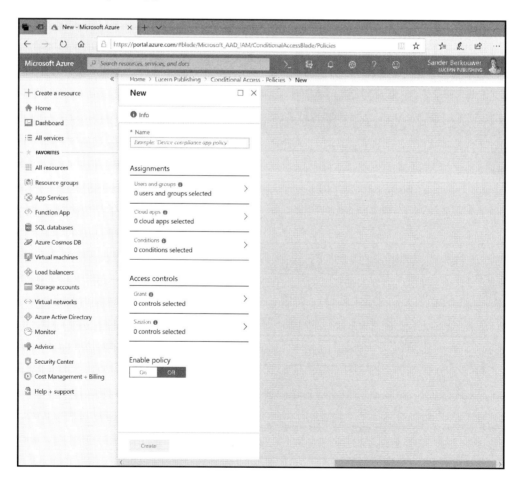

7. To create the policy to require multi-factor authentication, make these changes:
   1. Provide a **Name** for the new Conditional Access policy.
   2. In the **Assignments** region, click **0 users and groups selected**:
      1. Select the **All users** option.
      2. Click **Done** at the bottom of the **Users and groups** pane.
   3. In the **Assignments** region, click **0 cloud apps selected**:
      1. Select the **Select apps** option.
      2. Click **None** and select the Azure AD-integrated application from the list or search for it.
8. Click the **Select** button at the bottom of the **Select** pane.
9. Click **Done** on the **Cloud apps** pane.
10. In the **Access Controls** region, click **0 controls selected** under **Grant**:
    1. Select **Require multi-factor authentication** as a control.
    2. Click the **Select** button on the bottom of the **Grant** pane.
11. Select **On** for **Enable policy**.
12. Click **Create** at the bottom of the pane.

Perform these steps to configure Conditional Access to allow all users to access any Azure AD-integrated applications only when they use a Hybrid Azure AD-joined device when they are visiting sensitive countries:

1. Navigate your browser to `https://portal.azure.com`.
2. Sign in with an account in Azure Active Directory that has the **Global administrator** role or the **Conditional access administrator** role assigned.
3. Perform multi-factor authentication when prompted.
4. In the left-hand navigation pane, click **Azure Active Directory**.
5. In the **Azure Active Directory** pane, click **Conditional Access**.
6. In the **Conditional Access** pane, click **Named locations**.
7. On the **Conditional Access - Named locations** pane, click **+ New location**:
   1. Provide a **Name** for the new Named location.
   2. Select the **Countries/Regions** option.

3. From the drop-down list, select the country or countries you want to add to the Named location:

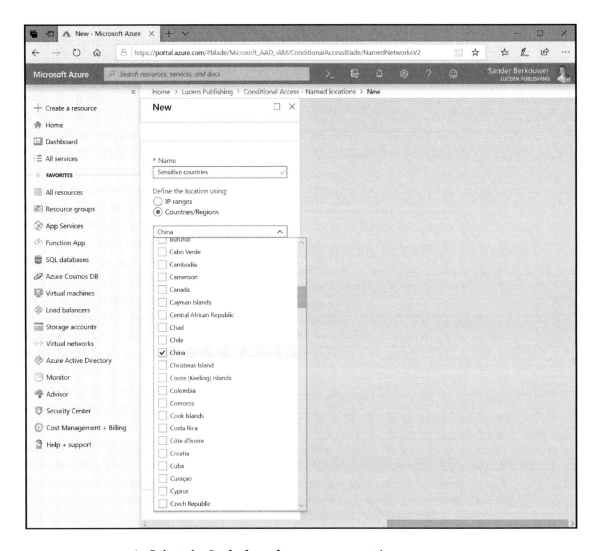

4. Select the **Include unknown areas** option.

8. Click **Create** at the bottom of the pane.
9. Click **Policies** at the top of the **Conditional Access** pane.
10. In the main pane of the **Conditional Access - Policies** pane, click **+ New policy**.

11. To create the policy to allow access on Hybrid Azure AD-joined devices only at a certain location, make these changes:
    1. Provide a **Name** for the new Conditional Access policy.
    2. In the **Assignments** region, click **0 users and groups selected**:
        1. Select the **All users** option.
        2. Click **Done** at the bottom of the **Users and groups** pane.
    3. In the **Assignments** region, click **0 cloud apps selected**:
        1. Select the **All cloud apps** option.
        2. Click **Done** on the **Cloud apps** pane.
    4. In the **Assignments** region, click **0 conditions selected**:
        1. On the **Conditions** pane, for **Locations**, click the **Not configured** text.
        2. Select **Yes** to **Configure**. Click **Selected locations**.

12. Click **None** under **Select**.
13. In the **Select** pane, select the named location created earlier.
14. Click **Select** at the bottom of the **Select** pane.
15. Click **Done** at the bottom of the **Locations** pane.
16. Click **Done** at the bottom of the **Conditions** pane.
17. In the **Access Controls** region, click **0 controls selected** under **Grant**:
    1. Select **Require Hybrid Azure AD joined device** as a control.
    2. Click the **Select** button on the bottom of the **Grant** pane.
18. Select **On** for **Enable policy**.
19. Click **Create** at the bottom of the pane.

Perform these steps to block legacy authentication:

1. Navigate your browser to `https://portal.azure.com`.
2. Sign in with an account in Azure Active Directory that has the **Global administrator** role or the **Conditional access administrator** role assigned.
3. Perform multi-factor authentication when prompted.
4. In the left-hand navigation pane, click **Azure Active Directory**.
5. In the **Azure Active Directory** pane, click **Conditional Access**.
6. In the main pane of the **Conditional Access - Policies** pane, click **+ New policy**.
7. To create the policy to block legacy authentication, make these changes:
    1. Provide a **Name** for the new Conditional Access policy.

2. In the **Assignments** region, click **0 users and groups selected**.

    1. Select the **All users** option.

    2. Click **Done** at the bottom of the **Users and groups** pane.

3. In the **Assignments** region, click **0 cloud apps selected**:

    1. Select the **All apps** option.

    2. Click **Done** on the **Cloud apps** pane.

4. In the **Assignments** region, click **0 conditions selected**:

    1. On the **Conditions** pane, for **Client apps**, click the **Not configured** text.

    2. Select **Yes** to **Configure**.

8. Deselect the **Browser** option.

9. Deselect **Modern authentication clients** and **Exchange ActiveSync clients**.

10. Make sure the **Other clients** option is selected:

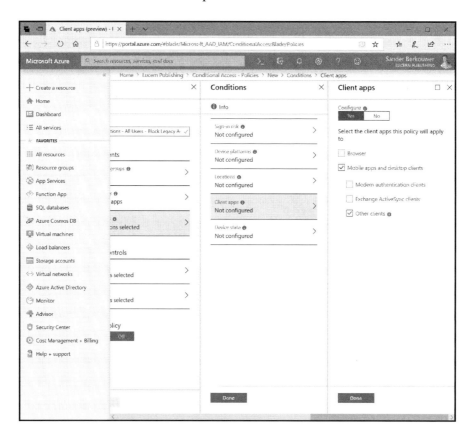

11. Click **Done** at the bottom of the **Client apps** pane.
12. Click **Done** at the bottom of the **Conditions** pane.
13. In the **Access Controls** region, click **0 controls selected** under **Grant**.
14. Select **Block access** as a control.
15. Click the **Select** button on the bottom of the **Grant** pane.
16. Select **On** for **Enable policy**.
17. Click **Create** at the bottom of the pane.

How it works...

In on-premises networks, access is typically governed by group memberships; when you authenticate on a domain-joined system, the groups an account is a member of dictate the level of access. Dynamic Access Control and Authentication Policies, introduced in Windows Server 2012, showed the possibilities of attribute-based access control with claims in Kerberos.

For cloud applications, services, and systems, a more granular form of access control is needed. Microsoft introduced the controls organizations need with Conditional Access. Access can be allowed or denied, per Azure AD account and/or group, and per Azure AD-integrated applications, including on-premises claims-based applications and applications that are published through the Azure AD Application Proxy.

Access can be allowed or denied based on conditions, such as the sign-in risk, the device used, and its state (marked as compliant or Hybrid Azure AD-joined), the location from where the authentication originates, and/or the client app used and its state (approved or non-approved).

Access can be subject to performing multi-factor authentication or accepting a Terms of Use. Additionally, access to SharePoint can be limited to read-only or non-download.

The possibilities to control access based on these conditions are virtually endless. To make the most of Conditional Access policies, it's good to know that, by default, everyone has access to everything, at any time, anywhere. Every time an admin tries to add a policy that enforces this same principal, the **Save** button at the bottom of the Conditional Access policy pane is grayed-out.

The **All Users** options in Conditional Access contain all users, including guest users.

To avoid locking out admins, Conditional Access features a **What If** feature. Before creating a policy, the **What If** feature allows you to input the conditions and run a preliminary analysis of the impact. Using this process, policies can be applied without unnecessarily locking out the wrong people. Embracing a more formalized process, the four-eyes principle can be applied by creating the policy but setting **Enable policy** to **Off**.

In terms of naming, it's wise to start with a consistent naming convention for Conditional Access policies. As the organization embraces the possibilities, many policies may be created. A naming convention with the environment (D, T, A, or P), app name(s), scope, and measures is recommended, resulting in the following Conditional Access policy names:

- P - HR Application - All Users - Require MFA
- P - All applications - All Users - Compliant devices only in China
- P - All applications - All Users - Block Legacy Authentication

See also

To use device state with Conditional Access, refer to the *Configuring Azure AD Join* recipe in this chapter and the *Configuring Hybrid Azure AD Join* recipe from `Chapter 13`, *Handling Synchronization in a Hybrid World (Azure AD Connect)*.

Accessing Azure AD Connect Health

This recipe shows the benefits of using Azure AD Connect Health to monitor and troubleshoot a hybrid identity implementation.

Getting ready

To complete this recipe, you'll need to sign into the Azure AD tenant with an account that has the Global administrator role assigned to it. Access to the Azure AD Connect Health dashboard can be delegated through its role-based access-control (IAM) settings.

The Azure AD Connect Health functionality requires Azure AD Premium P1 licenses, or Microsoft licenses that include the P1 license, such as Azure AD Premium P2, EMS E3, EMS A3, Microsoft 365 E3, or Microsoft 365 Business licenses.

Azure AD Connect Health agents communicate using TCP port 5671. Make sure this network traffic is allowed to the internet from the agents.

How to do it...

Perform these steps:

1. Navigate your browser to `https://portal.azure.com`.
2. Sign in with an account in Azure Active Directory that has the **Global administrator** role assigned.
3. Perform multi-factor authentication when prompted.
4. In the left-hand navigation pane, click **Azure Active Directory**.
5. In the **Azure Active Directory** pane, click **Azure AD Connect**.
6. In the **Azure AD Connect** main pane, under **Health and analytics**, follow the **Azure AD Connect Health** link:

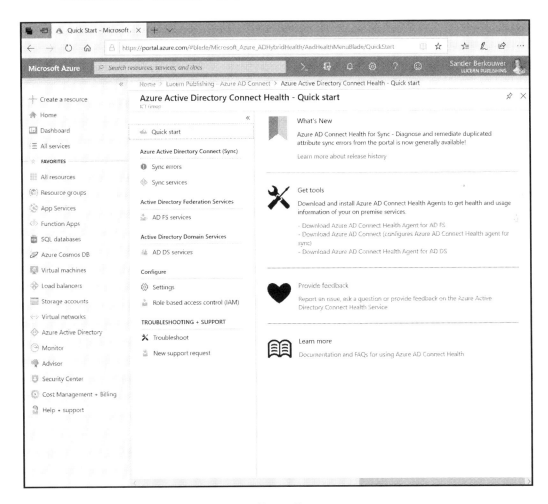

7. In the **Azure AD Connect Health** navigation pane, click **Sync errors** to examine the synchronization errors.

8. In the **Azure AD Connect Health** navigation pane, click **Sync services** to examine the Azure AD Connect installations, associated with the Azure AD tenant.

9. In the **Azure AD Connect Health** navigation pane, click **Settings** to optionally disable automatic upgrades of the Azure AD Connect Health agents with the latest version, or allow Microsoft access to the tenant's health data for troubleshooting purposes.

How it works...

By default, the Azure AD Connect Health agent is installed with Azure AD Connect and, by default, it provides data to Azure AD on the synchronization status. This data is exchanged using a network connection over TCP port 5671, if this network traffic is allowed.

Older Azure AD Connect Health agents may still require connectivity, based on TCP port 5671 for Azure AD Connect Health to work.

The data is available in the Azure AD Connect Health dashboard in Azure portal, but only accessible when at least one Azure AD Premium P1 license is attached to the Azure AD tenant per configured Azure AD Connect installation.

The Azure AD Connect Health dashboard provides information on the following:

- Azure AD Connect synchronization services
    - The Azure AD Connect Servers in use:
        - Their status
        - Their alerts
        - Their Azure AD Connect versions, database settings, and service accounts
        - Their operating systems, domains, time zones, last reboots, machine types, and dimensions in terms of CPU and physical memory
        - The Azure AD Connect Health Agent version
        - The time of their last export to Azure AD
        - Their run-profile latency in seconds

- Settings for uploaded data; whether to upload all error logs
- Azure AD Connect synchronization errors
    - Viewing of the following synchronization errors:
        - Duplicate attribute errors
        - Data mismatch errors
        - Data validation failures
        - Large attribute errors
        - Federated domain changes
        - Existing admin role conflicts
    - Exporting the preceding errors
    - Notification settings for errors

Microsoft's strategy is that admins can troubleshoot hybrid identity upon being notified of problems in their environment.

There's more...

By default, people with accounts in the Global administrator role receive notifications for Azure AD Connect Health. The list of email addressees can be expanded to include email addresses for people and/or distribution lists. Perform the following steps to configure, while signed in and in the **Azure AD Connect Health** dashboard:

1. In the **Azure AD Connect Health** navigation pane, click **Sync errors**.
2. In the top ribbon, click **Notification Settings**.
3. In the field under **Additional email recipients**, enter the email address of a mailbox or distribution list within your organization, outsourcing organization, or partner organization. New fields appear automatically to accommodate your needs.
4. Deselect the **Notify All Global Administrators** option if it is no longer needed.
5. Click **Save** at the top of the **Notification** pane.

Configuring Azure AD Connect Health for AD FS

Azure AD Connect Health can be expanded to include monitoring of the **Active Directory Federation Services** (**AD FS**) servers and Web Application Proxies of your organization's AD FS implementation. This recipe shows how to do this.

Getting ready

To complete this recipe, you'll need to sign into the Azure AD tenant with an account that has the Global administrator role assigned to it. Access to the Azure AD Connect Health dashboard can be delegated through its role-based access-control (IAM) settings.

The **Azure AD Connect Health** functionality requires Azure AD Premium P1 licenses, or Microsoft licenses that include the P1 license, such as Azure AD Premium P2, EMS E3, EMS A3, Microsoft 365 E3, or Microsoft 365 Business licenses.

Azure AD Connect Health agents communicate using TCP port `5671`. Make sure this network traffic is allowed to the internet from the agents.

Make sure all AD FS servers and Web Application Proxies run Windows PowerShell 4.0 or above.

How to do it...

Configuring Azure AD Connect Health for AD FS consists of three steps:

1. Downloading the agent.
2. Installing and configuring the agent.
3. Consuming the information in the Azure AD Connect Health dashboard.

Downloading the agent

Follow these steps to download the Azure AD Connect Health Agent for AD FS:

1. Navigate your browser to `https://portal.azure.com`.
2. Sign in with an account in Azure Active Directory that has the **Global administrator** role assigned.

3. Perform multi-factor authentication when prompted.
4. In the left-hand navigation pane, click **Azure Active Directory**.
5. In the **Azure Active Directory** pane, click **Azure AD Connect**.
6. In the **Azure AD Connect** main pane, under **Health and analytics**, follow the **Azure AD Connect Health** link.
7. In the **Azure AD Connect Health - Quick Start** pane, click the **Download Azure AD Connect Health Agent for AD FS** link.
8. Download the agent to a location where it is accessible to the AD FS servers and Web Application Proxies, or download it and copy it to the hard disks of these servers.

Installing and configuring the agent

Follow these steps to install and configure the Azure AD Connect Health Agent for AD FS on each AD FS server and each Web Application Proxy in your environment:

1. Run `AdHealthAdfsAgentSetup.exe`.
2. In the **Azure AD Connect Health AD FS Agent** window, click the **Install** button.
3. In the **Setup Successful** screen, click the **Configure Now** button. A Windows PowerShell window appears. Then the **Sign in to Azure AD Connect Health Agent** window appears.
4. Sign in with an account in Azure Active Directory that has the **Global administrator** role assigned.
5. Perform multi-factor authentication when prompted.
6. Close the Windows PowerShell window.

Consuming the information in the Azure AD Connect Health dashboard

Perform these steps to consume the information from the Azure AD Connect Health Agent for AD FS installations in the Azure AD Connect Health dashboard:

1. Navigate your browser to `https://portal.azure.com`.
2. Sign in with an account in Azure Active Directory that has the **Global administrator** role or the **Conditional access administrator** role assigned.
3. Perform multi-factor authentication when prompted.
4. In the left-hand navigation pane, click **Azure Active Directory**.

5. In the **Azure Active Directory** pane, click **Azure AD Connect**.
6. In the **Azure AD Connect** main pane, under **Health and analytics**, follow the **Azure AD Connect Health** link.
7. In the **Azure AD Connect Health** navigation pane, click **AD FS services**.
8. In the **AD FS services** pane, click the service name of the AD FS farm you want to monitor:

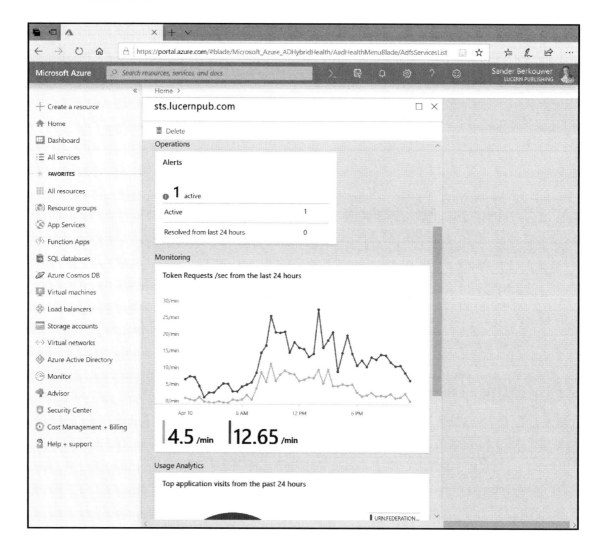

How it works...

The Azure AD Connect Health Agent for AD FS is an additional agent that can be installed on AD FS servers and Web Application Proxies of an AD FS implementation. Microsoft recommends installing the agent on all AD FS servers and Web Application Proxies for complete insights.

 Older Azure AD Connect Health agents for AD FS exchange data with Azure AD using a network connection over TCP port 5671. In this case, TCP port 5671 needs to be directly available from the individual AD FS servers and Web Application Proxies for Azure AD Connect Health to work.

Azure AD Connect Health's data is not sent by the Web Application Proxies on behalf of the AD FS servers, as outside authentication requests are.

The data is available in the Azure AD Connect Health dashboard in the Azure portal, but only accessible when at least one Azure AD Premium P1 license is attached to the Azure AD tenant per configured Azure AD Connect installation. For correct licensing, every monitored AD FS server and every monitored Web Application Proxy requires an additional 25 Azure AD Premium P1 licenses attached to the Azure AD tenant.

The Azure AD Connect Health dashboard provides information on the following:

- The AD FS servers
    - Their status
    - Their alerts
    - Their operating systems, domains, time zones, last reboots, machine types, and dimensions in terms of CPU and physical memory
    - The Azure AD Connect Health Agent version
    - Statistical information for the last week, day, or past 6 hours in graphs on the following aspects:
        - Token requests per second
        - AD FS private bytes
        - Extranet Account Lockouts
        - Established TCP connections
        - Credential authentication failures
        - Credential authentication failures per second
        - Used memory (percentage)
        - User processor (percentage)

- The Web Application Proxies
    - Their status
    - Their alerts
    - Their operating systems, domains, time zones, last reboots, machine types, and dimensions in terms of CPU and physical memory
        - The Azure AD Connect Health Agent version
        - Statistical information for the last week, day, or past 6 hours in graphs on the following aspects:
            - Token requests per second
            - Outstanding token requests (proxy)
            - Rejected token requests per second (proxy)
            - Established TCP connections
            - Token request latency
            - Used memory as a percentage of the total memory
            - User processor (percentage)
- Combined statistical information for the last week, day, or past 6 hours in graphs on the information that is available in the preceding individual graphs
- Usage analytics in terms of total requests, total failed requests and user count per application (relying party trust), server, authentication method, network location, and for workplace-joined devices only
- Reports for the last 30 days on bad password attempts and risky IP addresses

Configuring Azure AD Connect Health for AD DS

Azure AD Connect Health can be expanded to include monitoring of the domain controllers of your organization's Active Directory implementation. This recipe shows how to do this.

Getting ready

To complete this recipe, you'll need to sign into the Azure AD tenant with an account that has the Global administrator role assigned to it. Access to the Azure AD Connect Health dashboard can be delegated through its role-based access-control (IAM) settings.

The **Azure AD Connect Health** functionality requires Azure AD Premium P1 licenses, or a Microsoft license that includes the P1 license, such as Azure AD Premium P2, EMS E3, EMS A3, Microsoft 365 E3, or Microsoft 365 Business licenses.

Make sure all domain controllers run Windows PowerShell 4.0 or above.

How to do it...

Configuring Azure AD Connect Health for AD DS consists of three steps:

1. Downloading the agent.
2. Installing and configuring the agent.
3. Consuming the information in the Azure AD Connect Health dashboard.

Downloading the agent

Follow these steps to download the Azure AD Connect Health Agent for AD DS:

1. Navigate your browser to `https://portal.azure.com`.
2. Sign in with an account in Azure Active Directory that has the **Global administrator** role assigned.
3. Perform multi-factor authentication when prompted.
4. In the left-hand navigation pane, click **Azure Active Directory**.
5. In the **Azure Active Directory** pane, click **Azure AD Connect**.
6. In the **Azure AD Connect** main pane, under **Health and analytics**, follow the **Azure AD Connect Health** link.
7. In the **Azure AD Connect Health – Quick Start** pane, click the **Download Azure AD Connect Health Agent for AD DS** link.
8. Download the agent to a location where it is accessible to the domain controllers, or download it and copy it to the hard disks of these servers.

Installing and configuring the agent

Follow these steps to install and configure the Azure AD Connect Health Agent for AD DS on each domain controller in your environment:

1. Run `AdHealthAdfsAgentSetup.exe`.
2. In the **Azure AD Connect Health AD FS Agent** window, click the **Install** button.
3. In the **Setup Successful** screen, click the **Configure Now** button. A PowerShell window appears. Then the **Sign in to Azure AD Connect Health Agent** window appears.
4. Sign in with an account in Azure Active Directory that has the **Global administrator** role assigned.
5. Perform multi-factor authentication when prompted.
6. Close the PowerShell window.

Consuming the information in the Azure AD Connect Health dashboard

Perform these steps to consume the information from the Azure AD Connect Health Agent for AD DS installations in the Azure AD Connect Health dashboard:

1. Navigate your browser to `https://portal.azure.com`.
2. Sign in with an account in Azure Active Directory that has the **Global administrator** role or the **Conditional access administrator** role assigned.
3. Perform multi-factor authentication when prompted.
4. In the left-hand navigation pane, click **Azure Active Directory**.
5. In the **Azure Active Directory** pane, click **Azure AD Connect**.
6. In the **Azure AD Connect** main pane, under **Health and analytics**, follow the **Azure AD Connect Health** link.
7. In the **Azure AD Connect Health** navigation pane, click **AD DS services**.
8. In the **AD DS services** pane, click the service name of the Active Directory forest you want to monitor:

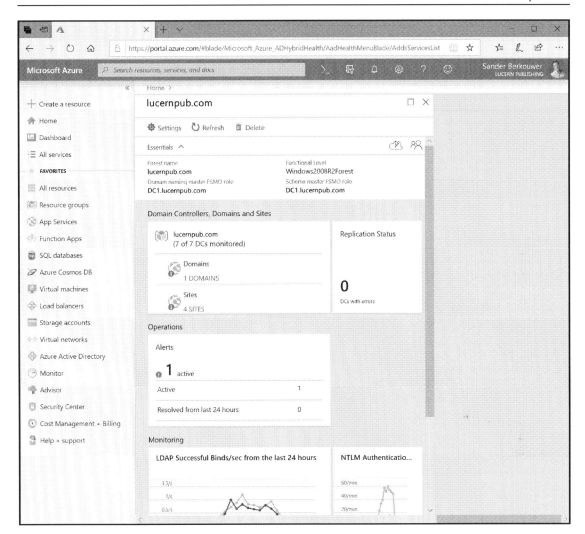

How it works...

The Azure AD Connect Health Agent for AD DS is an additional agent that can be installed on domain controllers. Microsoft recommends installing the agent on all domain controllers for complete insights.

Older versions of the Azure AD Connect Health agents for AD DS exchange data with Azure AD using a network connection over TCP port 5671. In this case, TCP port 5671 needs to be directly available from the individual domain controllers for Azure AD Connect Health to work.

The data is available in the Azure AD Connect Health dashboard in the Azure portal, but only accessible when at least one Azure AD Premium P1 license is attached to the Azure AD tenant per configured Azure AD Connect installation. For correct licensing, every monitored domain controller requires an additional 25 Azure AD Premium P1 licenses attached to the Azure AD tenant.

The Azure AD Connect Health dashboard provides information on the following:

- The Active Directory forest
    - The domain controller that holds the Domain Naming Master FSMO role
    - The domain controller that holds the Schema Naming Master FSMO role
    - Its **Forest Functional Level (FFL)**
- The Active Directory domains
    - Its replication statuses
    - The domain controllers and their sites, FSMO roles, status, active alerts, and whether they are global catalogs
- Alerts
- Combined statistical information for the last week, day, or past 6 hours in graphs on the following aspects:
    - Successful LDAP binds per second
    - Kerberos authentications per second
    - NTLM authentications per second
    - Replication queue length

Configuring Azure AD Privileged Identity Management

This recipe shows how to get the most out of Azure AD **Privileged Identity Management (PIM)**.

Getting ready

To complete this recipe, you'll need to sign into the Azure AD tenant with an account that has the Global administrator role assigned to it.

The PIM functionality requires Azure AD Premium P2 licenses, or Microsoft licenses that include the P2 license, such as EMS E5, EMS A5, Microsoft 365 E5, or Microsoft 365 Business Premium licenses.

People whose Azure AD accounts are assigned privileges roles in PIM, and are required to perform multi-factor authentication to unlock the role, should already have registered their multi-factor authentication methods.

 Microsoft recommends configuring two multi-factor authentication methods that are not tied to the same mobile number or mobile device.

How to do it...

Perform these steps to set up a person with the **Conditional Access administrator** privileged role in PIM, which requires multi-factor authentication and a justification for unlocking:

1. Navigate your browser to `https://portal.azure.com`.
2. Sign in with an account in Azure Active Directory that has the **Global administrator** assigned.
3. Perform multi-factor authentication when prompted.
4. In the left-hand navigation pane, click **All services**.
5. In the **Search Everything** search box, type **Azure AD Privileged Identity Management**.
6. If this is the first time you're using PIM, do the following:
    1. In the **Privileged Identity Management** navigation pane, click **Consent to PIM**.
    2. Perform multi-factor authentication when prompted.
    3. In the action bar of the **Consent to PIM** pane, click **Consent**.
    4. Click **Yes**.
7. In the **Privileged Identity Management** navigation pane, click **Azure AD roles**.
8. If this is the first time you're using Azure AD Roles, do the following:

1. In the **Azure AD Roles** navigation pane, click **Sign up PIM for Azure AD Roles**.
2. In the action bar of the **Sign up PIM for Azure AD Roles**, click **Sign up**. You are redirected to the **Azure AD roles - Overview** pane.
3. Click **Quick Start** in the **Azure AD Roles** navigation pane.

9. In the **Azure AD roles - Quick start** pane, click **Assign eligibility**.
10. In the top ribbon, click **+ Add Member**.
11. In the **Add managed members** pane, click **No role was selected** under **Select a role**.
   The **Select a role** pane appears:

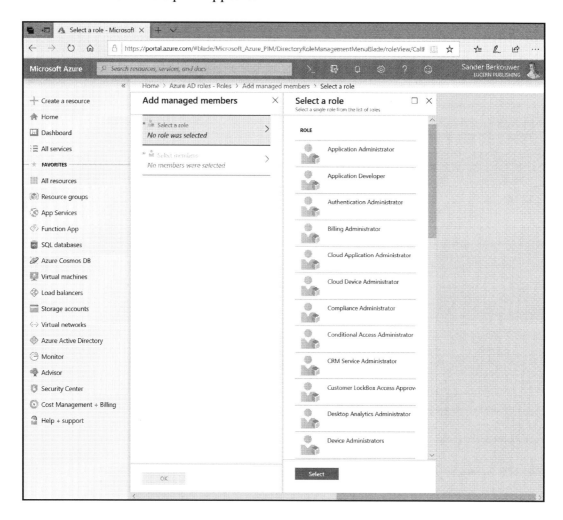

12. In the **Select a role** pane, select the **Conditional Access administrator** role.

13. Click **Select** at the bottom of the **Select a role** pane.

14. In the **Add managed members** pane, click **No members were selected** under **Select members**.

15. Select a user or multiple users in the **Select members** pane.

16. Click **Select** at the bottom of the **Select members** pane.

17. Click **OK** at the bottom of the **Add managed members** pane.

18. In the **Privileged Identity Management** navigation pane, click **Settings**.

19. In the **Roles** pane, select either the **Default for all roles** or the **Conditional Access administrator** role.

    Let's choose the **Default for all roles** option. Its properties blade appears:

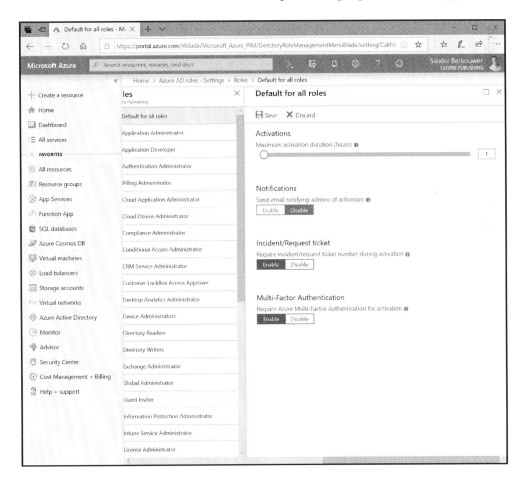

20. For **Notifications,** select **Enable** when you want the person activating the role to receive an email. This helps in detecting unauthorized activations.
21. For **Incident/Request ticket**, select **Enable** to require an incident or request ticket during activation.
22. For **Multi-Factor Authentication**, select **Enable** to require multi-factor authentication for activation.
23. Click **Save** at the top of the **Settings** pane.

How it works...

Azure AD PIM offers management, control, and monitoring of privileged access. By minimizing the number of admins and the time these people are actually equipped as admins with their privileges, Azure AD tenants can be hardened.

Always-on administrative privileges might seem like a good idea, but are not. Even the most dedicated admin would only need these privileges 10 out of 24 hours and only on some weekends. Azure AD PIM offers a solution to this situation: automatically-expiring privileges that admins need to specifically unlock.

In its most basic form, up to four people are assigned permanent Global administrator privileges. One account is configured as a break-glass account and also has these privileges. The roles for these accounts are out of scope of PIM. All the other people that need administrative privileges are provided with just-in-time, time-bound privileges in restricted admin roles, such as the **SharePoint administrator**, **Exchange administrator**, and **Intune administrator** roles. Their roles are in scope for PIM.

When a role is in scope for a PIM, unlocking the privileges of this role can be configured to require multi-factor authentication, require a justification (such as a support ticket number) and/or require an approval. Notifications can be configured, as well as Access Reviews. Every unlock is audited.

The maximum activation duration of the privileges for a role can be configured between 0.5 hours and 72 hours. The default duration (1 hour) might not be sufficient time for certain scripts for certain people in certain roles to complete. Address these situations by expanding the activation duration under **Activations** for the role under **Settings**.

There's more...

Azure AD PIM also offers the ability to convert permanent roles into roles that are eligible for activation through PIM. Start this guided experience by clicking **Wizard** in the **Privileged Identity Management** navigation pane and selecting the **Convert members to eligible** wizard.

Configuring Azure AD Identity Protection

Azure Identity Protection offers additional protection to organizations that worry about password breaches. This recipe shows how to configure the MFA registration policy.

Getting ready

The **Azure AD Identity Protection** functionality requires Azure AD Premium P2 licenses, or Microsoft licenses that include the P2 license, such as EMS E5, EMS A5, Microsoft 365 E5, Microsoft 365 Information Protection & Compliance, or Microsoft 365 Business Premium licenses.

How to do it...

Perform these steps:

1. Navigate your browser to `https://portal.azure.com`.
2. Sign in with an account in Azure Active Directory that has the **Global administrator** assigned.
3. Perform multi-factor authentication when prompted.
4. In the left-hand navigation pane, click **+ Create a resource**.
5. In the **Search the Marketplace** search box, type **Identity Protection**.

6. Click **Azure AD Identity Protection** from the search results.
   You are presented with the **Azure AD Identity Protection** marketplace item:

7. Click **Create**.
8. At the bottom of the **Azure AD Identity Protection** pane, click **Create** again.
9. In the left-hand navigation pane, click **All services**.
10. In the **Search Everything** search box, type **Identity Protection**.
11. Click **Azure AD Identity Protection** from the search results.

12. In the **Azure AD Identity Protection** navigation pane, click **MFA registration**.
13. In the **Assignments** region, confirm **All users**.
14. In the **Controls** region, click **Select a control**.
15. In the **Access** pane, select the **Require Azure MFA registration** option.

16. Click **Select** at the bottom of the pane.
17. Select **On** for **Enforce Policy**:

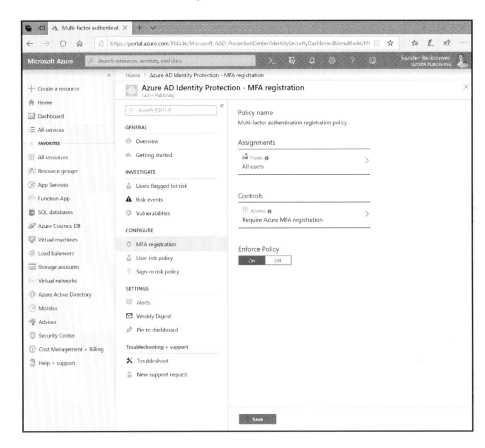

18. Click **Save** at the bottom of the **MFA registration** pane.

How it works...

Azure AD Identity Protection is enabled for every Azure AD account and every Microsoft account, formerly known as Windows Live ID. Every authentication goes through the Identity Protection funnel, where Microsoft's **Machine Learning** (**ML**) tries to distinguish risky and bad sign-ins from valid ones. Accounts that see a lot of risky and bad sign-ins, or have their password breached, become marked as risky users.

Azure Identity Protection offers additional investigation and configuration mechanisms for risky sign-ins and risky users. In the **Azure AD Identity Protection** dashboard, admins can do the following:

- Investigate users flagged for risk, risk events, and vulnerabilities
- Configure MFA registration, user risk policies, and sign-in risk policies

The investigation options provide admins with a way to find out why people are required to perform multi-factor authentication or change their password more often than they (think they) should. In many tenants, the **Sign-ins from unfamiliar locations** trigger often for travelling colleagues and these risk events trigger multi-factor authentication for them. It is recommended to review and dismiss false positives for **Users flagged for risk** and **risk events** when colleagues report complaints.

The vulnerabilities warn of common tenant misconfigurations, such as stale accounts in privileged roles. It is recommended to review the **Vulnerabilities** regularly.

The **All Users** options in Azure AD Identity Protection contains all users, including guest users.

MFA registration

Registering all users for MFA provides admins with a second layer of security, beyond just usernames and passwords.

Admins can configure the MFA registration policy. The policy requires selected users to register for Azure MFA. Switch the state of the policy to **On**.

When enabled, people who authenticate their accounts for the first time will need to register for MFA. Optionally, you can allow them a 14-day window for this registration.

User risk policies

With the user risk policy turned on, Azure AD Identity Protection calculates the probability that a user account has been compromised. As an admin, you can configure a user risk conditional access policy to automatically respond to a specific user risk level. For example, you can block access to your resources or require a password change to get a user account back into a clean state. Only when returned to a clean state is the user allowed to sign in normally.

In Azure AD Identity Protection, you can configure the user risk remediation policy. For the users in this policy, you need to set the conditions (risk level) under which the policy triggers and whether access is blocked when the policy is triggered. Switch the state of the policy to **On**.

Sign-in risk policies

Turning on the sign-in risk policy ensures that suspicious sign-ins are challenged for MFA.

In Azure AD Identity Protection, admins can configure the sign-in risk remediation policy. For the users in this policy, admins set the conditions (risk level) that trigger the policy. Switch the state of the policy to **On**.

When people who haven't registered MFA on their account trigger the user risk policy and/or sign-in risk policy that requires MFA, they are blocked from accessing their account. Make sure the MFA registration policy is **On** for all users who are a part of the user risk policy and/or sign-in risk policy.

There's more...

Even when Azure AD Identity Protection is not available for the Azure AD tenant, admins can still review **Users flagged for risk** and **Risk events**. To access the basic information available on these topics in every Azure AD tenant by default, perform these steps:

1. Navigate your browser to `https://portal.azure.com`.
2. Sign in with an account in Azure Active Directory that has the **Global administrator** role assigned.
3. Perform multi-factor authentication when prompted.
4. In the left-hand navigation pane, click **Azure Active Directory**.
5. In the **Azure Active Directory** pane, click **Users flagged for risk**.
6. Review users flagged for risk in the last 90 days in the **Users flagged for risk** main pane.
7. In the **Azure Active Directory** pane, click **Risk events**.
8. Review risk events for the last 90 days in the **Risk events** main pane.

Other Books You May Enjoy

If you enjoyed this book, you may be interested in these other books by Packt:

Identity with Windows Server 2016: Microsoft 70-742 MCSA Exam Guide
Vladimir Stefanovic, Sasha Kranjac

ISBN: 978-1-83855-513-9

- Install, configure, and maintain Active Directory Domain Services (AD DS)
- Manage Active Directory Domain Services objects
- Configure and manage Active Directory Certificate Services
- Configure and manage Group Policy
- Design, implement, and configure Active Directory Federation Services
- Implement and configure Active Directory Rights Management Services

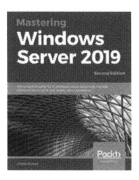

Mastering Windows Server 2019 - Second Edition
Jordan Krause

ISBN: 978-1-78980-453-9

- Work with the updated Windows Server 2019 interface, including Server Core and Windows Admin Center
- Secure your network and data with new technologies in Windows Server 2019
- Learn about containers and understand the appropriate situations to use Nano Server
- Discover new ways to integrate your data center with Microsoft Azure
- Harden your Windows Servers to help keep the bad guys out
- Virtualize your data center with Hyper-V

Leave a review - let other readers know what you think

Please share your thoughts on this book with others by leaving a review on the site that you bought it from. If you purchased the book from Amazon, please leave us an honest review on this book's Amazon page. This is vital so that other potential readers can see and use your unbiased opinion to make purchasing decisions, we can understand what our customers think about our products, and our authors can see your feedback on the title that they have worked with Packt to create. It will only take a few minutes of your time, but is valuable to other potential customers, our authors, and Packt. Thank you!

Index

A

account expiration
  about 247
  setting 243
  setting, Active Directory Administrative Center
    used 245
  setting, Active Directory Users and Computers
    used 243, 245
  setting, command-line tools used 246
  setting, Windows PowerShell used 247
  using 243
account lockout policies
  applying 328
Account Operators 361
Active Directory Administrative Center
  about 328
  used, for creating OUs 136, 137
  used, for deleting OUs 139
  used, for modifying 141
  using 328, 362
Active Directory Domain Services (AD DS)
  about 373, 375
  Azure AD Connect Health, configuring 560
Active Directory Domain Services role
  installing 76, 77
Active Directory Domains and Trusts 26, 30
Active Directory domains
  versus OUs 135
Active Directory Federation Services (AD FS) farm
  15
Active Directory Federation Services (AD FS)
  about 372, 375, 415
  AD FS SSL certificate, updating 440
  Azure AD Connect Health, configuring 556, 559,
    560
  Azure AD trust, resetting 439

deploying 442, 443
  federated Azure AD domain 440
  federated login, verifying 444
  managing, with Azure AD Connect 437, 438,
    445
  Web Application Proxy server, adding 443
Active Directory functionality
  preparing for, adprep.exe used 15
Active Directory Groups
  managing 249
Active Directory Migration Tool (ADMT) 29
Active Directory Module
  installing on Windows Server, for Windows
    PowerShell 12, 14
  used, for Windows PowerShell 330
Active Directory preparation process
  domain, preparing 18
  forest, preparing 17
  forest, preparing for RODCs 17
  Group Policy permissions, fixing up 18
  preparation replication, verifying 19
  stages 16
  working 20
Active Directory Recycle Bin
  about 50
  enabling 50, 51, 53
  working 54
Active Directory Service Interfaces (ADSI) 292
Active Directory sites
  creating 156
  functioning 155
  recommendations 155
Active Directory snapshots
  working with 341
Active Directory Users and Computers
  used, for delegating OU control 145, 147
  using 361

Printed in Great Britain
by Amazon